D0523379

Microsoft® Project 2010
Step by Step

Carl Chatfield
Timothy Johnson

PUBLISHED BY
Microsoft Press
A Division of Microsoft Corporation
One Microsoft Way
Redmond, Washington 98052-6399

Copyright © 2010 by Carl Chatfield and Timothy Johnson

All rights reserved. No part of the contents of this book may be reproduced or transmitted in any form or by any means without the written permission of the publisher.

Library of Congress Control Number: 2010928745

Printed and bound in the United States of America.

2 3 4 5 6 7 8 9   WCT   5 4 3 2 1 0

A CIP catalogue record for this book is available from the British Library.

Microsoft Press books are available through booksellers and distributors worldwide. For further information about international editions, contact your local Microsoft Corporation office or contact Microsoft Press International directly at fax (425) 936-7329. Visit our Website at www.microsoft.com/mspress. Send comments to mspinput@microsoft.com.

Microsoft, Microsoft Press, Access, Excel, Fluent, Internet Explorer, PivotChart, PivotTable, PowerPoint, SharePoint, Visio, Visual Basic, and Windows are either registered trademarks or trademarks of the Microsoft group of companies. Other product and company names mentioned herein may be the trademarks of their respective owners.

The example companies, organizations, products, domain names, e-mail addresses, logos, people, places, and events depicted herein are fictitious. No association with any real company, organization, product, domain name, e-mail address, logo, person, place, or event is intended or should be inferred.

This book expresses the author's views and opinions. The information contained in this book is provided without any express, statutory, or implied warranties. Neither the authors, Microsoft Corporation, nor its resellers, or distributors will be held liable for any damages caused or alleged to be caused either directly or indirectly by this book.

Acquisitions Editor: Juliana Aldous
Developmental Editor: Maria Garguilo
Project Editor: Rosemary Caperton
Editorial Production: Custom Editorial Productions, Inc.
Technical Reviewer: Thuy Le
Cover: Girvin

Body Part No. X16-95365

Contents at a Glance

Contents

What do you think of this book? We want to hear from you!

Microsoft is interested in hearing your feedback so we can continually improve our books and learning resources for you. To participate in a brief online survey, please visit:

microsoft.com/learning/booksurvey

What do you think of this book? We want to hear from you!

Microsoft is interested in hearing your feedback so we can continually improve our books and learning resources
for you. To participate in a brief online survey, please visit:

microsoft.com/learning/booksurvey

Acknowledgments

The authors would like to thank our families for their patience and encouragement while we wrote this book. From Carl: *merci* Rebecca, Alden, Mona, and Lathan. From Tim: *khawp jai* Ratsamy (Mimi), Brian, and Brenda. The authors also wish to acknowledge and thank our technical reviewer, Thuy Le, PMP, EPM Solutions Architect at Microsoft, and Project program manager Adrian Jenkins, for their timely and valuable feedback and responses to our technical questions.

Finally, we thank our project editor, Rosemary Caperton, and our content editor, Susan McClung, for their outstanding work.

Introducing Microsoft Project 2010

Microsoft Project 2010 is a powerful program that helps you plan and manage a wide range of projects. From meeting crucial deadlines and budgets to selecting the right resources, Project 2010 offers easier and more intuitive experiences to help you be more productive and realize better results. You can use Project to:

- Create project plans at the level of detail that's right for your project. Work with summary data initially or shift to a more detailed approach when it's convenient. Control what tasks Project can schedule automatically or that you'll schedule manually.

- Manage tasks, costs, work, and resources at whatever level of detail is appropriate for your project's needs.

- See your project plan data in a variety of views. Apply grouping, highlighting, sorting, and filtering to see your data the way that you want.

- Track and manage your project plan throughout project execution.

- Collaborate and share data with others in your organization using a variety of productivity applications.

- Use resource pools, consolidated projects, and cross-project links to extend your project management focus across multiple projects.

Project 2010 builds on previous versions to provide powerful project management tools. This introduction provides an overview of new features that we explore throughout the book.

New Features

If you're upgrading to Project 2010 from a previous version, you're probably most interested in the differences between the old and new versions and how they will affect you. The following sections list new features you will want to be aware of, depending on the version of Project you are upgrading from.

If You Are Upgrading from Project 2007

If you have been using Project 2007, you might be wondering what new features and interface changes Microsoft has added to its desktop project management application. The list of new features includes the following:

- **The Microsoft Office Fluent interface (the "ribbon")** No more hunting through menus, submenus, and dialog boxes. This new interface organizes all the commands that most people use in a new way, making them quickly accessible from tabs at the top of the program window.

- **The Backstage view** Finally, all the tools you need to work with your files are accessible from one location.

- **Manually scheduled tasks** Begin creating tasks with whatever information (numeric or text data) you may have, and don't worry about automatic scheduling of tasks until you're ready. Manually scheduled tasks are not affected by changes in duration, start or finish dates, dependencies, or other issues that otherwise would cause Project to reschedule a task. You can then switch individual tasks or an entire project plan from manual to automatic scheduling.

- **Timeline view** Create a visually compelling "project at a glance" view that includes just the summary tasks, tasks, and milestones that you choose. Easily copy the Timeline view as a graphic image to paste into other applications.

- **Better pasting to Excel and Word** Paste Project data into Excel or Word and preserve the column headings and outline structure of your Project data.

- **Customizable ribbon** Create your own tabs and groups to suit the way you work.

- **Custom fields** Just start typing a numeric value, date value, or text string into the rightmost column in a table, and Project will identify the right data type.

- **AutoFilter improvements** Use Microsoft Excel–like filtering, as well as sorting and grouping, right from AutoFilter arrows on column headings.

- **Save as PDF or XPS** Create PDF or XPS format documents directly from Project.

- **Team Planner view (Project Professional only)** Perform actions like reassigning a task from one resource to another with simple dragging in the Team Planner view.

- **Inactivate tasks (Project Professional only)** Disable (but don't delete) selected tasks from a project plan so they have no effect on the overall schedule but can be reactivated later if you need them.

- **SharePoint Task List integration (Project Professional only)** Publish and synchronize tasks between Project and a new type of Microsoft SharePoint list called a Project Task List.

If You Are Upgrading from Project 2003

In addition to the features listed in the previous section, if you're upgrading from Project 2003, you'll want to take note of the new features that were introduced in Project 2007. The 2007 upgrade included several new and improved features, including the following:

- **Visual reports** Export Project task, resource, or assignment details to Excel or Visio in a highly structured graphical format.

- **Change highlighting** See what values changed throughout a project plan immediately after you make a change to a calculated task, resource, or assignment value.

- **Cost resources** Assign this special type of resource to tasks to accrue categories of costs you wish to track, like travel or entertainment. Cost resources have no effect on the scheduling of tasks to which they are assigned.

- **Task Inspector pane** Called the Task Driver pane in Project 2007, the Task Inspector pane shows you details that affect the scheduling of a selected task.

- **Multi-level Undo** Back out of a series of actions when you need to.

- **Calendar working time exceptions** Record not just the date, but also an explanation of a resource or project calendar working time exception.

Let's Get Started!

We've been working with Project since it debuted for Windows, and each version has offered something that made project planning and management a little easier. Project 2010 is a substantial update for desktop project management, and we look forward to showing you around.

Modifying the Display of the Ribbon

The goal of the Microsoft Office working environment is to make working with Office documents, including Microsoft Project plans, Microsoft Word documents, Microsoft Excel workbooks, Microsoft PowerPoint presentations, Microsoft Outlook e-mail messages, and Microsoft Access database tables, as intuitive as possible. You work with an Office document and its contents by giving commands to the program in which the document is open. All Office 2010 programs organize commands on a horizontal bar called the ribbon, which appears across the top of each program window whether or not there is an active document.

A typical program window ribbon.

Commands are organized on task-specific tabs of the ribbon, and in feature-specific groups on each tab. Commands generally take the form of buttons and lists. Some appear in galleries. Some groups have related dialog boxes or task panes that contain additional commands.

Throughout this book, we discuss the commands and ribbon elements associated with the program feature being discussed. In this topic, we discuss the general appearance of the ribbon, things that affect its appearance, and ways of locating commands that aren't visible on compact views of the ribbon.

See Also For detailed information about the ribbon in Microsoft Project, see the section "The Ribbon and Tabs: Finding the Features You Want," in Chapter 1, "A Guided Tour of Project." For information about customizing the ribbon and other parts of the Project interface, see Chapter 16, "Customizing Project."

Tip Some older commands no longer appear on the ribbon but are still available in the program. You can make these commands available by adding them to the Quick Access Toolbar. For more information, see the section "Customizing the Ribbon and Quick Access Toolbar," in Chapter 16, "Customizing Project."

Dynamic Ribbon Elements

The ribbon is dynamic, meaning that the appearance of commands on the ribbon changes as the width of the ribbon changes. A command might be displayed on the ribbon in the form of a large button, a small button, a small labeled button, or a list entry. As the width of the ribbon decreases, the size, shape, and presence of buttons on the ribbon adapt to the available space.

For example, when sufficient horizontal space is available, the buttons on the Task tab of the Project program window are spread out and you're able to see more of the commands available in each group.

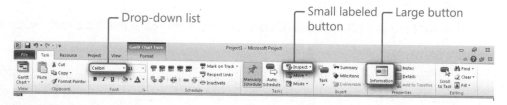

The Task tab of the Project program window at 1280 pixels wide.

If you decrease the width of the ribbon, small button labels disappear and entire groups of buttons hide under one button that represents the group. Click the group button to display a list of the commands available in that group.

The Task tab of the Project program window at 800 pixels wide.

When the window becomes too narrow to display all the groups, a scroll arrow appears at its right end. Click the scroll arrow to display hidden groups.

The Task tab of the Project program window at 393 pixels wide.

Changing the Width of the Ribbon

The width of the ribbon depends on the horizontal space available to it, which in turn depends on these three factors:

- **The width of the program window** Maximizing the program window provides the most space for ribbon elements. You can resize the program window by clicking the button in its upper-right corner or by dragging the border of a non-maximized window.

  Tip On a computer running Windows 7, you can maximize the program window by dragging its title bar to the top of the screen.

- **Your screen resolution** Screen resolution is the size of your screen display expressed as pixels wide × pixels high. The greater the screen resolution, the greater the amount of information that will fit on one screen. Your screen resolution options depend on your monitor. At the time of writing, possible screen resolutions range from 800 × 600 to 2048 × 1152. In the case of the ribbon, the greater the number of pixels wide (the first number), the greater the number of buttons that can be shown on the ribbon, and the larger those buttons can be.

  On a computer running Windows 7, you can change your screen resolution from the Screen Resolution window of Control Panel.

You set the resolution by dragging the pointer on the slider.

● **The density of your screen display** You might not be aware that you can change the magnification of everything that appears on your screen by changing the screen magnification setting in Windows. Setting your screen magnification to 125% makes text and user interface elements larger on screen. This increases the legibility of information, but it also means that less fits onto each screen.

On a computer running Windows 7, you can change the screen magnification from the Display window of Control Panel.

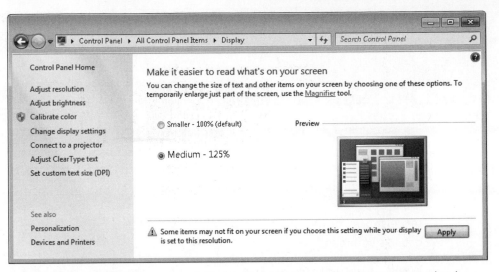

You can choose one of the standard display magnification options or create another by setting a custom text size.

The screen magnification is directly related to the density of the text elements on screen, which is expressed in dots per inch (dpi) or points per inch (ppi). (The terms are interchangeable, and in fact, they are both used in the Windows dialog box in which you change the setting.) The greater the dpi, the larger the text and user interface elements appear on screen. By default, Windows displays text and screen elements at 96 dpi. Choosing the Medium - 125% display setting changes the dpi of text and screen elements to 120 dpi. You can choose a custom setting of up to 500% magnification, or 480 dpi, in the Custom DPI Setting dialog box.

You can choose a magnification of up to 200% from the lists or choose a greater magnification by dragging across the ruler from left to right.

See Also For more information about display settings, refer to *Windows 7 Step by Step* (Microsoft Press, 2009), *Windows Vista Step by Step* (Microsoft Press, 2006), or *Windows XP Step by Step* (Microsoft Press, 2002) by Joan Lambert Preppernau and Joyce Cox.

Adapting Exercise Steps

The screen images shown in the exercises in this book were captured at a screen resolution of 1280 × 800, at 100% magnification, and the default text size (96 dpi). If any of your settings are different, the ribbon on your screen might not look the same as the one shown in the book. For example, you might see more or fewer buttons in each of the groups, the buttons you see might be represented by larger or smaller icons than those shown, or the group might be represented by a button that you click to display the group's commands.

When we instruct you to give a command from the ribbon in an exercise, we do it in this format:

● On the **Project** tab, in the **Properties** group, click **Project Information**.

If the command is in a list, we give the instruction in this format:

● On the **View** tab, in the **Data** group, click **Tables** and then click **Cost**.

The first time we instruct you to click a specific button in each exercise, we display an image of the button in the page margin to the left of the exercise step.

If differences between your display settings and ours cause a button on your screen to look different from the one shown in the book, you can easily adapt the steps to locate the command. First, click the specified tab. Then locate the specified group. If a group has been collapsed into a group list or group button, click the list or button to display the group's commands. Finally, look for a button that features the same icon in a larger or smaller size than that shown in the book. If necessary, point to buttons in the group to display their names in ScreenTips.

If you prefer not to have to adapt the steps, set up your screen to match ours while you read and work through the exercises in the book.

Features and Conventions of This Book

This book has been designed to lead you step by step through many of the tasks you're most likely to want to perform in Microsoft Project Professional 2010 or Microsoft Project Standard 2010. If you start at the beginning and work your way through all the exercises, you will gain enough proficiency to be able to create and work with a wide range of Project features. However, each topic is self contained. If you have worked with a previous version of Project, or if you completed all the exercises and later need help remembering how to perform a procedure, the following features of this book will help you locate specific information:

- **Detailed table of contents** Search the listing of the topics and sidebars within each chapter.

- **Chapter thumb tabs** Easily locate the beginning of the chapter you want.

- **Topic-specific running heads** Within a chapter, quickly locate the topic you want by looking at the running heads at the top of odd-numbered pages.

- **Glossary** Look up the meaning of a word or the definition of a concept.

- **Detailed index** Look up specific tasks and features in the index, which has been carefully crafted with the reader in mind.

You can save time when reading this book by understanding how the *Step by Step* series shows exercise instructions, keys to press, buttons to click, and other information.

Convention	Meaning
SET UP	This paragraph preceding a step-by-step exercise indicates the practice files that you will use when working through the exercise. It also indicates any requirements that you should attend to or actions that you should take before beginning the exercise.
CLEAN UP	This paragraph following a step-by-step exercise provides instructions for saving and closing open files or programs before moving on to another topic. It also suggests ways to reverse any changes you made to your computer while working through the exercise.
1 2	Blue numbered steps guide you through hands-on exercises in each topic.
1 2	Black numbered steps guide you through procedures in sidebars and expository text.

Convention	Meaning
Important	This paragraph points out information that you need to know to complete a procedure.
Note	This paragraph describes information that merits special attention.
See Also	This paragraph directs you to more information about a topic in this book or elsewhere.
Tip	This paragraph provides a helpful hint or shortcut that makes working through a task easier.
Ctrl+G	A plus sign (+) between two keys means that you must press those keys at the same time. For example, "Press Ctrl+G" means that you should hold down the Ctrl key while you press the G key.
	Pictures of buttons appear in the margin the first time the button is used in a chapter.
Black bold	In exercises that begin with SET UP information, the names of program elements, such as buttons, commands, windows, and dialog boxes, as well as files, folders, or text that you interact with in the steps, are shown in black, bold type.
Blue bold	In exercises that begin with SET UP information, text that you should type is shown in blue bold type.
Blue bold italic	Terms that are defined in the Glossary are formatted this way.

Using the Practice Files

Before you can complete the exercises in this book, you need to copy the book's practice files to your computer. These practice files, as well as other information, can be downloaded from the book's detail page, located at:

http://go.microsoft.com/fwlink/?LinkId=191765

Display the detail page in your Web browser and follow the instructions for downloading the files.

Important The Microsoft Project 2010 program is not available from this Website. You should purchase and install that program before using this book.

The following table lists the practice files for this book.

Note The same set of practice files works with both Microsoft Project Professional 2010 and Microsoft Project Standard 2010. Differences between the two editions of Project are explained where needed throughout the book.

Chapter	File
Chapter 1: A Guided Tour of Project	Guided Tour_Start.mpp
Chapter 2: Creating a Task List	(no initial practice file)
Chapter 3: Setting Up Resources	Simple Resources_Start.mpp
Chapter 4: Assigning Resources to Tasks	Simple Assignments_Start.mpp
Chapter 5: Formatting and Sharing Your Plan	Simple Formatting_Start.mpp
Chapter 6: Tracking Progress on Tasks	Simple Tracking_Start.mpp
Chapter 7: Fine-Tuning Task Details	Advanced Tasks A_Start.mpp
	Advanced Tasks B_Start.mpp
Chapter 8: Fine-Tuning Resource Details	Advanced Resources_Start.mpp
Chapter 9: Fine-Tuning Assignment Details	Advanced Assignments A_Start.mpp
	Advanced Assignments B_Start.mpp
Chapter 10: Fine-Tuning the Project Plan	Advanced Plan_Start.mpp
Chapter 11: Organizing Project Details	Advanced Organizing_Start.mpp
Chapter 12: Tracking Progress on Tasks and Assignments	Advanced Tracking A_Start.mpp
	Advanced Tracking B_Start.mpp
	Advanced Tracking C_Start.mpp
	Advanced Tracking D_Start.mpp
Chapter 13: Viewing and Reporting Project Status	Reporting Status_Start.mpp

Chapter	File
Chapter 14: Getting Your Project Back on Track	Back on Track_Start.mpp
Chapter 15: Applying Advanced Formatting and Printing	Advanced Formatting_Start.mpp
Chapter 16: Customizing Project	Customizing A_Start.mpp
	Customizing B_Start.mpp
Chapter 17: Sharing Project Information with Other Programs	Sample Task List.xls
	Sharing_Start.mpp
Chapter 18: Consolidating Projects and Resources	Consolidating A_Start.mpp
	Consolidating B_Start.mpp

Getting Help

Every effort has been made to ensure the accuracy of this Microsoft Press book. If you run into problems please contact the appropriate source, listed in the following sections, for help and assistance.

Getting Help with This Book and Its Practice Files

The practice files referred to throughout this book are available as Web downloads. For more information, see "Using the Practice Files," at the beginning of this book.

If your question or issue concerns the content of this book or its practice files, please first consult the book's errata page, which can be accessed at:

http://go.microsoft.com/fwlink/?LinkId=191765

This page provides information about known errors and corrections to the book. If you do not find your answer on the errata page, send your question or comment to Microsoft Press Technical Support at:

mspinput@microsoft.com

Getting Help with Project 2010

If your question is about Microsoft Project 2010, not about the content of this book or its practice files, please search Microsoft Support or the Microsoft Knowledge Base at:

http://support.microsoft.com

In the United States, Microsoft software product support issues not covered by the Microsoft Knowledge Base are addressed by Microsoft Product Support Services. The Microsoft software support options available from Microsoft Product Support Services are listed at:

http://support.microsoft.com/gp/selfoverview/

Part 1

Simple Scheduling

Chapter at a Glance

Walk through the new tabs and ribbons in the Project interface, page 5.

Explore the Backstage view, the central interface for file management, and other features, page 7.

See how different types of commands work, page 10.

Use different views to see Project data the way you want it, page 15.

1 A Guided Tour of Project

In this chapter, you will learn how to:

✔ Use the Backstage view to open and save Project files.

✔ Work with commands on different tabs of the ribbon interface, the major visual change introduced in Project 2010.

✔ Use different views to see Project information presented in different ways.

Microsoft Project 2010 can be your go-to tool in your project management toolbox. This book explains how to use Project to build project plans complete with *tasks* and *resources,* use the extensive formatting features in Project to organize and format the project plan details, track actual work against the plan, and take corrective action when things get off track.

Project management is a broadly practiced art and science. If you're reading this book, chances are that you're either seriously involved in project management, or you want to be.

Tip Terms formatted *like this* are defined in the Glossary at the end of this book.

At its heart, project management is a combination of skills and tools that help you predict and control the outcomes of endeavors undertaken by your organization. Your organization might be involved in other work apart from projects. *Projects* (such as publishing a new children's book) are distinct from *ongoing operations* (such as running payroll services). Projects are defined as temporary endeavors undertaken to create some unique deliverable or result. With a good project management system in place, you should be able to answer such questions as:

- What tasks must be performed, and in what order, to produce the deliverable of the project?
- When should each task be performed, and what is the final *deadline*?
- Who will complete these tasks?

- How much will it cost?

- What if some tasks are not completed as scheduled?

- What's the best way to communicate project details to those who have an interest in the project?

Good project management does not guarantee the success of every project, but poor project management often leads to failure.

Tip If you are new to project management, please read Appendix A, "A Short Course in Project Management," before proceeding with this chapter. It won't take long, and it will help you to assess and organize your specific project-scheduling needs properly and build solid plans in Project.

This chapter leads you on a fast-paced tour of Project. If you are new to Project, you'll see the essential features and activities that make it such a powerful application. If you are upgrading from a previous version, you'll see notes about some of the major new features introduced in the 2010 edition.

Project 2010 is available in two different editions:

- Project Standard is the entry-level desktop application with which you can create and modify project plans.

- Project Professional includes all the functionality of Project Standard plus a few additional features you can use to create and modify project plans. In addition, Project Professional can connect to Microsoft Project Server, the *Enterprise Project Management* (EPM) solution from Microsoft.

This book focuses on the desktop functionality in Project Standard and Project Professional. When a desktop feature that is unique to Project Professional appears, you'll see special instructions for users of both Project Standard and Project Professional.

Most of the exercises in this book revolve around a fictitious children's book publishing company, Lucerne Publishing. Each new book (even this one) constitutes its own project; in fact, some are fairly complex projects involving costly resources and aggressive deadlines. We think you'll be able to recognize many of the scheduling problems that the project managers at Lucerne Publishing encounter and apply their solutions to your own scheduling needs.

Practice Files Before you can complete the exercises in this chapter, you need to copy the book's practice files to your computer. A complete list of practice files is provided in "Using the Practice Files" at the beginning of this book. For each exercise that has a practice file, simply browse to where you saved the book's practice file folder.

Important If you are running Project Professional, you may need to make a one-time setting change. This helps ensure that the practice files you work with in this chapter do not affect your Project Server data. For more information, see Appendix C, "Using the Practice Files if Connected to Project Server."

Introducing Project

You can start Project from the Start menu or by opening a Project file. In this exercise, you'll start Project without opening a project plan and then examine the major parts of the interface.

1. On the **Windows** taskbar, click **Start**.

   The Start menu appears.

2. On the **Start** menu, point to **All Programs**, click **Microsoft Office**, and then click **Microsoft Project 2010**.

   Project appears. Your screen should look similar to the following illustration:

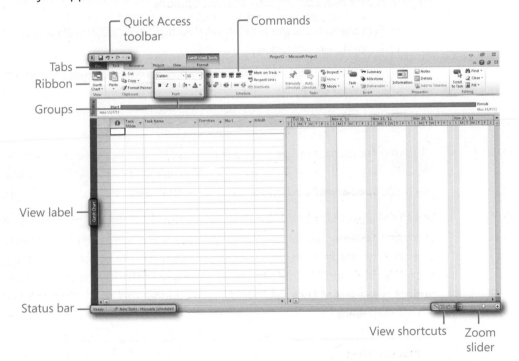

What you see on your screen might differ from what's shown in this book. This may depend on your screen resolution and any previous customizations made to Project on your computer.

You may notice that the user interface of Project 2010 is quite different from previous versions of Project. For its 2010 release, Project has adopted the Fluent interface (commonly called the *ribbon interface*) that was first introduced in some Microsoft Office 2007 applications, like Word and Excel.

Let's walk through the major parts of the Project interface:

○ The **Quick Access toolbar** is a customizable area of the interface where you can add your favorite or frequently used commands. For more information, see Chapter 16, "Customizing Project."

○ **Tabs** and the active **ribbon** replace the pull-down menus and toolbars that you may be familiar with. Tabs group high-level focus areas of Project together. One tab is always selected, and its ribbon is visible. The ribbon contains the commands that you use to control Project.

○ **Groups** are collections of related commands. Each ribbon is divided into multiple groups.

○ **Commands** are the specific features you use to control Project. Each ribbon contains several commands. Some commands, like Cut on the Task tab, perform an immediate action. Other commands, like Change Working Time on the Project tab, display a dialog box or prompt you to take further action in some other way. You can see a description of most commands by pointing the mouse pointer at the command.

Point at a command to see its description in a ScreenTip.

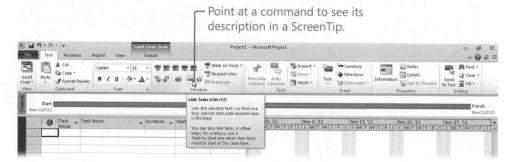

○ The active view appears in the main window of Project. Project can display a single view or multiple views in separate panes.

○ The **View label** appears along the left edge of the active view. Project includes dozens of views, so this is a handy reminder of what your active view is.

○ **View shortcuts** let you quickly switch between some of the more frequently used views in Project. The **Zoom slider** zooms the active view in or out.

- The **Status bar** displays some important details like the scheduling mode of new tasks (manual or automatic), and if a filter has been applied to the active view.

- *Shortcut menus* and **mini-toolbars** are accessible via right-clicking most items you see in a view.

If you are upgrading from a previous version of Project, you might wonder what happened to some parts of the interface not mentioned here:

- Menus and toolbars have been replaced by the tabs and ribbons.

- The entry bar (also called the formula bar) is hidden by default. To display it, on the File tab, click Options. In the Project Options dialog box, click the Display tab. Under "Show these elements," click the "Entry bar" check box.

Next, you'll use the Backstage view to open a sample project plan.

The Backstage: Managing Files and Setting Options

The Backstage view is a standard part of the Fluent interface, and you will see a similar Backstage view in most other Office 2010 applications. The Backstage contains customization and sharing options, as well as the essential commands for file management like Open, New, and Save.

In this exercise, you navigate to the Backstage view and see its major parts.

1. Click the **File** tab.

Project displays the Backstage view.

2. On the left side of the **Backstage** view, click **Help**.

Project displays options for getting assistance and details about your installed version.

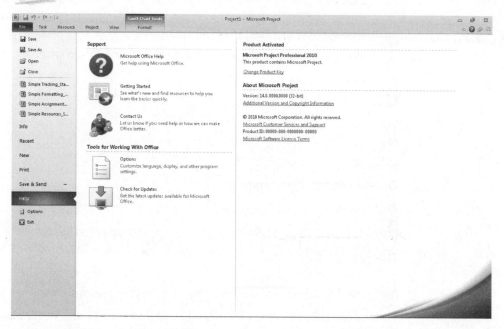

Here is a brief list of the features in the Backstage view. In most cases, you can click the tab name to see more options.

- ○ **Save**, **Save As**, **Open,** and **Close** are standard file management commands.

- ○ **Info** gives you access to the Organizer, a feature used to share customized elements like views between project plans; the Organizer is described in Chapter 16. Info also shows you project information like start and finish date, statistics, and advanced properties. You work with advanced properties and project statistics in Chapter 2, "Creating a Task List."

- ○ **Recent** displays the last several Project files that you have opened.

- ○ **New** displays options for creating a new project plan, either from scratch or based on a template. You'll use the New command in the next section.

- ○ **Print** includes options for printing a project plan, as well as the print preview.

- ○ **Save & Send** includes options for attaching a project plan to an e-mail message, generating a Portable Document Format (PDF) or XML Paper

Specification (XPS) format file of the project plan, and other options for collaborating. You'll work with these features in Chapter 15, "Applying Advanced Formatting and Printing."

○ **Help** gives you options for viewing the online Help installed with Project, as well as various Web resources. Help also includes the "About Microsoft Project" details, including your edition of Project: Standard or Professional.

○ **Options** displays the Project Options dialog box (similar to the Options command on the Tools menu in previous versions of Project). This dialog box itself contains several tabs through which you can adjust a wide range of behaviors in Project, such as the default view you want to see when Project starts.

○ **Exit** closes Project.

Note If you are running Project Standard, you will not see some options relating to Project Professional and integration with Project Server.

Next, you'll open the practice file that you'll work with through the rest of this chapter.

3. On the **File** tab, click **Open**.

The Open dialog box appears.

4. Open **Guided Tour_Start** from the Chapter01 practice file folder.

The practice file opens.

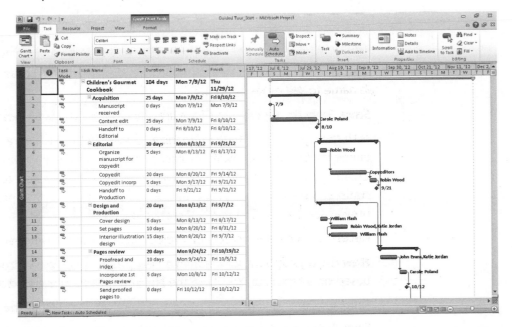

Next, you'll save the practice file with a different name.

5. On the **File** tab, click **Save As**.

   The Save As dialog box appears.

6. In the **File name** box, type **Guided Tour**, and then click **Save**.

Templates: Avoid Reinventing the Wheel

Instead of creating a project plan from scratch, you may be able to use a *template* that includes much of the initial information you need, like task names and relationships. Sources of templates include:

- Templates installed with Project. These can vary depending on the installation options that were selected when Project was installed on your computer.

- Templates from the Office Online Web site, *www.office.com*. Microsoft makes a large number of Project templates available for free download via the Web.

- Templates within your organization. You may be in an organization that has a central library of templates. Often such templates contain detailed task definitions, resource assignments, and other details that are unique to the organization.

- Templates that you casually share with other Project users you know.

To see available templates, click the File tab and then click New.

You can also create templates from your project plans for later use or to share. One common concern with sharing project plans is they may contain sensitive information like resource pay rates. You can save a project plan as a template and clear such information, as well as schedule progress. To do this, on the File tab, click Save As. In the "Save as type" box, click Project Template, enter the template file name that you want, and then click Save. When the Save As Template dialog box appears, select the types of information, such as pay rates, that you want removed from the template. The original project plan is not affected.

The Ribbon and Tabs: Finding the Features You Want

Project 2010 joins other Office applications in adopting the Fluent interface. The most prominent parts of this new interface are the tabs and ribbon that span the top of the Project window. In this section, you'll work with the tabs to see how they are organized.

To begin, look at the tab labels. These labels logically group the commands that apply to major parts of Project together:

- The **Tasks** and **Resources** tabs relate to the data you frequently work with in Project.

- The **Project** tab contains commands that usually apply to the entire project plan.

- The **View** tab helps you control what you see in the Project window and how that information appears.

- The **Format** tab is a contextual tab; the commands displayed on the Format tab vary, depending on what kind of information is displayed in the active view, or what kind of item is selected at the time. For example, when a task view, like the *Gantt Chart view*, is displayed, the commands on the Format tab apply to tasks and Gantt Chart items like Gantt bars. The current context of the Format tab appears above the tab label—Gantt Chart Tools, for example.

Let's look more closely at the Task tab.

Like all tabs, the Task tab contains a large number of commands, and these commands are organized into groups. The Task tab includes the View, Clipboard, Font, and other groups.

Some commands perform an immediate action, while other commands lead you to more options. You'll look at some examples on different tabs.

1. Click the **Resource** tab label.

   The Resource ribbon replaces the Task ribbon.

2. In the **Assignments** group, click **Assign Resources**.

   This command has an immediate effect; it displays the Assign Resources dialog box.

You can leave the Assign Resources dialog box displayed while you perform other actions in Project. For now, though, you'll close it.

3. In the **Assign Resources** dialog box, click **Close**.

4. Click the **View** tab label.

This tab contains a mixture of command types. As you can see some commands, like New Window, just have a command label and icon.

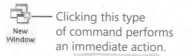 Clicking this type of command performs an immediate action.

In most cases, such commands perform an immediate action.

Other commands, like Sort, include a label and an arrow.

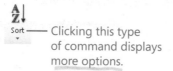 Clicking this type of command displays more options.

5. On the **View** tab, in the **Data** group, click **Sort**.

This command displays a list of sorting options.

Corey, 2010
Nov 1, 2010

Another type of command can either perform an immediate action or show you more options. You'll look at one example now.

6. On the **View** tab, in the **Task Views** group, click the graphic image portion of the **Calendar** button.

Some commands are split into two parts; clicking the arrow displays more options.

Clicking the graphic image portion of the command performs the command with its current setting; in this case, Project switched from the Gantt Chart view to the Calendar view.

7. On the **View** tab, in the **Task Views** group, click the graphic image portion of the **Gantt Chart** button.

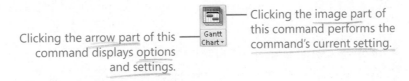

Clicking the arrow part of this command displays options and settings.

Clicking the image part of this command performs the command's current setting.

Project switches the active view back to the Gantt Chart view.

8. On the **View** tab, in the **Task Views** group, click the down arrow below the **Gantt Chart** button.

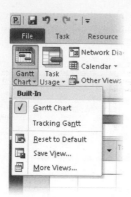

Clicking the text label portion of the command (or just the arrow for commands that have an arrow but no text label) shows you the available settings for that command. In this case, you can see some other types of Gantt chart views and other options. If you select, say, Tracking Gantt, then the next time you click the Gantt chart button image, you'll switch from whatever view you were in to the Tracking Gantt view.

Tip Throughout this book, when you see an instruction to click a command that has a graphic image as well as an arrow that displays more options, we mean to click the graphic image (unless otherwise noted).

9. On the **Format** tab, in the **Gantt Chart Style** group, click the **More** button to display the predefined color styles.

   A gallery of preformatted Gantt bar options appears.

You'll work with these options in Chapter 5, "Formatting and Sharing Your Plan."

10. Press the Esc key or click the **Format** tab to close the gallery.

    There are still more Gantt bar formatting options to see.

11. On the **Format** tab, in the **Gantt Chart Style** group, click the **Format Bar Styles** button in the lower-right corner of the group.

    The Bar Styles dialog box appears.

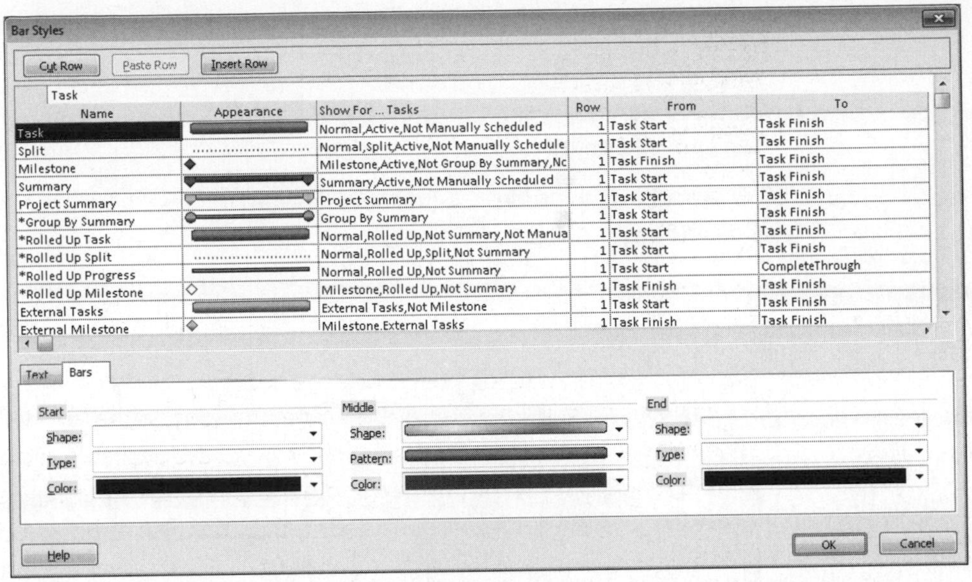

The Format Bar Styles button is an example of a dialog box launcher. Unlike the Assign Resources dialog box you saw earlier, you must close the Bar Styles dialog box before you can perform other actions.

12. Click **Cancel** to close the **Bar Styles** dialog box.

There are other ways of accessing commands in Project, but what you've seen in this exercise covers most command interfaces in Project.

Next, you'll change the active view and other details that you work with in Project.

Views: Working with Schedule Details the Way You Want

The working space in Project is called a *view*. Project contains dozens of views, but you normally work with just one view (or sometimes two) at a time. You use views to enter, edit, analyze, and display your project information. The default view—the one that you see when Project starts—is the Gantt with Timeline view.

In general, views focus on task, resource, or *assignment* details. The Gantt Chart view, for example, lists task details in a table on the left side of the view and graphically represents each task as a bar in the chart on the right side of the view. The Gantt Chart view is a common way to represent a project plan, especially when presenting it to others. It is also useful for entering and fine-tuning task details and for analyzing your project.

In this exercise, you'll start at the Gantt Chart view and then switch to other views that highlight different aspects of a project plan.

1. On the **View** tab, in the **Zoom** group, click the down arrow next to the **Timescale** box and click **Days**.

Project adjusts the timescale to show individual days. Nonworking days, such as weekends, are formatted in light gray.

You can adjust the Timescale to change how much of your project plan is visible.

A Gantt Chart view includes this table portion...

...and this chart portion.

You can adjust the timescale in the Gantt Chart view in several ways. Here, you used the Timescale box on the View tab. You can also use the Zoom In and Zoom Out controls on the View toolbar in the lower-right corner of the Project window.

Next, you'll display a second view.

2. On the **View** tab, in the **Split View** group, click the **Timeline** check box.

Project displays the Timeline view. The Timeline view is a handy way of seeing the "big picture" of the project plan.

This Timeline view has been populated for you with some details from the project plan. You'll create a custom Timeline view in Chapter 5.

3. Click anywhere in the **Timeline** view.

Note that the label above the Format tab changed to Timeline Tools. The commands displayed on the Format tab now are specific to the Timeline view. Throughout this exercise, as you see different views, note that the label above the Format tab changes accordingly.

4. On the **View** tab, in the **Split View** group, clear the **Timeline** check box.

Project hides the Timeline view. (The information in the view is not lost; it's just hidden for now.)

Next, you'll switch to a sheet view.

5. On the **View** tab, in the **Resource Views** group, click **Resource Sheet**.

The Resource Sheet view replaces the Gantt Chart view.

The Resource Sheet view displays details about resources in a row-and-column format (called a table), with one resource per row. This view is called a sheet view. Another sheet view, called the Task Sheet view, lists the task details.

Note that the Resource Sheet view doesn't tell you anything about the tasks to which resources might be assigned. To see that type of information, you'll switch to a different view.

6. On the **View** tab, in the **Resource Views** group, click **Resource Usage**.

The Resource Usage view replaces the Resource Sheet view. This usage view groups the tasks to which each resource is assigned and shows you the work assignments per resource on a timescale, such as daily or weekly.

In the timescaled grid on the right side of the usage table you can see some of Carole Poland's work assignments in the project plan. Currently, this usage view's timeline shows assigned work per day. As with the Gantt Chart timescale, you can adjust this timescale using the Timescale command on the View tab, or the Zoom In and Zoom Out controls on the View toolbar in the lower-right corner of the Project window.

Another usage view, the Task Usage view, flips the data around to display all the resources assigned to each task. You'll work more with usage views in Chapter 7, "Fine-Tuning Task Details."

7. On the **View** tab, in the **Task Views** group, click **Gantt Chart**.

   The Gantt Chart view appears.

   To conclude this exercise, you'll display a different split view.

8. If necessary, scroll the chart portion of the Gantt Chart view so that task 12 is visible.

9. In the **Task name** column, click the name of task 12, *Set pages*.

10. On the **View** tab, in the **Split View** group, click **Details**.

    The Task Form appears below the Gantt Chart view.

In this type of split view, the Gantt Chart is the primary view and the Task Form is the details pane. Details about the selected task in the Gantt Chart view appear in the Task Form. You can also edit values directly in the Task Form. You will work with the Task Form in Chapter 4, "Assigning Resources to Tasks," and with the similar Resource Form in Chapter 3, "Setting Up Resources."

11. On the **View** tab, in the **Split View** group, clear the **Details** check box.

    The Task Form closes.

There are many other views in Project. You can see them by clicking the Other Views command and then clicking More Views in the Task Views or Resource Views group on the View tab. It is important to understand that, in all these views as well as all the other views in Project, you are looking at different aspects of the same set of details about a project plan. Even a simple project plan can contain too much data to display at one time. Use views to help you focus on the specific details you want.

 CLEAN UP Close the Guided Tour file.

Key Points

- The Backstage view is the central location for managing files and customizing Project.

- The Fluent user interface, commonly called the ribbon interface, is a major visual change introduced in Project 2010. Commands are grouped on tabs for quick access.

- The main working space in Project is a view. One view (or sometimes two views) are typically displayed at a time. The Gantt with Timeline view is the default; the Gantt Chart is probably the best-known view in Project, and the Gantt chart is the best-known concept in project management as a whole.

Chapter at a Glance

Create a task list, page 27.

Change the project's working time, page 46.

Create summary tasks, page 35.

Link tasks and create dependencies, page 37.

Control if tasks are manually or automatically scheduled, page 43.

Add notes and hyperlinks to the Web, page 50.

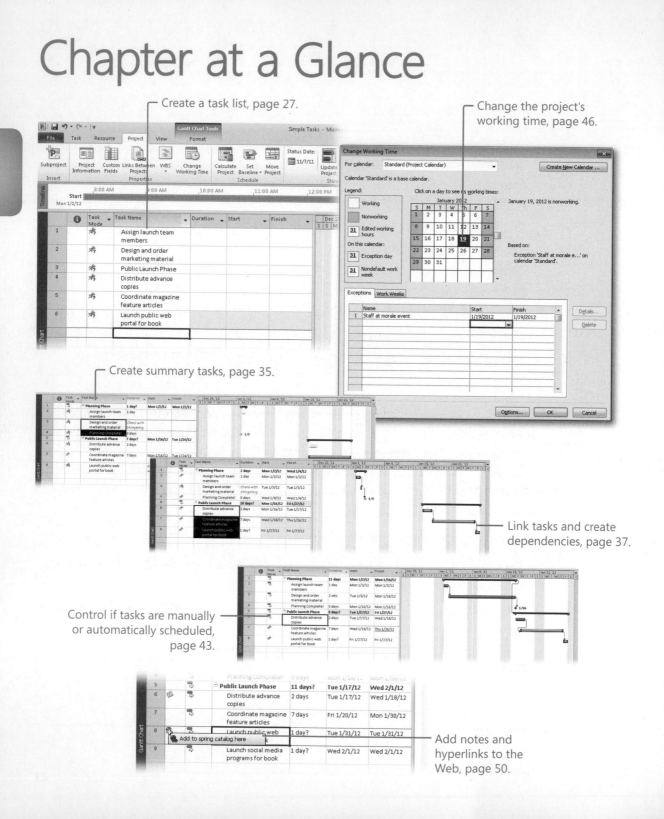

2 Creating a Task List

In this chapter, you will learn how to:

✔ Start Microsoft Project Standard or Professional and save a new project plan.

✔ Enter task names.

✔ Estimate and record how long each task should last.

✔ Create a milestone to track an important event.

✔ Organize tasks into phases.

✔ Create task relationships by linking tasks.

✔ Switch task scheduling from manual to automatic.

✔ Set nonworking days for the project plan.

✔ Check the project plan's overall duration.

✔ Record task details in notes and insert a hyperlink to content on the Web.

Tasks are the most basic building blocks of any project—tasks represent the work to be done to accomplish the goals of the project. Tasks describe project work in terms of *sequence*, *duration*, and resource requirements. In Project, there are several different kinds of tasks. These include summary tasks, subtasks, and milestones (all discussed in this chapter). More broadly, what are called tasks in Project are sometimes also called activities or work packages.

In this chapter, you will manage the scheduling of tasks in two different ways:

● Enter tasks as manually scheduled to quickly capture some details without actually scheduling tasks.

● Work with automatically scheduled tasks to begin to take advantage of the powerful scheduling engine in Project.

Practice Files Before you can complete the exercises in this chapter, you need to copy the book's practice files to your computer. A complete list of practice files is provided in "Using the Practice Files" at the beginning of this book. For each exercise that has a practice file, simply browse to where you saved the book's practice file folder.

> **Important** If you are running Project Professional, you may need to make a one-time setting change. This helps ensure that the practice files you work with in this chapter do not affect your Project Server data. For more information, see Appendix C, "Using the Practice Files if Connected to Project Server."

Creating a New Project Plan

A project plan is essentially a model that you construct of some aspects of a project you are anticipating—what you think will happen, or what you want to happen (it's usually best if these are not too different). This model focuses on some, but not all, aspects of the real project—tasks, resources, time frames, and possibly their associated costs. Note that throughout this book, we'll refer to the types of documents that Project works with as project plans, not documents or schedules.

As you might expect, Project focuses primarily on time. Sometimes you might know the planned start date of a project, the planned finish date, or both. However, when working with Project, you specify only one date, not both: the project start date or the project finish date. Why? Because after you enter the project start or finish date and the durations of the tasks, Project calculates the other date for you. Remember that Project is not just merely a static repository of your schedule information or a Gantt chart drawing tool; it is an active scheduling engine.

Most projects should be scheduled from a start date, even if you know that the project should finish by a certain deadline date. Scheduling from a start date causes all tasks to start as soon as possible, and it gives you the greatest scheduling flexibility. In this and later chapters, you will see this flexibility in action as we work with a project that is scheduled from a start date.

Project Management Focus: Project Is Part of a Larger Picture

Depending on your needs and the information to which you have access, the project plans that you develop might not deal with other important aspects of your projects. For example, many large projects are undertaken in organizations that have a formal change management process. Before a major change to the scope of a project is allowed, it must be evaluated and approved by the people managing and implementing the project. Even though this is an important project management activity, it is not something done directly within Project.

Now that you've had a brief look at the major parts of the Project interface in Chapter 1, "A Guided Tour of Project," you are ready to create the project plan you will use throughout Part 1 of this book, "Simple Scheduling." You'll play the role of a project manager at Lucerne Publishing, a book publisher that specializes in children's books. Lucerne is about to publish a major new book and you've been asked to develop a plan for the book launch. In this exercise, you create a new project plan, set its start date, and save it.

SET UP Start Project if it's not already running.

1. Click the **File** tab.

   Project displays the Backstage view.

2. Click the **New** tab.

   Project displays your options for creating a new project plan.

   These options include using templates installed with Project or available on the Web. For this exercise, you will create a new blank project plan.

3. Under **Available Templates**, make sure that **Blank project** is selected, and then click the **Create** button on the right side of the Backstage view.

   Project creates a new project plan. You may see a note briefly reminding you that new tasks are created in manually scheduled mode. This information remains visible on the status bar as well.

Notice the thin orange vertical line in the chart portion of the Gantt Chart view. This indicates the current date. When you create a new project plan, Project sets the plan's start date to the current date. Next you'll change the plan's start date.

4. On the **Project** tab, in the **Properties** group, click **Project Information**.

The Project Information dialog box appears.

Important If you are using Project Professional rather than Project Standard, the Project Information and some other dialog boxes contain additional options relating to Project Server. Throughout this book we won't use Project Server, so you can ignore these options. For more information about Project Server, see Appendix C.

5. In the **Start Date** box, type **1/2/12**, or click the down arrow to display the calendar and select **January 2, 2012**.

Tip In the calendar, you can navigate to any month and then click the date you want, or click Today to quickly choose the current date.

Project Standard users do not see this portion of the dialog box.

6. Click **OK** to accept this start date and close the **Project Information** dialog box.

7. On the **File** tab, click **Save**.

Because this project plan has not been previously saved, the Save As dialog box appears.

8. Locate the Chapter02 folder in the Project 2010 Step by Step folder on your hard disk. The default location for the Project 2010 Step by Step folder is \Documents\ Microsoft Press.

9. In the **File name** box, type **Simple Tasks**.

10. Click **Save** to close the **Save As** dialog box.

Entering Task Names

As mentioned previously, tasks represent the work to be done to accomplish the goals of the project. For this reason, it's worth developing good practices about how you name tasks in your project plans.

Task names should be recognizable and make sense to the people who will perform the tasks and to other stakeholders who will see the task names. Here are some guidelines for creating good task names:

● Use short verb phrases that describe the work to be done, such as "Edit manuscript."

● If tasks will be organized into *phases*, don't repeat details from the summary task name in the subtask name unless it adds clarity.

● If tasks will have resources assigned to them, don't include resource names in the task names.

Keep in mind that you can always edit task names later, so don't worry about getting exactly the right task names when you're initially entering them into a project plan. Do aim to use concise, descriptive phrases that communicate the required work and make sense to you and others who will perform the work.

In this exercise, you enter some initial tasks required for the new book launch events.

1. Click the cell directly below the **Task Name** column heading.

2. Type **Assign launch team members**, and then press the Enter key.

The task you entered is given an ID number. Each task has a unique ID number, but it does not necessarily represent the order in which tasks occur. Your screen should look similar to the following illustration.

The indicators in this column tell you whether a task is manually or automatically scheduled.

Because this is a manually scheduled task (as indicated in the Task Mode column), no duration or date values appear, and the task does not yet have a Gantt bar in the chart portion of the Gantt Chart view. Later you will work with automatically scheduled tasks that always have duration, start, and finish dates. Think of a manually scheduled task as an initial placeholder that you can create at any time without affecting the rest of the schedule. You might not know more than a task name at this time, and that's OK. As you discover or decide more details about the task, such as when it should occur, you can add those details to the project plan.

3. Enter the following task names, pressing Enter after each task name:

Design and order marketing material

Public Launch Phase

Distribute advance copies

Coordinate magazine feature articles

Launch public web portal for book

Your screen should look similar to the following illustration.

Project Management Focus: Defining the Right Tasks for the Deliverable

Every project has an ultimate goal or intent: the reason that the project was started. This is called the project deliverable. This deliverable might be a tangible product, such as a new book, or a service or event, such as a product launch party. Defining the right tasks to create the deliverable is an essential skill for a project manager. The task lists you create in Project should describe all the work required, and only the work required, to complete the project successfully.

When developing your task lists, you might find it helpful to distinguish product scope from project scope. Product scope describes the quality, features, and functions of the deliverable of the project. In the scenario used in Part 1 of this book, for example, the deliverable is a new children's book, and the product scope might include its number of pages and illustrations. Project scope, on the other hand, describes the work required to deliver such a product or service. In our scenario, the project scope includes detailed tasks relating to generating publicity and advance reviews for the book.

Entering Durations

In this section, you begin to work with task durations—the amount of time you expect it will take to complete the task. Project can work with task durations that range from minutes to months. Depending on the scope of your project, you'll probably want to work with task durations on the scale of hours, days, and weeks.

Let's explore durations with an example. Let's say a project has a project calendar with working time defined as 8 A.M. through 5 P.M. with one hour off for lunch breaks Monday through Friday, leaving nonworking time defined as evenings (after 5 P.M.) and weekends. If you estimate that a task will take 16 hours of working time, you could enter its duration as 2d, to schedule work over two eight-hour workdays. You should then expect that by starting the task at 8 A.M. on a Friday means that it wouldn't be completed until 5 P.M. on the following Monday. No work would be scheduled over the weekend because Saturday and Sunday have been defined as nonworking time.

Tip Project determines the overall duration of a project plan by calculating the difference between the earliest start date and the latest finish date of the plan's tasks. The plan's duration is also affected by other factors, such as task relationships, which are discussed in the "Linking Tasks" section later in this chapter. Because Project distinguishes between working and nonworking time, a task's duration doesn't necessarily correlate to elapsed time.

When working in Project, you can use abbreviations for durations.

If you enter this abbreviation	It appears like this	And it means
m	min	Minute
h	hr	Hour
d	day	Day
w	wk	Week
mo	mon	Month

Automatically scheduled tasks always have a duration (one day by default). *Manually scheduled tasks*, however, do not initially have any duration. A task's duration is essential for Project to schedule a task, so it makes sense that a manually scheduled task, which is not scheduled by Project, does not require a duration. You can, however, enter duration values for manually scheduled tasks—you'll do so in this section.

With manually scheduled tasks, you can enter regular duration values using the abbreviations shown previously; for example, 3d for three days. You can also enter text values, such as "Check with Bob." Such text values are replaced with the default 1-day duration value when you convert a task from manual to automatic scheduling.

Project uses standard values for minutes and hours for durations: 1 minute equals 60 seconds, and 1 hour equals 60 minutes. For the durations of days, weeks, and months you can use Project's defaults (for example, 20 days per month) or set your own values. To do this, on the File tab, click Options, and in the Options dialog box, click the Schedule tab, as illustrated here:

With a setting of 8 hours per day, entering a two-day task duration (2d) is the same as entering 16 hours (16h).

With a setting of 40 hours per week, entering a three-week task duration (3w) is the same as entering 120 hours (120h).

With a setting of 20 days per month, entering a one-month task duration (1mo) is the same as entering 160 hours (8 hours per day × 20 days per month).

The exercises in this chapter use the default values: 8 hours per day, 40 hours per week, and 20 days per month.

In this exercise, you enter various duration values for the tasks you've created.

1. Click the cell below the **Duration** column heading for task 1, *Assign launch team members*.

   The **Duration** field for task 1 is selected.

2. Type **1d**, and then press Enter.

   The value *1 day* appears in the Duration field. Project draws a Gantt bar for the task, starting at the project start date you previously set.

	ⓘ	Task Mode	Task Name	Duration	Start	Finish	Dec 25, '11	Jan 1, '12
							S S M T W T F	S S M T W T F
1		🏃	Assign launch team members	1 day				
2		🏃	Design and order marketing material					
3		🏃	Public Launch Phase					
4		🏃	Distribute advance copies					
5		🏃	Coordinate magazine feature articles					
6		🏃	Launch public web portal for book					

Until the tasks are linked or a specific start or finish date is set, Project will set all new tasks that have a duration value to start at the Project Start date. This is true whether the tasks are manually or automatically scheduled.

3. Enter the following durations or text phrases for the following tasks:

Task ID	Task name	Duration
2	Design and order marketing material	**Check with Marketing team**
3	Public Launch Phase	(press Enter to skip this task for now)
4	Distribute advance copies	**2d**

For task 5, *Coordinate magazine feature articles*, you'll enter start and finish dates and Project will calculate the duration.

4. In the **Start** field (not the Duration field) for task 5, type or select **1/16/12**, and then press the Tab key.

5. In the **Finish** field for the same task, type or select **1/24/12**, and then press Enter.

Project calculates the duration as seven days. Note that this is seven working days: Monday through Friday of the first week, and then Monday and Tuesday of the following week. Project also draws the Gantt bar for the task to span these working days plus the nonworking days (the weekend) between them, as shown here.

The project calendar's nonworking days, in this case ——
Saturday and Sunday, are formatted in gray.

6. For task 6, *Launch public web portal for the book*, you don't know a duration or start or finish date yet, but you can still capture what you do know.

7. In the **Start** field for task 6, type **About two weeks before launch complete**, and then press Enter.

As with the duration value of a manually scheduled task, you can also enter a text string for a start or finish date, or both. When the task is switched to be automatically scheduled, the text strings will be replaced with specific dates.

Project Management Focus: How Do You Come Up with Accurate Task Durations?

You should consider two general rules when estimating task durations:

- Overall project duration often correlates to task duration; long projects tend to have tasks with longer durations than do tasks in short projects.

- If you track progress against your project plan (described in Chapter 6, "Tracking Progress on Tasks," and in Part 2, "Advanced Scheduling"), you need to consider the level of detail that you want to apply to your project's tasks. If you have a multiyear project, for example, it might not be practical or even possible to track tasks that are measured in minutes or hours. In general, you should measure task durations at the lowest level of detail or control that is important to you, but no lower.

For the projects you work on in this book, the durations are usually supplied for you. For your projects, you will often have to estimate task durations. Good sources of task duration estimates include:

- Historical information from previous, similar projects

- Estimates from the people who will complete the tasks

- The expert judgment of people who have managed similar projects

- The standards of professional or industrial organizations that carry out projects similar to yours

For complex projects, you probably would combine these and other strategies to estimate task durations. Because inaccurate task duration estimates are a major source of *risk* in any project, making good estimates is well worth the effort expended.

One general rule of thumb to consider is called the *8/80 rule*. This rule suggests that task durations between 8 hours (or one day) and 80 hours (10 working days, or two weeks) are generally sized about right. Tasks shorter than one day might be too granular, and tasks longer than two weeks might be too long to manage properly. There are many legitimate reasons to break this rule, but for most tasks in your projects, it's worth considering.

Entering a Milestone

In addition to entering tasks to be completed, you might want to account for an important event for your project, such as when a major phase of the project will end. To do this, you will create a milestone task.

Milestones are significant events that are either reached within the project (such as completion of a phase of work) or imposed upon the project (such as a deadline by which to apply for funding). Because the milestone itself doesn't normally include any work, milestones are represented as tasks with zero duration.

In this exercise, you create a milestone task.

1. Click the name of task 3, *Public Launch Phase*.

2. On the **Task** tab, in the **Insert** group, click **Milestone**.

   Project inserts a row for a new task and renumbers the subsequent tasks. Project names the new task "<New Milestone>" and gives it a zero-day duration. As with the other new tasks, the milestone is initially scheduled at the project start date of January 2.

3. Type **Planning complete!** and then press Enter.

   The milestone task is added to your plan.

On the Gantt chart, the milestone appears as a diamond.

Tip You can mark a task of any duration as a milestone. Double-click the task name to display the Task Information dialog box, and then click the Advanced tab and select the "Mark task as milestone" option.

Organizing Tasks into Phases

It is helpful to organize groups of closely related tasks into phases. When reviewing a project plan, seeing tasks organized into phases helps you and your *stakeholders* think in terms of major work items. For example, it is common to divide book publishing projects into Editorial, Design, and Production phases. You create phases by indenting and outdenting tasks. In Project, phases are represented by summary tasks, and the tasks indented below the summary task are called *subtasks*.

When a summary task is manually scheduled, its duration will be calculated based on its subtasks, just like the duration of an automatically scheduled summary task. However, you can edit the duration of a manually scheduled task and Project will keep track of both the manual duration that you entered and the calculated duration.

The duration of an automatically scheduled summary task is calculated by Project as the span of time from the earliest start date to the latest finish date of its subtasks. If you directly edit the duration of an automatically scheduled summary task, or its start or finish date, it will be switched to a manually scheduled task.

Project Management Focus: Top-Down and Bottom-Up Planning

The two most common approaches to developing tasks and phases are top-down and bottom-up planning:

- *Top-down planning* identifies major phases or components of the project before filling in the tasks required to complete those phases. Complex projects can have several layers of phases. This approach works from general to specific.

- *Bottom-up planning* identifies as many of the bottom-level detailed tasks as possible before organizing them into logical groups called *phases* or *summary tasks*. This approach works from specific to general.

Creating accurate tasks and phases for most complex projects requires a combination of top-down and bottom-up planning. It is common for the project manager to begin with established, broad phases for a project (top-down), and for the resources who will execute the project to provide the detailed tasks that fill out each phase (bottom-up).

In this exercise, you organize the new book launch plan into two phases.

1. Select the names of tasks 5 through 7.

   These are the tasks you want to make subtasks of the public launch phase.

Indent Task

2. On the **Task** tab, in the **Schedule** group, click **Indent Task**.

   Project promotes task 4 to a summary task. Or you can think of it as Project demoting tasks 5 through 7 to subtasks; either way, the project plan now includes a summary task.

Summary task

Summary task bar in the Gantt chart

	ⓘ	Task Mode	Task Name	Duration	Start	Finish
1		馬	Assign launch team members	1 day		
2		馬	Design and order marketing material	*Check with Marketing*		
3		馬	Planning Complete!	0 days		
4		⬛	⊟ Public Launch Phase	7 days?	**Mon 1/16/12**	**Tue 1/24/12**
5		馬	Distribute advance copies	2 days		
6		⚓	Coordinate magazine feature articles	7 days	Mon 1/16/12	Tue 1/24/12
7		馬	Launch public web portal for book		*About two weeks before*	

Subtasks

Notice the scheduling effect of creating the summary task. Since task 6 had specific start and finish dates already, Project set the start date of the summary task (and its other subtask with a duration) to the same date, January 16.

Next you'll create another summary task in a different way.

3. Select the name of task 1, *Assign launch team members*.

4. On the **Task** tab, in the **Insert** group, click **Summary**.

   Project inserted a row for a new task, indented the task directly below it, and renumbered the subsequent tasks. Project names the new task "<New Summary Task>."

5. With the name of the new summary task selected, type **Planning Phase** and press Enter.

6. Select the names of tasks 3 and 4. You will indent these tasks under the summary task 1.

7. On the **Task** tab, in the **Schedule** group, click **Indent Task**.

Now the project plan is organized into two phases of work.

Linking Tasks

Most projects require tasks to be performed in a specific order. For example, the task of writing a chapter of a book must be completed before the task of editing the chapter can occur. These two tasks have a finish-to-start relationship (also called a *link* or a *dependency*), which has two aspects:

- The second task must occur after the first task; this is a sequence.

- The second task can occur only if the first task is completed; this is a dependency.

In Project, the first task ("write the chapter") is called the *predecessor* because it precedes tasks that depend on it. The second task ("edit the chapter") is called the *successor* because it succeeds, or follows tasks on which it is dependent. Any task can be a predecessor for one or more successor tasks. Likewise, any task can be a successor to one or more predecessor tasks.

Although this might sound complicated, tasks can have one of only four types of task relationships.

This task relationship	Means	Looks like this in the Gantt chart	Example
Finish-to-start (FS)	The finish date of the predecessor task determines the start date of the successor task.		A book chapter must be written before it can be edited.
Start-to-start (SS)	The start date of the predecessor task determines the start date of the successor task.		Ordering prepress and ordering paper are closely related, and they should occur simultaneously.
Finish-to-finish (FF)	The finish date of the predecessor task determines the finish date of the successor task.		Tasks that require specific equipment must end when the equipment rental period ends.
Start-to-finish (SF)	The start date of the predecessor task determines the finish date of the successor task.		The time when the print run is scheduled determines when a binder selection task must end.

Tip You can adjust the schedule relationship between predecessor and successor tasks with lead and lag time. For example, you can set a two-day lag between the end of a predecessor task and the start of its successor task. For more information, see Chapter 7, "Fine-Tuning Task Details."

Representing task relationships and handling changes to scheduled start and finish dates are two areas where the use of a scheduling engine such as Project really pays off. For example, you can change task durations or add or remove tasks from a chain of linked tasks, and Project will reschedule tasks accordingly.

Task relationships appear in several ways in Project, including the following:

- In the Gantt Chart and Network Diagram views, task relationships appear as the lines connecting tasks.

- In tables, such as the *Entry table*, task ID numbers of predecessor tasks appear in the Predecessor fields of successor tasks. (You might need to drag the vertical divider bar to the right to see the Predecessor column.)

You create task relationships by creating links between tasks. In this exercise, you use different methods to create links between several tasks, thereby creating finish-to-start relationships.

First, you'll create a finish-to-start dependency between two tasks.

1. Select the names of tasks 2 and 3.

Link Tasks

2. On the **Task** tab, in the **Schedule** group, click **Link Tasks**.

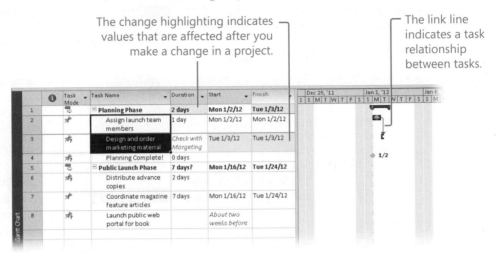

The change highlighting indicates values that are affected after you make a change in a project.

The link line indicates a task relationship between tasks.

Tasks 2 and 3 are linked with a finish-to-start relationship. Note that task 3 previously had no start or finish date, but by making it a successor of task 2, you gave Project enough information to give task 3 a start date: January 3, the next working day following the end of task 2.

Have you noticed the light blue highlighting of some of the Duration, Start, and Finish fields as you linked tasks? Project highlights the values that are affected after each change you make in a project plan.

Tip To unlink tasks, select the tasks you want to unlink, and then click Unlink Tasks in the Schedule group on the Task tab.

Next, you'll link tasks 3 and 4 using a different means.

3. Select the name of task 4, *Planning complete!*

4. On the **Task** tab, in the **Properties** group, click **Information**.

    The Task Information dialog box appears.

5. Click the **Predecessors** tab.

6. Click the empty cell below the **Task Name** column heading, and then click the down arrow that appears.

7. On the **Task Name** list, click *Design and order marketing material*.

8. Click **OK** to close the **Task Information** dialog box.

Tasks 3 and 4 are linked with a finish-to-start relationship.

Tip Recall that any task can have multiple predecessor tasks. One way you can specify additional predecessor tasks is to add them on the Predecessors tab of the Task Information dialog box. For finish-to-start relationships (the default link type), the predecessor with the later finish date will determine the start date of the successor task.

Next you'll link all the subtasks under Public Launch Phase in one action.

9. Select the names of tasks 6 through 8.

10. On the **Task** tab, in the **Schedule** group, click **Link Tasks**.

Tasks 6 through 8 are linked.

Tip To select tasks that are not adjacent, select the first task, hold down the Ctrl key, and then select the second task.

There are several ways of linking tasks, and you'll use one more to link the two phases of the new book launch plan.

11. In the chart portion of the Gantt Chart view, point the mouse pointer at the Gantt bar for task 1, *Planning Phase*, and then click and drag to the Gantt bar for task 5, *Public Launch Phase*.

When the mouse pointer is over task 5, note the link line and icon that appear. Release the mouse pointer.

This tooltip can help you — link tasks using the mouse.

The mouse pointer changes to — indicate that you are linking tasks.

The summary tasks 1 and 5 are linked with a finish-to-start relationship.

So far, you've used three different techniques to link tasks. As you use Project more, you'll probably find you prefer one of these or another way of linking tasks.

Tip When working with summary tasks, you can either link summary tasks directly (as you did previously), or link the latest task in the first phase with the earliest task in the second phase. The scheduling result is the same in either situation, but it's preferable to link the summary tasks to better reflect the sequential nature of the two phases. Under no circumstances, however, can you link a summary task to one of its own subtasks. Doing so would create a circular scheduling problem, so Project doesn't allow it.

To conclude this exercise, you'll enter a specific duration value for task 3. The Marketing team has reported that their estimate is task 3 should have a two-week duration.

12. In the duration field for task 3, type **2w**, and then press Enter.

The red squiggly line indicates a potential scheduling problem.

Notice that the new duration for task 3 caused the Planning Phase summary task's duration to increase, but it did not affect the scheduling of the task 4 milestone. Why not? Remember that this task is still manually scheduled. You can force Project to adjust the start and finish dates of this task while leaving it as manually scheduled.

13. Select the name of task 4.

14. On the **Task** tab, in the **Schedule** group, click **Respect Links**.

Project reschedules task 4 to start following the completion of its predecessor, task 3.

You might have noticed that the start of the Public Launch Phase summary task does not respect its link to its predecessor, the Planning Phase summary task. Clicking the Respect Link button with the Public Launch Phase summary task selected will not cause it to be rescheduled, as it did for task 4. That's because the start and finish dates of the summary task are driven by the earliest start and latest finish dates of its subtasks, which in this case are still manually scheduled. You'll address this issue next by switching to automatic scheduling.

Switching Task Scheduling from Manual to Automatic

Up to now, you've worked with manually scheduled tasks in the new book project. Manually scheduled tasks let you focus on capturing basic task details, such as name and sequence, without dealing with the complexity of Project's powerful scheduling engine. As a project plan becomes more detailed, though, you'll be ready to switch some or all tasks to automatic scheduling and to change the default for new tasks to automatic scheduling.

In this exercise, you convert some tasks and then the entire project plan to automatic scheduling.

1. Select the names of tasks 2 through 4.

    These tasks are currently set to be manually scheduled, as indicated by the push-pin indicator in the **Task Mode** column.

2. On the **Task** tab, in the **Tasks** group, click **Auto Schedule**.

    Project switches these tasks to be automatically scheduled.

Indicators in the Task Mode column tell you that these tasks are now automatically scheduled.

The formatting of automatically scheduled task bars is different from that of manually scheduled tasks.

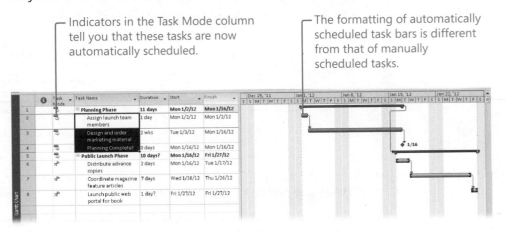

Project changes the Task Mode icons and formatting of the tasks' Gantt bars to indicate that they are now automatically scheduled.

3. Select the name of task 6, *Distribute advance copies*.

4. On the **Task** tab, in the **Tasks** group, click **Auto Schedule**.

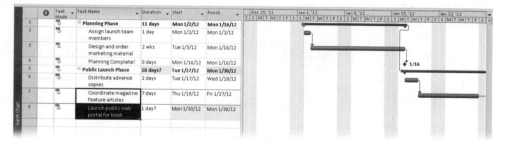

This time, task 6 was rescheduled to start later. Why did this happen? Recall the dependency between the two summary tasks. The dependency said in effect that the Public Launch Phase should start once the Planning Phase was complete. However, because task 6 and the other subtasks of the Public Launch Phase were manually scheduled, Project did not reschedule them to account for this dependency. As soon as you set task 6 to automatic scheduling, however, Project did just that and adjusted the start date of its summary task as well.

The remaining subtasks 7 and 8 are still manually scheduled, so Project left them alone. You'll switch these tasks next.

5. Select the names of task 7 and 8.

6. On the **Task** tab, in the **Tasks** group, click **Auto Schedule**.

Project reschedules the remaining tasks. This extends the duration of the Public Launch Phase and of the overall project.

Notice that Project supplied a one-day duration for task 8, which previously had a text note for its duration. Project did so because it requires a numeric time value for every automatically scheduled task's duration value. The question mark following the duration value indicates that this is an estimated duration; it has no effect on the scheduling of the task.

Right now, this project plan is set to treat all new tasks entered as manually sched-uled. You could leave this setting as is and then switch specific tasks to be auto-matically scheduled. However, this project plan is developed enough now to switch to automatic scheduling and later set some specific tasks to manually scheduled as needed.

7. On the **Task** tab, in the **Tasks** group, click **Mode** and then click **Auto Schedule**.

Tip You can also toggle the scheduling mode by clicking the New Tasks status bar text and then picking the other scheduling mode.

To see automatic scheduling in action, you'll add a new task to the project plan.

8. In the **Task Name** field, below task 8, type **Launch social media programs for book** and then press Enter.

Project adds the new task to the plan. By default, it is not linked to any other task and is scheduled to start at its summary task's start date. To end this exercise, you'll link it to another task.

9. Select the names of tasks 8 and 9.

10. On the **Task** tab, in the **Schedule** group, click **Link Tasks**.

Project links the two tasks. Notice that the duration of the Public Launch Phase summary task was updated automatically from 10 to 11 days.

Setting Nonworking Days

This exercise introduces calendars, the primary means by which you control when each task and resource can be scheduled for work in Project. In later chapters, you will work with other types of calendars; in this chapter, you work only with the project calendar.

The *project calendar* defines the general working and nonworking time for tasks. Project includes multiple calendars, called *base calendars*, any one of which serves as the project calendar for a project plan. You select the project calendar in the Project Information dialog box. Think of the project calendar as your organization's normal working hours. For example, this might be Monday through Fridays, 8 A.M. through 5 P.M., with a one-hour lunch break each day. Your organization or specific resources might have exceptions to this normal working time, such as holidays or vacation days. You'll address resource vacations in Chapter 3, "Setting Up Resources."

In this exercise, you'll create a working time exception in the project calendar.

1. If necessary, scroll the chart portion of the Gantt Chart view so the week of January 15 is visible.

You want to indicate that Thursday, January 19, will be a nonworking day for your organization.

2. On the **Project** tab, in the **Properties** group, click **Change Working Time**.

The Change Working Time dialog box appears.

3. In the **For calendar** box, click the down arrow.

The list that appears contains the three base calendars included with Project. These calendars are

- ○ **24 Hours**   Has no nonworking time
- ○ **Night Shift**   Covers a "graveyard" shift schedule of Monday night through Saturday morning, 11 P.M. to 8 A.M., with a one-hour break each day
- ○ **Standard**   The traditional working day, Monday through Friday from 8 A.M. to 5 P.M., with a one-hour break each day

Only one of the base calendars serves as the project calendar. For this project, you'll use the *Standard base calendar* as the project calendar, so leave it selected.

You know the entire staff will be at a morale event on January 19; therefore, no work should be scheduled that day. You will record this as a calendar exception.

4. In the **Name** field on the **Exceptions** tab in the lower portion of the dialog box, type **Staff at morale event**, and then click in the **Start** field.

5. In the **Start** field, type **1/19/12**, and then press Enter.

You could have also selected the date you want in the calendar above the Exceptions tab or from the drop-down calendar in the Start field.

The date is now scheduled as nonworking time for the project. In the dialog box, the date appears underlined and color formatting is applied to indicate an exception day.

6. Click **OK** to close the **Change Working Time** dialog box.

To verify the change to the project calendar, note in the chart that Thursday, January 19, is now formatted gray to indicate nonworking time (just like the weekends). The subsequent task is automatically rescheduled to start on the next working day, January 20.

In this section, you've made just one specific day a nonworking day. Other common examples of nonworking time include recurring holidays or unique working hours. You'll make such settings in Chapter 3, "Setting Up Resources."

Tip If needed, you can schedule tasks to occur during working and nonworking time. To do this, assign an *elapsed duration* to a task. You enter elapsed duration by preceding the duration abbreviation with an *e*. For example, type **3ed** to indicate three elapsed days. You might use an elapsed duration for a task that goes on around the clock rather than just during normal working hours. For instance, a construction project might have the tasks *Pour foundation concrete* and *Remove foundation forms* in a construction project. If so, you might also want a task called *Wait for concrete to cure* because you don't want to remove the forms until the concrete has cured. The task *Wait for concrete* to cure should have an elapsed duration because the concrete will cure over a contiguous range of days, whether they are working or nonworking days. If the concrete takes 48 hours to cure, you can enter the duration for that task as **2ed**, schedule the task to start on Friday at 9 A.M., and expect it to be complete by Sunday at 9 A.M. In most cases, however, you'll work with nonelapsed durations in Project.

Checking the Plan's Duration

At this point, you might want to know how long the project is expected to take. You haven't directly entered a total project duration or finish date, but Project has calculated these values based on individual task durations and task relationships. An easy way to view the project's scheduled start and finish dates is via the Timeline view and the Project Information dialog box.

In this exercise, you see the current total duration and scheduled finish date of the project based on the task durations and relationships you've entered.

1. In the Timeline view above the Gantt Chart view, note the project plan's current start and finish dates.

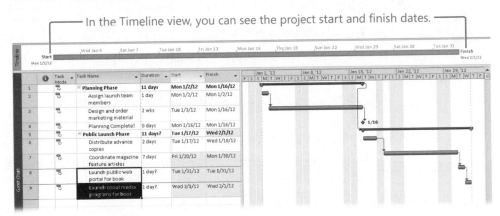

In the Timeline view, you can see the project start and finish dates.

Tip If the Timeline view is not shown, on the View tab, in the Split View group, click the Timeline check box.

The Timeline view is a handy way of seeing the "big picture" of the project plan. Here we're looking just at start and finish dates, but in later chapters, you'll work with the Timeline view in different ways.

Next you'll get a closer look at the plan's duration.

2. On the **Project** tab, in the **Properties** group, click **Project Information**.

   The Project Information dialog box appears.

   Here again you see the finish date: 2/1/12. You can't edit the finish date directly because this project plan is set to be scheduled from the start date. Project calculates the plan's finish date based on the span of working days required to complete the tasks, starting at the plan's start date. Any change to the start date will cause Project to recalculate the finish date.

   Next, let's look at the duration information in more detail.

3. Click **Statistics**.

Project Statistics for 'Simple Tasks'				
	Start		**Finish**	
Current		Mon 1/2/12		Wed 2/1/12
Baseline		NA		NA
Actual		NA		NA
Variance		0d		0d
	Duration	**Work**	**Cost**	
Current	22d?	0h	$0.00	
Baseline	0d	0h	$0.00	
Actual	0d	0h	$0.00	
Remaining	22d?	0h	$0.00	
Percent complete:				
Duration: 0%	Work: 0%		Close	

You don't need to understand all of these numbers yet, but the current duration is worth noting. The duration is the number of working days (not elapsed days) between the project's start date and finish date.

You can visually verify these numbers on the Gantt chart or Timeline view.

4. Click **Close** to close the **Project Statistics** dialog box.

Documenting Tasks and the Project Plan

You can record additional information about a task in a *note*. For example, you might have detailed descriptions of a task and still want to keep the task's name succinct. You can add such details to a task note. That way, the information resides in the project plan and can be easily viewed or printed.

There are three types of notes: task notes, resource notes, and assignment notes. You enter and review task notes on the Notes tab in the Task Information dialog box. Notes in Project support a wide range of text formatting options; you can even link to or store graphic images and other types of files in notes.

Hyperlinks allow you to connect a specific task to additional information that resides outside of the project plan—such as another file, a page on the Web, or a page on an intranet.

In this exercise, you enter task notes and hyperlinks to document important information about some tasks.

1. Select the name of task 6, *Distribute advance copies.*

2. On the **Task** tab, in the **Properties** group, click **Task Notes**.

    Tip You can also right-click the task name and click Notes in the shortcut menu that appears.

    Project displays the Task Information dialog box with the Notes tab visible.

3. In the **Notes** box, type **Get recipient list from publicist**.

4. Click **OK**.

    A note icon appears in the Indicators column.

5. Point to the note icon.

    The note appears in a ScreenTip. For notes that are too long to appear in a ScreenTip, you can double-click the note icon to display the full text of the note.

    To conclude this exercise, you create a hyperlink.

6. Right-click the name of task 8, *Launch public Web portal for book,* and then click **Hyperlink** on the shortcut menu.

    The Insert Hyperlink dialog box appears.

7. In the **Text to display** box, type **Add to spring catalog here**.

8. In the **Address** box, type **http://www.lucernepublishing.com/**

9. Click **OK**.

   A hyperlink icon appears in the Indicators column. Pointing to the icon displays the descriptive text you typed earlier.

To open the Web page in your browser, right-click on the hyperlink icon and in the shortcut menu that appears click Hyperlink, and then click Open Hyperlink.

To conclude this exercise, you'll record some information about the project plan. Like other Microsoft Office programs, Project keeps track of several file properties. Some of these properties are statistics, such as how many times the file has been revised. Other properties include information that you might want to record about a project plan, such as the project manager's name or keywords to support a file search. Project also uses properties in page headers and footers when printing.

In the following steps, you enter some properties that you will use later when printing and for other purposes.

10. Click the **File** tab.

    The Backstage view appears. The Info tab should be selected by default. Note the thumbnail image and key statistics such as the start date on the right side of the Backstage view.

11. Click the **Project Information** button directly below the thumbnail image. In the menu that appears, click **Advanced Properties**.

    The Properties dialog box appears with the Summary tab visible.

12. In the **Subject** box, type **New book launch schedule**.

13. In the **Author** box, type your name.

14. In the **Company** box, type **Lucerne Publishing**.

15. Select the **Save preview picture** check box.

The next time this file appears in the Open dialog box with the Preview option selected, a thumbnail image showing the first few tasks of the plan will be displayed.

16. Click **OK** to close the dialog box.

✖ **CLEAN UP** Close the Simple Tasks file.

Key Points

- Essential aspects of tasks in a project plan include their duration and order of occurrence.

- Task links, or relationships, cause the start or end of one task to affect the start or end of another task. A common task relationship is a finish-to-start relationship, in which the completion of one task controls the start of another task.

- In Project, phases of a schedule are represented as summary tasks.

- Tasks can be manually or automatically scheduled. For manually scheduled tasks, you can record whatever information you may have about a task's duration, start, and finish values.

- You use calendars in Project to control when work can be scheduled to occur.

- You can document additional details using task notes and create hyperlinks to the Web.

Chapter at a Glance

Create a list of resources, page 56.

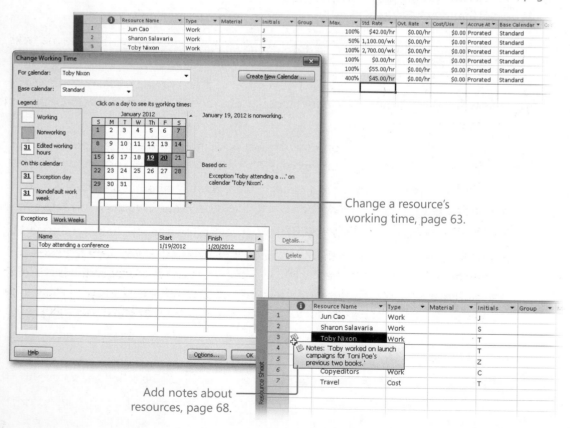

Change a resource's capacity to perform work, page 59.

Enter resource cost rates, page 60.

Change a resource's working time, page 63.

Add notes about resources, page 68.

3 Setting Up Resources

In this chapter, you will learn how to:

✔ Set up basic resource information for the people who work on projects.

✔ Adjust the maximum capacity of a resource to do work.

✔ Set up cost information for work resources.

✔ Change a resource's availability for work.

✔ Enter cost resource information for financial tracking.

✔ Record additional information about a resource in a note.

Microsoft Project 2010 supports three types of *resources*. These are work resources, as well as two special-purpose resources: cost and material. Briefly, here is how to think about the three resource types:

- *Work resources* include the people and equipment needed to complete the tasks in a project.

- *Cost resources* represent a financial cost associated with a task that you need to account for. Examples include categories of expenses like travel, entertainment, and so on.

- *Material resources* are consumables that you use up as the project proceeds. For example, a construction project might need to track steel or concrete as it is used throughout the project.

In this chapter you will set up work and cost resources. Material resources are described in Chapter 8, "Fine-Tuning Resource Details."

In this chapter, you will set up the work and cost resources that you need to complete the new book launch at Lucerne Publishing. Effective resource management is one of the most powerful advantages of using Project instead of task-focused planning tools, such as paper-based organizers. You do not need to set up resources and assign them to tasks in Project; however, without this information, you might be less effective in managing your schedule. Setting up resource information in Project takes a little effort, but the time is well spent if your project is primarily driven by time or cost constraints (and nearly all projects are driven by one, if not both, of these factors).

> **Practice Files** Before you can complete the exercises in this chapter, you need to copy the book's practice files to your computer. A complete list of practice files is provided in "Using the Practice Files" at the beginning of this book. For each exercise that has a practice file, simply browse to where you saved the book's practice file folder.

Important If you are running Project Professional, you may need to make a one-time setting change. This helps ensure that the practice files you work with in this chapter do not affect your Project Server data. For more information, see Appendix C, "Using the Practice Files if Connected to Project Server."

Setting Up Work Resources

Work resources are the people and equipment that do the work of the project. Project focuses on two aspects of work resources: their availability and their costs. Availability determines when specific resources can work on tasks and how much work they can perform, and costs refer to how much money will be required to pay for those resources.

Some examples of work resources are listed in this table.

Work Resource	Example
Individual people identified by name.	Jun Cao; Zac Woodall
Individual people identified by job title or function.	Publisher; Contract specialist
Groups of people who have common skills. (When assigning such interchangeable resources to a task, you might not be concerned about who the individual resource is so long as they have the right skills.)	Copyeditors; Typesetters
Equipment.	Offset lithography press

Equipment Resource Considerations

In Project, you set up people and equipment resources in exactly the same way; they are both examples of work resources. However, you should be aware of important differences in how you can schedule these two work resources. Most people resources have a working day of typically 8 and usually no more than 12 hours, but equipment resources might have much more varied capacities for work, ranging from short durations (followed by maintenance) to around the clock without interruption. Moreover, people resources might be flexible in the tasks they can perform, but equipment resources tend to be more specialized. For example, a content editor for a book project might also act as a copyeditor in a pinch, but a desktop copy machine cannot replace a printing press.

You do not need to track every piece of equipment that will be used in your project, but you might want to set up equipment resources when

- Multiple teams or people might need a piece of equipment to accomplish different tasks simultaneously, and the equipment might be overbooked.
- You want to plan and track costs associated with the equipment.

Consider these issues if your projects involve equipment resources.

Project can help you make smarter decisions about managing work resources and monitoring financial costs.

In this exercise, you enter the names of several people resources.

SET UP Start Project if it's not already running.

You need the Simple Resources_Start project plan located in your Chapter03 practice file folder to complete this exercise. Open the Simple Resources_Start project plan, and then follow these steps.

1. On the **File** tab, click **Save As**.

   Project displays the Save As dialog box.

2. In the **File name** box, type **Simple Resources**, and then click **Save**.

   Tip You can instruct Project to automatically save the active project plan at predefined intervals, such as every 10 minutes. On the File tab, click Options. In the Project Options dialog box, click Save, select the Auto Save Every check box, and then specify the time interval you want.

3. On the **View** tab, in the **Resource Views** group, click **Resource Sheet**.

You will use the Resource Sheet view to enter the initial list of resources for the new book launch project.

4. Click the cell directly below the **Resource Name** column heading.

5. Type **Jun Cao**, and press the Enter key.

Project creates a new resource.

6. On the next empty rows in the **Resource Name** column, enter the following names:

Sharon Salavaria

Toby Nixon

Toni Poe

Zac Woodall

When you create a new work resource, Project assigns it 100% Max. Units by default.

	ⓘ	Resource Name	Type	Material	Initials	Group	Max.	Std. Rate	Ovt. Rate	Cost/Use	Accrue At	Base Calendar	Co
1		Jun Cao	Work		J		100%	$0.00/hr	$0.00/hr	$0.00	Prorated	Standard	
2		Sharon Salavaria	Work		S		100%	$0.00/hr	$0.00/hr	$0.00	Prorated	Standard	
3		Toby Nixon	Work		T		100%	$0.00/hr	$0.00/hr	$0.00	Prorated	Standard	
4		Toni Poe	Work		T		100%	$0.00/hr	$0.00/hr	$0.00	Prorated	Standard	
5		Zac Woodall	Work		Z		100%	$0.00/hr	$0.00/hr	$0.00	Prorated	Standard	

These are all individual people. You can also have a resource that represents multiple people. You'll enter such a resource next.

7. In the **Resource Name** field, below the last resource, type **Copyeditors**, and then press Enter.

What Is the Best Way to Enter Resource Names?

In Project, work resource names can refer to specific people (Sharon Salavaria) or to specific job titles, such as Publisher or Contract Specialist. Use whatever naming convention makes the most sense to you and to those who will see your project plan information. The important questions are: who will see these resource names, and how will they identify the resources? The resource names that you choose will appear both in Project and in any resource information shared from Project. For example, in the default Gantt Chart view, the name of the resource appears next to the bars of the tasks to which that resource is assigned.

A resource might refer to somebody who is already on staff or to a position to be filled later. If you have not yet filled all the resource positions required, you might not have real people's names to enter. In that case, use descriptive placeholder names or job titles when setting up resources in Project.

Entering Resource Capacity

The Max. Units field represents the maximum capacity of a resource to accomplish any task. Specifying that a resource has 100% *maximum units* means that 100 percent of that resource's working time is available to work on assigned tasks in the project plan. Project will alert you if you assign the resource to more tasks than they can accomplish at 100% maximum units (in other words, if the resource becomes *overallocated*). 100% is the default Max. Units value for new resources.

For a resource that represents not a specific person, but a category of interchangeable people with a common skill set, you can enter a larger Max. Units value to indicate the number of available people. Entering a Max. Units setting such as 800% for such a resource means that you can expect that eight individual people who all belong to that resource category will be available to work full time every workday.

In this exercise, you adjust the Max. Units values to indicate one resource that represents multiple people, and another resource whose capacity to work in this project plan is less than full time.

1. Click the **Max. Units** field for the *Copyeditors* resource.

2. Type or select **400%**, and then press Enter.

   Tip When you click a numeric value in a field like Max. Units, up and down arrows appear. You can click these to display the number you want, or simply type the number in the field.

Next you'll update the Max. Units value for Sharon Salavaria to indicate that she works half time.

3. Click the **Max. Units** field for *Sharon Salavaria*, type or select **50%**, and then press Enter.

		Resource Name ▾	Type ▾	Material ▾	Initials ▾	Group ▾	Max. ▾	Std. Rate ▾	Ovt. Rate ▾	Cost/Use ▾	Accrue At ▾	Base Calendar ▾
1		Jun Cao	Work		J		100%	$0.00/hr	$0.00/hr	$0.00	Prorated	Standard
2		Sharon Salavaria	Work		S		50%	$0.00/hr	$0.00/hr	$0.00	Prorated	Standard
3		Toby Nixon	Work		T		100%	$0.00/hr	$0.00/hr	$0.00	Prorated	Standard
4		Toni Poe	Work		T		100%	$0.00/hr	$0.00/hr	$0.00	Prorated	Standard
5		Zac Woodall	Work		Z		100%	$0.00/hr	$0.00/hr	$0.00	Prorated	Standard
6		Copyeditors	Work		C		400%	$0.00/hr	$0.00/hr	$0.00	Prorated	Standard

Tip If you prefer, you can enter maximum units as partial or whole numbers (.5, 1, 4) rather than as percentages (50%, 100%, 400%). To use this format, on the File tab, click Options. In the Project Options dialog box, click the Schedule tab. In the Show assignment units as a box, click Decimal.

With these changes to Max. Units, Project will identify these resources as being overallocated when their assigned work exceeds their capacities. You will work with resource overallocation in Chapters 8 and 9.

Entering Resource Pay Rates

Almost all projects have some financial aspect, and cost limits the scope of many projects. Tracking and managing cost information allows the project manager to answer such important questions as the following:

- What is the expected total cost of the project based on our task durations and resource assignments?

- Are we using expensive resources to do work that less expensive resources could do?

- How much money will a specific type of resource or task cost over the life of the project?

- Are we spending money at a rate that we can sustain for the planned duration of the project?

You can enter standard rates and costs per use for work and material resources, as well as overtime rates for work resources. Cost resources do not use pay rates and are described later in this chapter.

When a work resource has a standard pay rate entered and is assigned to a task, Project calculates the cost of the assignment. Project does so by multiplying the assignment's work value by the resource's pay rate—both using a common increment of time (such as hours). You can then see cost per resource, cost per assignment, and cost per task (as well as costs rolled up to summary tasks and the entire project plan). You will assign resources to tasks in Chapter 4, "Assigning Resources to Tasks."

Project handles overtime expenses differently. Project will apply the overtime pay rate only when you specifically record overtime hours for an assignment. You will find more information about working with overtime in Chapter 14, "Getting Your Project Back On Track." Project does not automatically calculate overtime hours and associated costs because there's too great a chance that it would apply overtime when you did not intend it. In the new book launch project plan, Jun Cao's working schedule provides a good example. In the next exercise, you will set up a working schedule of 10 hours per day, four days per week for Jun. This is still a regular 40-hour workweek, even though 2 hours per day could be mistaken for overtime with the normal assumption of an 8-hour day.

In addition to or instead of cost rates, a resource can include a set fee that Project accrues to each task to which the resource is assigned. This is called a cost per use. Unlike cost rates, the cost per use does not vary with the task's duration or amount of work the resource performs on the task. You specify the cost per use in the Cost/Use field in the Resource Sheet view.

In this exercise, you enter standard and overtime pay rates for work resource.

1. In the **Resource Sheet**, click the **Std. Rate** field for *Jun Cao*.

2. Type **42** and press Enter.

   Jun's standard hourly rate of $42 appears in the Std. Rate column. Note that the default standard rate is hourly, so you did not need to specify cost per hour.

3. In the **Std. Rate** field for *Sharon Salavaria*, type **1100/w** and press Enter.

   Sharon's weekly pay rate appears in the Std. Rate column.

		Resource Name	Type	Material	Initials	Group	Max.	Std. Rate	Ovt. Rate	Cost/Use	Accrue At	Base Calendar
1		Jun Cao	Work		J		100%	$42.00/hr	$0.00/hr	$0.00	Prorated	Standard
2		Sharon Salavaria	Work		S		50%	1,100.00/wk	$0.00/hr	$0.00	Prorated	Standard
3		Toby Nixon	Work		T		100%	$0.00/hr	$0.00/hr	$0.00	Prorated	Standard
4		Toni Poe	Work		T		100%	$0.00/hr	$0.00/hr	$0.00	Prorated	Standard
5		Zac Woodall	Work		Z		100%	$0.00/hr	$0.00/hr	$0.00	Prorated	Standard
6		Copyeditors	Work		C		400%	$0.00/hr	$0.00/hr	$0.00	Prorated	Standard

4. Enter the following standard pay rates for the given resources:

Resource Name	Standard Rate
Toby Nixon	2700/w
Toni Poe	Leave at 0 (Toni is the book author and you're not tracking her rate-based costs in this project plan)
Zac Woodall	55
Copyeditors	45

		Resource Name	Type	Material	Initials	Group	Max.	Std. Rate	Ovt. Rate	Cost/Use	Accrue At	Base Calendar	C
	1	Jun Cao	Work		J		100%	$42.00/hr	$0.00/hr	$0.00	Prorated	Standard	
	2	Sharon Salavaria	Work		S		50%	1,100.00/wk	$0.00/hr	$0.00	Prorated	Standard	
	3	Toby Nixon	Work		T		100%	2,700.00/wk	$0.00/hr	$0.00	Prorated	Standard	
	4	Toni Poe	Work		T		100%	$0.00/hr	$0.00/hr	$0.00	Prorated	Standard	
	5	Zac Woodall	Work		Z		100%	$55.00/hr	$0.00/hr	$0.00	Prorated	Standard	
	6	Copyeditors	Work		C		400%	$45.00/hr	$0.00/hr	$0.00	Prorated	Standard	

As you can see, you can enter pay rates with a variety of time bases—hourly (the default), daily, weekly, and so on. In fact, you can enter pay rates in all the increments of time for which you can enter task durations—from minutes to years.

Next, you will enter an overtime pay rate for one of the resources.

5. In the **Overtime Rate** field for *Jun Cao*, type **67**, and then press Enter.

Tip If you work with a large number of resources who have the same standard or overtime pay rates, you can set up Project to apply these pay rates automatically whenever you add a new resource. You do this in the Advanced tab of the Project Options dialog box, which is accessible from the File tab.

Project Management Focus: Getting Resource Cost Information

Work resources can account for the majority of costs in many projects. To take full advantage of the extensive cost management features in Project, the project manager would ideally know the costs associated with each work resource. For people resources, it might be difficult to obtain such information. In many organizations, only senior management and human resource specialists know the pay rates of all resources working on a project, and they might consider this information confidential. Depending on your organizational policies and project priorities, you might not be able to track resource pay rates. If you cannot track resource cost information and your project is constrained by cost, your effectiveness as a project manager might be reduced, and the sponsors of your projects should understand this limitation. If you do include cost details in your project plan and this is considered sensitive information, consider requiring a password to open such project plans. To set a password, click the File tab, and then click Save As. In the Save As dialog box, click Tools and then click General Options.

Adjusting Working Time for Individual Resources

Project uses different types of calendars for different purposes. In Chapter 2, "Creating a Task List," you modified the *project calendar* to specify nonworking days for the entire project. In this exercise, you will focus on the resource calendar. A *resource calendar* controls the working and nonworking times of an individual resource. Project uses resource calendars to determine when work for a specific resource can be scheduled. Resource calendars apply only to work resources (people and equipment), not to material or cost resources.

When you initially create resources in a project plan, Project creates a resource calendar for each work resource. The initial working time settings for resource calendars exactly match those of the project calendar, which by default is the *Standard base calendar*. The Standard base calendar is built into Project and accommodates a default work schedule from 8 A.M. to 5 P.M., Monday through Friday, with an hour off for lunch each day. If all the working times of your resources match the working time of the project calendar, you do not need to edit any resource calendars. However, chances are that some of your resources will need exceptions to the working time in the project calendar—such as

- A flex-time work schedule
- Vacation time
- Other times when a resource is not available to work on the project, such as time spent training or attending a conference

Tip If you have a resource who is available to work on your project only part time, you might be tempted to set the working time of the resource in your project to reflect a part-time schedule, such as 8 A.M. to 12 P.M. daily. However, a better approach would be to adjust the availability of the resource as recorded in the Max. Units field to 50%, as you did for the previous exercise for the resource named Sharon Salavaria. Changing the unit availability of the resource keeps the focus on the capacity of the resource to work on the project rather than on the specific times of the day when that work might occur. You set the maximum units for a resource in the Resource Sheet view.

Changes that you make to the project calendar are reflected automatically in resource calendars derived from the same project calendar. For example, in Chapter 2, you specified a nonworking day for a staff morale event, and Project rescheduled all work to skip that day.

In this exercise, you specify the working and nonworking times for individual work resources.

1. On the **Project** tab, in the **Properties** group, click **Change Working Time**.

   The Change Working Time dialog box appears.

2. In the **For calendar** box, click *Toby Nixon*.

Toby Nixon's resource calendar appears in the Change Working Time dialog box. Toby has told you he will not be available to work on Thursday and Friday, January 19 and 20, because he plans to attend a book industry conference.

3. On the **Exceptions** tab in the **Change Working Time** dialog box, click in the first row directly below the **Name** column heading and type **Toby attending a conference**.

The description for the calendar exception is a handy reminder for you and others who may view the project plan later.

4. Click in the **Start** field and type or select **1/19/12**.

5. Click in the **Finish** field, type or select **1/20/12**, and then press the Enter key.

Tip Alternatively, in the calendar you can first select the date or date range for which you want to create an exception, and then enter the exception name. Project will insert the Start and Finish dates automatically based on your selection, and then press the Enter key.

Every work resource calendar is based on the project calendar; the default project calendar is the Standard base calendar.

Project will not schedule work for Toby on these dates.

Tip To set up a partial working time exception for a resource, such as a portion of a day when a resource cannot work, click Details. In the Details dialog box, you can also create recurring exceptions to the resource's availability.

To conclude this exercise, you will set up a "4 by 10" work schedule (that is, 4 days per week, 10 hours per day) for a resource.

6. In the **For** box, click *Jun Cao*.

7. When prompted to save the resource calendar changes that you made for Toby Nixon, click **Yes**.

8. Click the **Work Weeks** tab in the **Change Working Time** dialog box.

9. Click **[Default]** directly under the **Name** column heading, and then click **Details**.

Next, you will modify the default working week days and times for Jun Cao.

10. Under **Selected Day(s)**, select **Monday** through **Thursday**.

These are the weekdays Jun can normally work.

11. Click **Set day(s) to these specific working times**.

Next you'll modify Jun's regular daily schedule for the days she normally works.

12. In row 2, click **5:00 PM** and replace it with **7:00 PM**, and then press Enter.

Finally, you will mark Friday as a nonworking day for Jun.

13. Click **Friday**.

14. Click **Set days to nonworking time**.

Now Project can schedule work for Jun as late as 7 P.M. every Monday through Thursday, but it will not schedule work for her on Fridays.

15. Click **OK** to close the **Details** dialog box.

You can see in the calendar in the Change Working Time dialog box that Fridays (as well as Saturdays and Sundays) are marked as nonworking days for Jun Cao.

16. Click **OK** to close the **Change Working Time** dialog box.

Because you have not yet assigned these resources to tasks, you don't see the scheduling effect of their nonworking time settings. You will observe this in Chapter 4.

Tip If you find that you must edit several resource calendars in a similar way (to handle a night shift, for example), it may be easier to assign a different base calendar to a resource or collection of resources. This is more efficient than editing individual calendars, and it allows you to make project-wide adjustments to a single base calendar if needed. For example, if your project includes a day shift and a night shift, you can apply the Night Shift base calendar to those resources who work the night shift. You change a base calendar in the Change Working Time dialog box. For collections of resources, you can select a specific base calendar directly in the Base Calendar column on the Entry table in the Resource Sheet view.

Setting Up Cost Resources

Another type of resource that you can use in Project is the cost resource. You can use a cost resource to represent a financial cost associated with a task in a project. While work resources (people and equipment) can have associated costs (hourly rates and fixed costs per assignment), the sole purpose of a cost resource is to associate a particular type of cost with one or more tasks. Common types of cost resources might include categories of expenses you'd want to track on a project for accounting or financial reporting purposes, such as travel, entertainment, or training.

Cost resources do no work and have no effect on the scheduling of a task. The Max. Units Standard and Overtime pay rates and Cost/Use fields do not apply to cost resources. After you assign a cost resource to a task and specify the cost amount per task, you can then see the cumulative costs for that type of cost resource, such as total travel costs in a project.

The way in which cost resources generate cost values differs from that of work resources. When you assign a work resource to a task, the work resource can generate a cost based on a pay rate (such at $40 per hour for the length of the assignment), a flat per-use cost (such as $100 per assignment), or both. You set up such pay rates and cost per use amounts once for the work resource, as you did in the section "Entering Resource Pay Rates" earlier in this chapter. However, you enter the cost value of a cost resource only when you assign it to a task. You can do so in the Cost field of the Assign Resources dialog box or in the Cost field of the Task Form with the Cost detail shown.

Lucerne Publishing maintains a profit and loss (P&L) sheet for every book it publishes. Travel is a major expense incurred in a book launch.

In this exercise, you'll set up a cost resource.

1. In the **Resource Sheet**, click the next empty cell in the **Resource Name** column.

2. Type **Travel** and press the Tab key.

3. In the **Type** field, click **Cost**.

	ⓘ	Resource Name	Type	Material	Initials	Group	Max.	Std. Rate	Ovt. Rate	Cost/Use	Accrue At	Base Calendar	Co
1		Jun Cao	Work		J		100%	$42.00/hr	$67.00/hr	$0.00	Prorated	Standard	
2		Sharon Salavaria	Work		S		50%	1,100.00/wk	$0.00/hr	$0.00	Prorated	Standard	
3		Toby Nixon	Work		T		100%	2,700.00/wk	$0.00/hr	$0.00	Prorated	Standard	
4		Toni Poe	Work		T		100%	$0.00/hr	$0.00/hr	$0.00	Prorated	Standard	
5		Zac Woodall	Work		Z		100%	$55.00/hr	$0.00/hr	$0.00	Prorated	Standard	
6		Copyeditors	Work		C		400%	$45.00/hr	$0.00/hr	$0.00	Prorated	Standard	
7		Travel	Cost		T						Prorated		

You will assign a cost resource in Chapter 4.

Documenting Resources

You might recall from Chapter 2 that you can record any additional information about a task, resource, or assignment in a *note*. For example, if a resource has flexible skills that can help the project, it is a good idea to record this in a note. In that way, the note resides in the project plan and can be easily viewed or printed.

In this exercise, you enter resource notes relevant to the new book launch project. In Chapter 2, you entered a task note via the Task Notes button on the Task tab of the Properties group. You can enter resource notes in a similar way (via the Notes button on the Resource tab of the Properties group) but in this exercise, you'll use a different method. You'll use the Resource form, which allows you to view and edit notes for multiple resources more quickly.

In this exercise, you'll enter notes in the Resource Form.

1. In the **Resource Name** column, click *Toby Nixon*.

2. On the **Resource** tab, in the **Properties** group, click the **Details** button.

   Tip You can also click Details, Resource Form on the View tab of the Split View group.

   The Resource Form appears below the Resource Sheet view.

In this type of split view, details about the selected item in the upper view (a resource, in this case) appear in the lower view. You can quickly change the selected resource name in the upper view by clicking directly on a name, using the up arrow or down arrow keys, or by clicking Previous or Next in the Resource Form.

The Resource Form can display one of several details; initially it displays the Schedule details. Next you'll switch it to display the Notes details.

3. Click anywhere in the **Resource Form**.

4. On the **Format** tab, in the **Details** group, click **Notes**.

Tip You can also right-click in the gray background area of the Resource Form and, in the shortcut menu that appears, click Notes.

The Notes details appear in the Resource Form.

5. In the **Notes** box, type **Toby worked on launch campaigns for Toni Poe's previous two books.**

Notice that as soon as you started typing the note, the Previous and Next buttons changed to OK and Cancel.

6. Click **OK**.

In the Resource Sheet view, a note icon appears in the Indicators column.

7. Point to the note icon that appears next to Toby's name in the Resource Sheet.

	ⓘ	Resource Name ▼	Type ▼	Material ▼	Initials ▼	Group ▼	M
1		Jun Cao	Work		J		
2		Sharon Salavaria	Work		S		
3		Toby Nixon	Work		T		
4		Notes: 'Toby worked on launch campaigns for Toni Poe's previous two books.'			T		
5					Z		
6		Copyeditors	Work		C		
7		Travel	Cost		T		

The note appears in a ScreenTip. For notes that are too long to appear in a ScreenTip, you can double-click the note icon to display the full text of the note. You can also see more of long notes in the Resource Form or in the Resource Information dialog box.

To conclude this exercise, you'll add a note for one more resource.

8. In the **Resource Form**, click **Previous** to shift the focus to Sharon Salavaria and display her details.

Tip You can also click on Sharon's name in the Resource Sheet view above the Resource Form.

9. In the **Notes** box, type **Sharon's standard pay rate is adjusted for her half-time work schedule.** Then click **OK**.

	ⓘ	Resource Name ▼	Type ▼	Material ▼	Initials ▼	Group ▼	Max. ▼	Std. Rate ▼	Ovt. Rate ▼	Co
1		Jun Cao	Work		J		100%	$42.00/hr	$67.00/hr	
2		Sharon Salavaria	Work		S		50%	1,100.00/wk	$0.00/hr	
3		Toby Nixon	Work		T		100%	2,700.00/wk	$0.00/hr	
4		Toni Poe	Work		T		100%	$0.00/hr	$0.00/hr	
5		Zac Woodall	Work		Z		100%	$55.00/hr	$0.00/hr	
6		Copyeditors	Work		C		400%	$45.00/hr	$0.00/hr	
7		Travel	Cost		T					

Name: Sharon Salavaria | Initials: S | Max units: 50% | Previous | Next

Costs
Std rate: $1,100.00/w | Per use: $0.00 | Base cal: Standard
Ovt rate: $0.00/h | Accrue at: Prorated | Group:
| | | Code:

Sharon's standard pay rate is adjusted for her half-time work schedule.

Finally, you'll close the Resource Form.

10. On the **Resource** tab, in the **Properties** group, click the **Details** button.

The Resource Form is closed, leaving the Resource Sheet displayed.

In this exercise, you've entered notes for some resources. This information is unique to those resources.

❌ **CLEAN UP** Close the Simple Resources file.

Key Points

- Recording resource information in your project plans helps you better control who does what work when and at what costs.

- Work resources (people and equipment) perform the work in a project.

- Cost resources account for the types of expenses that you may wish to track across a project.

Chapter at a Glance

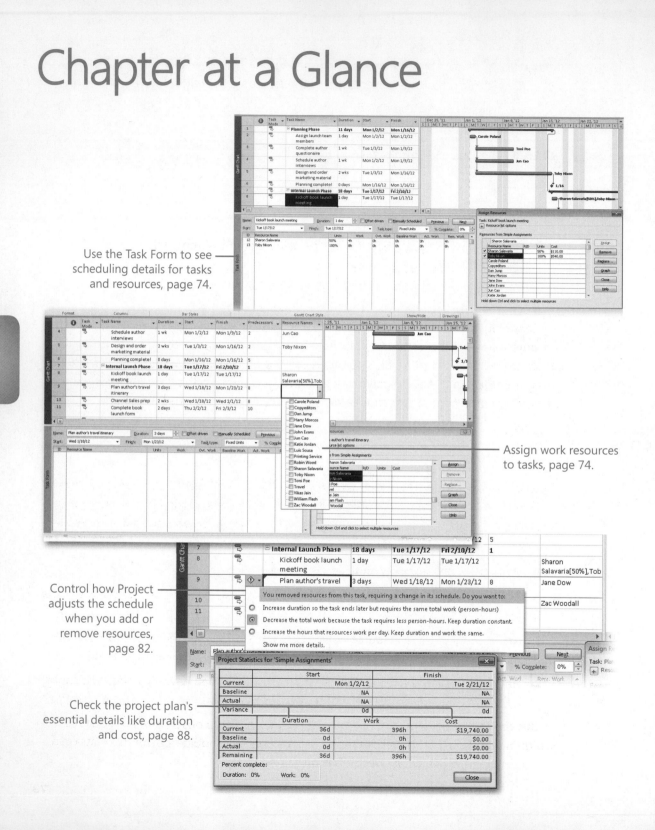

Use the Task Form to see scheduling details for tasks and resources, page 74.

Assign work resources to tasks, page 74.

Control how Project adjusts the schedule when you add or remove resources, page 82.

Check the project plan's essential details like duration and cost, page 88.

4 Assigning Resources to Tasks

In this chapter, you will learn how to:

✔ Assign work resources to tasks.

✔ Control how Project schedules additional resource assignments.

✔ Assign cost resources to tasks.

In Chapters 2 and 3, you created tasks and resources. You are now ready to assign resources to tasks. An *assignment* is the matching of a *resource* to a *task* to do work. From the perspective of a task, you might call the process of assigning a resource a task assignment; from the perspective of a resource, you might call it a resource assignment. It is the same thing in either case: a task plus a resource equals an assignment.

Important When we talk about resources throughout this chapter, we are talking about work resources (people and equipment) unless we specify material or cost resources. For a refresher on resource types, see Chapter 3, "Setting Up Resources."

You do not have to assign resources to tasks in Microsoft Project 2010; you could work only with tasks. However there are several good reasons for assigning resources in your project plan. When you assign resources to tasks, you can answer questions such as the following:

- Who should be working on what tasks and when?

- Do you have the correct number of resources to accomplish the scope of work that your project requires?

- Are you expecting a resource to work on a task at a time when that resource will not be available to work (for example, when someone will be on vacation)?

- Have you assigned a resource to so many tasks that you have exceeded the capacity of the resource to work—in other words, have you *overallocated* the resource?

In this chapter, you assign *work resources* to tasks, and you observe where resource assignments should affect task duration and where they should not. You then assign a *cost resource* and see what effect it has on a task.

> **Practice Files** Before you can complete the exercises in this chapter, you need to copy the book's practice files to your computer. A complete list of practice files is provided in "Using the Practice Files" at the beginning of this book. For each exercise that has a practice file, simply browse to where you saved the book's practice file folder.

Important If you are running Project Professional, you may need to make a one-time setting change. This helps ensure that the practice files you work with in this chapter do not affect your Project Server data. For more information, see Appendix C, "Using the Practice Files if Connected to Project Server."

Assigning Work Resources to Tasks

Assigning a work resource to a task enables you to track the progress of the resource's work on the task. If you enter resource pay rates, Project also calculates resource and task costs for you.

You might recall from Chapter 3 that the capacity of a resource to work is measured in units (a level of effort measurement), and recorded in the *Max. Units* field. Unless you specify otherwise, Project assigns 100 percent of the units for the resource to the task—that is, Project assumes that all the resource's work time can be allotted to the task. If the resource has less than 100 percent maximum units, Project assigns the resource's Max. Units value.

In this exercise, you make some initial resource assignments to tasks.

 SET UP Start Project if it's not already running.

You need the Simple Assignments_Start project plan located in your Chapter04 practice file folder to complete this exercise. Open the Simple Assignments_Start project plan, and then follow these steps.

1. On the **File** tab, click **Save As**.

   Project displays the Save As dialog box.

2. In the **File name** box, type **Simple Assignments**, and then click **Save**.

   Before making any resource assignments, you'll check the project plan's current duration and cost values for later comparison.

 3. On the **Project** tab, in the **Properties** group, click **Project Information**, and then click **Statistics**.

Note the current duration of 41 days and zero cost. After you assign work and cost resources, you'll check these values again.

4. Click **Close**.

Next you'll make your first resource assignment.

5. On the **Resource** tab, in the **Assignments** group, click **Assign Resources**.

The Assign Resources dialog box appears, in which you see the resource names you entered in Chapter 3, plus additional resources.

Except for assigned resources, which always appear at the top of the list, resources are sorted alphabetically in the Assign Resources dialog box.

Important If you are using Project Professional rather than Project Standard, the Assign Resources dialog box and some other dialog boxes you see will contain additional options relating to Project Server. Throughout this book, we won't use Project Server, so you can ignore these options.

6. In the **Task Name** column, click the name of task 2, *Assign launch team members*.

7. In the **Resource Name** column in the **Assign Resources** dialog box, click *Carole Poland*, and then click **Assign**.

The resources assigned to the selected task have a check mark next to their names in the Assigned Resources dialog box.

The names of assigned resources appear next to the Gantt bars.

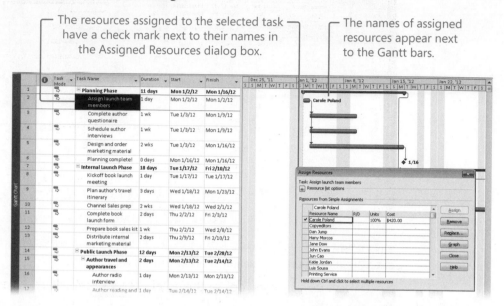

A cost value and check mark appears next to Carole's name, indicating that you have assigned her to the task. Carole's name also appears next to the task 2 Gantt bar. Because Carole has a standard cost rate recorded, Project calculates the cost of the assignment (Carole's standard pay rate times her scheduled amount of work on the task) and displays that value, $420, in the Cost field of the Assign Resources dialog box.

8. In the **Task Name** column, click the name of task 3, *Complete author questionnaire*.

9. In the **Resource Name** column in the **Assign Resources** dialog box, click *Toni Poe*, and then click **Assign**.

The names of assigned resources appear at the top of this list.

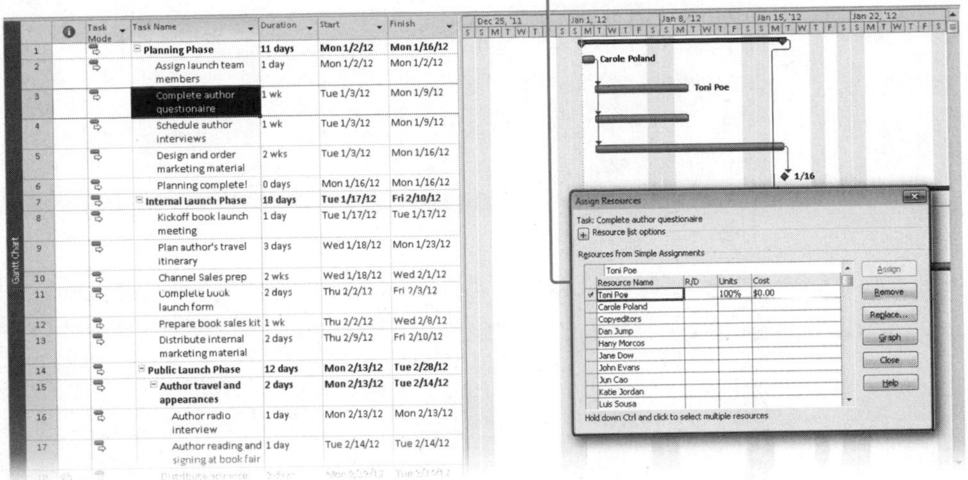

Tip To remove or unassign a resource from a selected task, in the Assign Resources dialog box, click the resource name, and then click Remove.

Next, you'll take a closer look at the details of task 3. You'll use a handy view called the Task Form.

10. On the **View** tab, in the **Split View** group, click **Details**.

Project splits the window into two panes. In the upper pane is the Gantt Chart view, and below it is the Task Form.

The names of the view or views displayed appear here.

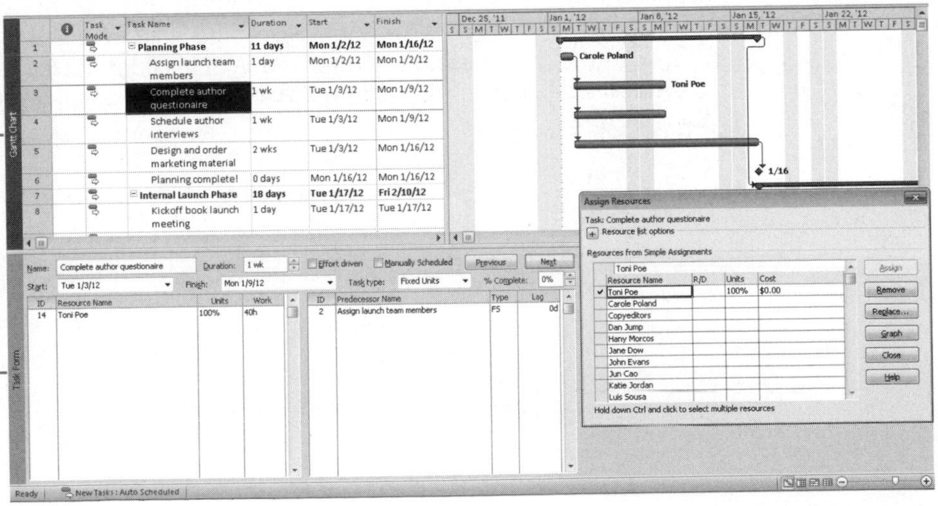

If you completed Chapter 3, you may recognize that the Task Form is similar to the Resource Form but shows different details. In this type of split view, the details about the selected item in the upper view (a task, in this case) appear in the lower view, similar to the Resource Form. The Task Form displays one of several details. Next you'll change the displayed details.

11. Click anywhere in the **Task Form** and then, on the **Format** tab, in the **Details** group, click **Work**.

The Work details appear.

Now, in the Task Form, you can see the essential scheduling values for this task: 1 week duration, 40 hours of work, and 100% assignment units. Because the Task Form is a handy way to see a task's duration, units, and work values, you'll leave it displayed for now.

12. Using the **Assign Resources** dialog box, assign the following resources to tasks. As you do so, note the **Duration**, **Units**, and **Work** values in the **Task Form**.

For this task	Assign this resource
4, Schedule author interviews	Jun Cao
5, Design and order marketing material	Toby Nixon

When you are finished, your screen should look similar to the following illustration.

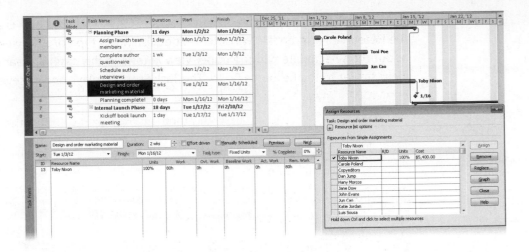

Next, you will assign two resources to a single task.

13. In the **Task Name** column, click the name of task 8, *Kickoff book launch meeting*.

14. In the Assign Resources dialog box, select the names of *Sharon Salavaria* and *Toby Nixon*, and then click **Assign**.

> **Tip** To select nonadjacent resource names, select the first name, hold down the Ctrl key, and then select additional names.

Sharon and Toby are assigned to the task. You can also see their names next to task 8's Gantt bar.

Recall from Chapter 3 that Sharon has a 50% Max. Units value to account for her half-time schedule. As a result, Project assigned her at 50% units.

To conclude this exercise, you'll use a different means of assigning resources.

15. In the Gantt Chart view, drag the vertical divider bar to the right until the Resource Names column is visible.

New In 2010

16. Click in the **Resource Names** column for task 9, *Plan author's travel itinerary*, and then click the arrow that appears.

The resource names appear.

Drag this vertical divider bar to see more or less — of the table portion of the Gantt Chart view.

17. In the list of resource names, click the check boxes for *Jane Dow* and *Zac Woodall*, and then press the Enter key.

Jane and Zac are assigned to task 9.

!	Task Mode	Task Name	Duration	Start	Finish	Predecessors	Resource Names
4		Schedule author interviews	1 wk	Mon 1/2/12	Mon 1/9/12	2	Jun Cao
5		Design and order marketing material	2 wks	Tue 1/3/12	Mon 1/16/12	2	Toby Nixon
6		Planning complete!	0 days	Mon 1/16/12	Mon 1/16/12	5	
7		⊟ **Internal Launch Phase**	**18 days**	**Tue 1/17/12**	**Fri 2/10/12**	**1**	
8		Kickoff book launch meeting	1 day	Tue 1/17/12	Tue 1/17/12		Sharon Salavaria[50%],Tob
9		Plan author's travel itinerary	3 days	Wed 1/18/12	Mon 1/23/12	8	Jane Dow,Zac Woodall
10		Channel Sales prep	2 wks	Wed 1/18/12	Wed 2/1/12	8	
11		Complete book launch form	2 days	Thu 2/2/12	Fri 2/3/12	10	

18. Click in the **Resource Names** column for task 10, *Channel Sales prep*, and then click the arrow that appears. In the list of resource names that appears, check *Zac Woodall* and then press the Enter key.

Zac is assigned to task 10.

Tip In this exercise, you assigned resources using the Assign Resources dialog box and the Resource Names column in the Gantt Chart view. In addition, you can assign resources in the Task Form and on the Resources tab of the Task Information dialog box, among other places. As you use Project, you'll likely develop your own preference for the way you assign resources.

The Scheduling Formula: Duration, Units, and Work

After you create a task, but before you assign a resource to it, the task has duration but no work associated with it. Why no work? Work represents the amount of effort a resource or resources will spend to complete a task. For example, if you have one person working full time, the amount of time measured as work is the same as the amount of time measured as duration. In general, the amount of work will match the duration unless you assign more than one resource to a task or the one resource you assign is not working full time.

Project calculates work using what is sometimes called the scheduling formula:

$$\text{Duration} \times \text{Units} = \text{Work}$$

Let's look at a specific example and find these values in the Task Form. The duration of task 3 is one week, or five working days. For our book launch project, five days equals 40 hours. When you assigned Toni Poe to task 3, Project applied 100 percent of Toni's working time to this task. The scheduling formula for task 3 looks like this:

40 hours (same as one week) task duration × 100% assignment units = 40 hours of work

In other words, with Toni assigned to task 3 at 100% units, the task should require 40 hours of work.

Here's a more complex example. You assigned two resources, Jane Dow and Zac Woodall, to task 9, each at 100% assignment units. The scheduling formula for task 9 looks like this:

24 hours (same as three days) task duration × 200% assignment units = 48 hours of work

The 48 hours of work is the sum of Jane's 24 hours of work plus Zac's 24 hours of work. In other words, as currently scheduled, both resources will work full time on the task in parallel for its three-day duration.

Controlling Work When Adding or Removing Resource Assignments

As you saw previously, you define the amount of work that a task represents when you initially assign a resource or resources to it. When using automatically scheduled tasks, Project gives you an option to control how it should calculate work on a task when you assign additional resources to the task or unassign resources from the task. This option is called *effort-driven scheduling*. You have a lot of flexibility in how you apply effort-driven scheduling. You can turn on effort-driven scheduling for an entire project plan or just specific tasks. You can also use the options in an Actions list to control how Project should recalculate work on a task immediately after making a resource assignment. Effort-driven scheduling applies only when you assign additional resources or remove resources from automatically scheduled tasks.

By now some time has passed since you made the initial resource assignments for the new book launch at Lucerne Publishing. You need to add and remove some assignments.

In this exercise, you adjust resource assignments on tasks and tell Project how it should adjust the tasks.

1. In the Gantt Chart view, click the name of task 5, *Design and order marketing material*.

   Currently, Toby is assigned to this task. A quick check of the scheduling formula looks like this:

   80 hours (the same as 10 days, or two weeks) task duration × 100% of Toby's assignment units = 80 hours of work

   Toby needs some help with this task, so you'll add a resource.

2. In the **Resource Name** column in the **Assign Resources** dialog box, click *Zac Woodall*, and then click **Assign**.

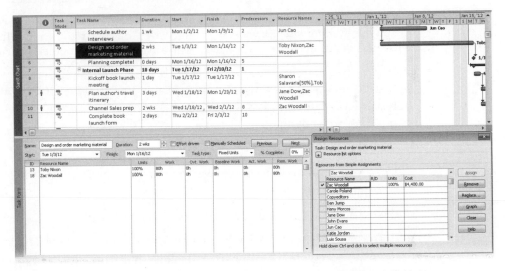

   Zac is added to the task and Project updates the scheduling formula values:

   80 hours (the same as 10 days, or two weeks) task duration × 200% (that is, the sum of Toby's and Zac's assignment units) = 160 hours work.

   Next, you will use a feature called the Actions list to control how Project schedules the work on a task when adding or removing resources. Note the small triangle in the upper-left corner of the name of task 5. This is a graphical indicator that an action is now available. Until you perform another action, you can use the Actions list to choose how you want Project to handle the additional resource assignment.

3. Click the name of task 5, and then click the **Actions** button that appears just to the left of the task name.

Look over the options on the list that appears.

	ⓘ	Task Mode	Task Name	Duration	Start	Finish	Predecessors	Resource Names
4		⇨	Schedule author interviews	1 wk	Mon 1/2/12	Mon 1/9/12	2	Jun Cao
5		⇨ ◈ ▾	Design and order	2 wks	Tue 1/3/12	Mon 1/16/12	2	Toby Nixon,Zac Woodall
6		⇨						
7		⇨						
8		⇨						Sharnn Salavaria[50%],Tob
9	⚹	⇨	itinerary					Jane Dow,Zac Woodall
10	⚹	⇨	Channel Sales prep	2 wks	Wed 1/18/12	Wed 2/1/12	8	Zac Woodall

You've added new resources to this task. Is it because you wanted to:

- ○ Reduce duration so the task ends sooner, but requires the same amount of work (person-hours)
- ◉ Increase total work because the task requires more person-hours. Keep duration constant.
- ○ Reduce the hours that resources work per day. Keep duration and work the same.

Show me more details.

These options allow you to choose the scheduling result that you want. You can adjust the task's duration, the resources' work, or the assignment units.

Tip You will see other Actions indicators while using Project. They generally appear when you might otherwise ask yourself, "Hmm, why did Project just do that?" (such as when a task's duration changes after you assign an additional resource). The Actions list gives you the chance to change how Project responds to your actions.

For this task, you want the additional assignment to mean additional work done in the original duration. This is the default setting, so you'll close the Actions list without making a change.

4. Click the **Actions** button again to close the list.

Next, you'll remove a resource from a task and then instruct Project how to schedule the remaining resource assignment on the task.

5. Click the name of task 9, *Plan author's travel itinerary*.

Currently both Jane and Zac are assigned to the task. Jane has told you that she needs to complete the planned work alone, but over a longer time period. This is acceptable to you, so you'll unassign Zac.

6. In the **Resource Name** column in the **Assign Resources** dialog box, click **Zac Woodall**, and then click **Remove**.

The small triangle in the upper-left corner of the field indicates that the Actions list is available. Click the field to see it.

Project unassigns Zac from the task. Next, you'll adjust how Project should handle the change in assignments.

7. Click the **Actions** button that appears just to the left of the task name.

8. Click **Increase duration so the task ends later but requires the same total work (person-hours)**.

Project increases the task's duration from three to six days, and increases Jane's work total from 24 to 48 hours. This 48 hours is the same total work on the task when both Jane and Zac were assigned, but now all the work belongs to Jane.

	ⓘ	Task Mode	Task Name	Duration	Start	Finish	Predecessors	Resource Names	
4			Schedule author interviews	1 wk	Mon 1/2/12	Mon 1/9/12	2	Jun Cao	
5			Design and order marketing material	2 wks	Tue 1/3/12	Mon 1/16/12	2	Toby Nixon,Zac Woodall	
6			Planning complete!	0 days	Mon 1/16/12	Mon 1/16/12	5		
7			⊟ **Internal Launch Phase**	**18 days**	**Tue 1/17/12**	**Fri 2/10/12**	**1**		
8			Kickoff book launch meeting	1 day	Tue 1/17/12	Tue 1/17/12		Sharon Salavaria[50%],Tob	
9			Plan author's travel itinerary	6 days	Wed 1/18/12	Thu 1/26/12	8	Jane Dow	
10			Channel Sales prep	2 wks	Wed 1/18/12	Wed 2/1/12	8	Zac Woodall	
11			Complete book launch form	2 days	Thu 2/2/12	Fri 2/3/12	10		

So far, you've been adjusting duration and work values as you add or remove resources from tasks. You can also change the default setting for a task such that as you add resources to the task, its duration is decreased. You'll do so next.

9. In the Gantt Chart view, click the name of task 10, *Channel Sales prep*.

Currently just Zac is assigned to this task, and it has a two-week duration.

10. In the **Task Form**, click **Effort-driven**, and then click **OK** in the upper-right corner of the **Task Form**.

There is no change to the duration, units, or work values for this task, but watch what happens when you assign an additional resource.

11. In the Gantt Chart view, click the name of task 10, and then, in the **Assign Resources** dialog box, click *Hany Morcos*, and then click **Assign**.

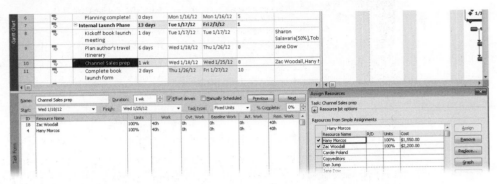

Task 10's duration is reduced from two weeks to one week. The total work on the task remains 80 hours, but now it is split evenly between Zac and Hany. This is the scheduling result that you wanted. If it wasn't, you could use the Actions list to change how Project responds to the additional resource assignment.

Tip By default, effort-driven scheduling is disabled for all tasks that you create in Project. To change the default setting for all new tasks in a project plan, on the File tab, click Options. In the Project Options dialog box, click the Schedule tab and then select "the New tasks are effort-driven" check box. To control effort-driven scheduling for a specific task or tasks, first select the task or tasks. Then, on the Task tab, in the Properties group, click Information, and on the Advanced tab of the Task Information dialog box, select or clear the "Effort driven" check box.

The order of your actions matters with regard to effort-driven scheduling. If you *initially assign two resources* to a task with a duration of three days (equal to 24 hours), Project schedules each resource to work 24 hours, for a total of 48 hours of work on the task. However, you might *initially assign one resource* to a task with a duration of 24 hours and later *add a second resource*. In this case, effort-driven scheduling will cause Project to schedule each resource to work 12 hours in parallel, for a total of 24 hours of work on the task. Remember that when it's turned on, effort-driven scheduling adjusts task duration only if you add or remove resources from a task.

> **Project Management Focus: When Should Effort-Driven Scheduling Apply?**
>
> You should consider the extent to which effort-driven scheduling should apply to the tasks in your projects. For example, if one resource should take 10 hours to complete a task, could 10 resources complete the task in 1 hour? How about 20 resources in 30 minutes? Probably not; the resources would likely get in each other's way and require additional coordination to complete the task. If the task is very complicated, it might require significant ramp-up time before a resource could contribute fully. Overall productivity might even decrease if you assign more resources to the task.
>
> No single rule exists about when you should apply effort-driven scheduling and when you should not. As the project manager, you should analyze the nature of the work required for each task in your project and use your best judgment.

Assigning Cost Resources to Tasks

Recall from Chapter 3 that cost resources are used to represent a financial cost associated with a task in a project. Cost resources do no work and have no effect on the scheduling of a task. Cost resources might include categories of expenses that you want to budget and track for accounting or financial reporting purposes. Broadly speaking, the costs that tasks can incur can include:

- Work resource costs, such as a person's standard pay rate times the amount of work they perform on the task.

- Cost resource costs, which are a fixed dollar amount that you enter when assigning the cost resource to a task. The amount is not affected by changes in duration or any other schedule changes to the task, although you can edit the amount at any time. You can also see cumulative costs resulting from assigning the same cost resource to multiple tasks.

For the new book launch project plan, you'd like to enter planned travel costs for certain tasks. Since work has not yet started on this project at this time, these costs represent planned costs (indeed, you should consider all costs that Project has calculated so far in the schedule to be planned costs, such as those resulting from work resource assignments to tasks). Later, you can enter actual costs if you wish to compare them with the budget.

In this exercise, you assign a work resource and a cost resource to a task and check the plan's overall duration and cost values.

1. Click the name of task 17, *Author reading and signing at book fair.*

   This task requires air travel by the author, and you've allocated $800 in anticipation of this expense.

   Currently task 17 has no assigned resource and no cost. First, you'll assign the author to the task.

2. In the **Resource Name** column in the **Assign Resources** dialog box, click *Toni Poe,* and then click **Assign**.

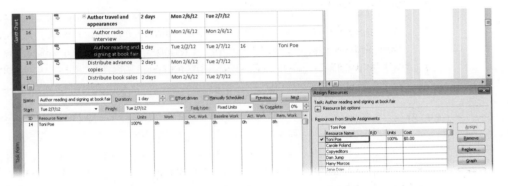

   Project assigns Toni Poe, a work resource, to the task. As you can see in the Cost field of the Assign Resources dialog box, this assignment has no cost. That's because this work resource, Toni Poe, has no cost rate or per-use cost. So even though the assignment generated work, there's no cost associated with it. Next, you'll assign the cost resource.

3. In the **Assign Resources** dialog box, select the **Cost** field for the **Travel** cost resource, type **800**, and then click **Assign**.

   Project assigns the cost resource to the task.

4. To see both assigned resources, scroll up the **Resource** list in the **Assign Resources** dialog box.

You can see the cost incurred by this assignment in the Cost column of the Assign Resources dialog box. The travel cost value will remain the same regardless of any changes made to the scheduling of the task, such as work resources being assigned or unassigned, or the task's duration changing.

Note the task has the same duration of one day and Toni Poe has the same units and work values as before. Assigning the cost resource affected only the cost incurred by this task.

To conclude this exercise, you'll revisit the project's overall duration and cost values now that you've made some resource assignments.

5. On the **Project** tab, in the **Properties** group, click **Project Information**, and then click **Statistics**.

Project Statistics for 'Simple Assignments'

	Start		Finish
Current	Mon 1/2/12		Tue 2/21/12
Baseline	NA		NA
Actual	NA		NA
Variance	0d		0d

	Duration	Work	Cost
Current	36d	396h	$19,740.00
Baseline	0d	0h	$0.00
Actual	0d	0h	$0.00
Remaining	36d	396h	$19,740.00

Percent complete:
Duration: 0%   Work: 0%

Note the shorter duration of 36 days (it had been 41 days) and the $19,740 cost. The shorter duration is the result of applying effort-driven scheduling to some tasks. The cost is the sum of work resource assignments plus the one cost resource assignment.

6. Click **Close**.

✖ **CLEAN UP** Close the Simple Assignments file.

Key Points

- In Project, a task normally has work associated with it after a work resource (which can be people or equipment) has been assigned to the task.

- You must assign resources to tasks before you can track resources' progress or cost.

- Project follows the scheduling formula Duration × Units = Work.

- Effort-driven scheduling determines whether work remains constant when you assign additional resources to tasks. Effort-driven scheduling is turned off by default.

- The easiest way to understand effort-driven scheduling is to ask yourself this question: If one person can do this task in 10 days, could two people do it in 5 days? If so, then effort-driven scheduling should apply to the task.

- Actions lists appear after you perform certain actions in Project. They allow you to quickly change the effect of your action to something other than the default effect.

- Assigning cost resources allows you to associate financial costs with a task other than those derived from work or material resources.

Chapter at a Glance

Create a custom-formatted
Gantt Chart view, page 94.

Customize the Timeline for a concise
project at a glance view, page 101.

Copy snapshots of
Project views to other
applications, page 106.

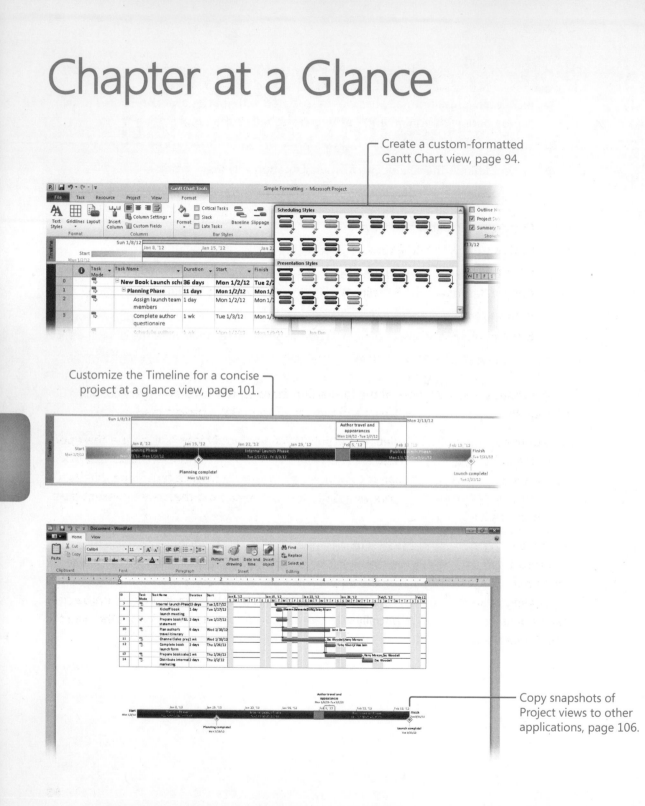

5 Formatting and Sharing Your Plan

In this chapter, you will learn how to:

✔ Customize a Gantt Chart view.

✔ Customize the Timeline view.

✔ Draw on the chart portion of a Gantt Chart view.

✔ Copy snapshots of the Timeline and Gantt chart views to another application.

✔ Print views.

✔ Edit and print reports.

In this chapter, you use some of the formatting features in Microsoft Project 2010 to change the way your data appears and then copy and print a project plan.

The primary way in which Project represents tasks graphically is as bars on the chart portion of a Gantt Chart *view*. These are called Gantt bars. On a Gantt chart, *tasks*, *summary tasks*, and *milestones* all appear as Gantt bars or symbols, and each type of bar has its own format. Whenever you work with Gantt bars, keep in mind that they represent tasks in a project plan.

In some respects, a project plan is really a database of information, not unlike a Microsoft Access database file. You don't normally see all the data in a project plan at one time. Instead, you focus on the aspect of the plan that you're currently interested in viewing. Views and reports are the most common ways to observe or print a project plan's data. In both cases (especially with views), you can substantially format the data to meet your needs.

Tip This chapter introduces you to some of the simpler view and report formatting features in Project. You'll find quite a bit more material about formatting, printing, and publishing your project plans in Chapter 11, "Organizing Project Details," and Chapter 15, "Applying Advanced Formatting and Printing."

> **Practice Files** Before you can complete the exercises in this chapter, you need to copy the book's practice files to your computer. A complete list of practice files is provided in "Using the Practice Files" at the beginning of this book. For each exercise that has a practice file, simply browse to where you saved the book's practice file folder.

Important If you are running Project Professional, you may need to make a one-time setting change. This helps ensure that the practice files you work with in this chapter do not affect your Project Server data. For more information, see Appendix C, "Using the Practice Files if Connected to Project Server."

Customizing the Gantt Chart View

The Gantt chart became a standard way of visualizing project plans when, in the early 20th century, American engineer Henry Gantt developed a bar chart showing the use of resources over time. For many people, a Gantt chart is synonymous with a project plan. In Project, the default view is the Gantt Chart view. You are likely to spend a lot of your time in this view when working in Project.

The Gantt Chart view consists of two parts: a table on the left and a bar chart on the right. The bar chart includes a timescale band across the top that denotes units of time. The bars on the chart graphically represent the tasks in the table in terms of start and finish dates, duration, and status (for example, whether work on the task has started or not). Other elements on the chart, such as link lines, represent relationships between tasks. The Gantt chart is a popular and widely understood representation of project information throughout the project management world.

Tip By default, Project displays a split view named Gantt with Timeline when you start the program. However, you can change this setting to display any view you want at startup. On the File tab, click Options. In the Project Options dialog box, click General. In the Default View box, click the view you want. The next time you start Project and create a new project plan, the view you have chosen will appear.

The default formatting applied to the Gantt Chart view works well for onscreen viewing, sharing with other programs, and printing. However, you can change the formatting of almost any element on the Gantt chart.

There are three distinct ways to format Gantt bars:

- Quickly apply predefined color combinations from the Gantt Chart Style group, which you can see on the Format tab when a Gantt Chart is displayed.

● Apply highly customized formatting to Gantt bars in the Bar Styles dialog box, which you can open by clicking the Format tab when a Gantt chart is displayed, then, in the Bar Styles group, click Format, Bar Styles. In this case, the formatting changes you make to a particular type of Gantt bar (a summary task, for example) apply to all such Gantt bars in the Gantt chart.

● Format individual Gantt bars directly. The direct formatting changes that you make have no effect on other bars in the Gantt chart. You can double-click a Gantt bar to view its formatting options, or, on the Format tab in the Bar Styles group, click Format, Bar. For more information, see Chapter 15.

In this exercise, you change the formatting of the Gantt chart view.

SET UP Start Project if it's not already running.

You need the Simple Formatting_Start project plan located in your Chapter05 practice file folder to complete this exercise. Open the Simple Formatting_Start project plan, and then follow these steps.

1. On the **File** tab, click **Save As**.

   Project displays the Save As dialog box.

2. In the **File name** box, type **Simple Formatting**, and then click **Save**.

   To begin, you will display the project summary task to see the top-level or rolled-up details of the project. Project automatically generates the project summary task but doesn't display it by default.

3. On the **Format** tab, in the **Show/Hide** group, click **Project Summary Task**.

   Project displays the project summary task at the top of the Gantt Chart view.

The project summary task and its taskbar display the project's overall duration.

The project summary task, which is always numbered as task 0, contains top-level information such as duration, work, and costs for the entire project. The name of the project summary task comes from the title entered in the plan's advanced properties in the Backstage view, or if that is blank, Project uses the file name as the project summary task's name.

Next, you will adjust the colors of the Gantt bars and milestones in the chart portion of the Custom Gantt Chart view. You'll begin by viewing the Gantt bar for a manual task so you can see how it is affected by the Gantt bar formatting.

4. In the **Task Name** column, click the name of task 9, *Prepare book P&L statement*.

5. On the **Task** tab, in the **Editing** group, click **Scroll to Task**.

   Tip You can accomplish the same thing by right-clicking the task name and in the shortcut menu that appears, clicking Scroll To Task.

   Project scrolls the chart portion of the Gantt Chart view to display the Gantt bar for a manually scheduled task that was previously added to the book launch plan.

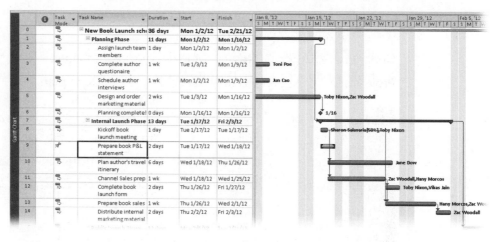

Keep an eye on this Gantt bar as we apply a different Gantt Chart style to the project plan.

6. On the **Format** tab, in the **Gantt Chart Style** group, click **More** to display the predefined color styles.

More

The formatting options under Scheduling Styles distinguish between manual and automatically scheduled tasks, but the Presentation Styles do not.

The Gantt Chart styles are divided into two groups:

- Scheduling Styles distinguish between manually and automatically scheduled tasks.

- Presentation Styles do not.

7. Under **Presentation Styles**, click the orange color scheme.

Project applies this style to the Gantt bars in the project plan.

The Gantt bar of task 9, the manually scheduled task, is no longer visually distinct from the automatically scheduled tasks.

Applying a presentation style to the Gantt Chart view is an option that you can use when you don't want to distinguish between manual and automatically scheduled tasks—when showing the Gantt chart to an audience for whom you do not want to make this distinction, for example.

Your next step in this exercise is to reformat a task name so it will visually stand out.

8. In the **Task Name** column, right-click the name of task 6, *Planning Complete!*

This is a milestone task that describes the end of the first phase of the new book launch at Lucerne Publishing. You'd like to highlight this task name.

In addition to the regular shortcut menu, note the mini-toolbar.

Background
Color

9. On the mini-toolbar, click the arrow next to the **Background Color** button, and under **Standard Colors**, click yellow.

Tip You can also click the Task tab, and in the Font group, click Background Color.

Project applies the yellow background color to the task name's cell.

I
Italic

10. Right-click the task name again, and on the mini-toolbar, click the **Italic** button.

This cell has been formatted
with direct formatting.

	ⓘ	Task Mode	Task Name	Duration	Start	Finish	Jan 8, '1
							S M T
0		⇨	⊟ New Book Launch sch	36 days	Mon 1/2/12	Tue 2/21/12	
1		⇨	⊟ Planning Phase	11 days	Mon 1/2/12	Mon 1/16/12	
2		⇨	Assign launch team members	1 day	Mon 1/2/12	Mon 1/2/12	
3		⇨	Complete author questionaire	1 wk	Tue 1/3/12	Mon 1/9/12	
4		⇨	Schedule author interviews	1 wk	Mon 1/2/12	Mon 1/9/12	
5		⇨	Design and order marketing material	2 wks	Tue 1/3/12	Mon 1/16/12	
6		⇨	*Planning complete!*	0 days	Mon 1/16/12	Mon 1/16/12	
7		⇨	⊟ Internal Launch Phase	13 days	Tue 1/17/12	Fri 2/3/12	
8		⇨	Kickoff book launch meeting	1 day	Tue 1/17/12	Tue 1/17/12	
9		📌	Prepare book P&L statement	2 days	Tue 1/17/12	Wed 1/18/12	

Now the milestone name stands out. You can also format the milestone indicator in the chart. You'll do this next.

11. On the **Format** tab, in the **Bar Styles** group, click **Format** and then click **Bar**.

12. In the **Format Bar** dialog box, under **Start**, click the **Shape** drop-down list.

Project displays the symbols you can use as a Gantt bar edge, or, in this case for a milestone, as a milestone symbol.

13. Click the star symbol, and then click **OK**.

Project uses the star symbol as the milestone symbol for this task.

This milestone symbol has been formatted with a custom shape.

Tip In this exercise, you used the Bar command to format a single Gantt bar. You can also customize entire categories of Gantt bars, such as all milestones, via the Bar Styles command. For more information, see Chapter 15.

To conclude this exercise, you will add horizontal gridlines to the chart portion of the Gantt Chart view so you can more easily associate Gantt bars with their tasks.

14. On the **Format** tab, in the **Format** group, click **Gridlines**, and then click **Gridlines**.

15. Under **Lines to change**, leave Gantt Rows selected, and in the **Type** box under **Normal**, select the small dashed line (the third option down), and then click **OK**.

Project draws dashed lines across the chart portion of the Gantt Chart view.

Customizing the Timeline View

New In
2010

The Timeline view is best suited to display some tasks from the Gantt Chart view in a less complicated format. The Timeline view is especially well suited for conveying quick summaries of project plans, as you will see in this exercise. Later in this chapter, you will also copy a Timeline view to another application as a quick "project at a glance" image.

In this exercise, you customize the Timeline view and adjust some display details on the Timeline.

1. Click anywhere in the Timeline view.

Project shifts focus to the Timeline view, and displays the Timeline Tools on the Format tab.

2. On the **Format** tab, in the **Insert** group, click **Existing Tasks**.

The Add Tasks to Timeline dialog box appears.

This dialog box contains an outline of the summary and subtasks in the project plan.

3. Check the boxes for the following task names:

- ○ **Planning Phase**
- ○ **Planning complete!**
- ○ **Internal Launch Phase**
- ○ **Public Launch Phase**
- ○ **Author travel and appearances**

Use this dialog box to quickly indicate tasks that you want to include in the Timeline view.

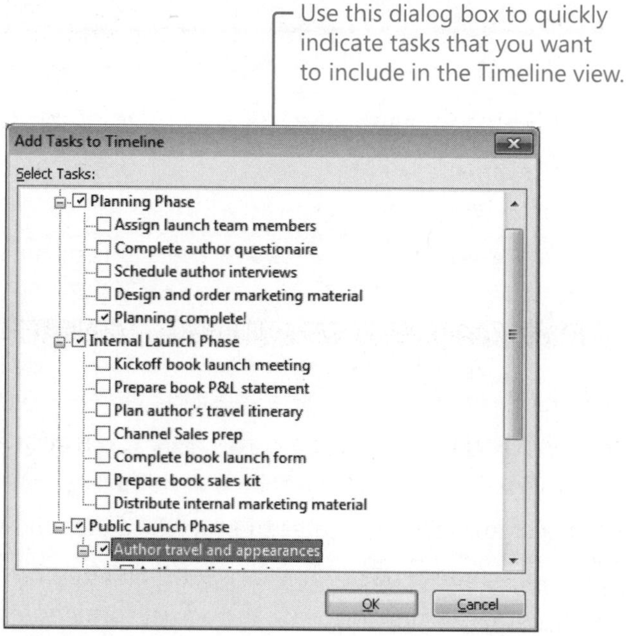

These tasks are summary tasks and a milestone task that you will add to the Timeline view.

4. Click **OK**.

Project adds the summary tasks and milestone to the Timeline view. If necessary, adjust the horizontal divider bar so you can see more of the Timeline view.

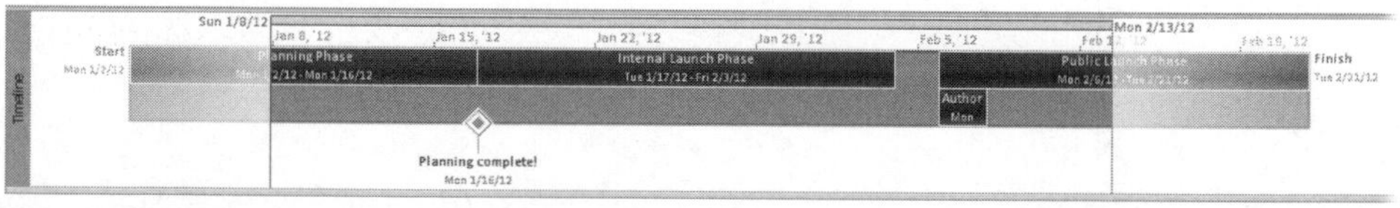

Next you'll adjust the formatting of the *Author travel and appearances* summary task on the Timeline.

5. In the **Timeline** view, click the bar for the *Author travel and appearances* summary task.

   Only a portion of the summary task name is visible. Hover over the bar name and Project displays a ScreenTip with the task's full name and other details.

6. On the **Format** tab, in the **Current Selection** group, click **Display as Callout**.

   Project displays this summary task as a callout, which for this task has the advantage of making the full task name visible.

   Next you'll add the final milestone task to the Timeline, but you'll use a different technique.

7. In the **Task Name** column, click the name of task 24, *Launch complete!*

8. On the **Task** tab, in the **Properties** group, click **Add to Timeline**.

   Tip You can also right-click the task name and click Add to Timeline in the shortcut menu that appears.

   Project adds this milestone task to the Timeline view.

   As you can see on the Timeline, Project displays the milestone tasks as callouts and uses the diamond marker that is a visual convention for milestones.

Pan and Zoom the Gantt Chart View from the Timeline View

Have you noticed the shading and the vertical lines and horizontal bar on the Timeline view? These are pan and zoom controls you can use to scroll the Gantt Chart view horizontally or to change its timescale.

Click and drag this bar left or right to pan the Gantt Chart view.

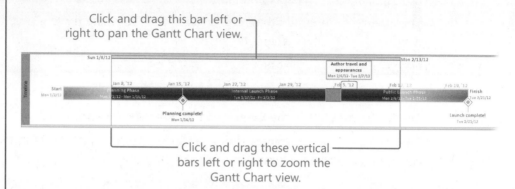

Click and drag these vertical bars left or right to zoom the Gantt Chart view.

These pan and zoom controls appear in the Timeline view when the Gantt chart's timeline shows less than the full project plan's duration on the screen.

To scroll the Gantt Chart view, click and drag the horizontal bar that appears above a portion of the Timeline. This is a convenient way to display a specific date range in the Gantt Chart view.

To change the timescale in the Gantt Chart view, drag the left or right vertical line on the edge of the scrolling bar in the Timeline view. As you do so, Project adjusts the timescale in the chart portion of the Gantt Chart view so that the time frame that appears in the unshaded portion of the Timeline view is also visible in the Gantt Chart view.

You may find the Timeline view useful not only for creating simplified representations of key details from your project plans, but also for navigating with the Gantt Chart view.

Drawing on a Gantt Chart

Project includes a Drawing tool with which you can draw objects directly on the chart portion of a Gantt chart. For example, if you would like to note a particular event or graphically call out a specific item, you can draw objects, such as text boxes, arrows, and other items, directly on a Gantt chart. You can also link a drawn object to either end of a Gantt bar or to a specific date on the timescale. Here's how to choose the type of link you need:

- Link objects to a Gantt bar when the object is specific to the task that the Gantt bar represents. The object will move with the Gantt bar if the task is rescheduled.

- Link objects to a date when the information the object refers to is date-sensitive. The object will remain in the same position relative to the timescale no matter which part of the timescale is displayed.

In this exercise, you add a text box to the Gantt Chart view.

1. Scroll the Gantt Chart view to the top of the table so task 0 is visible.

2. On the **Format** tab, in the **Drawings** group, click **Drawing**.

   The menu of drawing objects appears. This includes all the built-in shapes that you can draw, plus other commands for formatting shapes.

3. Click **Text Box**, and then drag a small box anywhere on the chart portion of the Gantt Chart view.

4. In the box that you just drew, type **Morale event Jan. 19**.

5. On the **Format** tab, in the **Drawings** group, click **Drawing**, and then click **Properties**.

   The Format Drawing dialog box appears.

   Tip You can also double-click the border of the text box to view its properties.

6. Make sure the **Line & Fill** tab is displayed, and in the **Color** box under the **Fill** label, click yellow.

   Next, you'll attach the text box to a specific date on the timescale.

7. Click the **Size & Position** tab.

8. Make sure that **Attach To Timescale** is selected, and in the **Date** box, type or click **1/19/12**.

9. In the **Vertical** box under **Attach To Timescale**, type **.5** (this is the number of inches below the timescale where the top of the box will be positioned), and then click **OK** to close the **Format Drawing** dialog box.

   Project colors the text box yellow and positions it below the timescale near the date you specified.

10. Click in an empty area of the Gantt Chart view to unselect the text box.

Double-click the border of a drawn object to change its formatting or other properties.

Because you attached the text box to a specific date on the timescale, it will always appear near this date even if you zoom the timescale in or out or scroll the chart left or right. Had you attached the text box to a Gantt bar, it would move with the Gantt bar if the task were rescheduled.

Copying Views

You may frequently need to share details of your project plans with colleagues who do not have Project, or who may prefer a simple schedule snapshot. In addition to the reports feature described later in this chapter, you can quickly copy or print views from Project. Copied views can then be pasted into e-mail messages, documents, presentations, and other elements.

Both the Gantt Chart and Timeline views are well suited for sharing schedule details—
the Timeline is a concise "project at a glance" view and the Gantt Chart is a widely used
format of schedules.

In this exercise, you copy the Gantt Chart and the Timeline views to another application.

1. In the **Task Name** column, click the name of task 7, *Internal Launch Phase*.

2. On the **Task** tab, in the **Editing** group, click **Scroll to Task**.

   The Gantt bars for the Internal Launch Phase summary task and its subtasks are
   displayed. This is close to the image you'd like to copy.

	❶	Task Mode	Task Name	Duration	Start	Finish						
6			*Planning complete!*	0 days	Mon 1/16/12	Mon 1/16/12			★ 1/16			
7			Internal Launch Phase	13 days	Tue 1/17/12	Fri 2/3/12						
8			Kickoff book launch meeting	1 day	Tue 1/17/12	Tue 1/17/12			Sharon Salavaria[50%],Toby Nixon			
9			Prepare book P&L statement	2 days	Tue 1/17/12	Wed 1/18/12						
10			Plan author's travel itinerary	6 days	Wed 1/18/12	Thu 1/26/12			Jane Dow			
11			Channel Sales prep	1 wk	Wed 1/18/12	Wed 1/25/12			Zac Woodall,Hany Morcos			
12			Complete book launch form	2 days	Thu 1/26/12	Fri 1/27/12			Toby Nixon,Vikas Jain			
13			Prepare book sales	1 wk	Thu 1/26/12	Wed 2/1/12				Hany Morcos,Zac Woodall		
14			Distribute internal marketing material	2 days	Thu 2/2/12	Fri 2/3/12				Zac Woodall		

3. In the Gantt Chart view, select the names of tasks 7 through 14.

   These are the *Internal Launch Phase* summary task and its subtasks.

4. On the **Task** tab, in the **Clipboard** group, click the arrow next to **Copy**, and then
   click **Copy Picture**.

   The Copy Picture dialog box appears.

Copy Picture	✕
Render image	
⦿ For screen	
○ For printer	
○ To GIF image file:	
[ ] Browse...	
Copy	
○ Rows on screen	
⦿ Selected rows	
Timescale	
⦿ As shown on screen	
○ From: Sun 1/8/12 ▼ To: Mon 2/13/12 ▼	
OK Cancel	

In this dialog box, you can control how Project copies details from the project plan
to the Clipboard or saves it to a file. The first two options under Render Image
control the size and resolution of the Gantt Chart image you copy; the third allows

you to save the copied image as a Graphics Interchange Format (GIF) image file. The Copy and Timescale options let you fine-tune what you want to copy.

For this exercise, you want to copy the selected rows for screen-resolution quality and leave the timescale as shown on the screen.

5. Click **OK**.

Project copies a graphic image of the Gantt chart for just the selected rows to the Windows Clipboard.

6. On the **Start** menu, click **All Programs**, and in the **Accessories** program group, click **WordPad**.

WordPad opens and creates a new document.

7. In WordPad, click **Paste**.

WordPad pastes the graphic image of the Gantt Chart view into the new document.

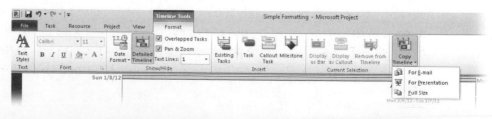

The Gantt Chart view is a standard format for presenting schedules, and it can show quite a bit of schedule detail.

8. Switch back to Project.

9. Click anywhere in the Timeline view.

10. On the **Format** tab, in the **Copy** group, click **Copy Timeline**.

The Copy Timeline options appear.

> **Tip** Feel free to experiment with the Copy Timeline options and pasting the results into whatever applications that are relevant for you. For this exercise, we'll paste into WordPad, a rich-text editor included with Windows.

11. Click **Full Size**.

    Project copies a graphic image of the timeline to the Clipboard.

12. Switch back to WordPad and then press the Enter key a few times to add some space below the Gantt chart image.

13. In WordPad, click **Paste**.

    WordPad pastes the graphic image of the Timeline view into the new document.

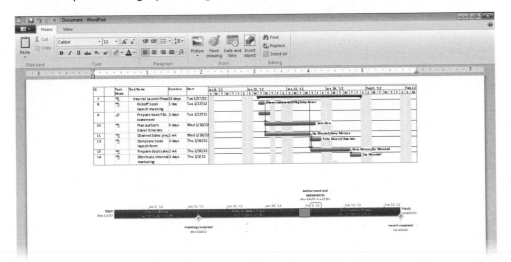

14. Close WordPad without saving the document, return to Project, and then click anywhere in the Gantt Chart view.

Printing Views

Printing views allows you to put on paper just about anything you see on your screen. For a project with many tasks, what you can see on your screen at one time may be a relatively small portion of the full project. When using standard letter-sized paper, it might require several sheets to print the full project plan. For example, a Gantt Chart view of a six-month project with 100 or so tasks can require 12 or more letter-size pages to print in its entirety. Printing out of Project can use quite a bit of paper; in fact, some heavy-duty Project users make poster-size printouts of their project plans using plotters. Whether you use a printer or plotter, it's a good idea to preview the views you intend to print.

Tip For advanced instructions on printing views, see Chapter 15.

In this exercise, you will see the Print Preview of the Gantt Chart and Timeline views.

1. On the **File** tab, click **Print**.

   The Print Preview appears in the Backstage view with the Gantt Chart in the preview.

Here, you can see the legend for the Gantt Chart view. You can control how it is displayed using the Page Setup dialog box.

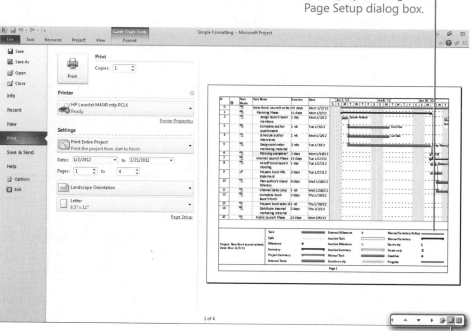

1 of 4

Use these buttons to navigate in the Print Preview.

The Print Preview has several options to explore. You will start with the page navigation buttons in the lower-right corner of the screen. To observe the broader view of the output, you'll switch to a multipage view.

2. Click **Multiple Pages**.

   Multiple Pages

   The full Gantt chart appears in the Print Preview. Assuming that you have a letter-size sheet as your paper size, you should see the Gantt chart spread across several sheets—what you see in the Print Preview may vary, depending on your specific printer. This is more information than you need to communicate right now, so you'll adjust the Print Preview to include just the portion of the Gantt chart that covers the month of January.

Note If you have a plotter selected as your default printer or have a different page size selected for your default printer, what you see in the Print Preview windows may differ from what's shown here. The next several steps will assume that you see the Gantt Chart view split across four sheets.

3. Under **Settings**, on the left side of the Print Preview window, click **Print Entire Project** to display additional printing options.

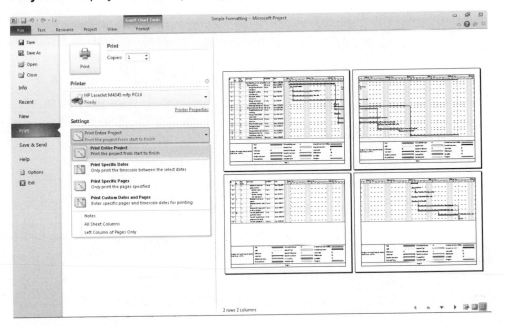

These options let you customize what details will be printed.

4. Click **Print Specific Dates**.

Notice the two date fields directly below the Print Specific Dates setting. In the first date field, *1/2/2012* should already be selected. This is the project start date.

5. In the **To date** field, select **1/31/2012**.

Project adjusts the Print Preview to include just the tasks that appear in the month of January.

6. Click the **Task** tab to close the Backstage view.

   Next you will work with the Timeline view.

7. Click anywhere in the Timeline view.

   This puts the focus on the Timeline. Project can print only a single view at a time, so when working with a split view, you must specify which view you intend to print.

8. On the **File** tab, click **Print**.

   The Print Preview appears in the Backstage view.

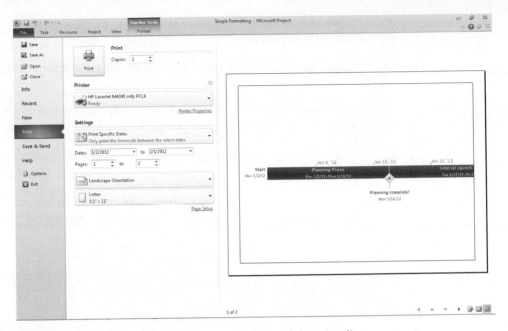

Page Right

9. Click **Page Right** to display the second page of the Timeline.

10. Click **Multiple Pages**.

The entire Timeline view appears in the Print Preview window.

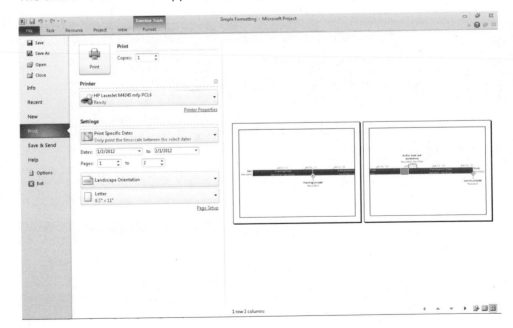

For a simple view like the Timeline, shrinking it to fit on a single page is fine for your communication needs. Next, you'll adjust the page setup options.

11. Click **Page Setup**; this appears at the bottom of the controls, to the left of the print preview.

The Page Setup dialog box appears—note that the dialog box title includes the word "Timeline." You can customize the page setup options that apply to this particular view.

12. Make sure the **Page** tab is visible, and then, under **Scaling**, click **Fit to 1 pages wide by 1 tall**.

Here, you can see the name of the view or report that you're working with. The tabs and options that are available depend on the type of view or report.

13. Click **OK**.

Project resized the Timeline print preview so it now fits on a single page.

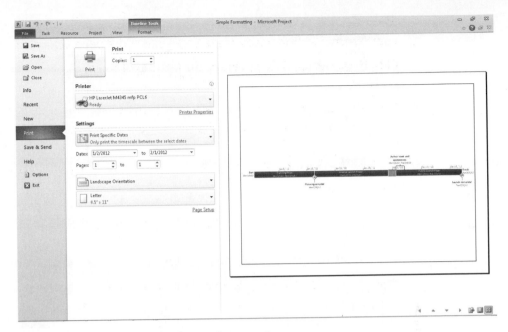

14. Click the **Task** tab to close the Backstage view.

Customizing and Printing Reports

Reports are intended for printing Project data. Unlike views, which you can either print or work with on the screen, reports are designed only for printing or for viewing in the Print Preview window. You do not enter data directly into a report. Project includes several predefined task, resource, and assignment reports that you can edit to obtain the information you want.

You can customize the way you print both views and reports; however, Project has few options for formatting reports. When printing, many of the same options exist for both views and reports, as well as some specific options unique to views or reports.

Tip For advanced instructions on printing reports, see Chapter 15.

In this exercise, you view reports in the Print Preview window and then edit their formats to include additional information.

1. On the **Project** tab, in the **Reports** group, click **Reports**.

The Reports dialog box appears, showing the categories of reports available.

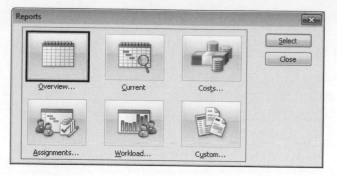

2. Click **Overview**, and then click **Select**.

The Overview Reports dialog box appears, listing the five predefined reports in Project that provide project-wide overview information.

3. In the **Overview Reports** dialog box, click **Project Summary**, and then click **Select**.

Project displays the print preview of the report in Backstage view.

This report is a handy summary of the project plan's tasks, resources, costs, and current status. You could use this report, for example, as a recurring status report that you share with the clients or other *stakeholders* of the project.

Depending on your screen resolution, the text in the report might not be readable when you view a full page.

4. In the **Print Preview** window, click the upper half of the page with the mouse pointer.

Project zooms in to show the page at a legible resolution.

At this point in the project life cycle, the most pertinent pieces of information in the report are the planned start and finish dates and the total cost. If any of these values did not fit within the expectations of the project *sponsor* or other stakeholders, now would be a good time to find out this information.

5. On the **Project** tab, in the **Reports** group, click **Reports**.

The Print Preview window closes, and the Reports dialog box reappears.

Next, you will preview and edit a different report. For a small, simple project such as the new book launch, a report is a simple way to communicate assignments to the resources involved. To do this, you will work with the Who Does What When report.

6. Click **Assignments**, and then click **Select**.

The Assignment Reports dialog box appears, listing four predefined reports in Project that provide resource assignment information.

7. In the **Assignment Reports** dialog box, click **Who Does What When**, and then click **Select**.

Project displays the multiple pages of the Who Does What When report in the Print Preview window.

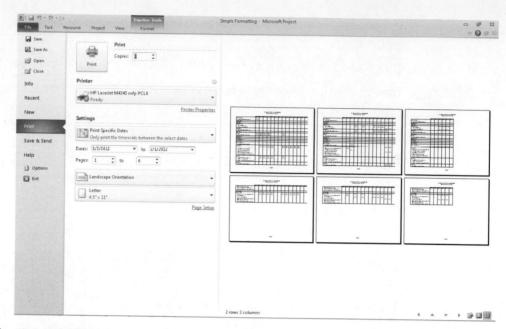

One Page

8. Click **One Page**.

The first page of the report appears in the Print Preview window; if it is not legible on your screen, click the upper half of the page with the mouse pointer to zoom in.

Use the pointer to zoom in or out of the print preview.

These details come from the values entered in the Properties dialog box.

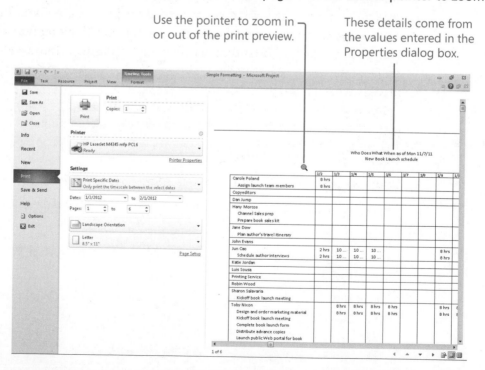

To conclude this exercise, you will reformat the project name as it appears in the report title.

9. Click **Page Setup** at the bottom of the controls in the print preview.

The Page Setup dialog box appears. This time, it shows the options that you can adjust when working with this report.

10. Click the **Header** tab.

In the upper portion of the tab, you see the preview of the report's header. Below that, you can see the codes that make up the header text. These codes include the project title and manager name, which are two properties of the project plan you may recall from Chapter 2, "Creating a Task List."

11. In the **Center** tab, select the text **&[Project Title]** and then click **Format Text Font**.

The Font dialog box appears.

12. Under **Font Style**, click **Bold**, and under **Size**, click **14**. Click **OK**.

The customized report header appears in the Page Setup dialog box.

13. Click **OK** to close the **Page Setup** dialog box.

The reformatted project name appears in the Print Preview window.

14. Click the **Task** tab to return to the Gantt Chart view.

You can change the headers and footers of views in the same way you change them in reports. Keep in mind that changes made to the page setup of any view or report apply only to that view or report. However, the general method used to customize the page setup is the same for any report or view.

✖ CLEAN UP Close the Simple Formatting file.

Key Points

- Presentation styles hide some Gantt chart details that the Scheduling Styles formatting options show.

- You can format individual Gantt bars or whole categories of Gantt bars by doing the following: On the Format tab, in the Bar Styles group, click either Bar or Bar Styles.

- Customize the Timeline view when you need to show a simplified graphical representation of a project plan.

- You can draw or insert graphic objects on the chart portion of a Gantt Chart view but not on the table portion.

- Use the Copy Picture feature (accessed by clicking the Task tab in the Clipboard group) to create a graphic image snapshot of the active view and copy it to the Clipboard. For the Timeline view, use the Copy Timeline feature (accessed by clicking the Format tab in the Copy group).

- Reports are intended for print-previewing or printing only; you cannot enter or edit data directly in a report.

Chapter at a Glance

Set a baseline to take a "snapshot" of the current schedule for future comparison, page 124.

Set progress on tasks through a specific date, page 128.

Enter percent complete on specific tasks, page 129.

Record actual work on tasks, page 132.

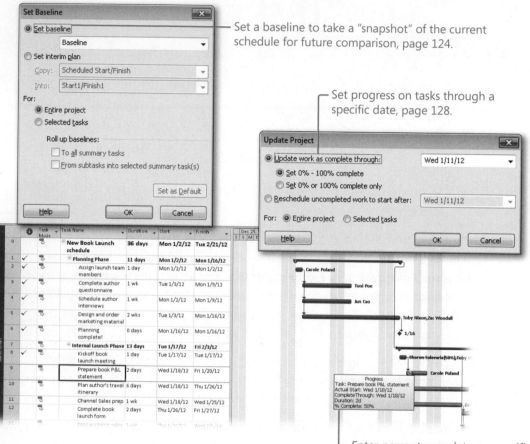

6 Tracking Progress on Tasks

In this chapter, you will learn how to:

✔ Save current values in a schedule as a baseline.

✔ Record progress on tasks through a specific date.

✔ Record a task's percentage of completion.

✔ Enter actual work and duration values for tasks.

Until now, you have focused on project *planning*—developing and communicating the details of a project plan before actual work begins. When work begins, so does the next phase of project management: *tracking* progress. Tracking means recording project details such as who did what work, when the work was done, and at what cost. These details are often called *actuals*.

Tracking actuals is essential to properly managing, as opposed to just planning, a project. The project manager must know how well the project team is performing and when to take corrective action. Properly tracking project performance and comparing it with the original plan allows you to answer such questions as the following:

● Are tasks starting and finishing as planned? If not, what will be the impact on the project's finish date?

● Are *resources* spending more or less time than planned to complete tasks?

● Are higher-than-anticipated task costs driving up the overall cost of the project?

Microsoft Project 2010 supports several ways to track progress. Your choice of a tracking method should depend on the level of detail or control required by you, your project sponsor, and other stakeholders. Tracking the fine details of a project requires additional work from you and possibly from the resources working on the project.

Therefore, before you begin tracking progress, you should determine the level of detail you need. The different levels of tracking detail include the following:

- Record project work as scheduled. This level works best if everything in the project occurs exactly as planned.

- Record each task's percentage of completion, either at precise values or at increments such as 25, 50, 75, or 100 percent.

- Record the actual start, actual finish, actual work, and actual and remaining duration for each task or assignment.

- Track assignment-level work by time period. This is the most detailed level of tracking. Here, you record actual work values per day, week, or other interval.

Because different portions of a project might have different tracking needs, you might need to apply a combination of these approaches within a single project plan. For example, you might want to track high-risk tasks more closely than low-risk ones. In this chapter, you will perform the first three actions in the preceding list; the fourth (tracking assignment-level work by time period) is addressed in Chapter 12, "Tracking Progress on Tasks and Assignments."

> **Practice Files** Before you can complete the exercises in this chapter, you need to copy the book's practice files to your computer. A complete list of practice files is provided in "Using the Practice Files" at the beginning of this book. For each exercise that has a practice file, simply browse to where you saved the book's practice file folder.

Important If you are running Project Professional, you may need to make a one-time setting change. This helps ensure that the practice files you work with in this chapter do not affect your Project Server data. For more information, see Appendix C, "Using the Practice Files if Connected to Project Server."

Saving a Project Baseline

After developing a project plan, one of a project manager's most important activities is to record actuals and evaluate project performance. To judge project performance properly, it is helpful to compare it with your original plan. This original plan is called the baseline plan, or just the *baseline*. A baseline is a collection of important values in a project plan such as the planned start dates, finish dates, and costs of the tasks, resources, and assignments. When you save a baseline, Project takes a "snapshot" of the existing values and saves it in your Project plan for future comparison.

The specific values saved in a baseline include the task, resource, and assignment fields, as well as the timephased fields.

Task Fields	Resource Fields	Assignment Fields
Start	Work and timephased work	Start
Finish	Cost and timephased cost	Finish
Duration		Work and timephased work
Work and timephased work		Cost and timephased cost

Tip *Timephased* fields show task, resource, and assignment values distributed over time. For example, you can look at a task with five days of work planned at the weekly, daily, or hourly level and see the specific baseline work values per time increment. In Chapter 12, you will work with timephased values.

You should save the baseline when

- You have developed the project plan as fully as possible. (However, this does not mean that you cannot add tasks, resources, or assignments to the project after work has started, for this is often unavoidable.)

- You have not yet started entering actual values, such as a task's percentage of completion.

Project supports not just 1 but up to 11 baselines in a single plan. The first one is called Baseline, and the rest are Baseline 1 through Baseline 10. Saving multiple baselines can be useful for projects with especially long planning phases in which you might want to compare different sets of baseline values. For example, you might want to save and compare the baseline plans every month as the planning details change. Or, you might want to save a new baseline at various points during the execution of the project plan. You could, for example, save the Baseline before work starts, then Baseline 1 a month after work starts, Baseline 2 two months after work starts, and so on. You can then view the various baselines and compare them to the actual schedule throughout the project's duration.

Tip Saving several baselines in a project plan can increase your file size.

The new book launch project plan at Lucerne Publishing is now fully developed, and actual work on the project will soon begin.

In this exercise, you save the baseline for a project plan and then view the baseline task values.

SET UP Start Project if it's not already running.

You need the Simple Tracking_Start project plan located in your Chapter06 practice file folder to complete this exercise. Open the Simple Tracking_Start project plan, and then follow these steps.

1. On the **File** tab, click **Save As**.

   Project displays the Save As dialog box.

2. In the **File name** box, type **Simple Tracking**, and then click **Save**.

3. On the **Project** tab, in the **Schedule** group, click **Set Baseline**, and then click **Set Baseline**.

   The Set Baseline dialog box appears.

   You'll set the baseline for the entire project by using the default settings of the dialog box.

4. Click **OK**.

   Project saves the baseline, even though there's no indication in the Gantt Chart view that anything has changed. You will now see some of the changes caused by saving the baseline.

5. On the **View** tab, in the **Task Views** group, click **Other Views** and then click **Task Sheet**.

   The Task Sheet view appears. Because this is a tabular view, it does not include the Gantt chart, so more room is available to see the fields in the table.

   Now you'll switch to the Variance table in the Task Sheet view. The Variance table is one of several predefined tables that include baseline values.

6. On the **View** tab, in the **Data** group, click **Tables**.

In the listed tables, note the check mark next to Entry. This means that the Entry table is currently displayed in the Task Sheet view. You'll switch to another table next.

7. Click **Variance**.

Tip You also can right-click the **Select All** button in the upper-left corner of the active table to switch to a different table.

The Variance table appears. This table includes both the scheduled and baseline start and finish columns, shown side by side for easy comparison.

	Task ▼	Task Name ▼	Start ▼	Finish ▼	Baseline Start ▼	Baseline Finish ▼	Start Var. ▼	Finish Var. ▼
0		New Book Launch	Mon 1/2/12	Tue 2/21/12	Mon 1/2/12	Tue 2/21/12	0 days	0 days
1		Planning Phase	Mon 1/2/12	Mon 1/16/12	Mon 1/2/12	Mon 1/16/12	0 days	0 days
2		Assign launch t	Mon 1/2/12	Mon 1/2/12	Mon 1/2/12	Mon 1/2/12	0 days	0 days
3		Complete auth	Tue 1/3/12	Mon 1/9/12	Tue 1/3/12	Mon 1/9/12	0 days	0 days
4		Schedule autho	Mon 1/2/12	Mon 1/9/12	Mon 1/2/12	Mon 1/9/12	0 days	0 days
5		Design and ord	Tue 1/3/12	Mon 1/16/12	Tue 1/3/12	Mon 1/16/12	0 days	0 days
6		Planning comp	Mon 1/16/12	Mon 1/16/12	Mon 1/16/12	Mon 1/16/12	0 days	0 days
7		Internal Launch Pl	Tue 1/17/12	Fri 2/3/12	Tue 1/17/12	Fri 2/3/12	0 days	0 days
8		Kickoff book la	Tue 1/17/12	Tue 1/17/12	Tue 1/17/12	Tue 1/17/12	0 days	0 days
9		Prepare book F	Wed 1/18/12	Fri 1/20/12	Wed 1/18/12	Fri 1/20/12	0 days	0 days
10		Plan author's tr	Wed 1/18/12	Thu 1/26/12	Wed 1/18/12	Thu 1/26/12	0 days	0 days
11		Channel Sales	Wed 1/18/12	Wed 1/25/12	Wed 1/18/12	Wed 1/25/12	0 days	0 days
12		Complete book	Thu 1/26/12	Fri 1/27/12	Thu 1/26/12	Fri 1/27/12	0 days	0 days
13		Prepare book s	Thu 1/26/12	Wed 2/1/12	Thu 1/26/12	Wed 2/1/12	0 days	0 days
14		Distribute inter	Thu 2/2/12	Fri 2/3/12	Thu 2/2/12	Fri 2/3/12	0 days	0 days
15		Public Launch Pha	Mon 2/6/12	Tue 2/21/12	Mon 2/6/12	Tue 2/21/12	0 days	0 days
16		Author travel a	Mon 2/6/12	Tue 2/7/12	Mon 2/6/12	Tue 2/7/12	0 days	0 days
17		Author radic	Mon 2/6/12	Mon 2/6/12	Mon 2/6/12	Mon 2/6/12	0 days	0 days
18		Author readi	Tue 2/7/12	Tue 2/7/12	Tue 2/7/12	Tue 2/7/12	0 days	0 days
19		Distribute adva	Mon 2/6/12	Tue 2/7/12	Mon 2/6/12	Tue 2/7/12	0 days	0 days
20		Distribute book	Mon 2/6/12	Tue 2/7/12	Mon 2/6/12	Tue 2/7/12	0 days	0 days
21		Coordinate ma	Wed 2/8/12	Thu 2/16/12	Wed 2/8/12	Thu 2/16/12	0 days	0 days
22		Launch public V	Wed 2/8/12	Tue 2/14/12	Wed 2/8/12	Tue 2/14/12	0 days	0 days
23		Launch social m	Wed 2/15/12	Tue 2/21/12	Wed 2/15/12	Tue 2/21/12	0 days	0 days
24		Launch comple	Tue 2/21/12	Tue 2/21/12	Tue 2/21/12	Tue 2/21/12	0 days	0 days

Because no actual work has occurred yet and no changes to the scheduled work have been made, the values in the Start and Baseline Start fields are identical, as are the values in the Finish and Baseline Finish fields. After actual work is recorded or later schedule adjustments are made, the scheduled start and finish values might differ from the baseline values. You would then see the differences displayed in the variance columns.

8. On the **View** tab, in the **Task Views** group, click **Gantt Chart**.

The Gantt Chart view appears.

Tip Project includes views that compare the current schedule to baseline, but here's one quick way to see baseline values in the Gantt Chart view: on the Format tab, in the Bar Styles group, click Baseline and then click the baseline (Baseline or Baseline1 through Baseline10) that you want to display. Project draws baseline Gantt bars for the baseline you choose.

Now that you've had a look at some baseline fields, it is time to enter some actuals!

Tracking a Project as Scheduled

The simplest approach to tracking progress is to report that the actual work is proceeding exactly as planned. For example, if the first month of a five-month project has elapsed and all its tasks have started and finished as scheduled, you can quickly record this in the Update Project dialog box. When you record progress through a specific date, Project calculates actual duration, remaining duration, actual costs, and other values up to the date you entered.

In the new book launch project, suppose that some time has now passed since saving the baseline. Work has started, and all is well.

In this exercise, you record project actuals by updating work to a specific date.

1. On the **Project** tab, in the **Status** group, click **Update Project**.

   The Update Project dialog box appears.

2. Make sure the **Update work as complete through** option is selected. In the adjacent date box, type or select **1/11/12**.

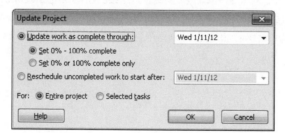

3. Click **OK**.

   Project records the completion percentage for the tasks that were scheduled to start before January 11. It displays that progress by drawing *progress bars* in the Gantt bars for those tasks.

Check marks appear in the Indicators column for tasks that have been completed.

Progress bars indicate the portion of each task that has been completed.

	ⓘ	Task Mode	Task Name	Duration	Start	Finish
0			⊟ New Book Launch schedule	36 days	Mon 1/2/12	Tue 2/21/12
1			⊟ Planning Phase	11 days	Mon 1/2/12	Mon 1/16/12
2	✓		Assign launch team members	1 day	Mon 1/2/12	Mon 1/2/12
3	✓		Complete author questionnaire	1 wk	Tue 1/3/12	Mon 1/9/12
4	✓		Schedule author interviews	1 wk	Mon 1/2/12	Mon 1/9/12
5			Design and order marketing material	2 wks	Tue 1/3/12	Mon 1/16/12
6			Planning complete!	0 days	Mon 1/16/12	Mon 1/16/12
7			⊟ Internal Launch Phase	13 days	Tue 1/17/12	Fri 2/3/12
8			Kickoff book launch meeting	1 day	Tue 1/17/12	Tue 1/17/12
9			Prepare book P&L statement	2 days	Wed 1/18/12	Fri 1/20/12

In the Gantt Chart view, the progress bar shows how much of each task has been completed. Because tasks 2, 3, and 4 have been completed, a check mark appears in the Indicators column for those tasks, and the progress bars extend through the full length of those tasks' Gantt bars. Task 5 is only partially completed, however.

Entering a Task's Completion Percentage

After work has begun on a task, you can quickly record its progress as a percentage. When you enter a completion percentage other than 0, Project changes the task's actual start date to match its scheduled start date. Project then calculates actual duration, remaining duration, actual costs, and other values based on the percentage you enter. For example, if you specify that a four-day task is 50 percent complete, Project calculates that it has had two days of actual duration and has two days of remaining duration.

Here are some ways of entering completion percentages:

● Use the 0%, 25%, 50%, 75%, and 100% Complete buttons in the Schedule group of the Task tab.

● Enter any percentage value you want in the Update Tasks dialog box (to access this dialog box, on the Task tab, in the Schedule group, click the down arrow to the right of the Mark on Track, and then click Update Tasks).

Tip If you can collect the actual start date of a task, it is a good practice to record the actual start date (described in the next section), and then record a completion percentage.

In this exercise, you record completion percentages of some tasks in the new book launch project plan.

1. In the **Task Name** column, select the name of task 5, *Design and order marketing material.*

   This task has some progress reported against it from the previous exercise, but has not yet been set as complete.

100% Complete

2. On the **Task** tab, in the **Schedule** group, click **100% Complete**.

   Project records the actual work for the task as scheduled and extends a progress bar through the length of the Gantt bar.

	ⓘ	Task Mode	Task Name	Duration	Start	Finish	Dec 25, '11	Jan 1, '12	Jan 8, '12	Jan 15, '12	Jan 22, '12
0			New Book Launch schedule	36 days	Mon 1/2/12	Tue 2/21/12					
1			Planning Phase	11 days	Mon 1/2/12	Mon 1/16/12					
2	✓		Assign launch team members	1 day	Mon 1/2/12	Mon 1/2/12		Carole Poland			
3	✓		Complete author questionnaire	1 wk	Tue 1/3/12	Mon 1/9/12			Toni Poe		
4	✓		Schedule author interviews	1 wk	Mon 1/2/12	Mon 1/9/12			Jun Cao		
5	✓		Design and order marketing material	2 wks	Tue 1/3/12	Mon 1/16/12				Toby Nixon,Zac Woodall	
6			Planning complete!	0 days	Mon 1/16/12	Mon 1/16/12				◆ 1/16	
7			Internal Launch Phase	13 days	Tue 1/17/12	Fri 2/3/12					
8			Kickoff book launch meeting	1 day	Tue 1/17/12	Tue 1/17/12					Sharon Salavaria[50%],Toby
9			Prepare book P&L statement	2 days	Wed 1/18/12	Fri 1/20/12					Carole Poland
10			Plan author's travel itinerary	6 days	Wed 1/18/12	Thu 1/26/12					
11			Channel Sales prep	1 wk	Wed 1/18/12	Wed 1/25/12					
12			Complete book launch form	2 days	Thu 1/26/12	Fri 1/27/12					
15			Prepare book sales	1 wk	Thu 1/26/12	Wed 2/1/12					

Next you'll record that the completion milestone for the Planning Phase and the first task of the Internal Launch Phase are complete.

3. In the **Task Name** column, select the name of task 6, *Planning complete!* and while holding down the Ctrl key, select the name of task 8, *Kickoff book launch meeting*.

4. On the **Task** tab, in the **Schedule** group, click **100% Complete**.

	ⓘ	Task Mode	Task Name	Duration	Start	Finish	Dec 25, '11	Jan 1, '12	Jan 8, '12	Jan 15, '12	Jan 22, '12
0			New Book Launch schedule	36 days	Mon 1/2/12	Tue 2/21/12					
1	✓		Planning Phase	11 days	Mon 1/2/12	Mon 1/16/12					
2	✓		Assign launch team members	1 day	Mon 1/2/12	Mon 1/2/12		Carole Poland			
3	✓		Complete author questionnaire	1 wk	Tue 1/3/12	Mon 1/9/12			Toni Poe		
4	✓		Schedule author interviews	1 wk	Mon 1/2/12	Mon 1/9/12			Jun Cao		
5	✓		Design and order marketing material	2 wks	Tue 1/3/12	Mon 1/16/12				Toby Nixon,Zac Woodall	
6	✓		Planning complete!	0 days	Mon 1/16/12	Mon 1/16/12				◆ 1/16	
7			Internal Launch Phase	13 days	Tue 1/17/12	Fri 2/3/12					
8	✓		Kickoff book launch meeting	1 day	Tue 1/17/12	Tue 1/17/12					Sharon Salavaria[50%],Toby
9			Prepare book P&L statement	2 days	Wed 1/18/12	Fri 1/20/12					Carole Poland
10			Plan author's travel itinerary	6 days	Wed 1/18/12	Thu 1/26/12					
11			Channel Sales prep	1 wk	Wed 1/18/12	Wed 1/25/12					
12			Complete book launch form	2 days	Thu 1/26/12	Fri 1/27/12					
15			Prepare book sales	1 wk	Thu 1/26/12	Wed 2/1/12					

Next, you'll get a better look at how progress is displayed in a task's Gantt bar. You will enter a completion percentage value for a different task.

5. Click the name of task 9, *Prepare book P&L statement*.

50%
50% Complete

6. On the **Task** tab, in the **Schedule** group, click **50% Complete**.

Project records the actual work for the task as scheduled and then draws a progress bar through part of the Gantt bar.

	❶	Task Mode	Task Name	Duration	Start	Finish
0		❸	⊟ **New Book Launch schedule**	**36 days**	**Mon 1/2/12**	**Tue 2/21/12**
1	✓	❸	⊟ **Planning Phase**	**11 days**	**Mon 1/2/12**	**Mon 1/16/12**
2	✓	❸	Assign launch team members	1 day	Mon 1/2/12	Mon 1/2/12
3	✓	❸	Complete author questionnaire	1 wk	Tue 1/3/12	Mon 1/9/12
4	✓	❸	Schedule author interviews	1 wk	Mon 1/2/12	Mon 1/9/12
5	✓	❸	Design and order marketing material	2 wks	Tue 1/3/12	Mon 1/16/12
6	✓	❸	Planning complete!	0 days	Mon 1/16/12	Mon 1/16/12
7		❸	⊟ **Internal Launch Phase**	**13 days**	**Tue 1/17/12**	**Fri 2/3/12**
8	✓	❸	Kickoff book launch meeting	1 day	Tue 1/17/12	Tue 1/17/12
9		❸	Prepare book P&L statement	2 days	Wed 1/18/12	Fri 1/20/12
10		❸	Plan author's travel itinerary	6 days	Wed 1/18/12	Thu 1/26/12
11		❸	Channel Sales prep	1 wk	Wed 1/18/12	Wed 1/25/12
12		❸	Complete book launch form	2 days	Thu 1/26/12	Fri 1/27/12
13		❸	Prepare book sales	1 wk	Thu 1/26/12	Wed 2/1/12

Note that although 50% of the work on task 9 is completed, the progress bar does not span 50% of the width of the Gantt bar. This is because Project measures duration in working time but draws the Gantt bars to extend over nonworking time, which in this case includes Thursday, January 19, the nonworking day.

Tip By default, Project shows Gantt bars in front of nonworking time (such as weekends), as you see in this section. However, Project can show nonworking time in front of task bars, visually indicating that no work on the task will occur during the nonworking time. If you prefer this type of presentation, right-click any shaded nonworking time in the chart portion of the Gantt Chart view, and click Nonworking Time in the shortcut menu. In the Timescale dialog box, click the "Non-working time" tab. Next to Draw, click "In front of task bars."

7. In the chart portion (on the right) in the Gantt Chart view, hold the mouse pointer over the progress bar in task 9's Gantt bar. When the mouse pointer changes to a percent symbol and right arrow, a Progress ScreenTip appears.

Depending on the type of bar or symbol you point to, in this case the progress bar, a ScreenTip pops up, providing information about that item.

The mouse pointer changes to a percent symbol and arrow when pointing to a progress bar.

The Progress ScreenTip informs you of the task's completion percentage and other tracking values.

Tip You can also set percent complete by pointing to a Gantt bar (or progress bar within a Gantt bar). When the mouse pointer changes to a percent symbol and right arrow, drag the mouse pointer from left to right within the Gantt bar. As you do so, note the "complete through" date value that appears in a ScreenTip.

So far, you have recorded actual work that started and finished on schedule. While this might prove true for some tasks, you often need to record actuals for tasks that lasted longer or shorter than planned, or occurred sooner or later than scheduled. This is the subject of the next topic.

Entering Actual Values for Tasks

A more detailed way to keep your schedule up to date is to record what actually happens for each task in your project. You can record each task's actual start, finish, work, and duration values. When you enter these values, Project uses the following rules:

- When you enter a task's actual start date, Project moves the scheduled start date to match the actual start date.

- When you enter a task's actual finish date, Project moves the scheduled finish date to match the actual finish date and sets the task to 100% complete.

● When you enter a task's actual work value, Project recalculates the task's remaining work value, if any.

● When you enter a task's actual duration, if it is less than the scheduled duration, Project subtracts the actual duration from the scheduled duration to determine the remaining duration.

● When you enter a task's actual duration, if it is equal to the scheduled duration, Project sets the task to 100% complete.

● When you enter a task's actual duration, if it is longer than the scheduled duration, Project adjusts the scheduled duration to match the actual duration and sets the task to 100% complete.

Suppose that a few more days have passed and work on the new book launch has progressed.

In this exercise, you record actual work values for some tasks as well as start dates and durations for other tasks.

1. On the **View** tab, in the **Data** group, click **Tables** and then click **Work**.

   The Work table appears.

   Tip You can display whichever table is most relevant to the details you are focused on while tracking progress in a project plan. Useful tables include the Work table, which focuses on work values, and the Cost table, which focuses on cost values. The Tracking table is a good all-around table when recording or viewing progress.

2. Drag the vertical divider bar to the right to expose the other columns in the Work table.

   This table includes both the total scheduled work (labeled "Work") and Actual and Remaining work columns. You'll refer to the values in these columns as you update tasks.

   In the chart portion of the Gantt Chart view, you can see that task 9 is partially complete. In the Work table, note the actual work value of 8 hours. This 8 hours is the result of setting the task at 50% complete in the previous exercise. The task had 16 hours of work total, so 50% complete equals 8 hours actual work completed and 8 hours remaining. You want to record that the task is now complete but required more actual work than expected.

3. In the **Actual** field for task 9, *Prepare book P&L statement*, type or select **24**, and then press the Enter key.

   Project records that 24 hours of work have been completed on task 9. Since 24 hours is greater than the originally scheduled 16 hours, Project marks the task as completed and extends the Gantt bar of the task to indicate its longer duration.

Actual work is rolled up from the subtasks to the summary tasks.

	Task Name	Work	Baseline	Variance	Actual	Remaining	% W. Comp	Jan 8, '12	Jan 15, '12	Jan 22, '12	Jan 29, '12
0	New Book Launch schedule	820 hrs	812 hrs	8 hrs	284 hrs	536 hrs	35%				
1	Planning Phase	248 hrs	248 hrs	0 hrs	248 hrs	0 hrs	100%				
2	Assign launch team members	8 hrs	8 hrs	0 hrs	8 hrs	0 hrs	100%				
3	Complete author questionnaire	40 hrs	40 hrs	0 hrs	40 hrs	0 hrs	100%	Toni Poe			
4	Schedule author interviews	40 hrs	40 hrs	0 hrs	40 hrs	0 hrs	100%	Jun Cao			
5	Design and order marketing material	160 hrs	160 hrs	0 hrs	160 hrs	0 hrs	100%		Toby Nixon,Zac Woodall		
6	Planning complete!	0 hrs	0 hrs	0 hrs	0 hrs	0 hrs	100%		◆ 1/16		
7	Internal Launch Phase	292 hrs	284 hrs	8 hrs	36 hrs	256 hrs	12%				
8	Kickoff book launch meeting	12 hrs	12 hrs	0 hrs	12 hrs	0 hrs	100%		Sharon Salavaria[50%],Toby Nixon		
9	Prepare book P&L statement	24 hrs	16 hrs	8 hrs	24 hrs	0 hrs	100%			Carole Poland	
10	Plan author's travel itinerary	48 hrs	48 hrs	0 hrs	0 hrs	48 hrs	0%			Jane Dow	
11	Channel Sales prep	80 hrs	80 hrs	0 hrs	0 hrs	80 hrs	0%			Zac Woodall,Hany Morcos	
12	Complete book launch form	32 hrs	32 hrs	0 hrs	0 hrs	32 hrs	0%			Toby Nixon,Vikas Jai	
13	Prepare book sales	80 hrs	80 hrs	0 hrs	0 hrs	80 hrs	0%				Han

Now suppose that more time has passed. To conclude this exercise, you will enter actual start dates and durations of other tasks in the Internal Launch Phase.

4. In the **Task Name** column, click task 10, *Plan author's travel itinerary*.

This task started one working day ahead of schedule (the Tuesday before its scheduled start date) and took a total of seven days to complete. You will record this information in the Update Tasks dialog box.

5. On the **Task** tab, in the **Schedule** group, click the down arrow to the right of the **Mark on Track** button, and then click **Update Tasks**.

The Update Tasks dialog box appears. This dialog box shows both the actual and scheduled values for the task's duration, start, and finish, as well as its remaining duration. In this box, you can update the actual and remaining values.

6. In the **Start** field in the **Actual** group on the left side of the dialog box, type or se-lect **1/17/12**.

7. In the **Actual dur** field, type or select **7d**.

Update Tasks		
Name:	Plan author's travel itinerary	Duration: 6d
% Complete: 0%	Actual dur: 7d	Remaining dur: 6d

Actual
Start: 1/17/12
Finish: NA

Current
Start: Wed 1/18/12
Finish: Thu 1/26/12

Help Notes... OK Cancel

8. Click **OK**.

Project records the actual start date, duration, and scheduled and actual work of the task. These values also roll up to the *Internal Launch Phase* summary task (task 7) and the project summary task (task 0), as indicated by the change highlighting.

	Task Name	Work	Baseline	Variance	Actual	Remaining	% W. Comp.
0	New Book Launch schedule	828 hrs	812 hrs	16 hrs	340 hrs	488 hrs	41%
1	Planning Phase	248 hrs	248 hrs	0 hrs	248 hrs	0 hrs	100%
2	Assign launch team members	8 hrs	8 hrs	0 hrs	8 hrs	0 hrs	100%
3	Complete author questionnaire	40 hrs	40 hrs	0 hrs	40 hrs	0 hrs	100%
4	Schedule author interviews	40 hrs	40 hrs	0 hrs	40 hrs	0 hrs	100%
5	Design and order marketing material	160 hrs	160 hrs	0 hrs	160 hrs	0 hrs	100%
6	Planning complete!	0 hrs	0 hrs	0 hrs	0 hrs	0 hrs	100%
7	Internal Launch Phase	300 hrs	284 hrs	16 hrs	92 hrs	208 hrs	31%
8	Kickoff book launch meeting	12 hrs	12 hrs	0 hrs	12 hrs	0 hrs	100%
9	Prepare book P&L statement	24 hrs	16 hrs	8 hrs	24 hrs	0 hrs	100%
10	Plan author's travel itinerary	56 hrs	48 hrs	8 hrs	56 hrs	0 hrs	100%
11	Channel Sales prep	80 hrs	80 hrs	0 hrs	0 hrs	80 hrs	0%
12	Complete book launch form	32 hrs	32 hrs	0 hrs	0 hrs	32 hrs	0%
13	Prepare book sales	80 hrs	80 hrs	0 hrs	0 hrs	30 hrs	0%

To conclude this exercise, you will record that task 11 started on time but took longer than planned to complete.

9. In the **Task Name** column, click task 11, *Channel Sales prep*.

10. On the **Task** tab, in the **Schedule** group, click the down arrow to the right of the **Mark on Track** button, and then click **Update Tasks**.

The Update Tasks dialog box appears.

11. In the **Actual dur** field, type **7d**, and then click **OK**.

Project records the actual duration of the task.

	Task Name	Work	Baseline	Variance	Actual	Remaining	% W. Comp.
0	New Book Launch schedule	860 hrs	812 hrs	48 hrs	452 hrs	408 hrs	53%
1	Planning Phase	248 hrs	248 hrs	0 hrs	248 hrs	0 hrs	100%
2	Assign launch team members	8 hrs	8 hrs	0 hrs	8 hrs	0 hrs	100%
3	Complete author questionnaire	40 hrs	40 hrs	0 hrs	40 hrs	0 hrs	100%
4	Schedule author interviews	40 hrs	40 hrs	0 hrs	40 hrs	0 hrs	100%
5	Design and order marketing material	160 hrs	160 hrs	0 hrs	160 hrs	0 hrs	100%
6	Planning complete!	0 hrs	0 hrs	0 hrs	0 hrs	0 hrs	100%
7	Internal Launch Phase	332 hrs	284 hrs	48 hrs	204 hrs	128 hrs	61%
8	Kickoff book launch meeting	12 hrs	12 hrs	0 hrs	12 hrs	0 hrs	100%
9	Prepare book P&L statement	24 hrs	16 hrs	8 hrs	24 hrs	0 hrs	100%
10	Plan author's travel itinerary	56 hrs	48 hrs	8 hrs	56 hrs	0 hrs	100%
11	Channel Sales prep	112 hrs	80 hrs	32 hrs	112 hrs	0 hrs	100%
12	Complete book launch form	32 hrs	32 hrs	0 hrs	0 hrs	32 hrs	0%
13	Prepare book sales	80 hrs	80 hrs	0 hrs	0 hrs	80 hrs	0%

Because you did not specify an actual start date, Project assumes that the task started as scheduled. However, the actual duration that you entered causes Project to calculate an actual finish date that is later than the originally scheduled finish date.

Tip You can apply all the tracking methods shown in this chapter to manually scheduled tasks. You can also record an actual start, actual finish, or remaining duration value for a manually scheduled task.

Project Management Focus: Is the Project on Track?

Evaluating a project's status properly can be tricky. Consider the following issues:

- For many tasks, it is very difficult to evaluate a completion percentage. When is an engineer's design for a new motor assembly 50 percent complete? Or when is a programmer's code for a software module 50 percent complete? Reporting work in progress is in many cases a "best guess" effort and inherently risky.

- The elapsed portion of a task's duration is not always equal to the amount of work accomplished. For example, a task might require relatively little effort initially, but require more work as time passes. (This is referred to as a back-loaded task.) When 50 percent of its duration has elapsed, far less than 50 percent of its total work will have been completed.

- The resources assigned to a task might have different criteria for what constitutes the task's completion than the criteria determined by the project manager or the resources assigned to successor tasks.

Good project planning and communication can avoid or mitigate these and other problems that arise in project execution. For example, developing proper task durations and status-reporting periods should help you identify tasks that have varied substantially from the baseline early enough to make adjustments. Having well-documented and well-communicated task completion criteria should help prevent "downstream" surprises. Nevertheless, large, complex projects will almost always vary from the baseline.

  CLEAN UP Close the Simple Tracking file.

Key Points

- Before tracking actual work in a project plan, you should set a baseline. This provides you with a "snapshot" of your initial project plan for later comparison against actual progress and is one way to tell whether your project is on track.

- The ability to track actual work in a project plan is a major advantage that a project management tool such as Project has over a list-keeping tool such as Microsoft Excel. In Project, you can track actual work at a very broad or very detailed level.

- To evaluate a project's status properly after you begin tracking requires a combination of recording accurate data in Project and using your good judgment when interpreting the results.

Part 2

Advanced Scheduling

Chapter at a Glance

Change how tasks are related to each other, page 142.

Apply constraints to control when tasks can be scheduled, page 147.

Interrupt work on a task, page 153.

Set working time for a specific task, page 155.

Fine-tune how Project responds to schedule changes, page 158.

Set up a recurring task, page 167.

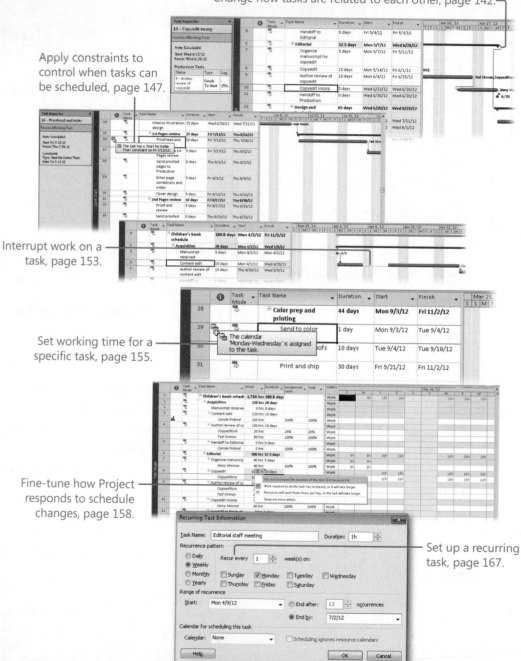

7 Fine-Tuning Task Details

In this chapter, you will learn how to:

✔ Adjust task links to have more control over how tasks are related.

✔ Apply a constraint to a task.

✔ Split a task to record an interruption in work.

✔ Create a task calendar and apply it to a task.

✔ Change a task type to control how Project schedules tasks.

✔ Record deadlines for tasks.

✔ Enter a fixed cost for a task.

✔ Set up a recurring task in the project schedule.

✔ View the project's critical path.

✔ Enter a specific duration value for a summary task.

✔ Inactivate tasks so they remain in the project plan but have no effect on the schedule (Project Professional only).

In this chapter, you examine and use a variety of advanced features in Microsoft Project 2010. These features focus on fine-tuning task details prior to saving a baseline, as well as commencing work on the project with the goal of developing the most accurate schedule representation of the tasks you anticipate for the plan.

> **Practice Files** Before you can complete the exercises in this chapter, you need to copy the book's practice files to your computer. A complete list of practice files is provided in "Using the Practice Files" at the beginning of this book. For each exercise that has a practice file, simply browse to where you saved the book's practice file folder.

Important If you are running Project Professional, you may need to make a one-time setting change. This helps ensure that the practice files you work with in this chapter do not affect your Project Server data. For more information, see Appendix C, "Using the Practice Files if Connected to Project Server."

Adjusting Task Relationships

You might recall from Chapter 2, "Creating a Task List," that there are four types of task dependencies, or relationships:

- Finish-to-start (FS): The finish date of the predecessor task determines the start date of the successor task.

- Start-to-start (SS): The start date of the predecessor task determines the start date of the successor task.

- Finish-to-finish (FF): The finish date of the predecessor task determines the finish date of the successor task.

- Start-to-finish (SF): The start date of the predecessor task determines the finish date of the successor task.

When you enter tasks in Project and link them by clicking the Link Tasks button on the Task tab, the tasks are given a finish-to-start relationship. This is fine for many tasks, but you will most likely change some task relationships as you fine-tune a project plan. The following are some examples of tasks that require relationships other than finish-to-start:

- You can start setting pages as soon as you start illustration work on a book project (a start-to-start relationship). This reduces the overall time required to complete the two tasks, as they are completed in parallel.

- Planning the editorial work for a book can begin before the manuscript is complete, but it cannot be finished until the manuscript is complete. You want the two tasks to finish at the same time (a finish-to-finish relationship).

Task relationships should reflect the sequence in which work should be performed. After you have established the correct task relationships, you can fine-tune your schedule by entering overlap (called lead time) or delay (called lag time) between the finish or start dates of predecessor and successor tasks.

Assuming that two tasks have a finish-to-start relationship:

- Lead time causes the successor task to begin before its predecessor task concludes.

- Lag time causes the successor task to begin some time after its predecessor task concludes.

The following is an illustration of how lead and lag time affect task relationships. Assume that you initially planned the following three tasks using finish-to-start relationships.

Initially the tasks are linked with finish-to-start relationships, so the successor task is scheduled to begin when the predecessor task finishes.

	Task Name	Predecessors
1	Copyedit	
2	Author review of copyedit	1
3	Copyedit incorp	2

Before task 2 can begin, you need to allow an extra day for the copyedited manuscript to be shipped to the author. You do not want to add a day to the duration of task 5 because no real work will occur on that day. Instead, you enter a one-day lag between tasks 1 and 2.

This lag time delays the start of the successor task by one day.

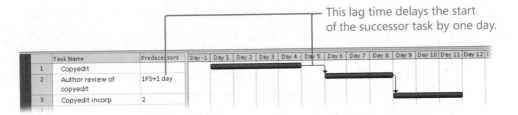

	Task Name	Predecessors
1	Copyedit	
2	Author review of copyedit	1FS+1 day
3	Copyedit incorp	2

However, task 3 can start as soon as task 2 is halfway completed. To make this happen, enter a 50 percent lead time between tasks 2 and 3.

This lead time schedules the successor task to start before the predecessor task finishes.

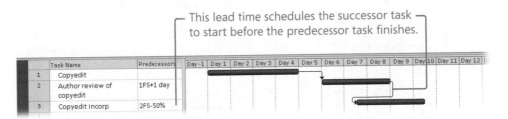

	Task Name	Predecessors
1	Copyedit	
2	Author review of copyedit	1FS+1 day
3	Copyedit incorp	2FS-50%

You can enter lead and lag time as units of time, such as two days, or as a percentage of the duration of the predecessor task, such as 50 percent. Lag time is entered in positive units and lead time in negative units (for example, –2d or –50%). You can apply lead or lag time to any type of task relationship: finish-to-start, start-to-start, and so on.

Places in which you can enter lead or lag time include the Task Information dialog box (Task tab), the Predecessors column in the Entry table, and the Task Dependency dialog box (viewable by double-clicking a link line between Gantt bars).

Lucerne Publishing is about to begin editorial and design work on a new children's book. At this stage, you have an initial project plan with task names, durations, and relationships, and resource assignments.

In this exercise, you enter lead and lag time and change task relationships between predecessor and successor tasks.

SET UP Start Project 2010 if it's not already running.

You need the Advanced Tasks A_Start project plan located in your Chapter07 practice file folder to complete this exercise. Open the Advanced Tasks A_Start project plan, and then follow these steps.

1. On the **File** tab, click **Save As**.

   The Save As dialog box appears.

2. In the **File name** box, type **Advanced Tasks A**, and then click **Save**.

3. On the **Task** tab, in the **Tasks** group, click **Inspect**.

   The Task Inspector pane appears. This pane succinctly reveals the scheduling factors that affect the selected task, such as predecessor task relationships, resource calendars, and/or task calendars. You can click any item in the Task Inspector that appears in blue to get more details. For example, you can click the assigned resource's name under Calendar to see the resource calendar.

4. Select the name of task 31, *Print and ship*.

   In the Task Inspector pane, you can view the scheduling factors affecting this task.

For task 31, you can see that its predecessor is task 30, *Generate proofs*. You can see in the pane that the two tasks have a finish-to-start relationship with zero lag time. Next, you'll adjust the lag value on the task relationship to account for the transit time of the proofs to the printer. Because you cannot edit this value directly in the pane, you'll display the Task Information dialog box. First, though, you'll display this task's Gantt bar so you can more easily observe the effect of adjusting the lag.

5. On the **Task** tab, in the **Editing** group, click **Scroll to Task**.

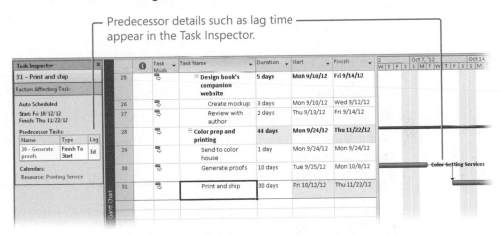

Next, you'll adjust the lag value between this task and its predecessor.

6. On the **Task** tab, in the **Properties** group, click **Information**.

The Task Information dialog box appears. It contains details about the currently selected task, 31.

7. Click the **Predecessors** tab.

8. In the **Lag** field for predecessor task 30, type **3d**, and then click **OK** to close the **Task Information** dialog box.

Predecessor details such as lag time appear in the Task Inspector.

Task 31 is now scheduled to start three working days after the end of task 30.

Next, you will adjust the lag time between two other tasks.

9. Click the name of task 10, *Copyedit incorp*.

You'd like to overlap this task with its predecessor; the *Copyedit incorp* task can start before the author review of copyedit is completed.

10. On the **Task** tab, in the **Properties** group, click **Information**, and then click the **Predecessors** tab.

11. In the **Lag** field for predecessor task 9, type **−25%**, and then click **OK**.

Entering lag time as a negative value produces lead time.

To see the adjustment you made more directly, you'll scroll to the task's Gantt bar again.

12. On the **Task** tab, in the **Editing** group, click **Scroll to Task**.

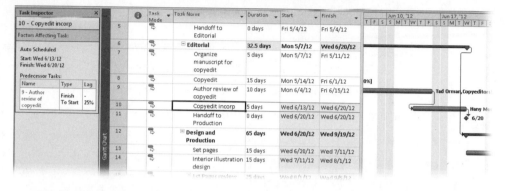

Task 10 is now scheduled to start at the 25 percent remaining point of the duration of task 9. Should the duration of task 9 change, Project will reschedule the start of task 10 so that it maintains a 25 percent lead time.

To conclude this exercise, you will change the task relationship between two tasks.

13. Double-click the name of task 14, *Interior illustration design*.

The Task Information dialog box appears. The Predecessors tab should be visible. Note also that the Task Inspector pane in the background updates to display the scheduling details for task 14, the currently selected task.

14. On the **Predecessors** tab, click in the **Type** column for predecessor task 13. Select **Start-to-Start (SS)**, and click **OK**.

Project changes the task relationship between tasks 13 and 14 to start-to-start.

Assigning tasks start-to-start relationships and entering lead times where appropriate are both excellent techniques to fine-tune task relationships so that you get the results you want. However, Project cannot automatically make such schedule adjustments for you. As project manager, you must analyze the sequences and relationships of your tasks and make those adjustments where necessary.

Setting Task Constraints

Every task that you enter into Project has some type of constraint applied to it. A constraint controls the start or finish date of a task and the degree to which that task can be rescheduled. There are three categories of constraints:

- **Flexible constraints** Project can change the start and finish dates of a task. The default constraint type in Project is that tasks start as soon as possible. This type of flexible constraint is called As Soon As Possible, or ASAP for short. No constraint date is associated with flexible constraints. Project does not display any special indicator in the Indicators column for flexible constraints.

- **Inflexible constraints** A task must begin or end on a certain date. For example, you can specify that a task must end on November 9, 2012. Inflexible constraints are sometimes called hard constraints. When an inflexible constraint has been applied to a task, Project displays a special indicator in the Indicators column. You can point to a constraint indicator, and the constraint details will appear in a ScreenTip.

- **Semi-flexible constraints** A task has a start or finish date boundary. However, within that boundary, Project has the scheduling flexibility to change the start and finish dates of a task. For example, let's say a task must finish no later than June 15, 2012. However, the task could finish before this date. Semi-flexible constraints are sometimes called soft or moderate constraints. When a semi-flexible constraint has been applied to a task, Project displays a special indicator in the Indicators column.

In total, there are eight types of task constraints.

This constraint category	Includes these constraint types	And means
Flexible	As Soon As Possible (ASAP)	Project will schedule a task to occur as soon as it can occur. This is the default constraint type applied to all new tasks when scheduling from the project start date. There is no constraint date for an ASAP constraint.
	As Late As Possible (ALAP)	Project will schedule a task to occur as late as it can occur. This is the default constraint type applied to all new tasks when scheduling from the project finish date. There is no constraint date for an ALAP constraint.
Semi-flexible	Start No Earlier Than (SNET)	Project will schedule a task to start on or after the constraint date that you specify. Use this constraint type to ensure that a task will not start before a specific date.
	Start No Later Than (SNLT)	Project will schedule a task to start on or before the constraint date that you specify. Use this constraint type to ensure that a task will not start after a specific date.
	Finish No Earlier Than (FNET)	Project will schedule a task to finish on or after the constraint date that you specify. Use this constraint type to ensure that a task will not finish before a specific date.
	Finish No Later Than (FNLT)	Project will schedule a task to finish on or before the constraint date that you specify. Use this constraint type to ensure that a task will not finish after a specific date.
Inflexible	Must Start On (MSO)	Project will schedule a task to start on the constraint date that you specify. Use this constraint type to ensure that a task will start on an exact date.
	Must Finish On (MFO)	Project will schedule a task to finish on the constraint date that you specify. Use this constraint type to ensure that a task will finish on an exact date.

These three constraint categories have very different effects on the scheduling of tasks:

- Flexible constraints, such as ASAP, allow tasks to be scheduled without any limitations other than their predecessor and successor relationships, and the project's start date (for ASAP task constraints) or finish date (for ALAP task constraints). No fixed start or end dates are imposed by these constraint types. Use these constraint types whenever possible.

- Semi-flexible constraints, such as Start No Earlier Than or Start No Later Than, limit the rescheduling of a task within the date boundary that you specify.

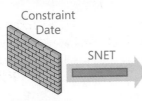

- Inflexible constraints, such as Must Start On, prevent the rescheduling of a task. Use these constraint types only when absolutely necessary.

Note You cannot change the constraint type or set a constraint date for a manually scheduled task. For more information about manually scheduled tasks versus automatically scheduled tasks, see Chapter 2.

The type of constraint that you apply to the tasks in your projects depends on what you need from Project. You should use inflexible constraints only if the start or finish date of a task is fixed by factors beyond the control of the project team. Examples of such tasks include handoffs to clients and the end of a funding period. For tasks without such limitations, you should use flexible constraints. Flexible constraints provide the most discretion in adjusting start and finish dates, and they allow Project to adjust dates if your project plan changes. For example, if you have used ASAP constraints and the duration of a predecessor task changes from four days to two days, Project adjusts, or "pulls in," the start and finish dates of all successor tasks. However, if a successor task had an inflexible constraint applied, Project could not adjust its start or finish dates.

In this exercise, you apply a constraint to a task.

1. Select the name of task 16, *Proofread and index*.

2. On the **Task** tab, in the **Editing** group, click **Scroll to Task**.

   Tip To select a task quickly, even a task you can't see in the current view, press Ctrl+G, and in the ID field of the Go To dialog box, enter a task number, and then click OK.

This task requires the children's book author, Tad Orman, to proofread his book at a certain stage in the design process. However, Tad has informed you that due to his travel schedule, he will be unable to start his review before July 13—later than currently scheduled.

3. On the **Task** tab, in the **Properties** group, click **Information**.

4. In the **Task Information** dialog box, click the **Advanced** tab.

5. In the **Constraint Type** box, select **Start No Earlier Than**.

6. In the **Constraint Date** box, type or select **7/13/12**, and then click **OK**.

Project applies a Start No Earlier Than constraint to the task, and a constraint icon appears in the Indicators column. You can point to the icon to see the constraint details in a ScreenTip.

Position your mouse pointer over a constraint indicator
(or any icon in the Indicators column) to see a ScreenTip.

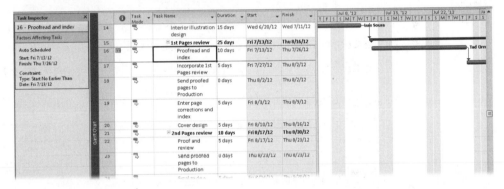

Because this constraint affects the scheduling of the task, the Task Inspector pane now includes the constraint details.

Task 16 is rescheduled to start on July 13 instead of July 11. All tasks that depend on task 16 are also rescheduled. One way to view this rescheduling is by the light blue change highlighting that Project applies to the Start and Finish dates of the successor tasks of task 16. Because the durations of the *1st Pages review* and *Design and Production* summary tasks were also changed by applying the constraint to task 16, the Duration and Finish fields for the those summary tasks are also highlighted. Change highlighting remains visible until you perform another editing action or save the file, and it is an effective visual way to see the broader effects of your specific actions in your schedule.

7. Click the **Close** button (the "X" button in the upper-right corner) on the Task Inspector pane.

Here are a few other things to keep in mind when applying constraints to tasks:

Note You cannot set constraints on manually scheduled tasks. The following issues apply only to automatically scheduled tasks. For more information about manually versus automatically scheduled tasks, see Chapter 2.

- Entering a Finish date for a task (for example, in the Finish column) applies a Finish No Earlier Than constraint to the task.

- Entering a Start date for a task (for example, in the Start column) or dragging a Gantt bar directly on the Gantt chart applies a Start No Earlier Than constraint to the task.

- In many cases, entering a deadline date is a preferable alternative to entering a semi-flexible or inflexible constraint. You will work with deadline dates later in this chapter.

- Unless you specify a time, Project schedules a constraint date's start or finish time using the Default Start Time or Default End Time values on the Schedule tab of the Project Options dialog box (to open this dialog box, on the File tab, click Options). In this project, the default start time is 8 A.M. If you want a constrained task to be scheduled to start at a different time, enter that time along with the start date. For example, if you want to schedule a task to start at 10 A.M. on July 12, enter 7/12/1/2 10AM in the Start field.

- To remove a constraint, first select the task or tasks and, on the Task tab, in the Properties group, click Information. In the Task Information dialog box, click the Advanced tab. In the Constraint Type box, select As Soon As Possible or (if scheduling from the project finish date) As Late As Possible.

- If you must apply semi-flexible or inflexible constraints to tasks in addition to task relationships, you might create what is called *negative slack*. For example, assume that you have a successor task that has a finish-to-start relationship with its predecessor task. If you entered a Must Start On constraint on the successor task earlier than the finish date of the predecessor task, this would result in negative slack and a scheduling conflict. By default, the constraint date applied to the successor task will override the relationship. However, if you prefer, you can set Project to honor relationships over constraints. On the **File** tab, click **Options**, and in the **Project Options** dialog box, click the **Schedule** tab. Clear the **Tasks Will Always Honor Their Constraint Dates** check box.

- If you must schedule a project from a finish date rather than a start date, some constraint behaviors change. For example, the As Late As Possible constraint type, rather than As Soon As Possible, becomes the default for new tasks. You should pay close attention to constraints when scheduling from a finish date to make sure that they create the effect that you intend.

Interrupting Work on a Task

When initially planning project tasks, you might know that work on a certain task will be interrupted. Rather than listing a task twice to account for a known interruption in work, you can *split* the task into two or more segments. The following are some reasons why you might want to split a task:

- You anticipate an interruption in a task. For example, a resource might be assigned to a weeklong task, but she needs to attend an event on Wednesday that is unrelated to the task.

- A task is unexpectedly interrupted. After a task is under way, a resource might have to stop work on the task because another task has taken priority. After the second task is completed, the resource can resume work on the first task.

In this exercise, you split a task to account for a planned interruption of work on that task.

1. Select the name of task 3, *Content edit*.

2. On the **Task** tab, in the **Editing** group, click **Scroll to Task**.

You have been informed that work on this task will be interrupted for three days starting Monday, April 9.

Split Task

3. On the **Task** tab, in the **Schedule** group, click **Split Task**.

A ScreenTip appears, and the mouse pointer changes.

4. Move the mouse pointer over the Gantt bar of task 3.

This ScreenTip is essential for accurately splitting a task because it contains the date at which you would start the second segment of the task if you dragged the mouse pointer from its current location on the Gantt bar. As you move the mouse pointer along the Gantt bar, you will see the start date in the ScreenTip change.

5. Move (but don't click) the mouse pointer over the Gantt bar of task 3 until the start date of Monday, April 9, appears in the ScreenTip.

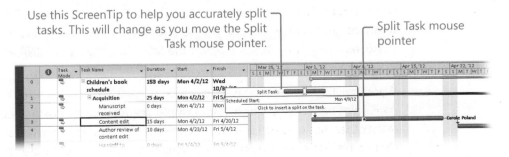

Use this ScreenTip to help you accurately split tasks. This will change as you move the Split Task mouse pointer.

Split Task mouse pointer

6. Click and drag the mouse pointer to the right until the start date of Thursday, April 12, appears in the ScreenTip, and then release the mouse button.

Project inserts a task split, represented in the Gantt chart as a dotted line, between the two segments of the task.

The split appears as a dotted line connecting the segments of the task. The split indicates an interruption of work on a task.

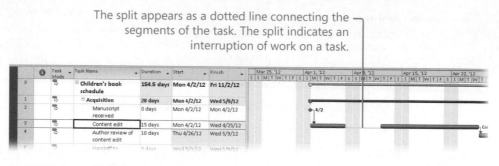

Tip Splitting tasks with the mouse might take a little practice. In step 6, if you didn't split task 3 so that the second segment starts on April 12, just point to the second segment again. When the mouse pointer changes to a four-headed arrow, drag the segment to the correct start date.

Here are a few other things to keep in mind when splitting tasks:

- You can split a task into multiple segments.

- You can drag a segment of a split task either left or right to reschedule the split.

- To rejoin two segments of a split task, drag one segment of the task until it touches the other segment.

- The time of the task split, represented by the dotted line, is not counted in the duration of the task. No work occurs during the split.

- If the duration of a split task changes, the last segment of the task is increased or decreased.

- If a split task is rescheduled (for example, if its start date changes), the entire task is rescheduled, splits and all. The task keeps the same pattern of segments and splits.

- Resource leveling or manually contouring assignments over time can cause tasks to split. You will contour assignments in Chapter 9, "Fine-Tuning Assignment Details," and level resources in Chapter 10, "Fine-Tuning the Project Plan."

- If you do not want to display splits as a dotted line, you can remove the dotted lines. On the Format tab, in the Format group, click Layout. In the Layout dialog box, clear the Show Bar Splits check box.

Adjusting Working Time for Individual Tasks

There may be times when you want specific tasks to occur at times that differ from the working time of the project calendar (or for assigned resources, the resource calendar). To accomplish this, you apply a task calendar to these tasks. As with the project calendar, you specify which base calendar to use as a task calendar. The following are some examples of when you might need a task calendar:

- You are using the Standard base calendar as your project calendar, and you have a task that must run overnight.
- You have a task that must occur on a specific weekday.
- You have a task that must occur over the weekend.

Unlike resources, Project does not create task calendars as you create tasks. (If you need a refresher on resource calendars, see Chapter 3, "Setting Up Resources.") When you need a task calendar, you assign one of the base calendars provided with Project (or, more likely, a new base calendar that you have created) to the task. For example, if you assign the 24 Hours base calendar to a task, Project will schedule that task according to a 24-hour workday rather than the working time specified in the project calendar.

For tasks that have both a task calendar and resource assignments, Project schedules work during the working times that are common between the task calendar and resource calendar(s). If there is no common working time, Project alerts you when you apply the task calendar or assign a resource to the task.

When you assign a base calendar to a task, you can choose to ignore resource calendars for all resources assigned to the task. Doing so causes Project to schedule the resources to work on the task according to the task calendar and not their own resource calendars (for example, to work 24 hours per day).

In the new book project, you need to record that a task has a more restrictive working time than the rest of the tasks. Task 29 relates to the handoff of final book proofs to a color setting services firm, who then prepares the book for commercial printing. However this firm starts new jobs only on Mondays through Wednesdays.

In this exercise, you create a new base calendar and apply it to account for the limited working time for a task.

1. On the **Project** tab, in the **Properties** group, click **Change Working Time**.

   The Change Working Time dialog box appears.

2. In the **Change Working Time** dialog box, click **Create New Calendar**.

   The Create New Base Calendar dialog box appears.

3. In the **Name** box, type **Monday-Wednesday**.

4. Make sure that the **Make a copy of** option is selected and that **Standard** is selected in the drop-down menu.

5. Click **OK**.

Tip The benefit of basing the new calendar on the Standard calendar is that all the working day exceptions from the Standard calendar, such as national holidays you may have entered, will also appear in the new calendar.

Note that *Monday-Wednesday* now appears in the For calendar box.

6. In the **Change Working Time** dialog box, click the **Work Weeks** tab.

Next, you'll enter the working time details for this new calendar.

7. Make sure that the **Name** value **[Default]** in Row 1 is selected, and then click **Details**.

8. In the **Select day(s)** box, select **Thursday** and **Friday**.

These are the days you want to change to nonworking days for this calendar.

9. Click **Set days to nonworking time**.

10. Click **OK** to close the **Details** dialog box, and then click **OK** again to close the **Change Working Time** dialog box.

Now that you've created the Monday-Wednesday calendar, you're ready to apply it to a task.

11. Select the name of task 29, *Send to color house.*

12. On the **Task** tab, in the **Properties** group, click **Information**.

   The Task Information dialog box appears.

13. Click the **Advanced** tab.

   As you can see in the Calendar box, the default for all tasks is "None."

14. In the **Calendar** box, select **Monday-Wednesday** from the list of available base calendars.

Task Information			
General	Predecessors	Resources	Advanced	Notes	Custom Fields

Name: Send to color house   **Duration:** 1 day   ☐ Estimated

Constrain task

Deadline: NA

Constraint type: As Soon As Possible   **Constraint date:** NA

Task type: Fixed Units   ☐ Effort driven

Calendar: Monday-Wednesday   ☐ Scheduling ignores resource calendars

WBS code: 4.1

Earned value method: % Complete

☐ Mark task as milestone

Help   OK   Cancel

15. Click **OK** to close the dialog box.

   Project applies the Monday-Wednesday calendar to task 29. A calendar icon appears in the Indicators column, reminding you that this task has a task calendar applied to it.

16. Point to the calendar icon.

	ⓘ	Task Mode	Task Name	Duration	Start	Finish	Mar 25, S S M T
28		⇨	⊟ **Color prep and printing**	**44 days**	**Mon 9/3/12**	**Fri 11/2/12**	
29	📅	⇨	Send to color	1 day	Mon 9/3/12	Tue 9/4/12	
30			The calendar 'Monday-Wednesday' is assigned to the task. oofs	10 days	Tue 9/4/12	Tue 9/18/12	
31		⇨	Print and ship	30 days	Fri 9/21/12	Fri 11/2/12	

A ScreenTip appears, showing the calendar details. Right now, this task is scheduled to be completed on a Monday, but as you further adjust the project plan, this is likely to change. Due to the custom calendar that has been applied to this task, it will not be scheduled on a Thursday or Friday or over the weekend.

Changing Task Types

You might recall from Chapter 4, "Assigning Resources to Tasks," that Project uses the following formula, called the scheduling formula, to calculate a task's work value:

Work = Duration × Assignment Units

where assignment units are normally expressed as a percentage. Remember also that a task has work when it has at least one work resource (people or equipment) assigned to it. Each value in the scheduling formula corresponds to a task type. A task type determines which of the three scheduling formula values remains fixed if the other two values change.

The default task type is fixed units: If you change a task's duration, Project will recalculate work. Likewise, if you change a task's work, Project will recalculate the duration. In either case, the units value is not affected.

The two other task types are fixed duration and fixed work. For these task types, Project uses a timephased field called peak units when responding to schedule changes.

For a fixed-work task:

- You can change the assignment units value and Project will recalculate the duration.

- You can change the duration value and Project will recalculate peak units per time period. The assignment units value is not affected.

Note You cannot turn off effort-driven scheduling for a fixed-work task.

For a fixed-duration task:

- You can change the assignment units value and Project will recalculate work.

- You can change the work value and Project will recalculate peak units per time period. The assignment units value is not affected.

Project also keeps track of the highest peak units value per assignment. This value is stored in the Peak field, which you'll work with in the sidebar.

Assignment Units, Peak, Peak Units, and the Scheduling Formula

In previous versions of Project, it was possible (in fact, it is likely) that a resource's initial assignment units value would change, and this led to unexpected results with regard to the scheduling formula. This behavior has changed in Project 2010. Project now tracks both the assignment units value and a calculated value called *peak* (or, when viewed on a timescale, *peak units*).

Project uses the assignment units value when initially scheduling or later rescheduling a task, but it uses peak units when reporting a resource's maximum peak units value. Here's one example. If you initially assigned a resource at 100% assignment units to a 1-day, fixed-unit task, Project used that value to initially calculate 8 hours of work. However if you then recorded 10 hours of actual work on the task, previous versions of Project would have recalculated the assignment units to be 120% to keep the scheduling formula accurate. If you then added more work or changed the duration of the task, Project would have scheduled the task using the 120% assignment units value—probably not the result you'd want. Project 2010, however, will record the 120% peak value, and if you later add work or change the duration of the task, Project will use the original assignment units value of 100% rather than the peak value of 120% to reschedule the task.

Which is the right task type to apply to each of your tasks? It depends on how you want Project to schedule that task. The following table summarizes the effects of changing any value for any task type. You read it like a multiplication table.

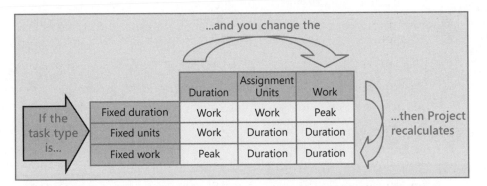

	Duration	Assignment Units	Work
Fixed duration	Work	Work	Peak
Fixed units	Work	Duration	Duration
Fixed work	Peak	Duration	Duration

Note You cannot change the task type of a manually scheduled task, and the effect of the task type on the scheduling of a task as described here applies only to automatically scheduled tasks. If you need a refresher on manually scheduled tasks, see Chapter 2.

To view the task type of the selected task, on the Task tab, in the Properties group, click Information. Then, in the Task Information dialog box, click the Advanced tab. You can also view the task type in the Task Form. (When in the Gantt Chart view, you can display the Task Form by clicking Details on the View tab, in the Split View group.) You can change a task type at any time. Note that characterizing a task type as fixed does not mean that its duration, assignment units, or work values are unchangeable. You can change any value for any task type.

In this exercise, you change a task type and some scheduling formula values.

1. On the **View** tab, in the **Task Views** group, click **Task Usage**.

   The Task Usage view appears.

2. In the **Task Name** column, select the name of task 8, *Copyedit*.

3. On the **Task** tab, in the **Editing** group, click **Scroll to Task**.

   Tip To select a task quickly, even a task you can't see in the current view, press Ctrl+G and in the ID field of the Go To dialog box, enter a task number, and then click OK.

ⓘ	Task Mode	Task Name	Work	Duration	Start	Details							May 20, '12					
							T		W		T		F		S	S	M	T	W	T
		Carole Poland	0 hrs		Wed 5/9/12	Work													
6		⊟ Editorial	420 hrs	32.5 days	Thu 5/10/12	Work	8h		8h		16h		16h				16h	16h	16h	16h
7		⊟ Organize manuscrip	40 hrs	5 days	Thu 5/10/12	Work	8h		8h											
		Hany Morcos	40 hrs		Thu 5/10/12	Work	8h		8h											
8		⊟ Copyedit	240 hrs	15 days	Thu 5/17/12	Work			16h		16h						16h	16h	16h	16h
		Copyeditors	240 hrs		Thu 5/17/12	Work			16h		16h						16h	16h	16h	16h
9		⊟ Author review of cc	100 hrs	10 days	Thu 6/7/12	Work														
		Copyeditors	20 hrs		Thu 6/7/12	Work														
		Tad Orman	80 hrs		Thu 6/7/12	Work														
10		⊟ Copyedit incorp	40 hrs	5 days	Mon 6/18/12	Work														
		Hany Morcos	40 hrs		Mon 6/18/12	Work														
11		⊟ Handoff to Product	0 hrs	0 days	Mon 6/25/12	Work														

Project displays the details for task 8, *Copyedit*, and its assignment.

The Task Usage view groups the assigned resources below each task and shows you, among other things, each task's duration and work—two of the three variables of the scheduling formula.

4. If necessary, drag the vertical divider bar to the right so that the **Finish** column is visible.

   Next, you'll add two columns to the Task Usage view so that you can see the assignment units (the third variable of the scheduling formula) and the peak values. You don't need to modify this view every time you want to use it, but for our purposes here, this is a good way to illustrate the effect of changing task types and scheduling formula values.

5. Click the **Start** column heading, and then, on the **Format** tab, in the **Columns** group, click **Insert Column**.

   A list of fields appears.

6. Click **Assignment Units**.

7. Click the **Start** column heading, and then, on the **Format** tab, in the **Columns** group, click **Insert Column**.

8. Click **Peak**.

Project inserts the Assignment Units and Peak columns to the left of the Start column. Peak is the resource's maximum units value at any time throughout the assignment's duration.

You can see that task 8 has a total work value of 240 hours, a resource assignment units value of 200%, and a duration of 15 days. Next, you will change the task's duration to observe the effects on the other values.

After a discussion between the two copyeditors about who will perform the copyedit, you all agree that the task's duration should increase and the resource's daily work on the task should decrease correspondingly.

9. In the **Duration** field for task 8, type or select **20d**, and press the Enter key.

Project changes the duration of task 8 to 20 days and increases the work to 320 hours. Note that the change highlighting applied to the Work and Duration values. You increased the duration and wanted the total work to remain the same (it didn't), so you will use the Action button to adjust the results of the new task duration.

10. Point at task 8's **Duration** field, and then click the **Action** button.

Review the options on the list that appears.

Because task 8's task type is fixed units (the default task type), the Action's default selection is to increase work as the duration increases. However, you'd like to keep the work value the same and decrease assignment units for the task's new duration.

11. On the **Actions** list, click **Resources will work fewer hours per day so that the task will take longer**.

The assignment units value decreases to 150%, and the total work on the task remains unchanged at 240 hours.

	ⓘ	Task Mode	Task Name	Work	Duration	Assignment Units	Peak	Details	T	W	T	F	S	May 20, '12 S	M	T	W
0			⊟ Children's book schedule	1,644 hrs	159.5 days			Work	8h	8h	12h	12h			12h	12h	12h
1			⊟ Acquisition	220 hrs	28 days			Work									
2			Manuscript received	0 hrs	0 days			Work									
3			⊟ Content edit	120 hrs	15 days			Work									
		👤	Carole Poland	120 hrs		100%	100%	Work									
4			⊟ Author review of content edit	100 hrs	10 days			Work									
			Copyeditors	20 hrs		25%	25%	Work									
			Tad Orman	80 hrs		100%	100%	Work									
5			⊟ Handoff to Editorial	0 hrs	0 days			Work									
			Carole Poland	0 hrs		100%	100%	Work									
6			⊟ Editorial	420 hrs	37.5 days			Work	8h	8h	12h	12h			12h	12h	12h
7			⊟ Organize manuscript for copyedit	40 hrs	5 days			Work	8h	8h							
			Hany Morcos	40 hrs		100%	100%	Work	8h	8h							
8			⊟ Copyedit	240 hrs	20 days			Work			12h	12h			12h	12h	12h
			Copyeditors	240 hrs		150%	150%	Work			12h	12h			12h	12h	12h
9			⊟ Author review of copyedit	100 hrs	10 days			Work									
			Copyeditors	20 hrs		25%	25%	Work									

Next, you will change a task type and then adjust the work on the task.

12. In the **Task Name** column, select the name of task 24, *Final review*.

13. On the **Task** tab, in the **Editing** group, click **Scroll to Task**.

Project displays work values for task 24, *Final review* in the timephased grid.

14. On the **Task** tab, in the **Properties** group, click **Information**.

The Task Information dialog box appears.

15. Click the **Advanced** tab.

The selected task describes the final review of the new book's page proofs. As you can see in the Task Type box, this task has the default task type of fixed-units. The task is scheduled for five days. You will make this a fixed-duration task.

16. In the **Task Type** box, select **Fixed Duration**.

17. Click **OK** to close the **Task Information** dialog box.

Next, you'll add work to the task.

18. In the **Work** field for task 24, *Final review*, type **150h**, and then press Enter.

	ⓘ	Task Mode	Task Name	Work	Duration	Assignment Units	Peak	Details		Sep 2, '12							Sep 9, '12	
									S	S	M	T	W	T	F	S	S	
21			⊟ 2nd Pages review	190 hrs	10 days			Work			19h	30h	30h	30h	30h			
22	⁑		⊟ Proof and review	40 hrs	5 days			Work			4h							
			Hany Morcos	40 hrs		100%	100%	Work			4h							
23			⊟ Send proofed pa:	0 hrs	0 days			Work			0h							
			Hany Morcos	0 hrs		100%	100%	Work			0h							
24	⁑		⊟ Final review	150 hrs	5 days			Work			15h	30h	30h	30h	30h			
			Carole Polan	50 hrs		100%	125%	Work			5h	10h	10h	10h	10h			
			Hany Morcos	50 hrs		100%	125%	Work			5h	10h	10h	10h	10h			
			Jane Dow	50 hrs		100%	125%	Work			5h	10h	10h	10h	10h			
25			⊟ Design book's comp	56 hrs	5 days			Work			8h							
26			⊟ Create mockup	24 hrs	3 days			Work										
			Luis Souza	24 hrs		100%	100%	Work										

Because this is a fixed-duration task and you've added work, Project adjusted the peak value to 125%; this represents an intentional overallocation. On the right side of the usage view, you can see that the resources assigned to task 24 now have 10 hours of work scheduled per day. Their original assignment units values of 100% each remain unaffected, however.

Task Types and Effort-Driven Scheduling

Many people misunderstand task types and effort-driven scheduling and conclude that these two issues are more closely related than they really are. Both settings can affect your schedule. Whereas the effect of a task type applies whenever you edit a task's work, duration, or unit values, effort-driven scheduling affects your schedule only when you're assigning or removing resources from tasks. For more information about effort-driven scheduling, see Chapter 4.

 CLEAN UP Close the Advanced Tasks A file.

Entering Deadline Dates

One common mistake made by new Project users is to place semi-flexible or inflexible constraints on too many tasks in their projects. Such constraints severely limit your scheduling flexibility.

Yet, if you know that a specific task must be completed by a certain date, why not enter a Must Finish On constraint? This is the reason: Assume that you have a five-day task that you want to see completed by April 13, and today is April 2. If you enter a Must Finish On constraint on the task and set it to April 13, Project will move it out so that it will indeed end on April 13.

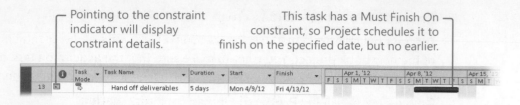

Pointing to the constraint indicator will display constraint details.

This task has a Must Finish On constraint, so Project schedules it to finish on the specified date, but no earlier.

Even if the task could be completed earlier, Project will not reschedule it to start earlier. In fact, by applying that constraint, you have increased the risk for this task. If the task is delayed for even one day for any reason (a required resource is sick, for example), the task will miss its planned finish date.

A better approach to scheduling this task is to use the default As Soon As Possible constraint and enter a deadline of April 13. A deadline is a date value you enter for a task that indicates the latest date by which you want the task to be completed, but the deadline date itself does not constrain the task.

The deadline indicator appears on the Gantt chart.

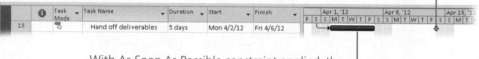

With As Soon As Possible constraint applied, the task starts earlier and leaves some time between the finish date and the deadline date.

Now the task has the greatest scheduling flexibility. It might be completed well before its deadline, depending on resource availability, predecessor tasks, and whatever other scheduling issues apply.

Entering a deadline date causes Project to display a deadline indicator on the chart portion of the Gantt Chart view. If the task's finish date moves past its deadline, Project displays a missed deadline indicator in the *Indicator* field for that task.

In this exercise, you enter a deadline date for a task.

Open Advanced Tasks B_Start from the Chapter07 practice file folder

1. On the **File** tab, click **Save As**.

   The Save As dialog box appears.

2. In the **File name** box, type **Advanced Tasks B**, and then click **Save**.

3. In the **Task Name** column, select the name of task 5, *Handoff to Editorial*.

4. On the **Task** tab, in the **Editing** group, click **Scroll to Task**.

This task is a milestone marking the scheduled finish date of the acquisition phase of the new book project. You want to make sure that the acquisition task concludes by Friday, May 11, 2012, so you will enter a deadline date for this milestone.

5. On the **Task** tab, in the **Properties** group, click **Information**.

The Task Information dialog box appears.

6. Click the **Advanced** tab.

7. In the **Deadline** box, type or select **5/11/12**, and then click **OK**.

Project displays a deadline indicator in the chart portion of the Gantt Chart view.

Deadline indicator ⌐

	ⓘ	Task Mode	Task Name	Duration	Start	Finish		
0			⊟ **Children's Book Schedule**	**159.5 days**	**Mon 4/2/12**	**Fri 11/9/12**		
1			⊟ **Acquisition**	**28 days**	**Mon 4/2/12**	**Wed 5/9/12**		
2			Manuscript received	0 days	Mon 4/2/12	Mon 4/2/12		
3			Content edit	15 days	Mon 4/2/12	Wed 4/25/12		
4			Author review of content edit	10 days	Thu 4/26/12	Wed 5/9/12		Tad Orman,Copy
5			Handoff to Editorial	0 days	Wed 5/9/12	Wed 5/9/12		◆ 5/9
6			⊟ **Editorial**	**37.5 days**	**Thu 5/10/12**	**Mon 7/2/12**		
7			Organize manuscript for copyedit	5 days	Thu 5/10/12	Wed 5/16/12		

You can now see at a glance how close the end of the acquisition phase, as currently scheduled, will come to meeting or missing its deadline. If the scheduled completion of the pre-production phase moves past May 11, Project will display a missed deadline indicator in the Indicators column.

Entering a deadline date has no effect on the scheduling of a summary or subtask. However, a deadline date will cause Project to alert you if the scheduled completion of a task exceeds its deadline date.

Tip To remove a deadline from a task, clear the Deadline field on the Advanced tab of the Task Information dialog box.

Entering Fixed Costs

For projects in which you must track budget or financial costs, you may need to work with several different sources of costs. These include costs associated with resources, as well as costs associated directly with a specific task.

For many projects, financial costs are derived mainly from costs associated with work resources, such as people and equipment, or with material resources. To handle costs of similar types for which you want to track aggregate sums (travel is one example in many projects), Project supports cost resources. If you need a refresher on cost resources, see Chapter 3.

However, you may occasionally want to associate a cost with a task that is not tied to resources or work and is not something you want to aggregate across the project. Project calls this a fixed cost, and it is applied per task. A fixed cost is a specific monetary amount budgeted for a task. It remains the same regardless of any resources assigned to the task. The following are common examples of fixed costs in projects:

- A setup fee, charged in addition to a per-day rental fee, for a piece of equipment

- A building permit

If you assign resources with cost rates, assign cost resources, or add fixed costs to a task, Project adds it all together to determine the task's total cost. If you do not enter resource cost information into a project plan (perhaps because you do not know how much your work resources will be paid), you can still gain some control over the project's total cost by entering fixed costs per task.

You can specify when fixed costs should accrue as follows:

- **Start** The entire fixed cost is scheduled for the start of the task. When you track progress, the entire fixed cost of the task is incurred as soon as the task starts.

- **End** The entire fixed cost is scheduled for the end of the task. When you track progress, the entire fixed cost of the task is incurred only after the task is completed.

- **Prorated** The fixed cost is distributed evenly over the duration of the task. When you track progress, the project incurs the cost of the task at the rate at which the task is completed. For example, if a task has a $100 fixed cost and is 75 percent complete, the project has incurred $75 against that task.

When you plan a project, the accrual method you choose for fixed costs determines how these costs are scheduled over time. This can be important in anticipating budget and cash-flow needs. By default, Project assigns the prorated accrual method for fixed costs, but you can change that to match your organization's cost accounting practices.

For the new book project, you've learned that the generating of page proofs by the color setting services firm will cost $500. Lucerne Publishing has a credit account with this firm, but to keep the book's P&L statement accurate, you'd like to accrue this expense when the color setting services firm completes the task.

In this exercise, you assign a fixed cost to a task and specify its accrual method.

1. On the **View** tab, in the **Task Views** group, click **Other Views**, and then click **Task Sheet**.

   The Task Sheet view appears.

2. On the **View** tab, in the **Data** group, click **Tables**, and then click **Cost**.

   The Cost table appears, replacing the Entry table.

3. In the **Fixed Cost** field for task 30, *Generate proofs*, type **500**, and press the Tab key.

4. In the **Fixed Cost Accrual** field, select **End**, and press Tab.

	Task Name	Fixed Cost	Fixed Cost Accrual	Total Cost	Baseline	Variance	Actual	Remaining
18	Send proofed pa:	$0.00	Prorated	$0.00	$0.00	$0.00	$0.00	$0.00
19	Enter page corre	$0.00	Prorated	$2,200.00	$0.00	$2,200.00	$0.00	$2,200.00
20	Cover design	$0.00	Prorated	$2,800.00	$0.00	$2,800.00	$0.00	$2,800.00
21	⊟ **2nd Pages review**	**$0.00**	**Prorated**	**$5,575.00**	**$0.00**	**$5,575.00**	**$0.00**	**$5,575.00**
22	Proof and review	$0.00	Prorated	$1,550.00	$0.00	$1,550.00	$0.00	$1,550.00
23	Send proofed pa:	$0.00	Prorated	$0.00	$0.00	$0.00	$0.00	$0.00
24	Final review	$0.00	Prorated	$4,025.00	$0.00	$4,025.00	$0.00	$4,025.00
25	⊟ **Design book's comp**	**$0.00**	**Prorated**	**$2,800.00**	**$0.00**	**$2,800.00**	**$0.00**	**$2,800.00**
26	Create mockup	$0.00	Prorated	$1,680.00	$0.00	$1,680.00	$0.00	$1,680.00
27	Review with auth	$0.00	Prorated	$1,120.00	$0.00	$1,120.00	$0.00	$1,120.00
28	⊟ **Color prep and printin**	**$0.00**	**Prorated**	**$810.00**	**$0.00**	**$810.00**	**$0.00**	**$810.00**
29	Send to color house	$0.00	Prorated	$310.00	$0.00	$310.00	$0.00	$310.00
30	Generate proofs	$500.00	End	$500.00	$0.00	$500.00	$0.00	$500.00
31	Print and ship	$0.00	Prorated	$0.00	$0.00	$0.00	$0.00	$0.00

Project will now schedule a $500 cost against the task *Generate proofs* at the task's end date, and the project will incur this cost when the task ends. This cost is independent of the task's duration and of any costs of resources that could be assigned to it.

Setting Up a Recurring Task

Many projects require repetitive tasks, such as attending project status meetings, creating and publishing status reports, or running quality-control inspections. Although it is easy to overlook the scheduling of such events, you should account for them in your project plan. After all, status meetings and similar events that indirectly support the project require time from resources, and such events take time away from your resources' other assignments.

To help account for such events in your project plan, create a recurring task. As the name suggests, a recurring task is repeated at a specified frequency such as daily, weekly, monthly, or yearly. When you create a recurring task, Project creates a series of tasks with Start No Earlier Than constraints, no task relationships, and effort-driven scheduling turned off.

In this exercise, you create a recurring task that will represent a weekly meeting associated with this project.

1. On the **View** tab, in the **Task Views** group, click **Gantt Chart**.

   The Gantt Chart view appears.

2. Select the name of task 1, *Acquisition*.

   You'll insert the recurring task above the first phase of the project plan, as it will occur throughout multiple phases of the plan.

3. On the **Task** tab, in the **Insert** group, click the down arrow below the **Task** button and then click **Recurring Task**.

   The Recurring Task Information dialog box appears.

4. In the **Task Name** box, type **Editorial staff meeting**.

5. In the **Duration** box, type **1h**.

6. Under **Recurrence pattern**, make sure **Weekly** is selected, and then select the **Monday** check box.

   Next, you will specify the date of its first occurrence. By default, it is the project start date. However, you want the weekly status meetings to begin one week later.

7. In the **Start** box, type or select **4/9/12**.

   Next, you will specify the end date. You'll plan for these staff meetings to continue until the project reaches the Design and Production phase. In the Gantt Chart, you can see that as currently scheduled, that phase starts on July 2, so you'll use that date for now. You can always update the recurring task later as needed.

8. In the **End by** box, type or select **7/2/12**.

![Recurring Task Information dialog box. Task Name: Editorial staff meeting, Duration: 1h. Recurrence pattern: Weekly selected, Recur every 1 week(s) on: Monday checked. Range of recurrence: Start Mon 4/9/12, End by 7/2/12 selected (End after 13 occurrences). Calendar: None.]

9. Click **OK** to create the recurring task.

Project inserts the recurring task. Initially, the recurring task is collapsed. A recurring task icon appears in the Indicators column.

10. To view the first occurrences of the recurring meeting's Gantt bars, on the **Task** tab, in the **Editing** group, click **Scroll To Task**.

⌐ This is a recurring task indicator.

⌐ Each bar represents a specific occurrence of the recurring task.

A Gantt bar for a recurring task shows only the occurrences or rollups of the individual occurrences of the task.

Next, you will assign resources to the recurring task.

11. Verify that task 1, *Editorial staff meeting*, is selected, and then, on the **Resource** tab, in the **Assignments** group, click **Assign Resources**.

12. In the **Assign Resources** dialog box, click **Carole Poland**. Then hold down the Ctrl key while clicking **Hany Morcos** and **Jun Cao**.

13. Click **Assign**, and then click **Close**.

The Assign Resources dialog box closes, and Project assigns the selected resources to the recurring task. Next, you will view the individual occurrences of the recurring task.

14. Click the plus sign next to the recurring task's title, *Editorial staff meeting*.

Each occurrence of the recurring task is sequentially numbered (if you wish to verify this, widen the Task Name column, or point to the task's name and note the content of the ScreenTip), and the resource assignments appear for the individual occurrences.

15. Click the minus sign next to the recurring task's title, *Editorial staff meeting*, to hide the individual occurrences.

Here are a few other things to keep in mind when creating recurring tasks:

- By default, Project schedules a recurring task to start at the Default Start Time value entered on the Calendar tab (on the **Tools** menu, click **Options**); in this project, that value is 8 A.M. If you want to schedule a recurring task to start at a different time, enter that time along with the start date in the **Start** box of the **Recurring Task Information** dialog box. For example, if you want the recurring staff meeting to be scheduled for 10 A.M. starting on April 9, you would enter **4/9/12 10 AM** in the **Start** box.

- As with a summary task, the duration of a recurring task spans the earliest start to latest finish date of the individual occurrences of the recurring task.

- When you schedule a recurring task to end on a specific date, Project suggests the current project end date. If you use this date, be sure to change it manually if the project end date changes later.

- If you want to assign the same resources to all occurrences of a recurring task, assign the resources to recurring tasks with the Assign Resources dialog box. Entering resource names in the Resource Name field of the summary recurring task assigns the resources to the summary recurring task only and not to the individual occurrences.

Viewing the Project's Critical Path

A critical path is the series of tasks that will push out the project's end date if the tasks are delayed. The word *critical* in this context has nothing to do with how important these tasks are to the overall project. It refers only to how their scheduling will affect the project's finish date; however, the project finish date is of great importance in most projects. If you want to shorten the duration of a project to bring in the finish date, you must begin by shortening (also referred to as *crashing*) the critical path.

Over the life of a project, the project's critical path is likely to change from time to time as tasks are completed ahead of or behind schedule. Schedule changes, such as changing task relationships or durations, can also alter the critical path. After a task on the critical path is completed, it is no longer critical because it cannot affect the project finish date. In Chapter 14, "Getting Your Project Back on Track," you will work with a variety of techniques to shorten a project's overall duration.

A key to understanding the critical path is to understand *slack*, also known as *float*. There are two types of slack: free and total. Free slack is the amount of time a task can be delayed before it delays another task. Total slack is the amount of time a task can be delayed before it delays the completion of the project.

A task is on the critical path if its total slack is less than a certain amount—by default, if it is zero days. In contrast, noncritical tasks have slack, meaning they can start or finish earlier or later within their slack time without affecting the completion date of a project. One way to see the critical path is to switch to the Detail Gantt view.

In this exercise, you view the project's critical path.

1. On the **View** tab, in the **Task Views** group, click the down arrow below the **Gantt Chart** button and then click **More Views**.

2. In the **More Views** dialog box, select **Detail Gantt**, and then click **Apply**.

   The project appears in the Detail Gantt view.

3. On the **View** tab, in the **Zoom** group, click **Entire Project**.

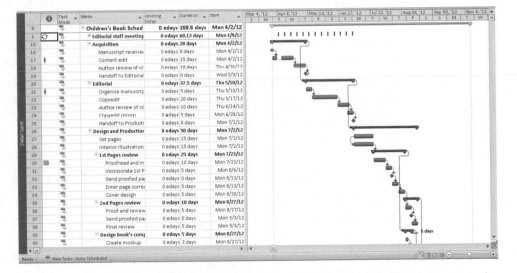

Because of the highly sequential nature of the task relationships in this project plan, almost all the tasks are on the critical path, and in the Detail Gantt view, their Gantt bars are formatted in red.

Notice the Gantt bar of task 41, *Review with author*. The blue bar represents the duration of the task. The thin teal line and the number next to it represent free slack for this task. As you can see, this particular task has some slack and is therefore a noncritical task. (Remember that the term *critical* in this sense has nothing to do with the task's importance, but only with how much or little total slack is associated with the task—and, ultimately, what effect the task has on the project's finish date.)

4. On the **View** tab, in the **Task Views** group, click the down arrow below the **Gantt Chart** button and then click **Gantt Chart**.

   Working with the critical path is the most important way to manage a project's overall duration. In later exercises, you will make adjustments that might extend the project's duration. Checking the project's critical path and, when necessary, shortening the overall project duration are important project management skills.

Here are a few other things to keep in mind when working with the critical path:

- By default, Project defines a task as critical if it has zero slack. However, you can change the amount of slack required for a task to be considered critical. You might do this, for example, if you wanted to more easily identify tasks that were within one or two days of affecting the project's finish date. On the File tab, click Options, and in the Project Options dialog box, click the Advanced tab. In the Tasks Are Critical If Slack Is Less Than Or Equal To box, enter the number of days you want. In this same dialog box, you can elect to display multiple critical paths.

- Project constantly recalculates the critical path even if you never display it.

- You see free slack represented in the chart portion of the Detail Gantt view, and you can also see the values of free and total slack in the Schedule table. You can apply the Schedule table to any Gantt Chart or Task Sheet view.

- You can toggle the formatting of critical tasks and slack directly in any Gantt Chart view. On the Format tab, in the Bar Styles group, select or clear the Critical Tasks and Slack check boxes.

Tip To learn more about managing a critical path, type **critical path** into the Search box in the upper-right corner of the Project window. The Search box initially contains the text "Type a question for help."

Scheduling Summary Tasks Manually

In Chapter 2, you worked with summary tasks and subtasks. Recall that the default behavior of Project is to automatically calculate a summary task's duration as the span of time between the earliest start and latest finish dates of its subtasks. For this reason, Project sets summary tasks as automatically scheduled—their durations are automatically determined by their subtasks, regardless if those subtasks are manually or automatically scheduled (or a mix).

There may be times, however, when you want to directly enter a duration value for a summary task that is independent of its calculated duration as determined by its subtasks. For example, a summary task might represent a phase of work for which you want to allocate 60 working days, and compare that duration with the calculated duration determined by the subtasks (their durations, task relationships, and other factors). This is especially true during the initial planning of a project plan, when you may need to account for the gap between how long you'd like a phase of work to take and its duration as determined by its subtasks.

Fortunately you can enter any duration you wish for a summary task. When you do so, Project switches the summary task from automatic to manually scheduled and reflects both the automatically calculated and manually entered durations as separate parts of the summary task's Gantt bar. If the summary task is a predecessor of another task, Project will reschedule the successor task based on the manual, not automatic duration.

Setting a manual duration for a summary task is a good way to apply a top-down focus to a project plan. You can, for example, introduce some slack or buffer to a phase of work by entering a manual duration for the summary task that is longer than its calculated duration.

In this exercise, you enter manual durations for some summary tasks.

To begin, you'll adjust the outline display of the project plan to display just its top-level summary tasks.

1. On the **View** tab, in the **Data** group, click **Outline**, and then click **Outline Level 1**.

   Project hides all subtasks and nested summary tasks, leaving only the top-level tasks visible.

2. On the **View** tab, in the **Zoom** group, click **Entire Project**.

Note that the minus signs next to the summary task names changed to plus signs, indicating that the subtasks are hidden.

In this view, you can more easily see and compare the durations of the individual summary tasks. Next, you'll enter some manual durations. You'll begin with the Editorial phase, which you'd like to see completed within 30 working days.

3. In the **Duration** field for the summary task 20, *Editorial*, type **30d** and press Enter.

A manually scheduled summary
task displays a two-part Gantt bar.

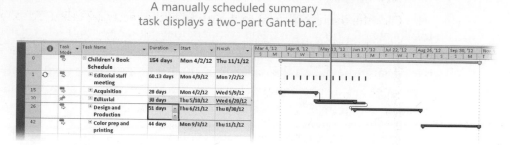

Project records your manually entered duration and makes some adjustments to the schedule:

○ The summary task is switched from automatically scheduled (the default for summary tasks) to manually scheduled. Note the pin icon in the Task Mode column that reflects the task's scheduling status.

○ Project drew a two-part Gantt bar for the summary task. The upper portion of the bar represents the manual duration, and the lower portion represents the automatically scheduled duration.

○ Project draws a red squiggly line under the new finish date to flag this as a potential scheduling conflict.

○ Project rescheduled the successor tasks throughout the schedule based on task 20's manually entered duration.

Looking at the updated schedule, you decide you'd like to allow a bit more time for the color prep and printing.

4. In the **Duration** field for the summary task 42, *Color prep and printing*, type **50d** and press Enter.

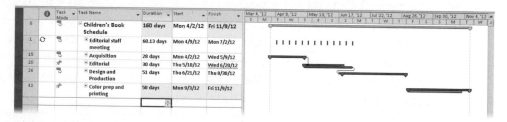

Project records your manually entered duration, switches the summary task to manually scheduled, and redraws the Gantt bar. To conclude this exercise, you'll adjust the display settings to see all subtasks.

5. On the **View** tab, in the **Data** group, click **Outline**, and then click **All Subtasks**.

Project expands the task list to show all subtasks. Next, you will collapse the recurring task.

6. Click the minus sign next to the name of the recurring task 1, *Editorial staff meeting*.

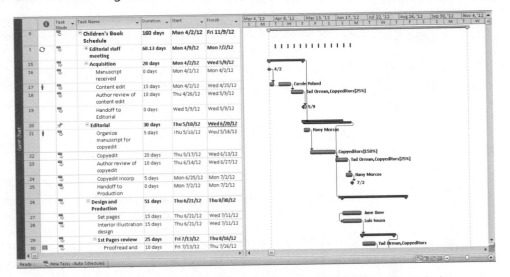

In the chart, you can see approximately where the tasks in the Editorial phase are extending beyond your preferred duration of the phase, and where there is a small amount of extra time, or buffer, in the Design and Production phase of the project plan.

Inactivating Tasks

New In
2010

Important The ability to inactivate tasks is available only in Project Professional and not in Project Standard. If you have Project Standard, skip this section.

You can include tasks in a project plan that you might later decide you don't want to have completed, but you also don't want to lose the details about those tasks by deleting them. You might for example develop tasks that pose "what-if" questions that you can't begin to answer until preliminary questions get answered. Or you could design a project plan that describes a likely-case scenario for completion but also includes more optimistic and pessimistic sets of tasks as well.

In Project, you can inactivate a single task or multiple tasks. Inactivating tasks may be preferable to deleting tasks, in that it keeps the task information in the project plan but removes the scheduling effect of those tasks. A task that drives the start of a successor task, for example, remains visible when inactivated, but it has strikethrough formatting applied in the Gantt Chart and other views, and its link relationship is broken and its successor is rescheduled.

Should you later wish to reactivate inactivated tasks, you can easily do so, and Project restores them as active tasks with the same scheduling impact as they previously had.

In this exercise, you inactivate a summary task and its subtasks.

1. Select the name of task 39, *Design book's companion website*.

   This summary task and its subtasks reflect an initial plan to account for the work of designing a Web site that would promote the new book at its launch. You still think you might want to include this work in the new book plan, but for now, you'd like to inactivate these tasks.

2. On the **Task** tab, in the **Schedule** group, click **Inactivate**.

   Project inactivates the summary task and its subtasks.

Inactive tasks are formatted as strikethrough text, and their Gantt bars appear as colorless outlines.

The original task information is still visible, but now it has no impact on the overall project plan. Later, should you decide to include these tasks in the project plan, you could reactivate them by clicking Inactivate again.

CLEAN UP Close the Advanced Tasks B file.

Key Points

- By using a combination of task relationships plus lead and lag time, you can more accurately model when work should be done.

- When entering lead time between a predecessor and successor task, entering a percentage lead time value offers some flexibility because Project recalculates the lead time value whenever the duration of the predecessor task changes.

- Think through the effects of semi-flexible and inflexible constraints on your schedules, and use them sparingly.

- You can often set a deadline date for a task instead of applying a hard constraint, such as Must Finish On (MFO).

- You can interrupt work on a task by splitting it.

- You can record any fixed cost value you wish per task, and it is not associated with resource costs.

- For tasks that must be completed at times other than of the project's normal working time (as specified by the project calendar), you can create a new base calendar and apply it to the task.

- The critical path indicates the series of tasks that determine the project's finish date. Project constantly recalculates the critical path, which may change as the details of your project plan change.

- Set up a recurring task for activities, such as status meetings, that occur on a regular frequency.

- You can enter a manual duration on a summary task in addition to its automatically scheduled duration.

- In Project Professional, inactivate tasks used in "what-if" scenarios or otherwise no longer needed in the project plan but that you don't want to delete permanently.

Chapter at a Glance

Resource Information

General | Costs | Notes | Custom Fields

Resource name: Copyeditors   Initials: C

Email: Group:

Windows Account...   Code:

Booking type: Committed ▼   Type: Work ▼

Material label:

Default Assignment Owner:

☐ Generic ☐ Budget
☐ Inactive

Change resource availability — Resource Availability
over time, page 179.

Change Working Time ...

Available From	Available To	Units
NA	4/30/2012	200%
5/1/2012	5/31/2012	300%
6/1/2012	NA	200%

Details... | OK | Cancel

Resource Information

General | Costs | Notes | Custom Fields

Resource Name: Hany Morcos

Cost rate tables

For rates, enter a value or a percentage increase or decrease from the previous rate. For instance, if a resource's Per Use Cost is reduced by 20%, type -20%.

A (Default) | B | C | D | E

Effective Date	Standard Rate	Overtime Rate	Per Use Cost
--	$45.00/h	$60.00/h	$0.00

Set up additional resource pay rates for different kinds of work, page 183.

Cost accrual: Prorated ▼

Help | Details... | OK | Cancel

Set up material resources to track costs of consumables, page 186.

13	Sharon Salavaria	Work		S		50%	1,100.00/wk	$0.00/hr	$0.00	Prorated	Standard
14	Tad Orman	Work		T			$0.00/hr	$0.00/hr	$0.00	Prorated	Standard
15	Toby Nixon	Work		T		100%	$0.00/hr	$0.00/hr	$0.00	Prorated	Standard
16	Travel	Cost		T		100%	2,700.00/wk	$0.00/hr	$0.00	Prorated	Standard
17	Vikas Jain	Work		V						Prorated	
18	William Flash	Work		W		100%	$22.00/hr	$0.00/hr	$0.00	Prorated	Standard
19	Zac Woodall	Work		Z		100%	$0.00/hr	$0.00/hr	$0.00	Prorated	Standard
20	Bound galley proof	Material	copy	B		100%	$55.00/hr	$0.00/hr	$0.00	Prorated	Standard
							$15.00		$0.00	Prorated	

8 Fine-Tuning Resource Details

In this chapter, you will learn how to:

✔ Set resource availability to change over time.

✔ Set up different pay rates for resources.

✔ Set up pay rates that will change over time for a resource.

✔ Set up a material resource.

Because *work resources* (people and equipment) are often the most expensive part of a project, understanding how to make the best use of resources' time is an important project planning skill. In this chapter, you use a variety of advanced Microsoft Project 2010 features relating to resources—their availability and costs.

> **Practice Files** Before you can complete the exercises in this chapter, you need to copy the book's practice files to your computer. A complete list of practice files is provided in "Using the Practice Files" at the beginning of this book. For each exercise that has a practice file, simply browse to where you saved the book's practice file folder.

Important If you are running Project Professional, you may need to make a one-time setting change. This helps ensure that the practice files you work with in this chapter do not affect your Project Server data. For more information, see Appendix C, "Using the Practice Files if Connected to Project Server."

Setting Up Resource Availability to Apply at Different Times

One of the values that Project stores for each work resource is the resource's *Max. Units* value. This is the maximum capacity of a resource to accomplish tasks. A resource's working time settings (recorded in the individual resource *calendars*) determine when work assigned to a resource can be scheduled. However, the resource's capacity to work (the resource's Max. Units value) determines the extent to which the resource can work within those hours without becoming *overallocated*. A resource's Max. Units value does not prevent a resource from becoming overallocated, but Project will indicate when the resource's assignments exceed their Max. Units capacity. You can specify that different Max. Units values be applied at different time periods for any resource.

Tip If you need a refresher on resource capacity or resource calendars, see Chapter 3, "Setting Up Resources."

Setting a resource's availability over time enables you to control exactly what a resource's Max. Units value is at any time. For example, you might have two copyeditors available for the first eight weeks of a project, three for the next six weeks, and then two for the remainder of the project.

In this exercise, you customize a resource's availability over time.

SET UP Start Project if it's not already running.

You need the Advanced Resources_Start project plan located in your Chapter08 practice file folder to complete this exercise. Open the Advanced Resources_Start project plan, and then follow these steps.

1. On the **File** tab, click **Save As**.

   The Save As dialog box appears.

2. In the **File name** box, type **Advanced Resources**, and then click **Save**.

   Next, you'll switch to a resource view.

3. On the **View** tab, in the **Resource Views** group, click **Resource Sheet**.

   The Resource Sheet view appears.

	ⓘ	Resource Name ▼	Type ▼	Material ▼	Initials ▼	Group ▼	Max. ▼	Std. Rate ▼	Ovt. Rate ▼	Cost/Use ▼	Accrue At ▼	Base Calendar ▼
1	◈	Carole Poland	Work		C		100%	2,100.00/wk	$0.00/hr	$0.00	Prorated	Standard
2		Color Setting Services	Work		C		100%	$0.00/hr	$0.00/hr	$0.00	Prorated	Standard
3		Copyeditors	Work		C		200%	$45.00/hr	$0.00/hr	$0.00	Prorated	Standard
4		Dan Jump	Work		D		50%	$75.50/hr	$0.00/hr	$0.00	Prorated	Standard
5	◈	Hany Morcos	Work		H		100%	1,550.00/wk	$0.00/hr	$0.00	Prorated	Standard
6		Jane Dow	Work		J		100%	$55.00/hr	$0.00/hr	$0.00	Prorated	Standard
7		John Evans	Work		J		100%	2,780.00/wk	$0.00/hr	$0.00	Prorated	Standard
8		Jun Cao	Work		J		100%	$42.00/hr	$67.00/hr	$0.00	Prorated	Standard
9		Katie Jordan	Work		K		100%	$48.00/hr	$0.00/hr	$0.00	Prorated	Standard
10		Luis Sousa	Work		L		100%	$70.00/hr	$0.00/hr	$0.00	Prorated	Standard
11		Printing Service	Work		P		100%	$0.00/hr	$0.00/hr	$0.00	Prorated	Standard
12		Robin Wood	Work		R		100%	$44.00/hr	$0.00/hr	$0.00	Prorated	Standard
13	✎	Sharon Salavaria	Work		S		50%	1,100.00/wk	$0.00/hr	$0.00	Prorated	Standard
14		Tad Orman	Work		T		100%	$0.00/hr	$0.00/hr	$0.00	Prorated	Standard
15		Toby Nixon	Work		T		100%	2,700.00/wk	$0.00/hr	$0.00	Prorated	Standard
16		Travel	Cost		T						Prorated	
17		Vikas Jain	Work		V		100%	$22.00/hr	$0.00/hr	$0.00	Prorated	Standard
18		William Flash	Work		W		100%	$0.00/hr	$0.00/hr	$0.00	Prorated	Standard
19		Zac Woodall	Work		Z		100%	$55.00/hr	$0.00/hr	$0.00	Prorated	Standard

As you may recall from Chapter 3, this is one view where you can see and edit resources' Max. Units values. The Max. Units values displayed here normally apply to the full duration of the project plan. Next, you will customize a resource's Max. Units value to vary at different times during this project plan.

4. In the **Resource Name** column, click the name of resource 3, *Copyeditors*.

The *Copyeditors* resource is not one specific person; it describes a job category that multiple people may occupy at various times throughout the duration of the project. Unlike individually named resources like Hany Morcos or Fabrikam, Ltd., the copyeditors are interchangeable. As a project manager, you are more concerned about the specific skill set of whoever may be in this job role than you are about who the specific person is.

5. On the **Resource** tab, in the **Properties** group, click **Information**.

Tip You can also double-click the *Resource Name* value to display the Resource Information dialog box.

The Resource Information dialog box appears. If the General tab is not visible, click it.

You expect to have two copyeditors available to work on this project from the start of the project through the month of April, three for the month of May, and then back to two for the remainder of the project.

6. Under **Resource Availability**, in the first row of the **Available From** column, leave **NA** (for Not Applicable).

7. In the **Available To** cell in the first row, type or select **4/30/12**.

8. In the **Units** cell in the first row, leave the **200%** value.

9. In the **Available From** cell in the second row, type or select **5/1/12**.

10. In the **Available To** cell in the second row, type or select **5/31/12**.

11. In the **Units** cell in the second row, type or select **300%**.

12. In the **Available From** cell in the third row, type or select **6/1/12**.

13. Leave the **Available To** cell in the third row blank. (Project will insert *NA* for you after you complete the next step.)

14. In the **Units** cell in the third row, type or select **200%**, and then press the Enter key.

For the month of May, you can schedule up to three copyeditors without over-allocating them. Before and after this period, you have just two copyeditors to schedule.

15. Click **OK** to close the **Resource Information** dialog box.

The Max. Units field for the *Copyeditors* resource will display 300% only when the current date, based on your computer's system clock or set in the Project Information dialog box (on the Project tab, in the Properties group, click Project Information), is within the May 1 through 31 date range. At other times, it will display 200%.

Entering Multiple Pay Rates for a Resource

Some work resources might perform different tasks with different pay rates. For example, in the new book project, the project editor could also serve as a content editor. Because the pay rates for project editor and content editor are different, you can enter two *cost rate tables* for the resource. Then, after you assign the resource to tasks, you specify which rate table should apply. Each resource can have up to five cost rate tables.

In this exercise, you create an additional cost rate table for a resource.

1. In the **Resource Sheet** view, click the name of resource 5, *Hany Morcos*.

2. On the **Resource** tab, in the **Properties** group, click **Information**.

   The Resource Information dialog box appears.

3. Click the **Costs** tab.

You see Hany's default pay rate of $1,550 per week on rate table A. Each tab (labeled A, B, and so on) corresponds to one of the five pay rates that a resource can have.

4. Under **Cost rate tables**, click the **B** tab.

5. Select the default entry of **$0.00/h** in the field directly below the column heading **Standard Rate**, and then type **45/h**.

6. In the **Overtime Rate** field in the same row, type **60/h**, and then press Enter.

Resource Information dialog box showing the Costs tab for resource Hany Morcos, with cost rate tables. Tab A (Default), B, C, D, E. The B tab shows Effective Date "--", Standard Rate $45.00/h, Overtime Rate $60.00/h, Per Use Cost $0.00. Cost accrual: Prorated.

7. Click **OK** to close the **Resource Information** dialog box.

Notice that on the Resource Sheet, Hany's standard pay rate is still $1,550 per week. (This is recorded in the Std. Rate column.) This matches the value in rate table A, the default rate table. This rate table will be used for all of Hany's task assignments unless you specify a different rate table. You will do this in Chapter 9, "Fine-Tuning Assignment Details."

Setting Up Pay Rates to Apply at Different Times

Resources can have both standard and overtime pay rates. By default, Project uses these rates for the duration of the project. However, you can change a resource's pay rates to be effective as of the date you choose. For example, you could initially set up a resource on January 1 with a standard rate of $40 per hour, planning to raise the resource's standard rate to $55 per hour on July 1.

Project uses these pay rates when calculating resource costs based on when the resource's work is scheduled. You can assign up to 25 pay rates to be applied at different times to each of a resource's five cost rate tables.

In this exercise, you enter different pay rates for a resource to be applied at a later date.

1. In the **Resource Name** column, select the name of resource 6, *Jane Dow*.

2. On the **Resource** tab, in the **Properties** group, click **Information**.

The Resource Information dialog box appears.

3. Click the **Costs** tab if it is not already selected.

   You'll enter a pay rate increase in cost rate table A.

4. In the **Effective Date** cell in the second row of cost rate table A, type or select **6/1/12**.

5. In the **Standard Rate** cell in the second row, type **15%**, and then press Enter.

Note that Project calculates the 15% increase to produce a rate of $63.25 per hour. The previous rate of $55 per hour plus 15% equals $63.25 per hour. You can enter a specific value or a percentage increase or decrease from the previous rate.

Tip In addition to or instead of cost rates, a resource can include a set fee that Project accrues to each task to which the resource is assigned. This is called a *cost per use*. Unlike cost rates, the cost per use does not vary with the task's duration or amount of work the resource performs on the task. You specify the cost per use in the *Cost/Use* field in the Resource Sheet view or in the *Per Use Cost* field in the Resource Information dialog box.

6. Click **OK** to close the **Resource Information** dialog box.

   Note that Jane Dow's initial rate, $55 per hour, appears in her *Std. Rate* field. This field will display $55 per hour until the current date changes to 6/1/12 or later. It will then display her new standard rate of $63.25 per hour.

Setting Up Material Resources

Material resources are consumables that you use up as the project proceeds. On a construction project, material resources might include nails, lumber, and concrete. You work with material resources in Project to track a fixed unit amount or a rate of consumption of the material resource and the associated costs. Although Project is not a complete system for tracking inventory, it can help you stay better informed about how quickly you are consuming your material resources, and at what cost.

For the new book project, galley proofs are the consumable resource that interests you most. These are high-fidelity mock-ups of the new book that are created before the book is commercially printed. Because these galley proofs are relatively expensive to have produced, you'd like to account for their costs in the project plan.

In this exercise, you enter information about a material resource.

1. In the **Resource Sheet**, click the next empty cell in the **Resource Name** column.

2. Type **Bound galley proof**.

3. In the **Type** field, click the down arrow, select **Material**, and press the Tab key.

4. In the **Material Label** field, type **copy**.

5. In the **Std. Rate** field, type **$15** and then press Enter.

   This is the per-unit cost of this material resource; put another way, each copy of a bound galley proof costs $15. In Chapter 9, you'll specify the unit quantity of the material resource when you assign it to tasks. Project will then calculate the cost of the material resource assignment as the per-unit cost that you entered above times the number of units on the assignment.

13	Sharon Salavaria	Work		S		50%	1,100.00/wk	$0.00/hr	$0.00 Prorated Standard
14	Tad Orman	Work		T		100%	$0.00/hr	$0.00/hr	$0.00 Prorated Standard
15	Toby Nixon	Work		T		100%	2,700.00/wk	$0.00/hr	$0.00 Prorated Standard
16	Travel	Cost		T					Prorated
17	Vikas Jain	Work		V		100%	$22.00/hr	$0.00/hr	$0.00 Prorated Standard
18	William Flash	Work		W		100%	$0.00/hr	$0.00/hr	$0.00 Prorated Standard
19	Zac Woodall	Work		Z		100%	$55.00/hr	$0.00/hr	$0.00 Prorated Standard
20	Bound galley proof	Material	copy	B			$15.00		$0.00 Prorated

The Material Label field applies only to material resources.

Note that you cannot enter a Max. Units value for a cost resource or material resource. Since neither type of resource performs work, the Max. Units value doesn't apply.

✖ **CLEAN UP** Close the Advanced Resources file.

Key Points

- When working with resource costs, you can specify different cost rates for different assignments and apply different cost rates at different times.

- You can account for variable resource availability over time (via a resource's Max. Units value), which allows you to control more finely when a resource will appear to be overallocated.

- Create material resources to track the cost of items that are consumed during the execution of the project.

Chapter at a Glance

Control when a resource starts work on an assignment, page 189.

Contour resource assignments manually or with built-in contour patterns, page 192.

Change the pay rate table to be applied to an assignment, page 196.

Assign material resources to track consumables, page 198.

Quickly assign and adjust resource assignments in the Team Planner view (Project Professional only), page 203.

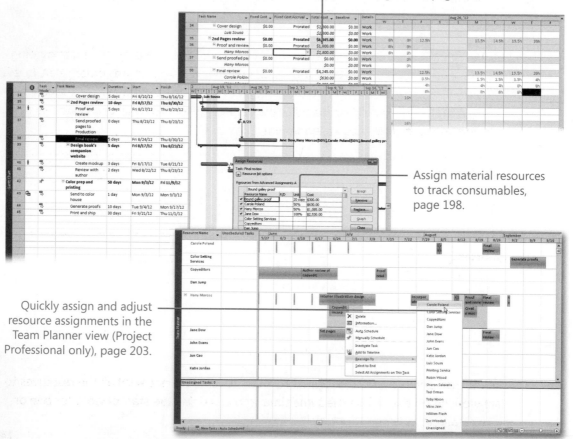

9 Fine-Tuning Assignment Details

In this chapter, you will learn how to:

✔ Delay the start of a resource assignment.

✔ Control how a resource's work on a task is scheduled by using work contours.

✔ Apply different cost rates for a resource to account for different kinds of work performed by the resource.

✔ Assign a material resource to a task.

✔ See resources' capacities to do work.

✔ Assign tasks in the Team Planner view (Project Professional only).

Because work *resources* are often the most expensive part of a project, understanding how to make the best use of their time is an important project management skill. In this chapter, you apply a variety of Microsoft Project 2010 features to manage resources' *assignments* to *tasks* and costs of assignments. Project Professional users also use the Team Planner view to manage assignments.

> **Practice Files** Before you can complete the exercises in this chapter, you need to copy the book's practice files to your computer. A complete list of practice files is provided in "Using the Practice Files" at the beginning of this book. For each exercise that has a practice file, simply browse to where you saved the book's practice file folder.

Important If you are running Project Professional, you may need to make a one-time setting change. This helps ensure that the practice files you work with in this chapter do not affect your Project Server data. For more information, see Appendix C, "Using the Practice Files if Connected to Project Server."

Delaying the Start of Assignments

If more than one resource is assigned to a task, you might not want all the resources to start working on the task at the same time. You can delay the start of work for one or more resources assigned to a task.

For example, assume that four resources have been assigned a task. Three of the resources initially work on the task, and the fourth later inspects the quality of the work. The inspector should start work on the task later than the other resources.

In this exercise, you delay the start of a resource assignment on a task.

SET UP Start Project if it's not already running.

You need the Advanced Assignments A_Start project plan located in your Chapter09 practice file folder to complete this exercise. Open the Advanced Assignments A_Start project plan, and then follow these steps.

1. On the **File** tab, click **Save As**.

   The Save As dialog box appears.

2. In the **File name** box, type **Advanced Assignments A**, and then click **Save**.

3. On the **Task** tab, in the **View** group, click the down arrow below the **Gantt Chart** button, and in the menu that appears, click **Task Usage**.

   As you may recall from Chapter 7, "Fine-Tuning Task Details," the Task Usage view groups the assigned resources below each task.

4. In the **Task Name** column, below task 18, *Author review of content edit*, click the assigned resource *Copyeditors*.

5. On the **Task** tab, in the **Editing** group, click **Scroll to Task**.

![Screenshot of Microsoft Project Task Usage view showing the Advanced Assignments A project plan with tasks including Children's book schedule, Editorial staff meeting, Acquisition, Content edit, Author review of content edit with Copyeditors and Tad Orman resources, Handoff to Editorial, Editorial, Organize manuscript, and Copyedit.]

As you can see, this task currently has two resources assigned to it: a copyeditor and the new book's author, Tad Orman.

The intent of task 18 is that the author will review the edits made to his book man-uscript, and shortly afterward, the copyeditor will begin to incorporate the author's feedback. Right now, both resources are assigned work throughout the duration of the task, but you'd like to delay the start of the copyeditor's work by two days. You'll make this adjustment in the Task Usage view.

6. On the **Format** tab, in the **Assignment** group, click **Information**.

The Assignment Information dialog box appears. Click the **General** tab if it is not already selected.

7. In the **Start** box, type or select **4/30/12**.

Assignment Information		
General	Tracking	Notes

Task:	Author review of content edit			
Resource:	Copyeditors			
Work:	80h		Units:	100%
Work contour:	Flat			
Start:	Mon 4/30/12		Booking type:	Committed
Finish:	Wed 5/9/12		Cost:	$3,600.00
Cost rate table:	A		Assignment Owner:	

OK   Cancel

8. Click **OK** to close the **Assignment Information** dialog box.

Project adjusts the copyeditor's assignment on this task so that he works no hours on Thursday or Friday.

The duration of this task has increased as the work is over a longer period of time.

	❶	Task Mode	Task Name	Work	Duration	Start	Details		T	W	T	F	S	S	M	T	W	T	
0			⊟ Children's book schedu	1,847 hrs	159 day	Mon 4/2/12	Work		0h	8h	8h	8h			19h	16h	16h	16h	
1	⟳		⊞ Editorial staff meeting	39 hrs	60.13 days	Mon 4/9/12	Work								3h				
15			⊟ Acquisition	280 hrs	30 days	Mon 4/2/12	Work		8h	8h	8h	8h			16h	16h	16h	16h	
16			Manuscript receiver	0 hrs	0 days	Mon 4/2/12	Work												
17	ⓘ		⊟ Content edit	120 hrs	15 days	Mon 4/2/12	Work		8h	8h									
	📊		Carole Poland	120 hrs		Mon 4/2/12	Work		8h	8h									
18			⊟ Author review of cc	160 hrs	12 days	Thu 4/26/12	Work			8h	8h				16h	16h	16h	16h	
			Copyeditors	80 hrs		Mon 4/30/12	Work			0h	0h				8h	8h	8h	8h	
			Tad Orman	80 hrs		Thu 4/26/12	Work			8h	8h				8h	8h	8h	8h	
19			⊟ Handoff to Editorial	0 hrs	0 days	Fri 5/11/12	Work												
			Carole Poland	0 hrs		Fri 5/11/12	Work												
20			⊟ Editorial	420 hrs	30 days	Thu 5/10/12	Work												
21	ⓘ		⊟ Organize manuscrip	40 hrs	5 days	Thu 5/10/12	Work												
			Hany Morcos	40 hrs		Thu 5/10/12	Work												
22			⊟ Copyedit	240 hrs	20 days	Thu 5/17/12	Work												
			Copyeditors	240 hrs		Thu 5/17/12	Work												

Now, in the timephased portion of the view, you can see that zero hours of work are scheduled for the copyeditor on Thursday and Friday, April 26 and 27. The other resource assigned to the task is not affected. Note that the total work of this task did not change, but its duration did—the finish date moved out two working days.

Tip If you want an assignment to start at a specific time as well as on a specific date, you can specify the time in the Start box. For example, if you want the copyeditor's assignment to start at 1 P.M. on April 30, type **4/30/12 1:00 PM**. Otherwise, Project uses the default start time. To change the default start time, on the File tab, click Options. In the Project Options dialog box, click the Schedule tab, and in the "Default start time" field, enter the value that you want.

Applying Contours to Assignments

In the Resource Usage and Task Usage views, you can see exactly how each resource's assigned work is distributed over time. In addition to viewing assignment details, you can change the amount of time a resource works on a task in any given time period. There are various ways to do this:

- Apply a predefined work contour to an assignment. Predefined *contours* generally describe how work is distributed over time in terms of graphical patterns. For example, the Bell predefined contour distributes less work to the beginning and end of the assignment and distributes more work toward the middle. If you were to graph the work over time, the graph's shape would resemble a bell.

- Edit the assignment details directly. For example, in the Resource Usage or Task Usage view, you can change the assignment values directly in the timescaled grid.

How you contour or edit an assignment depends on what you need to accomplish. Predefined contours work best for assignments in which you can predict a likely pattern of effort—for example, a task that requires gradual ramp-up time might benefit from a back-loaded contour to reflect the likelihood that the resource will work the most toward the end of the assignment.

In this exercise, you apply a predefined contour to an assignment and manually edit another assignment.

1. In the **Task Name** column, below task 38, *Final review*, click the assigned resource *Carole Poland*.

2. On the **Task** tab, in the **Editing** group, click **Scroll to Task**.

	❶	Task Mode	Task Name	Work	Duration	Start	Details	W	T	F	S	S	M	T	W	T	F
34			⊟ Cover design	40 hrs	5 days	Fri 8/10/12	Work										
			Luis Sousa	40 hrs		Fri 8/10/12	Work										
35			⊟ 2nd Pages review	120 hrs	10 days	Fri 8/17/12	Work	8h	8h	16h			16h	16h	16h	16h	
36	❶		⊟ Proof and review	40 hrs	5 days	Fri 8/17/12	Work	8h	8h								
			Hany Morcos	40 hrs		Fri 8/17/12	Work	8h	8h								
37			⊟ Send proofed pa	0 hrs	0 days	Thu 8/23/12	Work			0h							
			Hany Morcos	0 hrs		Thu 8/23/12	Work			0h							
38			⊟ Final review	80 hrs	5 days	Fri 8/24/12	Work			16h			16h	16h	16h	16h	
			Carole Poland	20 hrs		Fri 8/24/12	Work			4h			4h	4h	4h	4h	
			Hany Morcos	20 hrs		Fri 8/24/12	Work			4h			4h	4h	4h	4h	
			Jane Dow	40 hrs		Fri 8/24/12	Work			8h			8h	8h	8h	8h	
39			⊟ Design book's comp	80 hrs	5 days	Fri 8/17/12	Work	16h	16h								
40	❶		⊟ Create mockup	48 hrs	3 days	Fri 8/17/12	Work										
			Hany Morcos	24 hrs		Fri 8/17/12	Work										
			Luis Sousa	24 hrs		Fri 8/17/12	Work										
41			⊟ Review with auth	32 hrs	2 days	Wed 8/22/12	Work	16h	16h								
			Luis Sousa	16 hrs		Wed 8/22/12	Work	8h									

As you can see in the timescaled data at the right, two resources are scheduled to work on this task four hours per day (that is, 50 percent of their available working time) and a third resource is scheduled to work full time on this task. All these assignments have a flat *contour*; that is, work is distributed evenly over time. This is the default work contour type that Project uses when scheduling work.

You want to change Carole Poland's assignment on this task so that she starts with a brief daily assignment and increases her work time as the task progresses. To accomplish this, you will apply a back-loaded contour to the assignment. Note that task 38, *Final review* is a fixed-duration task type, not the default fixed-units task type.

3. On the **Format** tab, in the **Assignment** group, click **Information**.

   The Assignment Information dialog box appears. Click the **General** tab if it is not already selected.

4. Click the down arrow to display the options in the **Work Contour** box.

These are all predefined work contours, and some of the names of the contours are graphical representations of a resource's work over time with that contour applied.

5. Select **Back Loaded**, and then click **OK** to close the **Assignment Information** dialog box.

   Project applies the contour to this resource's assignment and reschedules her work on the task.

The contour indicator matches the type of contour applied—back-loaded in this case.

The back-loaded contour causes Project to assign very little work to the resource initially and then add more work each day.

You see that in each successive day of the task's duration, Carole Poland is assigned slightly more time to work on the assignment. You also see a contour indicator in the Indicators column displaying the type of contour that is applied to the assignment.

6. Point to the contour indicator.

Project displays a ScreenTip describing the type of contour applied to this assignment.

Tip Applying a contour to a fixed-duration task will cause Project to recalculate the resource's work value so that the resource works less in the same time period. For example, Carole's total work on task 38 was reduced from 20 to 12 hours when you applied the contour. Depending on the task type, applying a contour to this assignment may cause the overall duration of the task to be extended. Task 38 is a fixed-duration task, so applying the contour did not change the task's duration. For a fixed-work or fixed-unit task, however, it would. If you do not want a contour to extend a task's duration, change the task type (on the Advanced tab of the Task Information dialog box) to Fixed Duration before applying the contour.

Next, you will directly edit another task's assignment values.

7. In the **Task Name** column, below task 38, *Final review*, click the assigned resource *Hany Morcos*.

Note that Hany is currently assigned four hours per day for each day of the assignment's duration. Why four hours? Hany normally has eight working hours per day on these particular days (as determined by her resource calendar). She was assigned to this task at 50 percent assignment units, however, so the resulting scheduled work is only four hours per day.

You want to increase Hany's work on the last two days of this task so that she will work full time on it. To accomplish this, you will manually edit her assignment values.

8. In the timescaled grid in the right pane of the Task Usage view, select Hany Morcos's four-hour assignment for Wednesday, August 29.

Tip Point to each day label in the timescale (M, T, W and so on) and that day's date value will appear in a ScreenTip.

9. Type **8h**, and then press the Tab key.

10. In Hany's assignment for Thursday, type **8h**, and then press Enter.

	ⓘ	Task Mode	Task Name	Work	Duration	Start	Details	W	T	F	S	S	M	T	W	T	F
34			⊟ Cover design	40 hrs	5 days	Fri 8/10/12	Work										
			Luis Sousa	40 hrs		Fri 8/10/12	Work										
35		⚙	⊟ 2nd Pages review	120 hrs	10 days	Fri 8/17/12	Work	8h	8h	12.5h			13.5h	14.5h	19.5h	20h	
36	⚑	⚙	⊟ Proof and review	40 hrs	5 days	Fri 8/17/12	Work	8h	8h								
			Hany Morcos	40 hrs		Fri 8/17/12	Work	8h	8h								
37		⚙	⊟ Send proofed pa	0 hrs	0 days	Thu 8/23/12	Work			0h							
			Hany Morcos	0 hrs		Thu 8/23/12	Work			0h							
38		⚙	⊟ Final review	80 hrs	5 days	Fri 8/24/12	Work			12.5h			13.5h	14.5h	19.5h	20h	
	▁ll		Carole Polan	12 hrs		Fri 8/24/12	Work			0.5h			1.5h	2.5h	3.5h	4h	
	▓		Hany Morcos	28 hrs		Fri 8/24/12	Work			4h			4h	4h	8h	8h	
			Jane Dow	40 hrs		Fri 8/24/12	Work			8h			8h	8h	8h	8h	
39		⚙	⊟ Design book's comp	80 hrs	5 days	Fri 8/17/12	Work	16h	16h								
40	⚑	⚙	⊟ Create mockup	48 hrs	3 days	Fri 8/17/12	Work										
			Hany Morcos	24 hrs		Fri 8/17/12	Work										
			Luis Sousa	24 hrs		Fri 8/17/12	Work										
41		⚙	⊟ Review with auth	32 hrs	2 days	Wed 8/22/12	Work	16h	16h								
			Luis Sousa	16 hrs		Wed 8/22/12	Work	8h	8h								

Hany is now assigned eight hours per day on these days. Project displays a contour indicator in the Indicators column showing that a manually edited contour has been applied to the assignment.

Tip If you want to document details about contouring an assignment or anything pertaining to an assignment, you can record the details in an assignment note. In the Task Usage or Resource Usage view, select the assignment, and then click the Notes button in the Assignment group on the Format tab. Assignment notes are similar to task and resource notes.

Here are a few more capabilities that you can apply in a usage view:

● In addition to editing work values manually at the resource level as you did before, you can edit work values at the task level. When you change a work value at the task level, Project adjusts the resulting work value per resource in accordance with each resource's units value on that assignment. For example, assume that on a specific day, two resources were assigned four hours each to a task that had a total work value of eight hours. If you then change the total work on the task for that day to 12 hours, Project will increase the work per resource from four to six hours.

- You can split a task in the Gantt Chart view to account for an interruption in the task, as you did in Chapter 7. You can also split a task in the Task Usage view by entering "0" work values in the task's row in the timephased grid for the date range that you want. To preserve the total work on the task, you should add the same amount of work to the end of the task as you subtracted with the split. For example, assume that a task starts on Monday and has eight hours of total work per day for four days. Its work pattern (in hours per day) is 8, 8, 8, and 8. You interrupt work on the task on Tuesday and then add those eight hours to the end of the task (in this case, Friday). The new work pattern would be 8, 0, 8, 8, and 8.

- When editing values in the timephased grid, you can work with the cells somewhat like you might work in a Microsoft Excel worksheet—you can drag and drop values and use the AutoFill handle to copy values to the right or downward.

Applying Different Cost Rates to Assignments

Recall from Chapter 8, "Fine-Tuning Resource Details," that you can set as many as five pay rates per resource, which allows you to apply different pay rates to different assignments for a resource; for example, a different pay rate might depend on the skills required for different assignments. For each assignment, Project initially uses rate table A by default, but you can specify that another rate table should be used.

In the "Entering Multiple Pay Rates for a Resource" section of Chapter 8, you set up a second rate table for Hany Morcos to be applied for any assignments in which she is functioning as a content editor. Hany is currently assigned to task 36, *Proof and review*, as a content editor rather than her default role of a project editor, but her assignment still reflects her default pay rate as a project editor.

In this exercise, you change the pay rate table to be applied to an assignment.

1. In the **Task Name** column, below task 36, *Proof and review*, click the assigned resource *Hany Morcos*.

   Next, you'll view the cost of Hany's assignment.

2. On the **View** tab, in the **Data** group, click **Tables** and then click **Cost**.

   Project displays the Cost table. Note the current cost of Hany's assignment to this task: $1,550.00.

In the Cost table you can see the tasks and each assignment's total cost. To see other assignment cost values such as actual cost or variance, scroll the table to the right.

Task Name	Fixed Cost	Fixed Cost Accrual	Total Cost	Baseline	Details	W	T	F	S	S	M	T	W	T	F
34	⊟ Cover design	$0.00	Prorated	$2,800.00	$0.00	Work										
	Luis Sousa			$2,800.00	$0.00	Work										
35	⊟ **2nd Pages review**	**$0.00**	**Prorated**	**$5,795.00**	**$0.00**	Work	8h	8h	12.5h			13.5h	14.5h	19.5h	20h	
36	⊟ Proof and review	$0.00	Prorated	$1,550.00	$0.00	Work	8h	8h								
	Hany Morcos			$1,550.00	$0.00	Work	8h	8h								
37	⊟ Send proofed pag	$0.00	Prorated	$0.00	$0.00	Work		8h								
	Hany Morcos			$0.00	$0.00	Work		8h								
38	⊟ Final review	$0.00	Prorated	$4,245.00	$0.00	Work			12.5h			13.5h	14.5h	19.5h	20h	
	Carole Poland			$630.00	$0.00	Work			0.5h			1.5h	2.5h	3.5h	4h	
	Hany Morcos			$1,085.00	$0.00	Work			4h			4h	4h	8h	8h	
	Jane Dow			$2,530.00	$0.00	Work			8h			8h	8h	9h		
39	⊟ **Design book's comp**	**$0.00**	**Prorated**	**$3,730.00**	**$0.00**	Work	16h	16h								
40	⊟ Create mockup	$0.00	Prorated	$2,610.00	$0.00	Work										
	Hany Morcos			$930.00	$0.00	Work										
	Luis Sousa			$1,680.00	$0.00	Work										
41	⊟ Review with auth	$0.00	Prorated	$1,120.00	$0.00	Work		16h								

3. On the **Format** tab, in the **Assignment** group, click **Information**.

   The Assignment Information dialog box appears. Click the **General** tab if it is not already selected.

4. In the **Cost Rate Table** box, type or select **B**, and then click **OK** to close the **Assignment Information** dialog box.

   Project applies Hany's cost rate table B to the assignment.

Task Name	Fixed Cost	Fixed Cost Accrual	Total Cost	Baseline	Details	W	T	F	S	S	M	T	W	T	F
34	⊟ Cover design	$0.00	Prorated	$2,800.00	$0.00	Work										
	Luis Sousa			$2,800.00	$0.00	Work										
35	⊟ **2nd Pages review**	**$0.00**	**Prorated**	**$6,045.00**	**$0.00**	Work	8h	8h	12.5h			13.5h	14.5h	19.5h	20h	
36	⊟ Proof and review	$0.00	Prorated	$1,800.00	$0.00	Work	8h	8h								
	Hany Morcos			$1,800.00	$0.00	Work	8h	8h								
37	⊟ Send proofed pag	$0.00	Prorated	$0.00	$0.00	Work		0h								
	Hany Morcos			$0.00	$0.00	Work		0h								
38	⊟ Final review	$0.00	Prorated	$4,245.00	$0.00	Work			12.5h			13.5h	14.5h	19.5h	20h	
	Carole Poland			$630.00	$0.00	Work			0.5h			1.5h	2.5h	3.5h	4h	
	Hany Morcos			$1,085.00	$0.00	Work			4h			4h	4h	8h	8h	
	Jane Dow			$2,530.00	$0.00	Work			8h			8h	0h	9h		
39	⊟ **Design book's comp**	**$0.00**	**Prorated**	**$3,730.00**	**$0.00**	Work	16h	16h								
40	⊟ Create mockup	$0.00	Prorated	$2,610.00	$0.00	Work										
	Hany Morcos			$930.00	$0.00	Work										
	Luis Sousa			$1,680.00	$0.00	Work										
41	⊟ Review with auth	$0.00	Prorated	$1,120.00	$0.00	Work	16h	16h								

The new cost of the assignment, $1,800.00, appears in the Total Cost column. The new cost value is also accounted for in the summary tasks and project summary task.

Tip If you frequently change cost rate tables for assignments, you will find it quicker to display the Cost Rate Table field directly in the Resource Usage or Task Usage view. Display the right edge of the table portion of a usage view, click Add New Column, and then select Cost Rate Table.

Assigning Material Resources to Tasks

In Chapter 8, you created the *material resource* named *Bound galley proofs*. As you may recall from Chapter 8, material resources are used up or "consumed" as a project progresses. Common examples for a construction project include lumber and concrete.

When assigning a material resource, you can handle consumptions and cost in one of two ways:

- Assign a fixed-unit quantity of the material resource to the task. Project will multiply the unit cost of this resource by the number of units assigned to determine the total cost. (You'll use this method in the following exercise.)

- Assign a variable-rate quantity of the material resource to the task. Project will adjust the quantity and cost of the resource as the task's duration changes.

In our new book project, we are interested in tracking the use and cost of the bound galley proofs of the new children's book.

In this exercise, you assign a material resource to a task and enter a fixed-unit quantity of consumption.

1. On the **Task** tab, in the **View** group, click **Gantt Chart**.

2. In the **Task Name** column, click the name of task 38, *Final review*.

   You anticipate that you'll need 20 bound galley proof copies for this review.

3. On the **Task** tab, in the **Editing** group, click **Scroll to Task**.

4. On the **Resource** tab, in the **Assignments** group, click **Assign Resources**.

   The Assign Resources dialog box appears.

5. In the **Assign Resources** dialog box, select the **Units** field for the *Bound galley proofs* resource.

6. Type or select **20**, and then click **Assign**.

   Project assigns the material resource to the task and calculates the $300 cost of the assignment ($15 per copy times 20 copies).

When you assign a material resource to a task, its label value appears in the Units column and next to the Gantt bar to which it is assigned.

Because *Bound galley proof* is a material resource, it cannot do work. Therefore, assigning a material resource does not affect the duration of a task.

7. Click **Close** to close the **Assign Resources** dialog box.

Variable Consumption Rates for Material Resources

You just assigned a material resource with a fixed amount, or *fixed consumption rate,* to a task. Another way to use material resources is to assign them with a *variable consumption rate.* The difference between the two rates is as follows:

- A fixed consumption rate means that, regardless of the duration of the task to which the material resource is assigned, an absolute quantity of the resource will be used. For example, pouring concrete for a house foundation requires a fixed amount of concrete no matter how long it takes to pour it.

- A variable consumption rate means that the quantity of the material resource consumed depends on the duration of the task. When operating a generator, for example, you will consume more fuel in four hours than in two, and you can determine an hourly rate at which you consume the fuel. You enter a variable consumption rate in units per time period; for example, you enter "2/h" to record the consumption of two gallons of fuel per hour. After you enter a variable consumption rate for a material resource's assignment, Project calculates the total quantity of the material resource consumed based on the task's duration.

The advantage of using a variable rate of consumption is that the rate is tied to the task's duration. If the duration changes, the calculated quantity and cost of the material resource will change as well. When you need this level of cost tracking for a material resource, use a variable consumption rate.

Viewing Resource Capacity

Recall that the amount of time that a resource is able to work on tasks in a project plan is called its resource capacity, and in Project, this is measured in units. By default, such units are presented as a percentage value, with 0% meaning no capacity and 100% meaning the full or maximum capacity of a single resource with a normal working schedule of 40 hours per week. In Project, a resource's maximum capacity to do work is tracked as the resource's *Max Units* value.

Even experienced project managers have been known to overestimate resource capacity for the people allocated to work on a given project. This can lead to problems during the execution of a project and unhappy resources, especially when the project manager has also underestimated the amount of work required to complete the tasks in the project plan. There are many legitimate reasons to expect some variability with task work estimates—especially in the initial planning stage of a project. Resource capacity, however, should be easier to estimate more accurately. This section introduces some useful tools in Project that can help you better see and understand resource capacity.

At this point in the planning for the new book project, you've set up an initial task list and initial resource details, as well as some of the resources' working time exceptions such as planned days off. Viewing the working capacity per resource now will give you a better understanding of overall capacity for this project. This in turn can help inform you and the project's stakeholders about any possible adjustments to the scope of the project to better match that capacity of the team (or vice versa). Normally, at this stage of project planning you can expect one of the following conditions:

- Planned work is less than the working capacity of the team. You may be able to use some portion of your resources' time for other projects, or to do more work in this project.

- Planned work exceeds the working capacity of the team. You may need to reduce the scope of work or secure more resources.

- Planned work is approximately equal to the working capacity of the team.

Tip This way of understanding project scope and resource capacity is explored more in Appendix A, "A Short Course in Project Management."

In this exercise, you'll look at individual resource capacity per day, week, and month during the time span in which the project plan is now scheduled.

1. On the **View** tab, in the **Resource Views** group, click **Resource Usage**.

   Project displays the Resource Usage view.

Recall that in this view, the left pane organizes tasks under the resources to which the tasks are assigned. The right pane shows assignment and other values organized on the timeline.

Here, our focus is on seeing availability for the resources. To begin, you'll switch the timephased view to show resource availability.

2. On the **Format** tab, in the **Details** group, select the **Remaining Availability** check box.

3. On the **Format** tab, in the **Details** group, clear the **Work** check box.

   Project hides the Work details, leaving the Remaining Availability detail visible.

4. Click the **Resource Name** column heading.

5. On the **View** tab, in the **Data** group, click **Outline** and then click **Hide Subtasks**.

Now you can see the daily remaining availability values for all work resources. The full-time resources, like Carole Poland, have the expected 8 hours per day available for the days in which they have no assignments. Dan Jump, the half-time resource with 50% max. units, has just 4 hours per day available.

Next, you'll adjust the zoom level of the timephased view to see availability per month.

6. On the **View** tab, in the **Zoom** group, click **Months** in the **Timescale** box.

Project shows available hours per resource, per month.

CLEAN UP Close the Advanced Assignments A file.

7. Do one of the following:

○ If you have Project Standard, proceed to the next chapter.

○ If you have Project Professional, proceed to the next section in this chapter.

Adjusting Assignments in the Team Planner View

New In
2010

Important The Team Planner view is available only in Project Professional, not in Project Standard. If you have Project Standard, skip this section.

The Task and Resource Usage views are powerful views in which you can accomplish intricate goals, like manually contouring resource assignments. If these views present more details than you want, Project Professional includes a simple but powerful view called the Team Planner view.

In the Team Planner view, you see tasks organized by the resource to which they are assigned (like the Resource Usage view) and any unassigned tasks. Both assigned and unassigned tasks may be either:

- **Scheduled tasks** Scheduled for a specific time period and displayed in the Team Planner view at a specific point in time.

- **Unscheduled tasks** Manually scheduled tasks, with or without an assigned resource.

What the Team Planner view enables that the usage views do not is a simple drag-and-drop method of rescheduling or reassigning tasks.

In this exercise, you examine resource assignments and address some overallocation problems, as well as assign some unassigned and unscheduled tasks in the new book project plan.

SET UP You need the Advanced Assignments B_Start project plan located in your Chapter09 practice file folder to complete this exercise. Open the Advanced Assignments B_Start project plan, and then follow these steps.

1. On the **File** tab, click **Save As**.

   The Save As dialog box appears.

2. In the **File name** box, type **Advanced Assignments B**, and then click **Save**.

3. On the **View** tab, in the **Resource Views** group, click **Team Planner**.

   The Team Planner view appears.

4. In the **Resource Name** column, select *Carole Poland*.

5. On the **Task** tab, in the **Editing** group, click **Scroll to Task**.

Carole Poland's initial resource assignments come into view.

The Team Planner view includes four
sections: assigned but unscheduled tasks...

...assigned and
scheduled tasks...

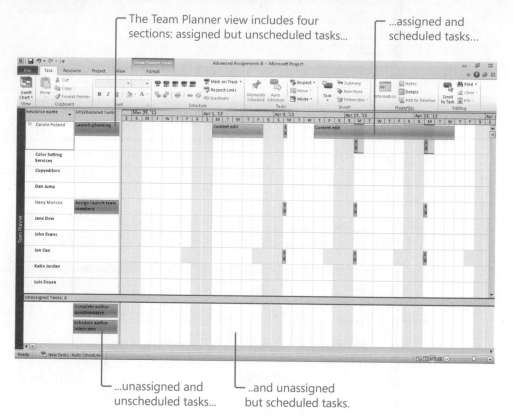

...unassigned and
unscheduled tasks...

..and unassigned
but scheduled tasks.

First, you'll schedule the assigned but unscheduled (that is, *manually scheduled*) tasks. Carole has one unscheduled task, as well as several scheduled tasks. In fact, her scheduled tasks have caused her to be overallocated. The red formatting of her name communicates the fact that she is overallocated, and the red horizontal lines that run through the middle and end of April tell you when she is overallocated.

You'd like Carole's unscheduled task, *Launch planning,* to start in the beginning of August, so you'll move it there.

6. Horizontally scroll the view until the week of August 5th is visible in the timescale.

7. Click and drag Carole's unscheduled task, *Launch planning,* in Carole's row so that the task start date is Monday, August 6.

As on the Gantt Chart, the width of a scheduled task bar corresponds to its duration. Depending on the timescale zoom level, you may not see full task names in some task bars.

8. Point your mouse pointer at the task that you just scheduled.

A ScreenTip appears and contains the essential task details.

Note that although this task is now scheduled for a specific time, it is still a manually scheduled task, and it will remain so until it is switched to *automatic scheduling*.

Next, you'll schedule the unscheduled task assigned to Hany Morcos, and you'll also reassign it to Carole. You'd like this task to be completed in early August as well.

9. Click and drag the name of Hany Morcos's unscheduled task, *Assign launch team members*, to Carole's Poland's row so that the task start date is Tuesday, August 7.

Project schedules and reassigns the task.

Next, you'll assign the two unassigned and unscheduled tasks. Both of these tasks should be assigned to Hany Morcos.

10. Click and drag the first unassigned task, *Complete author questionnaire*, to Hany Morcos's row so that the task start date is Monday, August 13.

11. Click and drag the remaining unassigned task, *Schedule author interviews*, to Hany Morcos's row so that the task start date is Tuesday, August 14.

Now both tasks are assigned and scheduled, though they remain manually scheduled tasks.

To conclude this exercise, you'll address some of the resource overallocation problems that are visible in the Timeline view.

12. On the **View** tab, in the **Zoom** group, click the down arrow next to the **Timescale** box and click **Weeks**.

The timescale adjusts to show more of the project plan.

13. Scroll the view horizontally until the week of June 24 is visible in the timescale.

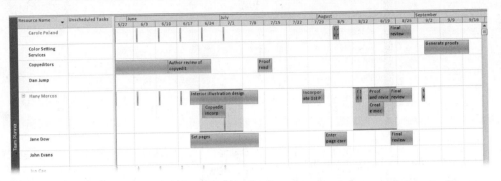

Most of the resource overallocations in the project plan are due to the weekly editorial status meeting overlapping with other tasks. Since each occurrence of the editorial status meeting is only one hour long, you're not concerned with addressing this level of overallocation. You can see a more severe overallocation for Hany Morcos the week of June 24, however.

Because you need Hany's full attention on the *Interior illustration and design* task, you'll reassign the *Copyedit incorp* task to someone else.

14. Right-click Hany's task, *Copyedit incorp*, and in the shortcut menu that appears, click **Reassign To**, and then select *Carole Poland*.

Project reassigns the task but does not change the task's start or finish dates or duration.

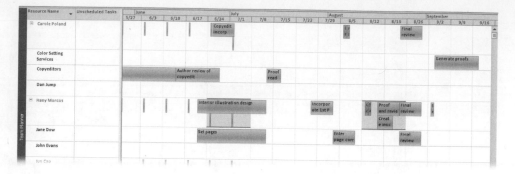

Tip You can also reassign tasks by dragging them from one resource to another. To better control the scheduling of tasks when you reassign them this way, set the timescale to daily (to do this, on the View tab, in the Zoom group, click Days in the Timescale box).

There are still overallocation issues in the project plan, but they are minor issues that don't require additional attention.

 CLEAN UP Close the Advanced Assignments B file.

Key Points

- You can change when a resource will start work on an assignment without affecting other resources assigned to the same task.

- Project includes several predefined work contours that you can apply to an assignment.

- When working with resource costs, you can specify different cost rates for different assignments.

- When assigned to a task, material resources can have a fixed or variable consumption rate.

- In a usage view, you can see remaining availability of work resources at whatever time increment you wish.

- The Team Planner view allows easy dragging of assignments between resources (Project Professional only).

Chapter at a Glance

View work assignments per day, week, month, or other time period, page 211.

Edit resource assignments to manually resolve overallocations, page 217.

Use resource leveling to automatically resolve resource overallocation problems, page 220.

Check a project plan's cost and duration statistics, page 227.

10 Fine-Tuning the Project Plan

In this chapter, you will learn how to:

✔ Look at how resources are scheduled to work over the duration of a project.

✔ Edit a resource assignment to resolve a resource overallocation.

✔ Resolve resource overallocations automatically.

✔ See the project's overall cost and finish date.

In the previous three chapters, you have focused on details about tasks, resources, and assignments. Now, you will examine the results of your previous work on the schedule and dive deeper into resource assignments. You'll also observe the overall project duration and cost.

> **Practice Files** Before you can complete the exercises in this chapter, you need to copy the book's practice files to your computer. A complete list of practice files is provided in "Using the Practice Files" at the beginning of this book. For each exercise that has a practice file, simply browse to where you saved the book's practice file folder.

Important If you are running Project Professional, you may need to make a one-time setting change. This helps ensure that the practice files you work with in this chapter do not affect your Project Server data. For more information, see Appendix C, "Using the Practice Files if Connected to Project Server."

Examining Resource Allocations over Time

In this section, you will focus on resource allocation—how the task assignments you've made affect the workloads of the *work resources* (people and equipment) of a project. A resource's capacity to work in a given time period is determined by his or her *Max. Units* and *resource calendar*. The relationship between a resource's capacity and his or her task assignments is called *allocation*. Each work resource is in one of three states of allocation:

- **Underallocated** The resource's assignments do not fill the resource's maximum capacity to do work. For example, a full-time resource who has only 25 hours of work assigned in a 40-hour workweek is *underallocated*.

- **Fully allocated** The resource's assignments fill the resource's maximum capacity. For example, a full-time resource who has 40 hours of work assigned in a 40-hour workweek is *fully allocated*.

- **Overallocated** The resource's assignments exceed the resource's maximum capacity for any period of time. For example, a full-time resource who has 65 hours of work assigned in a 40-hour workweek is *overallocated*.

These states of allocation apply to work resources. *Cost* and *material resources* do not do work; therefore, their assignments do not affect the overall duration of a project.

In Project, a resource's capacity to work is measured in units; the maximum capacity of a given resource is called *maximum units*. Units are measured either as numbers (such as three units) or as a percentage (such as 300% units).

Project Management Focus: Evaluating Resource Allocation

It is tempting to say that fully allocating all resources on every occasion is every project manager's goal, but that would be an oversimplification. Depending on the nature of your project and the resources working on it, some underalloca-tions might be perfectly fine. Overallocation might not always be a problem either, depending on the amount of overallocation. If one resource is overallocated for just a half-hour, Project will flag the overallocation, but such a minor overalloca-tion might not be a problem that you need to solve, depending on the resource involved and the nature of the assignment. Severe overallocation—for example, a resource being assigned twice the work he or she could possibly accomplish in one week—is always a problem, however, and you should know how to identify it and maintain strategies for addressing it. This chapter helps you identify and remedy resource overallocation.

In this exercise, you look at resource allocations and focus on a resource who is overallocated.

SET UP Start Project if it's not already running.

You need the Advanced Plan_Start project plan located in your Chapter10 practice file folder to complete this exercise. Open the Advanced Plan_Start project plan, and then follow these steps.

1. On the **File** tab, click **Save As**.

   The Save As dialog box appears.

2. In the **File name** box, type **Advanced Plan**, and then click **Save**.

3. On the **View** tab, in the **Resource Views** group, click **Resource Usage**.

   The Resource Usage view appears.

4. On the **Task** tab, in the **Editing** group, click **Scroll to Task**.

   Project scrolls the right side of the view to show some assignment details.

On the left side of the view is a table (the Usage table, by default) that shows assignments grouped per resource, the total work assigned to each resource, and each assignment's work. This information is organized into an *outline* that you can expand or collapse.

The right side of the view contains assignment details (work, by default) arranged on a timescale. You can horizontally scroll the timescale to see different time periods. You can also change the tiers on the timescale to display data in units of weeks, days, hours, and so on.

Notice the name in the first row, *Unassigned*. This item lists any tasks to which no specific resources are assigned.

Next, you will collapse the outline in the table to see total work per resource over time.

5. Click the **Resource Name** column heading.

6. On the **View** tab, in the **Data** group, click **Outline** and then click **Hide Subtasks**.

Tip You can also do this by pressing Alt+Shift+−.

Project collapses the outline (assignments per resource) in the Resource Usage view.

7. In the **Resource Name** column, click the name *Carole Poland*.

		Resource Name	Work	Add New Column	Details			Apr 1, '12								Apr 8, '12		
						F	S	S	M	T	W	T	F	S	S	M	T
		⊞ Unassigned	0 hrs		Work												
1	◇	⊞ Carole Poland	213 hrs		Work				8h	8h	8h	8h	8h			1h	0h
2		⊞ Color Setting Service	80 hrs		Work												
3		⊞ Copyeditors	300 hrs		Work												
4		Dan Jump	0 hrs		Work												
5	◇	⊞ Hany Morcos	393 hrs		Work												
6	◇	⊞ Jane Dow	240 hrs		Work											1h	
7		⊞ Jun Cao	13 hrs		Work												
8		⊞ Luis Sousa	200 hrs		Work											1h	
9		⊞ Printing Service	240 hrs		Work												
10		⊞ Tad Orman	296 hrs		Work												
11		Travel			Work												
12		Bound galley proof	0 copy		Work (												

Resource assignments are currently hidden in the Usage table, and the resources' total work values over time appear in the timescaled grid on the right.

Next, you will look at two work resources and their allocations.

8. Point to the **M** column heading (for Monday) for the week of April 1 at the top of the timescaled grid.

A ScreenTip appears with the date of the assignment: 4/2/12.

In timescaled views, you can get details about dates by placing your mouse pointer over the timescale.

		Resource Name	Work	Add New Column	Details			Apr 1, '12	
						F	S	S	M	T
		⊞ Unassigned	0 hrs		Work				4/2/12
1	◇	⊞ Carole Poland	213 hrs		Work				8h	8h
		⊞ Color Setting Service	80 hrs		Work				

Such ScreenTips are handy in timescaled views, such as the Resource Usage view or the Gantt Chart view.

Currently, the timescale is set to display weeks and days. You will now change the timescale to see the work data summarized more broadly.

9. On the **View** tab, in the **Zoom** group, in the **Timescale** box, click **Months**.

   Project changes the timescaled grid to show scheduled work values per month.

	Resource Name	Work	Add New Column	Details	1st Quarter			2nd Quarter			3rd Quarter			4th Quarter			1s
					Jan	Feb	Mar	Apr	May	Jun	Jul	Aug	Sep	Oct	Nov	Dec	
	Unassigned	0 hrs		Work													
1	Carole Poland	213 hrs		Work				124h	4h	44h	1h	40h					
2	Color Setting Service	80 hrs		Work									80h				
3	Copyeditors	300 hrs		Work				8h	248h	24h	20h						
4	Dan Jump	0 hrs		Work													
5	Hany Morcos	393 hrs		Work				4h	44h	60h	89h	100h	96h				
6	Jane Dow	240 hrs		Work						56h	64h	120h					
7	Jun Cao	13 hrs		Work				4h	4h	4h	1h						
8	Luis Sousa	200 hrs		Work							56h	64h	80h				
9	Printing Service	240 hrs		Work									48h	184h	8h		
10	Tad Orman	296 hrs		Work				24h	56h	80h	80h	16h	40h				
11	Travel			Work													
12	Bound galley proof	0 copy		Work (													
				Work													
				Work													
				Work													
				Work													

Notice that the names of Carole Poland and some other resources appear in red. The red formatting means that these resources are overallocated: at one or more points in the schedule, their assigned tasks exceed their capacity to work.

As you can see in the timescaled grid, Carole Poland is overallocated in April and June. She is underallocated for the other months in which she has assignments. Notice that Carole's June work value of 44 hours is formatted in red. Even though 44 hours within a month isn't an overallocation for a full-time resource, at some point in June (perhaps even for just one day), Carole is scheduled to work more hours than she can accommodate.

You will focus on Carole Poland first by changing the timescale settings.

10. On the **View** tab, in the **Zoom** group, in the **Timescale** box, click **Days**.

    Project adjusts the timescale to its previous setting.

11. Click the plus sign next to Carole's name in the **Resource Name** column.

    Project expands the Resource Usage view to show Carole's individual assignments.

12. Scroll the Resource Usage view horizontally to the right to see Carole's assignments the week of April 15.

    Carole's total work that Monday, April 16, is 9 hours. This is formatted red, indicating the overallocation.

These two assignments make up the
9 hours to work scheduled for Monday.

	Resource Name	Work	Add New Column	Details	Apr 15, '12							Apr 22, '12			
					S	S	M	T	W	T	F	S	S	M	T	W
	⊞ Unassigned	0 hrs		Work												
1	⊟ Carole Poland	213 hrs		Work			9h	8h	8h	8h	8h			9h	8h	8h
	Handoff to Edito	0 hrs		Work												
	Copyedit incorp	40 hrs		Work												
	Content edit	120 hrs		Work			8h	8h	8h	8h	8h			8h	8h	8h
	Final review	12 hrs		Work												
	Editorial staff mi	1 hr		Work			1h									
	Editorial staff mi	1 hr		Work												
	Editorial staff mi	1 hr		Work										1h		
	Editorial staff mi	1 hr		Work												
	Editorial staff mi	1 hr		Work												
	Editorial staff mi	1 hr		Work												
	Editorial staff mi	1 hr		Work												
	Editorial staff mi	1 hr		Work												
	Editorial staff mi	1 hr		Work												
	Editorial staff mi	1 hr		Work												
	Editorial staff mi	1 hr		Work												
	Launch planning	20 hrs		Work												
	Assign launch te	8 hrs		Work												
2	⊞ Color Setting Servici	80 hrs		Work												

Carole has two assignments on April 16: eight hours on the *Content edit* task and the one-hour task *Editorial staff meeting 2* (one instance of a *recurring task*).

These two tasks have been scheduled at times that overlap between the hours of 8 A.M. and 9 A.M. (If you want to observe this, adjust the timescale to display hours.) This is a real overallocation: Carole probably cannot complete both tasks simultaneously. However, it is a relatively minor overallocation given the scope of the project, and you don't need to be too concerned about resolving this level of overallocation. However, there are other, more serious overallocations in the schedule that you will remedy later in this chapter.

13. Click the minus sign next to Carole's name in the **Resource Name** column.

Here are a few other things to keep in mind when viewing resource allocation:

● A quick way to navigate to resource overallocations in the Resource Usage view is to use the Next Overallocation button on the Resources tab in the Level group.

● By default, the Resource Usage view displays the Usage table; however, you can display different tables. On the View tab, in the Data group, click Table and then click the table you want displayed.

● By default, the Resource Usage view displays work values in the timescaled grid. However, you can display additional assignment values, such as cost and remaining availability. To do this, on the Format tab, in the Details group, click the value that you want displayed.

● Instead of using the Timescale box on the View tab to change the timescale, you can click the Zoom In and Zoom Out buttons on the status bar. However, this method might not produce the exact level of detail that you want.

● To see allocations for each resource graphed against a timescale, you can display the Resource Graph: on the View tab, in the Resource Views group, click OtherViews and then click Resource Graph. Use the arrow keys or horizontal scroll bar to switch between resources in this view.

● Project Professional users can use the Team Planner view to see assignments per resource in a simpler format. For more information about the Team Planner view, see Chapter 9, "Fine-Tuning Assignment Details."

Resolving Resource Overallocations Manually

In this section and the next, you will continue to focus on resource allocation—how the task assignments you have made affect the workloads of the work resources of the project. In this section, you will manually edit an assignment to resolve a resource overallocation. In the next section, you will automatically resolve resource overallocations.

Editing an assignment manually is just one way to resolve a resource overallocation. Other solutions include the following:

● Replace the overallocated resource with another resource using the Replace button in the Assign Resources dialog box.

● Reduce the value in the Units field in the Assignment Information or Assign Resources dialog box.

● Assign an additional resource to the task so that both resources share the work.

● Add leveling delay to an assignment manually.

If the overallocation is not too severe (such as assigning 9 hours of work in a normal 8-hour workday), you can often leave the overallocation in the project plan.

In this exercise, you will use the Resource Usage view to examine one overallocated resource's assignments and edit the assignment to eliminate the overallocation.

1. On the **View** tab, in the **Zoom** group, in the **Timescale** box, click **Weeks**.

    At the weekly setting, you can more easily spot overallocations that may need to be addressed. Assigned work well over 40 hours per week for a full-time resource could be a serious problem.

		Resource Name	Work	Add New Column	Details	April 3/25	4/1	4/8	4/15	4/22	May 4/29	5/6	5/13	5/20	5/27	June 6/3	6/10
		Unassigned	0 hrs		Work												
1		Carole Poland	213 hrs		Work		40h	17h	41h	25h	1h	1h	1h	1h	1h	1h	27h
2		Color Setting Service	80 hrs		Work												
3		Copyeditors	300 hrs		Work					0h	40h	40h	32h	80h	69.5h	10h	8.5h
4		Dan Jump	0 hrs		Work												
5		Hany Morcos	393 hrs		Work			1h	1h	1h	1h	17h	25h	1h	1h	1h	1h
6		Jane Dow	240 hrs		Work			1h	1h	1h	1h	1h	1h	1h	1h	1h	1h
7		Jun Cao	13 hrs		Work												
8		Luis Sousa	200 hrs		Work												
9		Printing Service	240 hrs		Work												
10		Tad Orman	296 hrs		Work						16h	40h	24h		6h	40h	34h
11		Travel			Work												
12		Bound galley proof	0 copy		Work (												

Note that several names appear in red. These are overallocated resources.

2. Horizontally scroll the usage view to the right to examine the more severe overallocations per week.

You see several cases of minor overallocation, such as 41 hours per week, and some cases of overallocations where the total work is less than 40 hours per week. Note the more severe overallocations that affect Hany Morcos and Jane Dow starting the week of August 19.

		Resource Name	Work	Add New Column	Details	August 7/29	8/5	8/12	8/19	8/26	September 9/2	9/9	9/16	9/23	October 9/30	10/7	10/14
		Unassigned	0 hrs		Work												
1		Carole Poland	213 hrs		Work				4.5h	35.5h							
2		Color Setting Service	80 hrs		Work						32h	40h	8h				
3		Copyeditors	300 hrs		Work												
4		Dan Jump	0 hrs		Work												
5		Hany Morcos	393 hrs		Work	32h		16h	52h	16h	48h	40h	8h				
6		Jane Dow	240 hrs		Work	8h	32h			16h	64h						
7		Jun Cao	13 hrs		Work												
8		Luis Sousa	200 hrs		Work			8h	40h	32h							
9		Printing Service	240 hrs		Work								8h	40h	40h	40h	40h
10		Tad Orman	296 hrs		Work					16h		40h					
11		Travel			Work												
12		Bound galley proof	0 copy		Work (												

These overallocations are severe enough that they merit more investigation. You'll begin with Hany's overallocation of 52 hours the week of August 19.

3. Click the plus sign next to Hany's name in the **Resource Name** column.

Next, you'd like to get a better look at the tasks that are overallocating Hany this week.

4. On the **View** tab, in the **Zoom** group, in the **Timescale** box, click **Days**.

5. Horizontally scroll the usage view to display the August 19 timeframe.

At the daily setting, you can see that Hany is overallocated on Monday and Tuesday, August 20 and 21.

You decide to reduce Hany's work on both the *Proof and review* and the *Create mockup* tasks.

6. In the timephased grid of the **Resource Usage** view, select Hany's assignment of 8 hours on Monday, August 20, on the task *Proof and review*.

7. Type **4h**, and then press the Tab key.

8. With Hany's 8-hour assignment on the same task for Tuesday, August 21, selected, type **4h**, and then press Tab.

9. Select Hany's assignment of 8 hours on Monday, August 20, on the task *Create mockup*.

10. Type **4h**, and then press Tab.

11. With Hany's 8-hour assignment on the same task for Tuesday, August 21, selected, type **4h**, and then press Tab.

You've addressed her overallocation for the week by reducing her work on the two tasks. Note that by taking this action, you have reduced not just Hany's work on these tasks, but the total work in the project plan. As a project manager, you have to use your judgment to determine the best course of action in such cases: reduce work, change resource assignments, or spread the work over a longer period of time.

Next, you will look at other resource overallocations in the new book plan that you can resolve automatically with resource leveling.

Leveling Overallocated Resources

In the previous section, you read about resource allocation, discovered what causes overallocation, and resolved an overallocation manually. *Resource leveling* is the process of delaying or splitting a resource's work on a task to resolve an overallocation. The options in the Level Resources dialog box enable you to set parameters concerning how you want Project to resolve resource overallocations. Project will attempt to resolve such overallocations when you choose to level resources. Depending on the options you choose, this might involve delaying the start date of an assignment or task or splitting the work on the task.

Important Although the effects of resource leveling on a schedule might be significant, resource leveling does not change who is assigned to tasks nor the total work or assignment unit values of those assignments.

For example, consider the following tasks, all of which have the same full-time resource assigned.

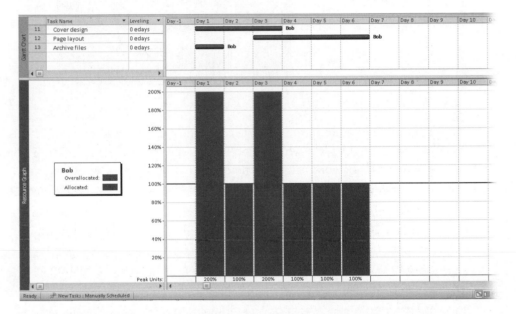

In this split view, the Resource Graph view appears below the Gantt Chart view. On day 1, the resource is overallocated at 200%. On day 2, the resource is fully allocated at 100%. On day 3, he is again overallocated at 200%. After day 3, the resource is fully allocated at 100%.

When you perform resource leveling, Project delays the start dates of the second and third tasks so that the resource is not overallocated.

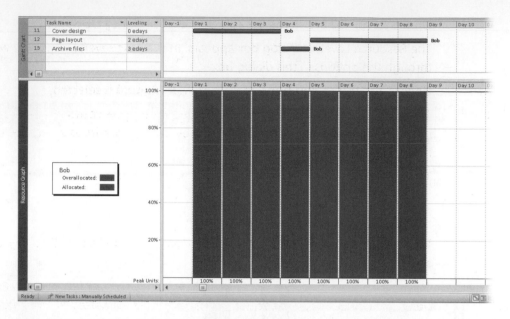

Note that the finish date of the latest task has moved from day 6 to day 8. This is common with resource leveling, which often pushes out the project finish date. There was a total of eight days of work before leveling, but two of those days overlapped, causing the resource to be overallocated on those days. After leveling, all eight days of work are still there, but the resource is no longer overallocated.

Resource leveling is a powerful tool, but it accomplishes only a few basic things: it delays tasks, splits tasks, and delays resource assignments. It does this following a fairly complex set of rules and options that you specify in the Resource Leveling dialog box. (These options are explained in the following exercise.) Resource leveling is a great fine-tuning tool, but it cannot replace your good judgment about resource availability, task durations, relationships, and constraints. Resource leveling will work with all this information as it is entered into your project plan, but it might not be possible to fully resolve all resource overallocations within the time frame desired unless you change some of the basic task and resource values in the project plan.

Tip To learn more about resource leveling, click the Help button (which looks like a question mark) in the upper-right corner of the Project window, and in the Help Search box, type **Level resource assignments**.

In this exercise, you level resources and view the effects on assignments and the project finish date.

1. On the **View** tab, in the **Resource Views** group, click **Resource Sheet**.

   The Resource Sheet view appears. Note that a few resource names appear in red and display the Overallocated icon in the Indicators column.

2. On the **Resource** tab, in the **Level** group, click **Leveling Options**.

   The Resource Leveling dialog box appears. In the next several steps, you will walk through the options in this dialog box.

3. Under **Leveling calculations**, make sure that **Manual** is selected.

   This setting determines whether Project levels resources constantly (Automatic) or only when you tell it to (Manual). Automatic leveling occurs as soon as a resource becomes overallocated.

   Tip All settings in the Resource Leveling dialog box apply to all project plans that you work with in Project, not only to the active project plan. Using automatic leveling might sound tempting, but it will cause frequent adjustments to project plans whether you want them or not. For this reason, we recommend you keep this setting on Manual.

4. In the **Look for overallocations on a . . . basis** box, make sure that **Day by Day** is selected.

   This setting determines the time frame in which Project will look for overalloca-tions. If a resource is overallocated, its name will be formatted in red. If it's over-allocated at the level you choose here, Project will also show the Overallocated indicator next to its name.

   Tip On most projects, leveling in finer detail than day by day can result in unrealistically precise adjustments to assignments. If you prefer not to see overallocation indicators for day-by-day overallocations, select Week by Week in the "Look for overallocations on a . . . basis" box and then click OK. Doing so will not level resources, but it will determine when Project displays overallocation indicators next to resource names.

5. Make sure that the **Clear leveling values before leveling** check box is selected.

   Sometimes you will need to level resources repeatedly to obtain the results that you want. For example, you might initially attempt to level week by week and then switch to day by day. If the "Clear leveling values before leveling" check box is selected, Project removes any existing leveling delays from all tasks and assign-ments before leveling. For example, if you previously leveled the project plan and then added more assignments, you might clear this check box before leveling again so that you wouldn't lose the previous leveling results.

6. Under **Leveling range for 'Advanced Plan',** make sure that **Level entire project** is selected.

   Here you choose to level either the entire project or only those assignments that fall within a date range you specify. Leveling within a date range is most useful after you have started tracking actual work and you want to level only the remain-ing assignments in a project.

7. In the **Leveling order** box, make sure that **Standard** is selected.

You control the priority that Project uses to determine which tasks it should delay to resolve a resource conflict. The ID Only option delays tasks only according to their ID numbers: numerically higher ID numbers (for example, 10) will be delayed before numerically lower ID numbers (for example, 5). You might want to use this option when your project plan has no task relationships or constraints. The Standard option delays tasks according to predecessor relationships, start dates, task constraints, *slack,* priority, and IDs. The Priority, Standard option looks at the task priority value before the other standard criteria. (*Task priority* is a numeric ranking between 0 and 1000 that indicates the task's appropriateness for leveling. Tasks with the lowest priority are delayed or split first.)

8. Make sure that the **Level only within available slack** check box is cleared.

    Tip Remember that to clear a check box means to remove a check from the check box, and to select a check box means to put a check in it. You toggle the selection state of a check box by clicking it.

    Clearing this check box allows Project to extend the project's finish date, if necessary, to resolve resource allocations.

    Selecting this check box would prevent Project from extending the project's finish date to resolve resource overallocations. Instead, Project would use only the free slack within the existing schedule. Depending on the project, this might not be adequate to fully resolve resource overallocations.

9. Make sure that the **Leveling can adjust individual assignments on a task** check box is selected.

    This allows Project to add leveling delay (or split work on assignments if "Leveling can create splits in remaining work" is also selected) independently of any other resources assigned to the same task. This might cause resources to start and finish work on a task at different times.

10. Make sure that the **Leveling can create splits in remaining work** check box is selected.

    This allows Project to split work on a task (or on an assignment if "Leveling can adjust individual assignments on a task" is also selected) as a way of resolving an overallocation.

11. Make sure that the **Level manually scheduled tasks** check box is selected.

    This allows Project to level a manually scheduled task just as it would an automatically scheduled task.

Important If you are using Project Professional rather than Project Standard, the Resource Leveling and some other dialog boxes contain additional options relating to Project Server. Throughout this book we won't use Project Server, so you can ignore these options for now. For more information about Project Server, see Appendix C.

12. Click **Level All**.

Tip After you have set the leveling options that you want in the Resource Leveling dialog box, you can level the project plan by clicking the Level All button on the Resource tab in the Level group. You don't need to return to the Resource Leveling dialog box unless you want to change leveling options.

Project levels the overallocated resources.

Notice that the Overallocated indicators are gone.

Note When leveling resources with Day By Day selected, you might see the overallocation icons disappear, but some resource names may still appear in red. This means that some resources are still overallocated hour by hour (or minute by minute), but not day by day.

Next, you will look at the project plan before and after leveling by using the Leveling Gantt view.

13. On the **View** tab, in the **Task Views** group, click **Other Views** and then click **More Views**.

14. In the **More Views** dialog box, click **Leveling Gantt**, and then click **Apply**.

Project switches to the Leveling Gantt view.

15. On the **View** tab, in the **Zoom** group, click **Entire Project**.

This view gives you a better look at some of the tasks that were affected by leveling.

16. Scroll the Leveling Gantt view vertically down to see task 46, the *Book launch prep* summary task.

In the Leveling Gantt view, the bars on the top represent the pre-leveled schedule of the task. The lower bars represent the schedule after leveling.

		Task Mode	Name	Leveling Delay	Duration	Start
41			Review with auth	0 edays	2 days	Wed 8/29/12
42			⊟ Color prep and printin	0 edays	50 days	Mon 9/3/12
43			Send to color house	0 edays	1 day	Mon 9/3/12
44			Generate proofs	0 edays	10 days	Tue 9/4/12
45			Print and ship	0 edays	30 days	Fri 9/21/12
46			⊟ Book launch prep	0 edays	18 days	Fri 8/31/12
47			Launch planning	0 edays	6 days	Fri 8/31/12
48			Assign launch team	0 edays	1 day	Mon 9/10/12
49			Complete author qu	0 edays	5 days	Tue 9/11/12
50			Schedule author int	0 edays	1 day	Tue 9/18/12
51			Design and order m	0 edays	5 days	Wed 9/19/12

These are some of the tasks that were more substantially affected by resource leveling. Notice that each task has two bars. The top bar represents the pre-leveled task. You can see a task's pre-leveled start, finish, and duration by pointing to a light tan–colored bar. The bottom bar represents the leveled task.

Project was able to resolve the resource overallocations. For this particular project, leveling did not extend the project finish date. The latest task in the plan (task 45, *Print and ship*) still has some slack due to the manual duration entered on its summary task.

Checking the Project's Cost and Finish Date

Not all project plans include cost information, but for those that do, keeping track of project costs can be as important as or more important than keeping track of the scheduled finish date. In this section, you examine both the cost and the finish date.

Two factors to consider when examining project costs are the specific types of costs you want to see and how you can best see them.

The types of costs that you might encounter over the life of a project include the following:

- **Baseline costs** The original planned task, resource, or assignment costs saved as part of a baseline plan.

- **Current (or scheduled) costs** The calculated costs of tasks, resources, and assignments in a project plan. As you make adjustments in a project plan, such as assigning or removing resources, Project recalculates current costs just as it recalculates task start and finish dates. After you start to incur actual costs (typically by tracking actual work), the current cost equals the actual cost plus the remaining cost per task, resource, or assignment. Current costs are the values you see in the fields labeled Cost or Total Cost.

- **Actual costs** The costs that have been incurred for tasks, resources, or assignments.

- **Remaining costs** The difference between the current or scheduled costs and the actual costs for tasks, resources, or assignments.

You might need to compare these costs (for example, baseline vs. actual) or examine them individually per task, resource, or assignment. Or you might need to examine cost values for summary tasks or for an entire project plan. Some common ways to view these types of costs include the following:

- You can see the project's cost values in the Project Statistics dialog box (you'll do so later).

- You can see or print formatted reports that include cash flow, budget, overbudgeted tasks or resources, and earned value (to do this, on the Project tab, in the Reports group, click Reports or Visual Reports).

- You can see task-, resource-, or assignment-level cost information in usage views by displaying the Cost table (to do this, on the View tab, in the Data group, click Tables and then click Cost).

In addition to cost, the finish date is a critical (often the most critical) measure of a project plan. A project's finish date is a function of its duration and start date. Most projects have a desired, or soft, finish date, and many projects have a "must hit," or hard, finish date. When managing projects like these, it is essential that you know the project's current or scheduled finish.

Tip In the language of project management, a project's finish date is determined by its *critical path*. The critical path is the series of tasks that will push out the project's end date if the tasks are delayed. For this reason, when evaluating the duration of a project, you should focus mainly on the tasks on the critical path, called critical tasks. Remember that the word *critical* has nothing to do with how important these tasks are to the overall project. The word refers only to how their scheduling will affect the project's finish date. If you need a refresher on critical path, see Chapter 7, "Fine-Tuning Task Details."

In this exercise, you look at the overall project costs, individual task costs, and the project's finish date.

 1. On the **View** tab, in the **Task Views** group, click **Other Views**, and then click **Task Sheet**.

Project switches to the Task Sheet view. Next, you will switch to the Cost table.

Tip Wonder where Project got this project summary task name shown for task 0? Project uses the title entered in the Advanced Plan Properties dialog box (on the File tab, in the Info group) as the project summary task name. Or, if nobody has entered a distinct title property, Project uses the file name as the project summary task name. If you change the project summary task once you've displayed it, Project updates the Title property, and vice versa.

 2. On the **View** tab, in the **Data** group, click **Tables** and then click **Cost**.

The Cost table appears.

	Task Name	Fixed Cost	Fixed Cost Accrual	Total Cost	Baseline	Variance	Actual	Remaining	Add New Column
0	Children's Book Sched	$0.00	Prorated	$74,017.25	$0.00	$74,017.25	$0.00	$74,017.25	
1	Editorial staff meeting	$0.00	Prorated	$1,732.25	$0.00	$1,732.25	$0.00	$1,732.25	
15	Acquisition	$0.00	Prorated	$9,900.00	$0.00	$9,900.00	$0.00	$9,900.00	
16	Manuscript receive	$0.00	Prorated	$0.00	$0.00	$0.00	$0.00	$0.00	
17	Content edit	$0.00	Prorated	$6,300.00	$0.00	$6,300.00	$0.00	$6,300.00	
18	Author review of cc	$0.00	Prorated	$3,600.00	$0.00	$3,600.00	$0.00	$3,600.00	
19	Handoff to Editorial	$0.00	Prorated	$0.00	$0.00	$0.00	$0.00	$0.00	
20	Editorial	$0.00	Prorated	$12,650.00	$0.00	$12,650.00	$0.00	$12,650.00	
21	Organize manuscrip	$0.00	Prorated	$1,550.00	$0.00	$1,550.00	$0.00	$1,550.00	
22	Copyedit	$0.00	Prorated	$8,100.00	$0.00	$8,100.00	$0.00	$8,100.00	
23	Author review of cc	$0.00	Prorated	$900.00	$0.00	$900.00	$0.00	$900.00	
24	Copyedit incorp	$0.00	Prorated	$2,100.00	$0.00	$2,100.00	$0.00	$2,100.00	
25	Handoff to Producti	$0.00	Prorated	$0.00	$0.00	$0.00	$0.00	$0.00	
26	Design and Production	$0.00	Prorated	$37,015.00	$0.00	$37,015.00	$0.00	$37,015.00	
27	Set pages	$0.00	Prorated	$7,590.00	$0.00	$7,590.00	$0.00	$7,590.00	
28	Interior illustration	$0.00	Prorated	$13,050.00	$0.00	$13,050.00	$0.00	$13,050.00	
29	1st Pages review	$0.00	Prorated	$7,780.00	$0.00	$7,780.00	$0.00	$7,780.00	
30	Proofread and in	$0.00	Prorated	$900.00	$0.00	$900.00	$0.00	$900.00	
31	Incorporate 1st P	$0.00	Prorated	$1,550.00	$0.00	$1,550.00	$0.00	$1,550.00	
32	Send proofed pa	$0.00	Prorated	$0.00	$0.00	$0.00	$0.00	$0.00	
33	Enter page correc	$0.00	Prorated	$2,530.00	$0.00	$2,530.00	$0.00	$2,530.00	
34	Cover design	$0.00	Prorated	$2,800.00	$0.00	$2,800.00	$0.00	$2,800.00	
35	2nd Pages review	$0.00	Prorated	$5,175.00	$0.00	$5,175.00	$0.00	$5,175.00	
36	Proof and review	$0.00	Prorated	$1,240.00	$0.00	$1,240.00	$0.00	$1,240.00	
37	Send proofed pa	$0.00	Prorated	$0.00	$0.00	$0.00	$0.00	$0.00	
38	Final review	$0.00	Prorated	$3,935.00	$0.00	$3,935.00	$0.00	$3,935.00	
39	Design book's comp	$0.00	Prorated	$3,420.00	$0.00	$3,420.00	$0.00	$3,420.00	
40	Create mockup	$0.00	Prorated	$2,300.00	$0.00	$2,300.00	$0.00	$2,300.00	
41	Review with auth	$0.00	Prorated	$1,120.00	$0.00	$1,120.00	$0.00	$1,120.00	

Ready   New Tasks : Auto Scheduled

Here, you can see many types of cost values for the overall project (the total cost of the project summary task 0), project phases (summary tasks), and individual tasks.

At this point in the project life cycle, the project plan does not yet include a baseline; therefore, the Baseline column contains only zero values. Similarly, the project plan does not yet contain any actual progress, so the Actual column contains only zero values.

Next, you'll check the project's finish date.

3. On the **Project** tab, in the **Properties** group, click **Project Information**.

   The Project Information dialog box appears.

Project Information for 'Advanced Plan'	☒

Start date:	Mon 4/2/12	Current date:	Wed 2/8/12
Finish date:	Fri 11/9/12	Status date:	NA
Schedule from:	Project Start Date	Calendar:	Standard
	All tasks begin as soon as possible.	Priority:	500

   Enterprise Custom Fields
   Department:

Custom Field Name	Value

   Help   Statistics...   OK   Cancel

   In the Project Information dialog box, you can see the finish date as the project is currently scheduled. Note that you can edit the start date of the project here, but not its finish date. Project has calculated this finish date based on the start date plus the overall duration of the project.

   Next, you will look at the duration values for this project.

4. In the **Project Information** dialog box, click **Statistics**.

   The Project Statistics dialog box appears. Here again, you can see the project's current start and finish dates.

This project currently has no baseline and actual work reported, so you see *NA* in the Baseline, Actual Start, and Actual Finish fields and zero values in the Actual Duration and Actual Work fields.

Note also that the cost value is the same as what you saw in the Task Sheet view.

5. Click **Close** to close the **Project Statistics** dialog box.

CLEAN UP Close the Advanced Plan file.

Key Points

● A work resource's maximum units (Max. Units) value and his or her working time (as set by the resource calendar) determine when the resource becomes overallocated.

● The Resource Usage view enables you to view the details of assignments that cause resource overallocation.

● You can manually or automatically resolve resource overallocations.

● You can view cost details from the individual assignment level all the way to the entire project level.

Chapter at a Glance

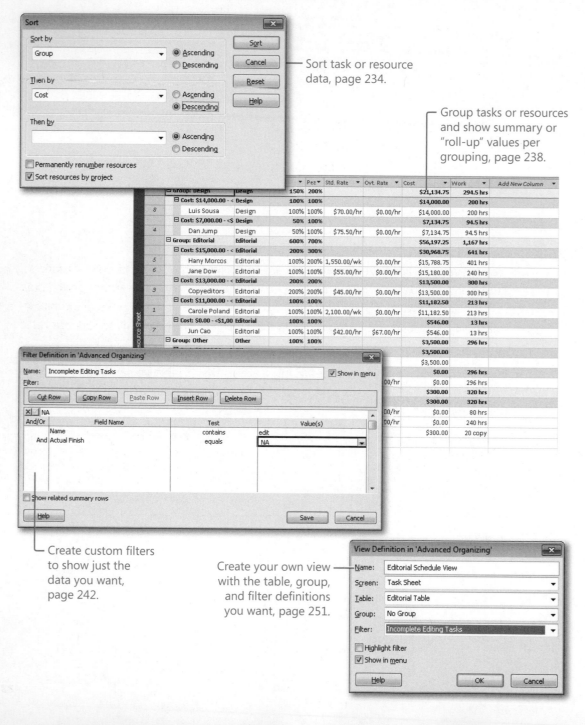

Sort task or resource data, page 234.

Group tasks or resources and show summary or "roll-up" values per grouping, page 238.

Create custom filters to show just the data you want, page 242.

Create your own view with the table, group, and filter definitions you want, page 251.

11 Organizing Project Details

In this chapter, you will learn how to:

✔ Sort task and resource data.

✔ Display task and resource data in groups.

✔ Filter or highlight task and resource data.

✔ Create a custom table.

✔ Create a custom view.

After you've built a project plan, chances are you will need to examine specific aspects of the plan for your own analysis or to share with other *stakeholders*. Although the built-in *views*, *tables*, and *reports* in Microsoft Project 2010 provide many ways to examine a project plan, you might need to organize information to suit your own specific needs.

In this chapter, you use some of the formatting tools in Project to change the way your data appears. Project includes many features that enable you to organize and analyze data that otherwise would require separate tools, such as a spreadsheet application.

> **Practice Files** Before you can complete the exercises in this chapter, you need to copy the book's practice files to your computer. A complete list of practice files is provided in "Using the Practice Files" at the beginning of this book. For each exercise that has a practice file, simply browse to where you saved the book's practice file folder.

Important If you are running Project Professional, you may need to make a one-time setting change. This helps ensure that the practice files you work with in this chapter do not affect your Project Server data. For more information, see Appendix C, "Using the Practice Files if Connected to Project Server."

Sorting Project Details

Sorting is the simplest way to reorganize task or resource data in Project. You can sort tasks or resources by predefined criteria, or you can create your own sort order with up to three levels of nesting. For example, you can sort resources by resource group (this is the value in the Group field—*Design, Editorial,* and so on) and then sort by cost within each resource group.

Like grouping and filtering, which you will work with later in this chapter, sorting does not (with one exception) change the underlying data of your project plan; it simply reorders the data you have in the active view. The one exception is the option that Project offers to renumber task or resource IDs after sorting.

When you sort data, the sort order applies to the active view regardless of the specific table currently displayed in the view. For example, if you sort the Gantt Chart view by start date while displaying the Entry table and then switch to the Cost table, you'll see the tasks sorted by start date in the Cost table. You can also sort in most views that do not include a table, such as the Resource Graph view.

It's fine to renumber tasks or resources permanently if that's what you intend to do. For example, when building a resource list, you might enter resource names in the order in which the resources join your project. Later, when the list is complete, you might want to sort them alphabetically by name and permanently renumber them.

In the new book plan at Lucerne Publishing, each resource is assigned to one of several resource groups. These groups have names such as *Design, Editorial,* and other names that pertain to a book publisher. For your project plans, you might use resource groups to represent functional teams, departments, or whatever most logically describes collections of similar resources.

Sorting all resources by resource group enables you to see the costs associated with each resource group more easily. This can help you plan your project's budget. You can also sort resources within each group by cost from most to least expensive.

In this exercise, you sort a resource view by cost.

SET UP Start Project if it's not already running.

You need the Advanced Organizing_Start project plan located in your Chapter11 practice file folder to complete this exercise. Open the Advanced Organizing_Start project plan, and then follow these steps.

1. On the **File** tab, click **Save As**.

   The Save As dialog box appears.

2. In the **File name** box, type **Advanced Organizing**, and then click **Save**.

3. On the **View** tab, in the **Resource Views** group, click **Resource Sheet**.

   The Resource Sheet view appears. By default, the Entry table appears in the Resource Sheet view; however, the Entry table includes pay rates but does not display the total cost field per resource. You will switch to the Summary table instead.

4. On the **View** tab, in the **Data** group, click **Tables** and then click **Summary**.

   The Summary table appears.

	Resource Name	Group	Max.	Pea	Std. Rate	Ovt. Rate	Cost	Work	Add New Column
1	Carole Poland	Editorial	100%	100%	2,100.00/wk	$0.00/hr	$11,182.50	213 hrs	
2	Color Setting Service	Production	200%	100%	$0.00/hr	$0.00/hr	$0.00	80 hrs	
3	Copyeditors	Editorial	200%	200%	$45.00/hr	$0.00/hr	$13,500.00	300 hrs	
4	Dan Jump	Design	50%	100%	$75.50/hr	$0.00/hr	$7,134.75	94.5 hrs	
5	Hany Morcos	Editorial	100%	200%	1,550.00/wk	$0.00/hr	$15,788.75	401 hrs	
6	Jane Dow	Editorial	100%	100%	$55.00/hr	$0.00/hr	$15,180.00	240 hrs	
7	Jun Cao	Editorial	100%	100%	$42.00/hr	$67.00/hr	$546.00	13 hrs	
8	Luis Sousa	Design	100%	100%	$70.00/hr	$0.00/hr	$14,000.00	200 hrs	
9	Printing Service	Production	100%	100%	$0.00/hr	$0.00/hr	$0.00	240 hrs	
10	Tad Orman	Other	100%	100%	$0.00/hr	$0.00/hr	$0.00	296 hrs	
11	Travel	Other		0%			$3,500.00		
12	Bound galley proof	Production		y/day	$15.00		$300.00	20 copy	

You are now ready to sort the Resource Sheet view.

New In
2010

5. Click the **AutoFilter** arrow in the **Cost** column heading, and in the menu that appears, click **Sort Largest to Smallest**.

   Tip If you do not see the AutoFilter arrows in the column headings, try this: on the View tab, in the Data group, in the Filter box, click Display AutoFilter.

   The Resource Sheet view is sorted by the Cost column in descending order.

You can quickly sort a table by clicking on the AutoFilter arrow. ⌐

	Resource Name	Group	Max.	Pea	Std. Rate	Ovt. Rate	Cost	Work	Add New Column
5	Hany Morcos	Editorial	100%	200%	1,550.00/wk	$0.00/hr	$15,788.75	401 hrs	
6	Jane Dow	Editorial	100%	100%	$55.00/hr	$0.00/hr	$15,180.00	240 hrs	
8	Luis Sousa	Design	100%	100%	$70.00/hr	$0.00/hr	$14,000.00	200 hrs	
3	Copyeditors	Editorial	200%	200%	$45.00/hr	$0.00/hr	$13,500.00	300 hrs	
1	Carole Poland	Editorial	100%	100%	2,100.00/wk	$0.00/hr	$11,182.50	213 hrs	
4	Dan Jump	Design	50%	100%	$75.50/hr	$0.00/hr	$7,134.75	94.5 hrs	
11	Travel	Other		0%			$3,500.00		
7	Jun Cao	Editorial	100%	100%	$42.00/hr	$67.00/hr	$546.00	13 hrs	
12	Bound galley proof	Production		y/day	$15.00		$300.00	20 copy	
2	Color Setting Service	Production	200%	100%	$0.00/hr	$0.00/hr	$0.00	80 hrs	
9	Printing Service	Production	100%	100%	$0.00/hr	$0.00/hr	$0.00	240 hrs	
10	Tad Orman	Other	100%	100%	$0.00/hr	$0.00/hr	$0.00	296 hrs	

Resource Sheet

This arrangement is fine for viewing resource costs in the entire project, but perhaps you'd like to see this data organized by resource group. To see this, you'll apply a two-level sort order.

6. On the **View** tab, in the **Data** group, click **Sort**, and then click **Sort By**.

   The Sort dialog box appears. In it, you can apply up to three nested levels of sort criteria.

7. Under **Sort By**, click **Group** on the drop-down list, and next to that, click **Ascending**.

   Tip When selecting items from a list like this, you can often begin typing the name of the item you want, and when its full name appears, select it.

   Group here refers to the Resource Group field, which, for the new book project, contains values like *Design* and *Editorial*; these are the groups with which most of the resources in the project plan are associated. These values were previously added to the project plan for you.

8. Under **Then By** (in the center of the dialog box), click **Cost** on the drop-down list, and next to that, click **Descending**.

   Tip You can sort by any field, not just the fields visible in the active view. However, it's helpful to see the field by which you sort—in this case, the *Cost* field.

9. Make sure that the **Permanently renumber resources** check box is cleared.

Sort		
Sort by		Sort
Group ▼	● Ascending / ○ Descending	Cancel
Then by		Reset
Cost ▼	○ Ascending / ● Descending	Help
Then by		
▼	● Ascending / ○ Descending	
☐ Permanently renumber resources		
☑ Sort resources by project		

Important The "Permanently renumber resources" (or, when in a task view, the "Permanently renumber tasks") check box in the Sort dialog box is a Project-level (that is, application) setting; if selected, it permanently renumbers resources or tasks in any Project plan in which you sort. Because you might not want to renumber resources or tasks permanently every time you sort, it's a good idea to keep this check box cleared.

10. Click **Sort**.

Project sorts the Resource Sheet view to display resources by group (*Design, Editorial*, and so on) and then by cost within each group.

	Resource Name ▼	Group ▼	Max. ▼	Pea▼	Std. Rate ▼	Ovt. Rate ▼	Cost ▼	Work ▼	Add New Column ▼
8	Luis Sousa	Design	100%	100%	$70.00/hr	$0.00/hr	$14,000.00	200 hrs	
4	Dan Jump	Design	50%	100%	$75.50/hr	$0.00/hr	$7,134.75	94.5 hrs	
5	Hany Morcos	Editorial	100%	200%	1,550.00/wk	$0.00/hr	$15,788.75	401 hrs	
6	Jane Dow	Editorial	100%	100%	$55.00/hr	$0.00/hr	$15,180.00	240 hrs	
3	Copyeditors	Editorial	200%	200%	$45.00/hr	$0.00/hr	$13,500.00	300 hrs	
1	Carole Poland	Editorial	100%	100%	2,100.00/wk	$0.00/hr	$11,182.50	213 hrs	
7	Jun Cao	Editorial	100%	100%	$42.00/hr	$67.00/hr	$546.00	13 hrs	
11	Travel	Other		0%			$3,500.00		
10	Tad Orman	Other	100%	100%	$0.00/hr	$0.00/hr	$0.00	296 hrs	
12	Bound galley proof	Production		y/day	$15.00		$300.00	20 copy	
2	Color Setting Service	Production	200%	100%	$0.00/hr	$0.00/hr	$0.00	80 hrs	
9	Printing Service	Production	100%	100%	$0.00/hr	$0.00/hr	$0.00	240 hrs	

This sort offers an easy way to identify the most expensive resources in each resource group working on the new book project.

To conclude this exercise, you'll re-sort the resource information to return it to its original order.

11. On the **View** tab, in the **Data** group, click **Sort**, and then click **by ID.**

Project re-sorts the resource list by resource ID.

Reordered ID numbers give you a visual indication that a task or resource view has been sorted. If you see that a sort has been applied but you don't know which one, you can look in the Sort By dialog box. You cannot save custom sort settings that you have specified as you can with grouping and filtering. However, the sort order that you most recently specified will remain in effect until you re-sort the view.

Grouping Project Details

As you develop a project plan, you can use the views available in Project to view and analyze your data in several ways. One important way to see the data in task and resource views is by grouping. *Grouping* allows you to organize task or resource information (or, when in a usage view, assignment information) according to criteria you choose. For example, rather than viewing the resource list in the Resource Sheet view sorted by ID, you can view resources sorted by cost. Grouping goes a step beyond just sorting, however. Grouping adds summary values, or "roll-ups," at intervals that you can customize. For example, you can group resources by their cost, with a $1,000 interval between groups.

Grouping changes the way that you view your task or resource data, allowing for a more refined level of data analysis and presentation. Grouping doesn't change the underlying structure of your project plan; it simply reorganizes and summarizes the data. As with sorting, when you group data in a view, the grouping applies to all tables that you can display in the view. You can also group the Network Diagram view, which does not contain a table.

Project includes several predefined group definitions for tasks and resources, such as grouping tasks by duration or resources by standard pay rate. You can also customize any of the built-in groups or create your own.

In this exercise, you group resources and create a custom grouping definition.

1. On the **View** tab, in the **Data** group, click the arrow on the **Group By:** button, and then click **Resource Group**.

New In
2010

Tip Since the Group column is visible in the Resource Sheet view, you can also click the AutoFilter arrow in the Group column heading, and in the menu that appears, click **Group on this field**.

Project reorganizes the resource data into resource groups, adds summary values per group, and presents the data in an expanded outline form.

	Resource Name	Group	Max.	Pea	Std. Rate	Ovt. Rate	Cost	Work	Add New Column
	⊟ **Group: Design**	**Design**	**150%**	**200%**			**$21,134.75**	**294.5 hrs**	
4	Dan Jump	Design	50%	100%	$75.50/hr	$0.00/hr	$7,134.75	94.5 hrs	
8	Luis Sousa	Design	100%	100%	$70.00/hr	$0.00/hr	$14,000.00	200 hrs	
	⊟ **Group: Editorial**	**Editorial**	**600%**	**700%**			**$56,197.25**	**1,167 hrs**	
1	Carole Poland	Editorial	100%	100%	2,100.00/wk	$0.00/hr	$11,182.50	213 hrs	
3	Copyeditors	Editorial	200%	200%	$45.00/hr	$0.00/hr	$13,500.00	300 hrs	
5	Hany Morcos	Editorial	100%	200%	1,550.00/wk	$0.00/hr	$15,788.75	401 hrs	
6	Jane Dow	Editorial	100%	100%	$55.00/hr	$0.00/hr	$15,180.00	240 hrs	
7	Jun Cao	Editorial	100%	100%	$42.00/hr	$67.00/hr	$546.00	13 hrs	
	⊟ **Group: Other**	**Other**	**100%**	**100%**			**$3,500.00**	**296 hrs**	
10	Tad Orman	Other	100%	100%	$0.00/hr	$0.00/hr	$0.00	296 hrs	
11	Travel	Other		0%			$3,500.00		
	⊟ **Group: Production**	**Production**	**300%**	**200%**			**$300.00**	**320 hrs**	
2	Color Setting Serv	Production	200%	100%	$0.00/hr	$0.00/hr	$0.00	80 hrs	
9	Printing Service	Production	100%	100%	$0.00/hr	$0.00/hr	$0.00	240 hrs	
12	Bound galley prod	Production		y/day	$15.00		$300.00	20 copy	

This grouping is similar to the sorting that you did in the previous section, but this time you will see summary cost values for each resource group.

Project applies light-colored formatting to the summary data rows. Because the summary data is derived from subordinate data, you cannot edit it directly. Displaying these summary values has no effect on the cost or schedule calculations of the project plan.

To give yourself more control over how Project organizes and presents the data, you'll now create a group.

Before you create a custom group and additional customizations throughout this chapter, however, you'll make one change to Project's settings. You'll make this adjustment to prevent this custom group from becoming available in other project plans that you may work with that are unrelated to this training material.

2. Click the **File** tab, and then click **Options**.

The Project Options dialog box appears.

3. Click the **Advanced** tab, and under **Display**, clear the **Automatically add new views, tables, filters, and groups to the global** check box.

4. Click **OK** to close the **Project Options** dialog box.

   With that housekeeping chore completed, you are ready to create a custom group.

5. On the **View** tab, in the **Data** group, click the arrow on the **Group By:** button, and then click **More Groups**.

   The More Groups dialog box appears.

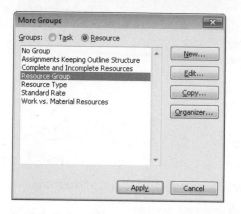

In this dialog box, you can see all of the available predefined groups for tasks (when in a task view) and resources (when in a resource view). Your new group will be most similar to the Resource Group, so you'll start by copying it.

6. Make sure that **Resource Group** is selected, and then click **Copy**.

   The Group Definition dialog box appears.

7. In the **Name** box, select the displayed text, and then type **Resource Groups by Cost**.

8. In the **Field Name** column, click the first empty cell below *Group*.

9. Type or select **Cost**.

10. In the **Order** column for the **Cost** field, select **Descending**.

    The resources will be grouped based on the values in the Group field, and then by the Cost field from highest to lowest.

Next, you'll fine-tune the cost intervals at which Project will group the resources.

11. With the **Cost** row still selected, click **Define Group Intervals**.

    The Define Group Interval dialog box appears.

12. In the **Group on** box, select **Interval**.

13. In the **Group interval** box, type **1000**.

14. Click **OK**.

15. Click **Save** to close the **Group Definition** dialog box.

    The new group, *Resource Groups by Cost*, now appears in the More Groups dialog box.

16. Click **Apply**.

Project applies the new group to the Resource Sheet view.

Resource Name	Group	Max.	Peak	Std. Rate	Ovt. Rate	Cost	Work	Add New Column
⊟ Group: Design	Design	150%	200%			$21,134.75	294.5 hrs	
⊟ Cost: $14,000.00 - <	Design	100%	100%			$14,000.00	200 hrs	
8 Luis Sousa	Design	100%	100%	$70.00/hr	$0.00/hr	$14,000.00	200 hrs	
⊟ Cost: $7,000.00 - <$	Design	50%	100%			$7,134.75	94.5 hrs	
4 Dan Jump	Design	50%	100%	$75.50/hr	$0.00/hr	$7,134.75	94.5 hrs	
⊟ Group: Editorial	Editorial	600%	700%			$56,197.25	1,167 hrs	
⊟ Cost: $15,000.00 - <	Editorial	200%	300%			$30,968.75	641 hrs	
5 Hany Morcos	Editorial	100%	200%	1,550.00/wk	$0.00/hr	$15,700.75	401 hrs	
6 Jane Dow	Editorial	100%	100%	$55.00/hr	$0.00/hr	$15,180.00	240 hrs	
⊟ Cost: $13,000.00 - <	Editorial	200%	200%			$13,500.00	300 hrs	
3 Copyeditors	Editorial	200%	200%	$45.00/hr	$0.00/hr	$13,500.00	300 hrs	
⊟ Cost: $11,000.00 - <	Editorial	100%	100%			$11,182.50	213 hrs	
1 Carole Poland	Editorial	100%	100%	2,100.00/wk	$0.00/hr	$11,182.50	213 hrs	
⊟ Cost: $0.00 - <$1,00	Editorial	100%	100%			$546.00	13 hrs	
7 Jun Cao	Editorial	100%	100%	$42.00/hr	$67.00/hr	$546.00	13 hrs	
⊟ Group: Other	Other	100%	100%			$3,500.00	296 hrs	
⊟ Cost: $3,000.00 - <$	Other		0%			$3,500.00		
11 Travel	Other		0%			$3,500.00		
⊟ Cost: $0.00 - <$1,00	Other	100%	100%			$0.00	296 hrs	
10 Tad Orman	Other	100%	100%	$0.00/hr	$0.00/hr	$0.00	296 hrs	
⊟ Group: Production	Production	300%	200%			$300.00	320 hrs	
⊟ Cost: $0.00 - <$1,00	Production	300%	200%			$300.00	320 hrs	
2 Color Setting S	Production	200%	100%	$0.00/hr	$0.00/hr	$0.00	80 hrs	
9 Printing Servic	Production	100%	100%	$0.00/hr	$0.00/hr	$0.00	240 hrs	
12 Bound galley p	Production		y/day	$15.00		$300.00	20 copy	

The resources are grouped by their resource group value (the bands that bind together *Design*, *Editorial*, and so on) and within each group by cost values at $1,000 intervals (the light blue bands).

To conclude this exercise, you'll remove the grouping.

17. On the **View** tab, in the **Data** group, click the arrow on the **Group By:** button, and click **Clear Group**.

Project removes the summary values and outline structure, leaving the original data. Again, displaying or removing a group has no effect on the data in the project.

Tip All predefined groups and any groups you create are available to you through the Group By: button on the View tab. The name of the active group appears in the box next to this button. Click the arrow on the Group By: button to see other group names. If no group is applied to the current table, the words *No Group* appear on the button.

Filtering Project Details

Another useful way to change the way you view Project task and resource information is by filtering. As the name suggests, *filtering* hides task or resource data that does not meet the criteria you specify, displaying only the data in which you're interested. Like grouping, filtering does not change the data in your Project plan; it merely changes the way that data appears.

There are two ways to use filters. You can either apply an AutoFilter or a predefined filter to a view:

- Use *AutoFilters* for ad hoc filtering in any table in Project. Small AutoFilter arrows appear next to the names of column headings. Click the arrow to display a list of criteria by which you can filter the data. Which criteria you see depends on the type of data contained in the column—for example, AutoFilter criteria in a date column include choices such as "Today" and "This month," as well as a Custom option, with which you can specify your own criteria. You use AutoFilter in Project in the same way you might use AutoFilter in Microsoft Excel.

- Apply a predefined or custom filter to view only the task or resource information that meets the criteria of the filter. For example, the Critical Task filter displays only the tasks on the critical path. Some predefined filters, such as the Task Range filter, prompt you to enter specific criteria—for example, a range of task IDs. If a task or resource sheet view has a filter applied, the "Filter Applied" message appears on the status bar. Both types of filters hide rows in task or resource sheet views that do not meet the criteria you specify. You might see gaps in the task or resource ID numbers. The "missing" data is only hidden and not deleted. As with sorting and grouping, when you filter data in a view, the filtering applies to all tables you can display in the view. Views that do not include tables, such as the Calendar and Network Diagram views, also support filtering (through the Filter button on the View tab), but not AutoFilters.

A very similar feature is highlighting. While applying a filter hides information that does not meet your criteria, applying a highlight applies a bright orange format to information that does meet your criteria. Otherwise the two features are nearly identical—you can perform ad hoc highlights or create custom highlights, just as with filters. When a highlight is applied, the message "Highlight Filter Applied" appears on the status bar.

In this exercise, you create a filter that displays only the tasks that include a certain term in their names. Later in the chapter, you'll combine this filter with a custom table in a custom view.

1. On the **View** tab, in the **Task Views** group, click **Gantt Chart**.

   The Gantt Chart view appears. Before you create a filter, you'll quickly see the tasks that you're interested in by applying an AutoFilter.

2. Click the **AutoFilter** arrow in the **Task Name** column heading, point to **Filters**, and then click **Custom**.

The Custom AutoFilter dialog box appears. You'd like to see only the tasks that contain the word *edit*.

3. Under **Name**, select **contains** in the first box.

4. In the adjacent box, type **edit**.

5. Click **OK** to close the **Custom AutoFilter** dialog box.

Project filters the task list to show only the tasks that contain the word *edit* and their summary tasks.

This is a visual indicator that an AutoFilter has been applied to this column.

The status bar indicates when an AutoFilter is applied.

Note that the funnel-shaped filter indicator appears next to the Task Name column label, and the message "AutoFilter Applied" appears on the status bar. These are visual indicators that a custom AutoFilter has been applied to this column.

Tip When an AutoFilter is applied, you can point to the filter indicator and a summary description of the applied filter appears in a ScreenTip. Pointing to the AutoFilter Applied label on the status bar tells you the fields that have been filtered.

Next, you turn off the AutoFilter and create a custom filter.

6. Click the funnel-shaped filter indicator in the **Task Name** column heading, and then click **Clear All Filters**.

    Project toggles the AutoFilter off, redisplaying all tasks in the project plan. Now you are ready to create a custom filter.

7. On the **View** tab, in the **Data** group, click the arrow next to **Filter:** and then click **More Filters**.

    The More Filters dialog box appears. In this dialog box, you can see all the pre-defined filters for tasks (when in a task view) and resources (when in a resource view) that are available to you.

8. Click **New**.

    The Filter Definition dialog box appears.

9. In the **Name** box, type **Incomplete Editing Tasks**.

10. In the first row in the **Field Name** column, type or select **Name**.

11. In the first row in the **Test** column, select **contains**.

12. In the first row in the **Value(s)** column, type **edit**.

    That covers the first criterion for the filter; next, you'll add the second criterion.

13. In the second row in the **And/Or** column, select **And**.

14. In the second row in the **Field Name** column, type or select **Actual Finish**.

15. In the second row in the **Test** column, select **equals**.

16. In the second row in the **Value(s)** column, type **NA**.

NA means "not applicable" and is the way that Project marks some fields that do not yet have a value. In other words, any editing task that does not have an actual finish date must be uncompleted.

17. Click **Save** to close the **Filter Definition** dialog box.

The new filter appears in the More Filters dialog box.

18. In the list of filters, select **Incomplete Editing Tasks**, and then click **Apply**.

Project applies the new filter to the Gantt Chart view.

The name of the applied filter appears here. ⌐

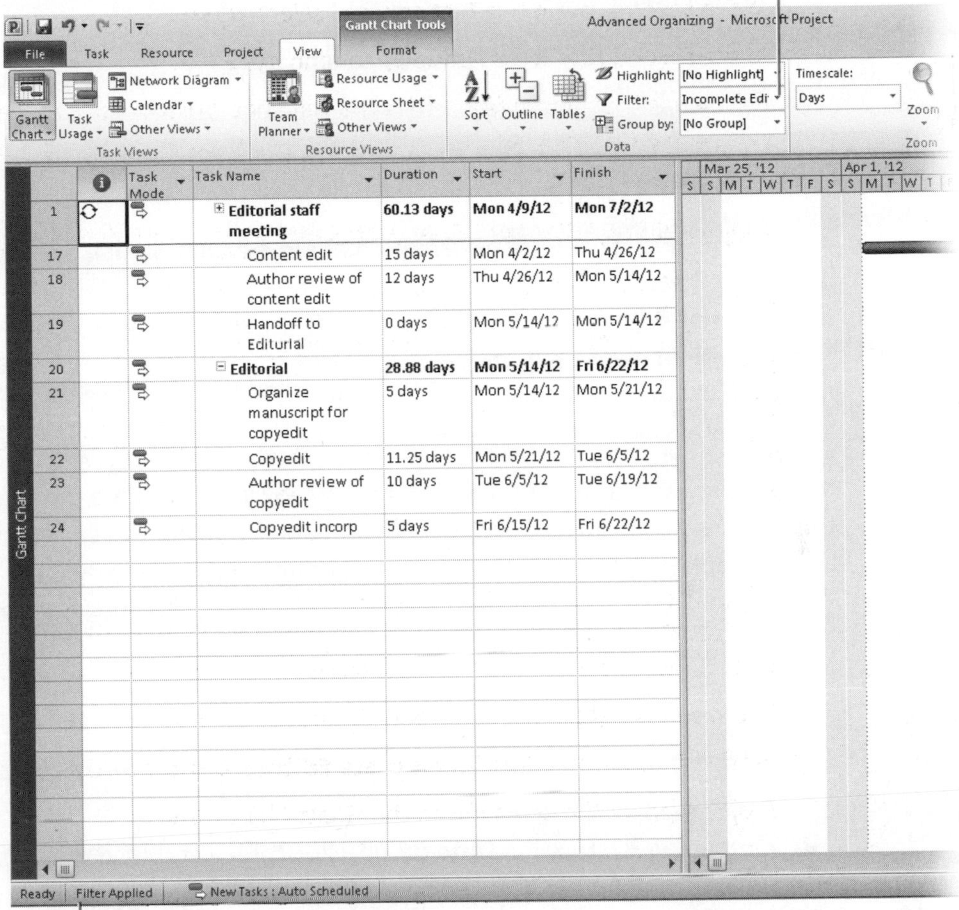

⌐ The status bar indicates when a filter is applied.

The tasks are now filtered to show only the uncompleted editing tasks. Because we haven't started tracking actual work yet, all the editing tasks are uncompleted at this time.

Tip When a filter has been applied, you can point to the Filter Applied label on the status bar to see the name of the filter.

To conclude this exercise, you will remove the filtering.

19. On the **View** tab, in the **Data** group, click the arrow next to **Filter:** and then click **Clear Filter**.

Project removes the filter. As always, displaying or removing a filter has no effect on the original data.

Customizing Tables

A *table* is a spreadsheet-like presentation of project data organized into vertical columns and horizontal rows. Each column represents one of the many fields in Project, and each row represents a single task or resource (or, in usage views, an assignment). The intersection of a column and a row can be called a *cell* (if you're oriented toward spreadsheets) or a *field* (if you think in database terms).

Project includes several tables that can be applied in views. You've already used some of these tables, such as the Entry and Summary tables. Chances are that most of the time, these tables will contain the fields that you want. However, you can modify any predefined table, or you can create a new table that contains only the data you want.

In this exercise, you create a table to display information about editorial tasks in the new book's project plan.

1. On the **View** tab, in the **Task Views** group, click **Other Views**, and then click **Task Sheet**.

Project displays the Task Sheet view.

2. On the **View** tab, in the **Data** group, click **Tables** and then click **More Tables**.

The More Tables dialog box appears. The Entry table should be selected.

In this dialog box, you can see all the available predefined tables for tasks (when in a task view) or resources (when in a resource view).

3. Make sure that **Entry** is selected, and then click **Copy**.

The Table Definition dialog box appears.

4. In the **Name** box, type **Editorial Table**.

Next, you will remove some fields and then add others.

5. In the **Field Name** column, click each of the following field names, and then click the **Delete Row** button after clicking each field name:

Indicators

Task Mode

Predecessors

Next, you will add a field to this table definition.

6. In the **Field Name** column, click **Duration**, and then click **Insert Row**.

Project inserts an empty row above *Duration*.

7. In the **Field Name** column, click the arrow in the new row's empty field name, and then select **Editorial Focus (Text9)** from the drop-down list.

The customized text field *Editorial focus* contains some notes about level of edit required per task. This information was previously customized for you in the project plan.

8. In the **Width** column, type or click **20**.

Table Definition in 'Advanced Organizing'

Name: Editorial Table   ☐ Show in menu
Table

[Cut Row] [Copy Row] [Paste Row] [Insert Row] [Delete Row]

☒ | 20

Field Name	Align Data	Width	Title	Align Title	Header Wrapping	Text Wrapping
ID	Center	6		Left	Yes	No
Name	Left	24	Task Name	Left	Yes	Yes
Editorial Focus	Left	20		Center		
Duration	Left	11		Left	Yes	No
Start	Left	13		Left	Yes	No
Finish	Left	13		Left	Yes	No
Resource Names	Left	17		Left	Yes	No

Date format: Default ▼   Row height: 1 ⬍

☑ Lock first column
☑ Auto-adjust header row heights
☑ Show 'Add New Column' interface

[Help]   [OK] [Cancel]

9. Click **OK** to close the **Table Definition** dialog box.

The new table appears in the More Tables dialog box.

10. Click **Apply**.

Project applies the new table to the Task Sheet view.

	Task Name	Editorial Focus	Duration	Start	Finish	Resource Names	Add New Column
0	⊟ Children's book schedu		158 days	Mon 4/2/12	Thu 11/8/12		
1	⊞ Editorial staff meeting		60.13 days	Mon 4/9/12	Mon 7/2/12		
15	⊟ Acquisition		30.25 days	Mon 4/2/12	Mon 5/14/12		
16	Manuscript receiver		0 days	Mon 4/2/12	Mon 4/2/12		
17	Content edit	Full developmental ec	15 days	Mon 4/2/12	Thu 4/26/12	Carole Poland	
18	Author review of co	Incorp must-fix issues	12 days	Thu 4/26/12	Mon 5/14/12	Tad Orman,Copyed	
19	Handoff to Editorial		0 days	Mon 5/14/12	Mon 5/14/12	Carole Poland	
20	⊟ Editorial		28.88 days	Mon 5/14/12	Fri 6/22/12		
21	Organize manuscrip	Address outstanding li	5 days	Mon 5/14/12	Mon 5/21/12	Hany Morcos,Dan Ji	
22	Copyedit	Style Guide complianc	11.25 days	Mon 5/21/12	Tue 6/5/12	Copyeditors[200%]	
23	Author review of co	Incorp must-fix issues	10 days	Tue 6/5/12	Tue 6/19/12	Tad Orman,Copyed	
24	Copyedit incorp	Incorp must-fix issues	5 days	Fri 6/15/12	Fri 6/22/12	Carole Poland,Dan	
25	Handoff to Producti		0 days	Fri 6/22/12	Fri 6/22/12	Hany Morcos	
26	⊟ Design and Production		53.25 days	Fri 6/22/12	Thu 9/6/12		
27	Set pages		15 days	Fri 6/22/12	Mon 7/16/12	Jane Dow	
28	Interior illustration		15.25 days	Fri 6/22/12	Mon 7/16/12	Luis Sousa,Hany Mc	
29	⊟ 1st Pages review		25 days	Mon 7/16/12	Mon 8/20/12		
30	Proofread and in		10 days	Mon 7/16/12	Mon 7/30/12	Tad Orman,Copyed	

Tip You can add or remove columns quickly in the current table. To add a column, first select the column to the right of the spot where you want to add a new column. Then, on the Format tab, in the Columns group, click Insert Column. Project displays all fields available for the type of table you have displayed (task or resource); select the one that you want to add. To remove a column, right-click the column heading and click Hide Column.

In the next section, you will combine the custom filter with this custom table to create an editorial schedule view for the new book project.

New In
2010

Create Custom Fields Quickly

In this section, you saw a custom field, *Text9,* that had been customized to say "Editorial focus" and contained details about editing activities in the new book's project plan. Project supports a wide range of custom fields, and you can add a custom field to any table easily. The rightmost column in a table is labeled "Add New Column," and you can either click the column heading and select any field you wish to add, or you can just start typing in a cell in the Add New Column column. Project detects the type of data you're typing and adds the correct custom field type. The custom fields supported by Project include:

- Cost (up to 10 cost fields)
- Date (up to 10 date fields)
- Duration (up to 10 duration fields)
- Flag (up to 20 "Yes" or "No" fields)
- Number (up to 20 number fields)
- Text (up to 30 text fields)

These custom fields are a great way to store additional information about tasks or resources in your project plans. Normally, none of these custom fields have any impact on the scheduling of tasks or resources.

Customizing Views

Nearly all work you perform in Project occurs in a *view.* A view might contain elements such as tables, groups, and filters. You can combine these with other elements (such as a timescaled grid in a usage view) or with graphic elements (such as the graphic representation of tasks in the chart portion of the Gantt Chart view).

Project includes dozens of views that organize information for specific purposes. You might find that you need to see your project information in some way that is not available in the predefined views. If Project's available views do not meet your needs, you can edit an existing view or create your own view.

In this exercise, you create a new view that combines the custom filter and custom table that you created in the previous sections.

1. On the **View** tab, in the **Task Views** group, click **Other Views**, and then click **More Views**.

   The More Views dialog box appears.

   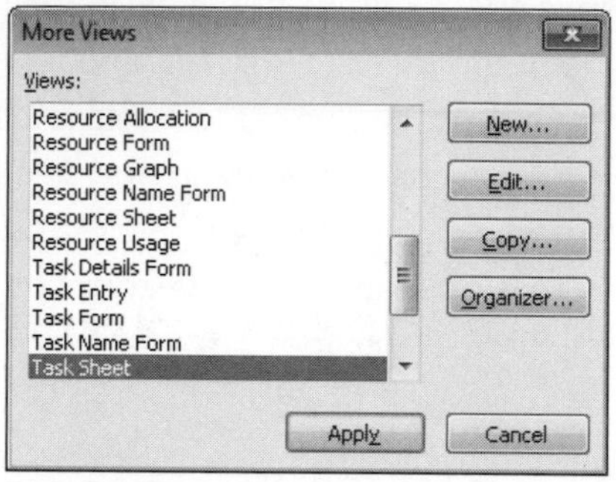
   More Views
Views:
Resource Allocation
Resource Form
Resource Graph
Resource Name Form
Resource Sheet
Resource Usage
Task Details Form
Task Entry
Task Form
Task Name Form
Task Sheet
New...
Edit...
Copy...
Organizer...
Apply
Cancel

   In this dialog box, you can see all the predefined views available to you.

2. Click **New**.

   The Define New View dialog box appears. Most views occupy a single pane, but a view can consist of two separate panes. In fact, the default view in Project is really a two-pane view: the Gantt Chart and the Timeline.

3. Make sure **Single View** is selected, and then click **OK**.

   The View Definition dialog box appears.

4. In the **Name** box, type **Editorial Schedule View**.

   This is the name that you will see in the Project interface later.

5. In the **Screen** box, select **Task Sheet** from the drop-down list.

   The Screen box lists the types of views available.

6. In the **Table** box, select **Editorial Table** from the drop-down list.

   Editorial Table is the custom table that you created earlier.

7. In the **Group** box, select **No Group** from the drop-down list.

8. In the **Filter** box, select **Incomplete Editing Tasks** from the drop-down list.

   Incomplete Editing Tasks is the custom filter that you created earlier.

   Note The specific tables, group, and filters listed in the drop-down lists depend on the type of view you selected in the Screen box in step 5.

9. Make sure that the **Show in menu** check box is selected.

View Definition in 'Advanced Organizing'	☒
Name:	Editorial Schedule View
Screen:	Task Sheet ▼
Table:	Editorial Table ▼
Group:	No Group ▼
Filter:	Incomplete Editing Tasks ▼

☐ Highlight filter
☑ Show in menu

| Help | | OK | Cancel |

10. Click **OK** to close the **View Definition in** dialog box.

The new view appears and should be selected in the More Views dialog box.

11. Click **Apply**.

Project applies the new view.

	Task Name	Editorial Focus ▼	Duration ▼	Start ▼	Finish ▼	Resource Names ▼	Add New Column ▼
1	⊞ **Editorial staff meeting**		**60.13 days**	**Mon 4/9/12**	**Mon 7/2/12**		
17	Content edit	Full developmental ec	15 days	Mon 4/2/12	Thu 4/26/12	Carole Poland	
18	Author review of cc	Incorp must-fix issues	12 days	Thu 4/26/12	Mon 5/14/12	Tad Orman,Copyed	
19	Handoff to Editorial		0 days	Mon 5/14/12	Mon 5/14/12	Carole Poland	
20	⊟ **Editorial**		**28.88 days**	**Mon 5/14/12**	**Fri 6/22/12**		
21	Organize manuscrip	Address outstanding li	5 days	Mon 5/14/12	Mon 5/21/12	Hany Morcos,Dan Ji	
22	Copyedit	Style Guide compliance	11.25 days	Mon 5/21/12	Tue 6/5/12	Copyeditors[200%]	
23	Author review of cc	Incorp must-fix issues	10 days	Tue 6/5/12	Tue 6/19/12	Tad Orman,Copyed	
24	Copyedit incorp	Incorp must-fix issues	5 days	Fri 6/15/12	Fri 6/22/12	Carole Poland,Dan	

The name of the custom view appears here.

Only uncompleted editorial tasks are now displayed, and the fields are presented in the way that you want them. Also, Project added *Editorial Schedule View* to the Other Views list in the Task Views group on the View tab. The new view appears under the Custom label, so it is always easily accessible in this project plan.

Because of the housekeeping adjustment that you performed earlier in this chapter, the new custom view is not available in other project plans. However when you create your own custom views, you probably will want them available in any project plan, so we'll change the display setting back to the default. That way, any custom views that you create in the future will be available in any project plan you work with.

12. Click the **File** tab, and then click **Options**.

    The Project Options dialog box appears.

13. Click the **Advanced** tab, and under **Display**, check the **Automatically add new views, tables, filters, and groups to the global** check box.

14. Click **OK** to close the **Project Options** dialog box.

✖ CLEAN UP Close the Advanced Organizing file.

Key Points

- Common ways of organizing data in Project include sorting, grouping, and filtering. In all cases, Project never deletes the data; it simply changes what is displayed and how it appears.

- Project includes many built-in sort orders, groupings, and filters, and you can also create your own.

- Whereas sorting and filtering rearrange or selectively show only some data in a project plan, grouping adds summary values or "roll-ups" of values, such as costs, based on whatever interval you choose.

- Tables are the primary elements of most views in Project. Project includes several built-in tables, and you can also create your own.

- You work with data in Project via views. Views may contain tables, groups, filters, and in some cases graphical charts. The Gantt Chart view, for example, consists of a table on the left and a timescaled chart on the right.

- Project contains many built-in views, and you can also create your own.

- By default, any new views, tables, filters, and groups you create in one project plan are also available in all other project plans you work with in Project. This behavior is controlled by the setting in the Project Options dialog box.

Chapter at a Glance

Update a baseline prior to tracking actual work, page 258.

Enter actual work values for tasks and assignments, page 263.

Enter timephased actual work for tasks and assignments, page 269.

Interrupt work on the project to restart after the date you specify, page 274.

12 Tracking Progress on Tasks and Assignments

In this chapter, you will learn how to:

✔ Update a previously saved baseline plan.

✔ Record actual work for tasks and assignments.

✔ Record actual work by time period.

✔ Interrupt work on a task and specify the date on which the task should start again.

Building, verifying, and communicating a sound project plan might take much or even most of your time as a project manager. However, *planning* is only the first phase of managing your projects. After the planning is completed, the implementation of the project starts—carrying out the plan that was previously developed. Ideally, projects are implemented exactly as planned, but this is seldom the case. In general, the more complex the project plan and the longer its planned duration, the more opportunity there is for variance to appear. *Variance* is the difference between what you thought would happen (as recorded in the project plan) and what really happened (as recorded by your tracking efforts).

Properly tracking actual work and comparing it against the original plan enables you to identify variance early and adjust the incomplete portion of the plan when necessary. If you completed Chapter 6, "Tracking Progress on Tasks," you were introduced to the simpler ways of *tracking actuals* in a project plan. These include recording the percentage of a task that has been completed as well as its actual start and finish dates. These methods of tracking progress are fine for many projects, but Microsoft Project 2010 also supports more detailed ways of tracking.

In this chapter, you track task-level and assignment-level *work* totals and work per time period, such as work completed per week or per day. Information distributed over time is commonly known as timephased, so tracking work by time period is sometimes referred to as tracking timephased actuals. This is the most detailed level of tracking progress available in Project.

As with simpler tracking methods, tracking timephased actuals is a way to address the most basic questions of managing a project:

● Are tasks starting and finishing as planned? If not, what will be the impact on the project's finish date?

● Are resources spending more or less time than planned to complete tasks?

● Is it taking more or less money than planned to complete tasks?

As a project manager, you must determine what level of tracking best meets the needs of your project plan and stakeholders. As you might expect, the more detailed the tracking level, the more effort required from you and the resources assigned to tasks. This chapter exposes you to the most detailed tracking methods available in Project.

In this chapter, you work with different means of tracking work and handling incomplete work. You begin, however, by updating the project baseline.

> **Practice Files** Before you can complete the exercises in this chapter, you need to copy the book's practice files to your computer. A complete list of practice files is provided in "Using the Practice Files" at the beginning of this book. For each exercise that has a practice file, simply browse to where you saved the book's practice file folder.

Important If you are running Microsoft Project Professional, you may need to make a one-time setting change. This helps ensure that the practice files you work with in this chapter do not affect your Project Server data. For more information, see Appendix C, "Using the Practice Files if Connected to Project Server."

Updating a Baseline

If you completed Chapter 6, you saved a baseline plan for a project plan. Recall that a *baseline* is a collection of important values in a project plan, such as the planned start dates, finish dates, and costs of *tasks*, *resources*, and *assignments*. When you save (or set) a baseline, Project takes a "snapshot" of the existing values and saves it in the Project plan for future comparison.

Keep in mind that the purpose of the baseline is to record what you expected the project plan to look like at one point in time. As time passes, however, you might need to change your expectations. After saving an initial baseline plan, you might need to fine-tune the project plan by adding or removing tasks or assignments, and so on. To keep an accurate baseline for later comparison, you have several options:

- **Update the baseline for the entire project.** This simply replaces the original baseline values with the currently scheduled values.

- **Update the baseline for selected tasks.** This does not affect the baseline values for other tasks or resource baseline values in the project plan.

- **Save a second or subsequent baseline.** You can save up to 11 baselines in a single plan. The first one is called Baseline, and the rest are Baseline 1 through Baseline 10.

Since you completed the initial planning for the new book project at Lucerne Publishing, the plan has undergone some additional fine-tuning. This includes some adjustments to task durations, a new task in the Editorial phase, and some deactivated (or deleted) tasks in the Design and Production phase. Because of these changes, the initial baseline does not quite match the project plan as it is currently scheduled.

In this exercise, you compare the project plan as it is currently scheduled with the baseline plan and update the baseline for the project plan.

SET UP Start Project if it's not already running.

You need the Advanced Tracking A_Start project plan located in your Chapter 12 practice file folder to complete this exercise. Open the Advanced Tracking A_Start project plan, and then follow these steps.

1. On the **File** tab, click **Save As**.

   The Save As dialog box appears.

2. In the **File name** box, type **Advanced Tracking A**, and then click **Save**.

   Next, you will switch to a different view to see baseline and scheduled values arranged for easy comparison.

3. On the **View** tab, in the **Task Views** group, click the down arrow below the **Gantt Chart** button and then click **Tracking Gantt**.

   The Tracking Gantt view appears.

In the chart portion of this view, the tasks as they are currently scheduled appear as blue bars (if they are not *critical tasks*) or red bars (if they are critical). Below them, the baseline values of each task appear as gray bars.

Tip In Gantt Chart views, the colors, patterns, and shapes of the bars represent specific things. To see what any item on the Gantt chart represents, just point your mouse pointer at it and a description will appear in a ScreenTip. To see a complete legend of Gantt chart items and their formatting, on the Format tab, in the Bar Styles group, click Format and then click Bar Styles.

4. In the **Task Name** column, click the name of task 18, *Original art review*.

5. On the **Task** tab, in the **Editing** group, click **Scroll to Task**.

   The Tracking Gantt view scrolls to display the Gantt bar for task 18, *Original art review*. This task was added to the plan after the initial baseline was saved. As you can see in the Tracking Gantt view, this task has no baseline bar, indicating that it has no baseline values.

   To get a broader look at the project plan's baseline, you'll adjust the zoom level.

6. On the **View** tab, in the **Zoom** group, in the **Timescale** box, click **Weeks**.

   You can see that currently none of the later tasks in the project plan match their baselines.

This task was added to the project plan after its initial —
baseline was saved, so this task has no baseline bar.

To conclude this exercise, you will resave the baseline for the project plan. Doing so will update all baseline information for tasks, resources, and assignments prior to tracking progress.

Tip This project plan includes a previously saved baseline that you will now overwrite. That's fine at this stage of the new book project, where the planning is complete and you'd like to have the most up-to-date baseline before recording any actual work. However, after work has been recorded, you should be careful about overwriting any previously saved baseline values. Once you overwrite a baseline, the original values are replaced and cannot be retrieved. Saving additional baselines is often a better strategy after work on the project has begun.

7. On the **Project** tab, in the **Schedule** group, click **Set Baseline**, and then click **Set Baseline**.

The Set Baseline dialog box appears.

8. Make sure that the **Set Baseline** option is selected. In the **For** area, make sure that the **Entire project** option is selected.

Tip To update a baseline just for selected tasks, you can click Selected Tasks under the For label. When you do this, the options under Roll Up Baselines become available. You can control how baseline updates should affect the baseline values for summary tasks. For example, you could resave a baseline for a subtask and update its related summary task baseline values if desired. To remove a baseline, on the Project tab, in the Schedule group, click the Set Baseline button and then click Clear Baseline.

9. Click **OK** to update the baseline.

   Project alerts you that you are about to overwrite the previously saved baseline values.

10. Click **Yes**.

   Project updates the baseline values for the project plan.

After resaving the baseline for the entire project,
the baseline start, finish, and duration values
(among others) match the scheduled values.

Task 18 now has a baseline, and all of the other tasks' baseline values now match their scheduled values.

CLEAN UP Close the Advanced Tracking A file.

Saving Interim Plans

After you've started tracking actual values or any time you've adjusted your schedule, you might want to take another snapshot of the current start and finish dates. You can do this with an interim plan. Like a baseline, an *interim plan* is a set of current values from the project plan that Project saves with the file. Unlike the baseline, however, an interim plan saves only the start and finish dates of tasks, not resource or assignment values. You can save up to 10 different interim plans during a project. (If you find that you need multiple snapshots of scheduled values in addition to start and finish dates, you should instead save additional baselines.)

Depending on the scope and duration of your projects, you might want to save an interim plan at any of the following junctures:

- At the conclusion of a major phase of work
- At preset time intervals, such as weekly or monthly
- Just before or after entering a large number of actual values

To save an interim plan, on the Project tab, in the Schedule group, click Set Baseline and then click Set Baseline. In the Set Baseline dialog box, select the "Set interim plan" option. To learn more about interim plans, click the Help button (which looks like a question mark) in the upper-right corner of the Project window, and in the Help Search box, type **Create an interim plan**.

Tracking Actual and Remaining Values for Tasks and Assignments

If you completed Chapter 6, you entered actual start, finish, and duration values for individual tasks. For tasks that have resources assigned to them, you can enter actual and remaining work values for the task as a whole or for specific assignments to that task. To help you understand how Project handles the actual values you enter, consider the following:

- If a task has a single resource assigned to it, the actual work values that you enter for the task or assignment apply equally to both the task and the resource. For example, if you record that the assignment started on April 23 and has five hours of actual work, those values apply to the task and to the assigned resource.

- If a task has multiple resources assigned to it, the actual work values that you enter for the task are distributed among or rolled down to the assignments according to their assignment units. This level of detail is appropriate if you aren't concerned about the details at the individual assignment level.

- If a task has multiple resources assigned to it, the actual work values that you enter for one assignment are rolled up to the task. However, the new actual work values do not affect the other assignments' work values on the task. This level of detail is appropriate if details at the individual assignment level are important to you.

In this exercise, you record task-level and assignment-level actuals and see how the information is rolled up or down between tasks and assignments.

Open Advanced Tracking B_Start from the Chapter12 folder, and then follow these steps.

1. On the **File** tab, click **Save As**.

   The Save As dialog box appears.

2. In the **File name** box, type **Advanced Tracking B**, and then click **Save**.

   This version of the project plan includes the updated baseline values that you previously saved, as well as the first actuals reported against the first tasks in the Acquisition phase.

3. On the **View** tab, in the **Task Views** group, click **Task Usage**.

   The Task Usage view appears. As you may recall from Chapter 7, "Fine-Tuning Task Details," the two sides of the usage view are split by a vertical divider bar. The Task Usage view lists resources under the tasks to which they're assigned. This information appears in the table on the left side. On the right side, you see rows organized under a timescale. The rows on the right side show you the scheduled work values for each task or assigned resource. The Task Usage view color-codes the rows on the right side: task rows have a shaded background, and assignment rows have a white background.

4. In the **Task Name** column, click the name of task 18, *Original art review*.

5. On the **Task** tab, in the **Editing** group, click **Scroll to Task**.

   The timephased grid on the right side of the view scrolls to display the first scheduled work for the task.

   Next, you'll switch the table and details shown in the view.

6. On the **View** tab, in the **Data** group, click **Tables** and then click **Work**.

   The Work table appears.

	Task Name	Work	Baseline	Variance	Actual	Details			T	W	T	F	S	Apr 22, '12 S	M	T	W	T	F
0	⊟ Children's Book Sched	2,337.5 hrs	2,337.5 hrs	0 hrs	127 hrs	Work		8h		8h	20h	24h			25.5h	24h	24h	19h	16l
1	⊞ Editorial staff meeting	45.5 hrs	45.5 hrs	0 hrs	7 hrs	Work									3.5h				
15	⊟ Acquisition	440 hrs	440 hrs	0 hrs	120 hrs	Work		8h		8h	20h	24h			22h	24h	24h	18h	16l
16	Manuscript receive·	0 hrs	0 hrs	0 hrs	0 hrs	Work													
17	⊟ Content edit	120 hrs	120 hrs	0 hrs	120 hrs	Work		8h		8h	8h	8h			7h	8h	8h	2h	
	Carole Poland	*120 hrs*	*120 hrs*	*0 hrs*	*120 hrs*	Work		8h		8h	8h	8h			7h	8h	8h	2h	
18	⊟ Original art review	160 hrs	160 hrs	0 hrs	0 hrs	Work					12h	16h			15h	16h	16h	16h	16l
	Hany Morcos	*80 hrs*	*80 hrs*	*0 hrs*	*0 hrs*	Work					6h	8h			7h	8h	8h	8h	8l
	Jane Dow	*80 hrs*	*80 hrs*	*0 hrs*	*0 hrs*	Work					6h	8h			8h	8h	8h	8h	8l
19	⊟ Author review of cc	160 hrs	160 hrs	0 hrs	0 hrs	Work													

This table includes the Actual Work and Remaining Work columns that you will work with shortly, although they might not yet be visible. The values in the Work column are the task and assignment totals for scheduled work. Note that each task's work value is the sum of its assignment work values. For example, the work total for task 18, 160 hours, is the sum of Hany Morcos' 80 hours of work on the task and Jane Dow's 80 hours.

Next, you'll change the details shown on the timephased grid on the right side of the view.

7. On the **Format** tab, in the **Details** group, click **Actual Work**.

For each task and assignment, Project now displays the Work and Actual Work rows on the timephased grid on the right side of the view.

When you display the actual work details, the Act. Work row appears in the timephased grid for every assignment, task, and summary task.

Tip You can change the details (that is, fields) shown under the timescale in a usage view. You can add or remove fields and change the formatting of the fields shown. For example, you can add the Baseline Cost field to the fields shown in the usage view and format it with a different colored background. To see the available fields and formatting options, on the Format tab, in the Details group, click Add Details.

In the timephased grid, you see the scheduled work values per day. If you were to add up the daily work values for a specific task or assignment, the total would equal the value in the Work column for that task or assignment. In a usage view, you see work values at two different levels of detail: the total value for a task or assignment and the more detailed timephased level. These two sets of values are directly related.

Next, you'll enter task-level and assignment-level actual work values and see how they are reflected in the timephased details.

8. Using the mouse, drag the vertical divider bar to the right until you can see all the columns in the Work table.

Tip When the mouse pointer is in the correct position to drag the vertical divider bar, it changes to a two-headed arrow that points left and right. Double-clicking the vertical divider bar will snap it to the nearest column's right edge.

To see more or less of the table on the left and the timephase grid on the right, drag the divider bar left or right. Double-clicking the divider bar will snap it to the nearest column.

Task Name	Work	Baseline	Variance	Actual	Remaining	%W. Comp.	Details	W	T	F	S	S	M	T	W
0 Children's Book Sched	2,337.5 hrs	2,337.5 hrs	0 hrs	127 hrs	2,210.5 hrs	5%	Work	8h	20h	24h			25.5h	24h	24h
							Act. W	8h	8h	8h			7h	8h	8h
1 Editorial staff meeting	45.5 hrs	45.5 hrs	0 hrs	7 hrs	38.5 hrs	15%	Work						3.5h		
							Act. W								
15 Acquisition	440 hrs	440 hrs	0 hrs	120 hrs	320 hrs	27%	Work	8h	20h	24h			22h	24h	24h
							Act. W	8h	8h	8h			7h	8h	8h
16 Manuscript received	0 hrs	0 hrs	0 hrs	0 hrs	0 hrs	100%	Work								
							Act. W								
17 Content edit	120 hrs	120 hrs	0 hrs	120 hrs	0 hrs	100%	Work	8h	8h	8h			7h	8h	8h
							Act. W	8h	8h	8h			7h	8h	8h
Carole Poland	120 hrs	120 hrs	0 hrs	120 hrs	0 hrs	100%	Work	8h	8h	8h			7h	8h	8h
							Act. W	8h	8h	8h			7h	8h	8h
18 Original art review	160 hrs	160 hrs	0 hrs	0 hrs	160 hrs	0%	Work		12h	16h			15h	16h	16h
							Act. W								
Hany Morcos	80 hrs	80 hrs	0 hrs	0 hrs	80 hrs	0%	Work		6h	8h			7h	8h	8h
							Act. W								
Jane Dow	80 hrs	80 hrs	0 hrs	0 hrs	80 hrs	0%	Work		6h	8h			8h	8h	8h
							Act. W								
19 Author review of co	160 hrs	160 hrs	0 hrs	0 hrs	160 hrs	0%	Work								
							Act. W								

9. In the **Actual** column for task 18, *Original art review*, type or click **90h**, and then press the Enter key.

Entering an actual value for the task causes Project to distribute the actual values among the assigned resources and adjust remaining work and other values.

Task Name	Work	Baseline	Variance	Actual	Remaining	%W. Comp.	Details	W	T	F	S	S	M	T	W
0 Children's Book Schedule	2,337.5 hrs	2,337.5 hrs	0 hrs	217 hrs	2,120.5 hrs	9%	Work	8h	20h	24h			25.5h	24h	24h
							Act. W	8h	20h	24h			22h	24h	24h
1 Editorial staff meeting	45.5 hrs	45.5 hrs	0 hrs	7 hrs	38.5 hrs	15%	Work						3.5h		
							Act. W								
15 Acquisition	440 hrs	440 hrs	0 hrs	210 hrs	230 hrs	48%	Work	8h	20h	24h			22h	24h	24h
							Act. W	8h	20h	24h			22h	24h	24h
16 Manuscript received	0 hrs	0 hrs	0 hrs	0 hrs	0 hrs	100%	Work								
							Act. W								
17 Content edit	120 hrs	120 hrs	0 hrs	120 hrs	0 hrs	100%	Work	6h	8h	8h			7h	8h	8h
							Act. W	8h	8h	8h			7h	8h	8h
Carole Poland	120 hrs	120 hrs	0 hrs	120 hrs	0 hrs	100%	Work	8h	8h	8h			7h	8h	8h
							Act. W	6h	8h	8h			7h	8h	8h
18 Original art review	160 hrs	160 hrs	0 hrs	90 hrs	70 hrs	56%	Work		12h	16h			15h	16h	16h
							Act. W		12h	16h			15h	16h	16h
Hany Morcos	80 hrs	80 hrs	0 hrs	44.5 hrs	35.5 hrs	56%	Work		6h	8h			7h	8h	8h
							Act. W		6h	8h			7h	8h	8h
Jane Dow	80 hrs	80 hrs	0 hrs	45.5 hrs	34.5 hrs	57%	Work		6h	8h			8h	8h	8h
							Act. W		6h	8h			8h	8h	8h
19 Author review of co	160 hrs	160 hrs	0 hrs	0 hrs	160 hrs	0%	Work								
							Act. W								

Project highlights the most recently changed values.

Several important things occurred when you pressed Enter:

○ Project applied change highlighting to the updated values in the table.

○ The amount of actual work you entered was subtracted from the Remaining column.

○ The actual work was distributed to the two assignments on the task, resulting in 44.5 hours of actual work being recorded for one resource and 45.5 hours for the other resource. (The difference in assignments is due to Hany's previously customized assignment values.) Likewise, the updated remaining work value was recalculated for each assignment.

○ The updated actual and remaining work values were rolled up to the *Acquisition* summary task.

○ The actual work values were also redistributed to the task and assignment timephased values.

In the timephased grid side of the view, you can see the daily scheduled work and actual work values for the three resources through Thursday, April 26. Because you entered an actual work value for the entire task, Project assumes that the work was done as scheduled and records these timephased values for the resource assignments.

To conclude this exercise, you will enter actual work values at the assignment level and see the effect on the task.

10. In the **Actual** column for Hany Morcos's assignment to task 18, type or click **60h**, and then press Enter.

Task Name	Work	Baseline	Variance	Actual	Remaining	%W. Comp.	Details	W	T	F	S	S	M	T	W
0	⊟ Children's Book Sched	2,337.5 hrs	2,337.5 hrs	0 hrs	232.5 hrs	2,105 hrs	10%	Work	8h	20h	24h			25.5h	24h	24h
								Act. W	8h	20h	24h			22h	24h	24h
1	⊞ Editorial staff meeting	45.5 hrs	45.5 hrs	0 hrs	7 hrs	38.5 hrs	15%	Work						3.5h		
								Act. W								
15	⊟ Acquisition	440 hrs	440 hrs	0 hrs	225.5 hrs	214.5 hrs	51%	Work	8h	20h	24h			22h	24h	24h
								Act. W	8h	20h	24h			22h	24h	24h
16	Manuscript receive	0 hrs	0 hrs	0 hrs	0 hrs	0 hrs	100%	Work								
								Act. W								
17	⊟ Content edit	120 hrs	120 hrs	0 hrs	120 hrs	0 hrs	100%	Work	8h	0h	8h			7h	8h	8h
								Act. W	8h	8h	8h			7h	8h	8h
	Carole Poland	120 hrs	120 hrs	0 hrs	120 hrs	0 hrs	100%	Work	8h	8h	8h			7h	8h	8h
								Act. W	8h	8h	8h			7h	8h	8h
18	⊟ Original art review	160 hrs	160 hrs	0 hrs	105.5 hrs	54.5 hrs	66%	Work		12h	16h			15h	16h	16h
								Act. W		12h	16h			15h	16h	16h
	Hany Morcos	80 hrs	80 hrs	0 hrs	60 hrs	20 hrs	75%	Work		6h	8h			7h	8h	8h
								Act. W		6h	8h			7h	8h	8h
	Jane Dow	80 hrs	80 hrs	0 hrs	45.5 hrs ▾	34.5 hrs	57%	Work		6h	8h			8h	8h	8h
								Act. W		6h	8h			8h	8h	8h
19	⊟ Author review of cc	160 hrs	160 hrs	0 hrs	▯ hrs	160 hrs	0%	Work								
								Act. W								

Entering actual work on this assignment updates remaining work and related values on the task.

Hany's actual and remaining work values are updated, and those updates also roll up to the task and its summary task (Project highlights the changed values). However, the actual and remaining work values for Jane Dow, the other resource assigned to the task, are not affected.

11. Drag the vertical divider bar back to the left to see more of the updated timephased values for the task.

The actual work value entered in the table
for the task and assignment is distributed
across the timephased grid.

Again, Project assumes that the actual work value that you entered for Hany was completed as scheduled; therefore, her work and actual work timephased values match through Monday, April 30.

CLEAN UP Close the Advanced Tracking B file.

Tip You entered actual work values in this exercise, but you can also enter remaining work values or percentage of work complete. All these values are related to each other—a change to one affects the others. You can update these values in the Work table or on the Tracking tab of the Assignment Information dialog box (when an assignment is selected).

Tracking a task's actual work complete value is more detailed than entering a simple percentage complete on a task. However, neither method is as detailed as entering time-phased actual work for tasks or assignments (as you will see in the next section). There's nothing wrong with tracking actual work at the task or assignment level (or simply entering a percentage complete value, for that matter) if that level of detail meets your needs. In fact, whether you see the timephased details or not, Project always distributes any percentage complete or task-level or assignment-level actual work value that you enter into corresponding timephased values, as you saw earlier. This is one reason why new Project users sometimes are surprised to encounter extremely precise values, such as 7.67 hours of work, scheduled for a particular day. If you generally understand the math that Project is following, however, you can figure out where such numbers come from. On the other hand, you might not care about this level of scheduling detail—and that's OK, too.

Entering Actual Costs Manually

Whenever you've entered actual work values in this chapter, Project has calculated actual cost values for the affected task, its summary task, the resources assigned to the task, and the entire project. By default, Project calculates actual costs and does not allow you to enter them directly. In most cases, this is what we recommend and what is done with the practice files used in this book. However, if you want to enter actual cost values yourself in your own project plans, follow these steps.

Important The following procedure is provided for your general information; however, do not follow this procedure now if you are completing the exercises in this book. Doing so will produce results that will not match those shown in this book.

1. On the **File** tab, click **Options**.

   The Project Options dialog box appears.

2. Click the **Schedule** tab.

3. Under the **Calculation options for this project** label, clear the **Actual costs are always calculated by Project** check box.

4. Click **OK**.

After automatic cost calculation is turned off, you can enter or import task- or assignment-level actual costs in the Actual field. This field is available in several locations, such as the Cost table. You can also enter actual cost values daily or at another interval in any timescale view, such as the Task Usage or Resource Usage view. With a usage view displayed, on the Format tab, in the Details group, click Actual Cost.

Tracking Timephased Actual Work for Tasks and Assignments

Entering timephased actuals requires more work on the project manager's part and might require more work from resources to inform the project manager of their daily or weekly actuals. However, doing so gives you far more detail about the project's task and resource status than the other methods used for entering actuals. Entering timephased values might be the best approach to take if you have a group of tasks or an entire project that includes the following:

- High-risk tasks
- Relatively short-duration tasks in which a variance of even one day could put the overall project at risk

- Tasks for which you'd like to develop or validate throughput metrics, or rates at which a given quantity of a deliverable can be completed over a given time period, such as *copyedit 3000 words per day*

- Tasks in which sponsors or other stakeholders have an especially strong interest

- Tasks that require hourly billing for labor

At this point in the new book project, the Acquisition work has been completed, and the Editorial phase has just begun. Because of the larger number of resources involved and the variability of the editorial work, these tasks are the riskiest ones so far in the project.

In this exercise, you enter some actuals for tasks for specific time periods.

Open Advanced Tracking C_Start from the Chapter12 folder, and then follow these steps.

1. On the **File** tab, click **Save As**.

   The Save As dialog box appears.

2. In the **File name** box, type **Advanced Tracking C**, and then click **Save**.

3. Click the minus sign next to task 15, *Acquisition*, to collapse this phase of the project plan.

4. In the **Task Name** column, click the name of task 22, *Organize manuscript for copyedit*, and then, on the **Task** tab, in the **Editing** group, click **Scroll to Task**.

   Project scrolls the timephased grid to display the first scheduled work values of the Editorial phase.

The first timephased actual work values that you will enter are at the task level and not for specific assignments.

5. In the timephased grid, click the cell at the intersection of the Wednesday, May 23 column and the task 22 actual work row. The actual work row is directly below the work row, which contains the value *12h*.

Tip If you point to the name of a day on the timescale, Project will display the full date of that day in a ScreenTip. You can change the formatting of the timescale to control the time period in which you enter actual values in the timephased grid. For example, you can format the timescale to show weeks rather than days; when you enter an actual value at the weekly level, that value is distributed over the week.

6. Type **9h**, and then press the Tab key.

Here is the first timephased actual work value you entered.

As soon as you entered the first actual value for the task, the scheduled work value changed to match it. Both work and actual work values rolled up to the summary task levels and were distributed among the specific assignments to the task. You can see this happen in the timephased grid on the right and the table on the left.

7. In the Thursday, May 24 actual work cell, type **15h**, and then press Tab.

8. For task 22, enter the following actual work values for the dates listed.

Date	Actual Hours
Friday, May 25	12
Monday, May 28	12
Tuesday, May 29	15

Task Name	Work	Baseline	Variance	Actual	Details	2							May 27, '12				
						M	T	W	T	F	S	S	M	T	W	T
0	Children's Book Schedule	2,364.5 hrs	2,337.5 hrs	27 hrs	551.5 hrs	Work	11.5h	8h	9h	15h	12h			15.5h	15h	16h	1
						Act. W	11.5h	9h	9h	15h	12h			12h	15h		
1	Editorial staff meeting	45.5 hrs	45.5 hrs	0 hrs	24.5 hrs	Work	3.5h							3.5h			
						Act. W	3.5h										
15	Acquisition	464 hrs	440 hrs	24 hrs	464 hrs	Work	8h	8h									
						Act. W	8h	8h									
21	Editorial	403 hrs	400 hrs	3 hrs	63 hrs	Work			9h	15h	12h			12h	15h	16h	1
						Act. W			9h	15h	12h			12h	15h		
22	Organize manuscrip	63 hrs	60 hrs	3 hrs	63 hrs	Work			9h	15h	12h			12h	15h		
						Act. W			9h	15h	12h			12h	15h		
	Dan Jump	21 hrs	20 hrs	1 hr	21 hrs	Work			3h	5h	4h			4h	5h		
						Act. W			3h	5h	4h			6h	5h		
	Hany Morcos	42 hrs	40 hrs	2 hrs	42 hrs	Work			6h	10h	8h			8h	10h		
						Act. W			6h	10h	8h			8h	10h		
23	Copyedit	180 hrs	180 hrs	0 hrs	0 hrs	Work										16h	1
						Act. W											
	Copyeditors	180 hrs	180 hrs	0 hrs	0 hrs	Work										16h	1
						Act. W											
24	Author review of co	100 hrs	100 hrs	0 hrs	0 hrs	Work											
						Act. W											

This step concludes the actual work for this task. Next, you'll enter actual work values for the assignments on the next task.

For task 23, *Copyedit*, you have weekly actual work values from the assigned resource. The copyeditors have completed the task. For this task, you'll adjust the timescale to record weekly actual values.

9. On the **View** tab, in the **Zoom** group, in the **Timescale** box, click **Weeks**.

10. Enter the following actual work values into the timephased grid for the Copyeditors' assignment to task 23, *Copyedit*.

Tip When entering actual work, you do not need to include the "h" abbreviation (to denote hours). You can simply enter the number and Project will record it as hours. Hours is the default work value for data entry. If you wish, you can change this. Click the File tab and then click Options. On the Schedule tab of the Project Options dialog box, in the Work Is Entered In box, select the default time increment you want.

Date (Week of)	Actual Hours
May 27	60
June 3	80
June 10	48

Task Name	Work	Baseline	Variance	Actual	Details				June					July			
						5/6	5/13	5/20	5/27	6/3	6/10	6/17	6/24	7/1	7/8	7/15
0	Children's Book Schedule	2,372.5 hrs	2,337.5 hrs	35 hrs	739.5 hrs	Work	79.5h	83.5h	55.5h	90.5h	83.5h	76.5h	53.5h	87h	97h	120h	12
						Act. W	79.5h	83.5h	55.5h	87h	80h	48h					
1	Editorial staff meeting	45.5 hrs	45.5 hrs	0 hrs	24.5 hrs	Work	3.5h	3.5h	3.5h	3.5h	3.5h	3.5h	3.5h	3.5h			
						Act. W	3.5h	3.5h	3.5h								
15	Acquisition	464 hrs	440 hrs	24 hrs	464 hrs	Work	76h	80h	16h								
						Act. W	76h	80h	16h								
21	Editorial	411 hrs	400 hrs	11 hrs	251 hrs	Work				36h	87h	80h	73h	50h	83.5h	1.5h	
						Act. W				36h	87h	80h	48h				
22	Organize manuscrip	63 hrs	60 hrs	3 hrs	63 hrs	Work				36h	27h						
						Act. W				36h	27h						
	Dan Jump	21 hrs	20 hrs	1 hr	21 hrs	Work				12h	9h						
						Act. W				12h	9h						
	Hany Morcos	42 hrs	40 hrs	2 hrs	42 hrs	Work				24h	18h						
						Act. W				24h	18h						
23	Copyedit	188 hrs	180 hrs	8 hrs	188 hrs	Work					60h	80h	48h				
						Act. W					60h	80h	48h				
	Copyeditors	188 hrs	180 hrs	8 hrs	188 hrs	Work					60h	80h	48h				
						Act. W					60h	80h	48h				
24	Author review of co	100 hrs	100 hrs	0 hrs	0 hrs	Work								25h	50h	25h	
						Act. W											

The resource's actual work values were rolled up to the task's actual work values. The original work values were saved in the baseline should you ever need to refer to them later.

CLEAN UP Close the Advanced Tracking C file.

Tip In this exercise, you have seen how task and assignment values are directly related; an update to one directly affects the other. However, you can break this relationship if you want. Doing so enables you to record progress for resource assignments, for example, and manually enter actual values for the tasks to which those resources are assigned. You normally should not break this relationship unless you have special reporting needs within your organization—for example, you must follow a status reporting methodology based on something other than the actual values recorded for assignments in project plans. To break this relationship, do the following. On the File tab, click Options. In the Project Options dialog box, click the Schedule tab and then under the Calculation options for this project label, clear the "Updating Task status updates resource status" check box. This setting applies to the entire project plan that you have open at the time; you cannot apply it to only some tasks within a project plan.

When you need to track actual work at the most detailed level possible, use the timephased grid in the Task Usage or Resource Usage view. In either view, you can enter actual work values for individual assignments daily, weekly, or at whatever time period you want (by adjusting the timescale). For example, if a task has three resources assigned to it and you know that two resources worked on the task for eight hours one day and the third resource worked for six hours, you can enter these as three separate values on a timephased grid.

If your organization uses a timesheet reporting system for tracking actual work, you might be able to use this timesheet data in Project as timephased actuals. You might not need to track at this level, but if resources complete timesheets for other purposes (billing other departments within the organization, for example), you can use their data and save yourself some work.

Project Management Focus: Collecting Actuals from Resources

The view that you used in the previous exercise is similar to a time card. In fact, to enter assignment-level actual work values, you might need some form of paper time card or its electronic equivalent. Several methods are used to collect such data from resources, assuming that you need to track actual and remaining work at this level of detail. Some collection methods include the following:

● Collect actual values yourself. This method is feasible if you communicate with only a small group of resources on a frequent basis, such as a weekly status meeting. It's also a good opportunity to talk directly to the resources about

> any blocking issues or surprises they might have encountered (either positive or negative) while performing the work.
>
> ● Collect actuals through a formal status reporting system. This technique might work through the already-existing hierarchy of your organization and serve additional purposes besides project status reporting.
>
> Regardless of the data collection methods you might use, be aware that resources might have some concern about how their actual work values might reflect on their overall performance. You may need to communicate to resources that schedule actuals help in managing the schedule, but performance evaluation is a business management focus, not a project management one.

Rescheduling Incomplete Work

During the course of a project, work might occasionally be interrupted for a specific task or for the entire project. Should this happen, you can have Project reschedule the remaining work to restart after the date you specify.

When you reschedule incomplete work, you specify the date after which work can resume—the rescheduled date. Here is how Project handles tasks in relation to the rescheduled date:

- If the task does not have any actual work recorded for it prior to the rescheduled date and does not have a constraint applied, the entire task is rescheduled to begin after that date.

- If the task has some actual work recorded prior to but none after the rescheduled date, the task is split so that all remaining work starts after the rescheduled date. The actual work is not affected.

- If the task has some actual work recorded for it prior to as well as after the rescheduled date, the task is not affected.

At this point in the new book project, work on the Editorial phase has been completed, and the team has started work on the next phase, Design and Production. However, you need to troubleshoot a delay in work caused by an unforeseen problem.

In this exercise, you reschedule uncompleted work.

Open Advanced Tracking D_Start from the Chapter12 folder, and then follow these steps.

1. On the **File** tab, click **Save As**.

   The Save As dialog box appears.

2. In the **File name** box, type **Advanced Tracking D**, and then click **Save**.

   The project plan is currently in the Task Usage view. Next, you'll switch to the Gantt Chart view.

3. On the **View** tab, in the **Task Views** group, click the down arrow below the **Gantt Chart** button, and then click **Gantt Chart**.

4. In the **Task Name** column, click the name of task 31, *Proofread and index*.

5. On the **Task** tab, in the **Editing** group, click **Scroll to Task**.

   The Gantt Chart view scrolls to display the Gantt bar for task 31, *Proofread and index*. Currently, this task has two days of actual work completed and several days of scheduled work remaining.

6. Scroll the Gantt Chart view up so that the *1st Pages review* (task 30) appears near the top of the view.

Progress bars indicate the portion of the task that has been completed.

	ⓘ	Task Mode	Task Name	Duration	Start	Finish
30			⊟ 1st Pages review	30.4 days	Thu 7/26/12	Thu 9/6/12
31	📅		Proofread and index	10.4 days	Thu 7/26/12	Thu 8/9/12
32			Incorporate 1st Pages review	10 days	Thu 8/9/12	Thu 8/23/12
33			Send proofed pages to Production	0 days	Thu 8/23/12	Thu 8/23/12
34			Enter page corrections and index	5 days	Thu 8/23/12	Thu 8/30/12
35			Cover design	5 days	Thu 8/30/12	Thu 9/6/12
36			⊟ 2nd Pages review	10 days	Thu 9/6/12	Thu 9/20/12
37	⦿		Proof and review	5 days	Thu 9/6/12	Thu 9/13/12
38			Send proofed pages to Production	0 days	Thu 9/13/12	Thu 9/13/12
39			Final review	5 days	Thu 9/13/12	Thu 9/20/12

You have learned that over the weekend of July 28, a water pipe burst in the proofreaders' office. None of the project's equipment or material was damaged, but the cleanup will delay work until Wednesday, August 1. This effectively stops work on the proofreading task for a few days. Next, you will reschedule incomplete work so that the project can begin again on Wednesday.

7. On the **Project** tab, in the **Status** group, click **Update Project**.

   The Update Project dialog box appears.

8. Select the **Reschedule uncompleted work to start after** option, and in the text box, type or select **7/31/12**.

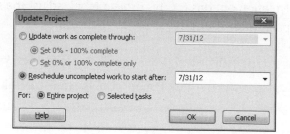

9. Click **OK** to close the **Update Project** dialog box.

Project splits task 31 so that the incomplete portion of the task is delayed until Wednesday.

Rescheduling work for the project causes Project to split the task and then reschedule the remainder of it (and all subsequent tasks) after the date you specified.

As you can see, although the duration of task 31 remains 10.4 working days, its finish date and subsequent start dates for successor tasks have been pushed out. Although we have addressed a specific problem, in doing so, we have created other problems in the remainder of the project. You will address this and other problems in the project plan in later chapters.

Here are a few other things to keep in mind when tracking progress:

● You can turn off Project's ability to reschedule incomplete work on tasks for which any actual work has been recorded. On the File tab, click Options. In the Project Options dialog box, click the Schedule tab, and then, under the Scheduling options for this project label, clear the "Split in-progress tasks" check box.

● If you use status dates for reporting actuals, Project supports several options for controlling the way completed and incomplete segments of a task are scheduled around the status date. You can see the options by doing the following: On the File tab, click Options. In the Project Options dialog box, click the Advanced tab, and then, under the Calculation options for this project label, adjust the settings "Move end of completed parts after status date back to status date" and the three other check boxes below it.

✖ CLEAN UP Close the Advanced Tracking D file.

Key Points

- Saving a baseline saves a large set of task, resource, and assignment values in a project plan. Saving an interim plan, however, saves only the start and finish dates of tasks.

- If you track work at the task level, work rolls down to the assignments. Conversely, if you track work at the assignment level, work rolls up to the task level.

- In usage views, you can change the time increments of the timescale to match the time period against which you wish to track. For example, if you wish to record actual work as full weeks, you can set the timescale to display weeks.

- Should work on a project be interrupted for some reason, you can reschedule the work to begin again on the date you specify.

Chapter at a Glance

Compare actual progress against baseline plan, page 280.

Use different views and tables to see variance, page 280.

See overbudget tasks, page 287.

Customize a field with a formula and graphical indicators, page 293.

Use the customized field to create a stoplight view that illustrates cost variance, page 293.

13 Viewing and Reporting Project Status

In this chapter, you will learn how to:

✔ Determine which tasks were started or completed late.

✔ View task costs at summary and detail levels.

✔ Examine resource costs and variance.

✔ Use custom fields to create a stoplight view that illustrates each task's cost variance.

After a project's *baseline* has been set and work has begun, the primary focus of the project manager shifts from planning to collecting, updating, and analyzing project performance details. For most projects, these performance details boil down to three primary questions or vital signs:

● How much *work* was required to complete a task?

● Did the *task* start and finish on time?

● What was the cost of completing the task?

Comparing the answers to these questions against the baseline provides the project manager and other *stakeholders* with a good way to measure the project's progress and to determine when corrective action might be necessary.

Communicating project status to key stakeholders, such as customers and sponsors, is arguably the most important function of a project manager and one that might occupy much of your time on the job. Although the perfect flow of communications cannot guarantee a project's success, a project with poor communications flow is almost guaranteed to fail.

A key to communicating project status properly is knowing the following:

- Who needs to know the project's status, and for what purpose?
- What format or level of detail do these people need?

The time to answer these questions is in the initial planning phase of the project. After work on the project is under way, your main communications task will be reporting project status. This can take several forms:

- Status reports that describe where the project is in terms of cost, scope, and schedule (the three sides of the *project triangle,* as described in Appendix A, "A Short Course in Project Management.")
- Progress reports that document the specific accomplishments of the project team
- Forecasts that predict future project performance

Where the scheduled or actual project performance differs from the baseline plan, you have variance. *Variance* is usually measured as time, such as days behind schedule, or as cost, such as dollars over budget. After initial project planning is complete, many project managers spend most of their time identifying, investigating, and, in many cases, responding to variance. However, before you can respond to variance, you must first identify it. That is the subject of this chapter.

> **Practice Files** Before you can complete the exercises in this chapter, you need to copy the book's practice files to your computer. A complete list of practice files is provided in "Using the Practice Files" at the beginning of this book. For each exercise that has a practice file, simply browse to where you saved the book's practice file folder.

Important If you are running Microsoft Project Professional, you may need to make a one-time setting change. This helps ensure that the practice files you work with in this chapter do not affect your Project Server data. For more information, see Appendix C, "Using the Practice Files if Connected to Project Server."

Identifying Tasks that Have Slipped

When tasks start or finish earlier or later than planned, schedule variance is the result. One cause of schedule variance is delays in starting or finishing tasks. You'd certainly want to know about tasks that started late or future tasks that might not start as scheduled. It's also helpful to identify completed tasks that did not start on time to try to determine why this occurred.

There are different ways to view tasks with variance, depending on the type of information you want:

- Apply the Tracking Gantt view to compare tasks' baseline dates graphically with their actual or scheduled dates. (To do this, on the View tab, in the Task Views group, click the down arrow below the Gantt Chart button and then click Tracking Gantt.)

- Apply the Detail Gantt view to show graphically each task's slippage from baseline. (To do this, on the View tab, in the Task Views group, click Other Views, click More Views, and then double-click Detail Gantt.)

- Apply the Variance table to a task view to see the number of days of variance for each task's start and finish dates. (To do this, on the View tab, in the Data group, click Tables and then click Variance.)

- Filter for delayed or slipping tasks with the Slipped/Late Progress, Slipping Tasks, or Late Tasks filter. (To do this, on the View tab, in the Data group, in the Filter box, select the filter that you want to apply.)

Project Management Focus: Is Variance Ever a Good Thing?

In project management, we generally look for variance that can have an adverse effect on a project, such as variance that pushes out the finish date or increases the cost of a project. However, the term *variance* refers to any difference between planned and actual schedule events—even differences that have a helpful effect, such as an earlier finish date or a lower-than-expected cost. Should you have the good fortune of managing a project that experiences such helpful variance, the techniques described here will help you identify the beneficial variance as well as any adverse variance. Your focus as a project manager is basically the same regardless of the nature of the variance—watch for it, and when it does occur, communicate it and its effects to project sponsors and other stakeholders and (if it's adverse variance) mitigate against it according to the nature of the project.

In this exercise, you use views and filters to identify variance.

 SET UP Start Project 2010 if it's not already running.

You need the Reporting Status_Start project plan located in your Chapter13 practice file folder to complete this exercise. Open the Reporting Status_Start project plan, and then follow these steps.

1. On the **File** tab, click **Save As**.

   The Save As dialog box appears.

2. In the **File name** box, type **Reporting Status**, and then click **Save**.

   To begin your analysis of tasks that have slipped, you'll start at the highest level—the project summary information.

3. On the **Project** tab, in the **Properties** group, click **Project Information**.

   The Project Information dialog box appears.

4. Click **Statistics**.

   The Project Statistics dialog box appears.

   Project Statistics for 'Reporting Status'

	Start	Finish
Current	Mon 4/2/12	Thu 12/20/12
Baseline	Mon 4/2/12	Fri 11/16/12
Actual	Mon 4/2/12	NA
Variance	0d	24.5d

	Duration	Work	Cost
Current	188d	2,609.1h	$104,506.50
Baseline	163.5d	2,337.5h	$93,742.00
Actual	115.89d	1,737.1h	$73,717.50
Remaining	72.11d	872h	$30,789.00

   Percent complete:

   Duration: 62%   Work: 67%

   Close

   In this dialog box, you can see (among other things) that the new book plan at Lucerne Publishing currently has substantial schedule variance on the finish date. The overall project finish date has slipped out by this number of days.

5. Click **Close** to close the **Project Statistics** dialog box.

   For the remainder of this exercise, you will use various techniques to examine the specific task variance.

6. On the **View** tab, in the **Task Views** group, click the down arrow below the **Gantt Chart** button and then click **Tracking Gantt**.

   Project displays the Tracking Gantt view.

7. On the **View** tab, in the **Zoom** group, click the down arrow next to the **Timescale** box and then click **Weeks**.

The timescale adjusts to show more of the project plan.

8. In the **Task Name** column, click the name of task 33, *Send proofed pages to Production*, and scroll the Tracking Gantt view up so that task 33 appears near the top of the view.

9. On the **Task** tab, in the **Editing** group, click **Scroll to Task**.

   Tip You can also right-click the task name and in the shortcut menu that appears, click Scroll to Task.

   In the chart portion of this view, the tasks as they are currently scheduled appear as blue bars (if they are not on the *critical path*) or red bars (if they are on the critical path). In the lower half of each task's row, the baseline start and finish dates of each task appear as gray bars.

A gray bar represents the original (baseline) schedule in the Tracking Gantt view.

A blue or red bar represents the task as it is currently scheduled or when it was completed.

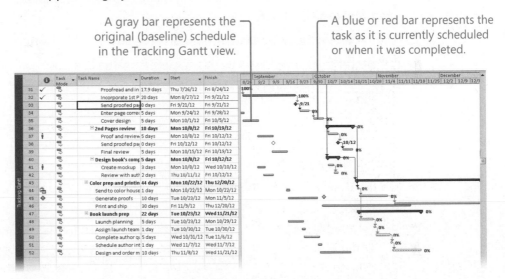

By comparing the currently scheduled Gantt bars with the baseline Gantt bars, you can see what tasks started later than planned or took longer to complete.

Tip To see details about any bar or other item in a Gantt Chart view, position the mouse pointer over it. After a moment, a ScreenTip appears with details.

To focus on only the slipping tasks, you will apply a filter.

10. On the **View** tab, in the **Data** group, click the arrow next to **Filter:** and then click **More Filters**.

The More Filters dialog box appears. In this dialog box, you can see all the predefined filters for tasks (when in a task view) and resources (when in a resource view) that are available to you.

11. Click **Slipping Tasks**, and then click **Apply**.

    Project filters the task list to show only those uncompleted tasks that, as they are now scheduled, have slipped from their baseline schedule.

    Note the gaps in the task ID numbers. Tasks 1 through 26, for example, do not appear with the filter applied because they are already complete.

    At this point in the schedule, the scheduled start date of the uncompleted tasks has slipped quite a bit. Most of these tasks' scheduled Gantt bars are formatted red to indicate that they are critical, meaning that any delay in completing these tasks will delay the project's finish date.

12. On the **View** tab, in the **Data** group, click the arrow next to **Filter:** and then click **Clear Filter**.

    Project removes the filter. As always, displaying or removing a filter has no effect on the original data.

    The Tracking Gantt view graphically illustrates the difference between scheduled, actual, and baseline project performance. To see this information in a table format, you will display the Variance table in the Task Sheet view.

13. On the **View** tab, in the **Task Views** group, click **Other Views** and then click **Task Sheet**.

    Project displays the Task Sheet view. Next, you'll switch to the Variance table.

14. On the **View** tab, in the **Data** group, click **Tables** and then click **Variance**.

    Tip You also can right-click the Select All button in the upper-left corner of the active table to switch to a different table.

    The Variance table appears in the Task Sheet view.

	Task ▼	Task Name ▼	Start ▼	Finish ▼	Baseline Start ▼	Baseline Finish ▼	Start Var. ▼	Finish Var. ▼
0		☐ Children's book sc	Mon 4/2/12	Thu 12/20/12	Mon 4/2/12	Fri 11/16/12	0 days	24.5 days
1		⊞ Editorial staff me	Mon 4/9/12	Wed 8/1/12	Mon 4/9/12	Mon 7/2/12	0 days	21 days
15		⊞ Acquisition	Mon 4/2/12	Tue 5/22/12	Mon 4/2/12	Mon 5/21/12	0 days	1.5 days
21		☐ Editorial	Wed 5/23/12	Tue 7/3/12	Mon 5/21/12	Fri 6/29/12	1.5 days	2.63 days
22		Organize manu	Wed 5/23/12	Tue 5/29/12	Mon 5/21/12	Mon 5/28/12	1.5 days	1.5 days
23		Copyedit	Wed 5/30/12	Wed 6/13/12	Mon 5/28/12	Tue 6/12/12	1.5 days	0.75 days
24		Author review	Wed 6/13/12	Fri 6/29/12	Tue 6/12/12	Tue 6/26/12	0.75 days	3.25 days
25		Copyedit incorp	Tue 6/26/12	Tue 7/3/12	Fri 6/22/12	Fri 6/29/12	2.63 days	2.63 days
26		Handoff to Prod	Tue 7/3/12	Tue 7/3/12	Fri 6/29/12	Fri 6/29/12	2.63 days	2.63 days
27		☐ Design and Produ	Thu 7/5/12	Fri 10/19/12	Fri 6/29/12	Mon 9/17/12	2.63 days	24.5 days
28		Set pages	Thu 7/5/12	Wed 7/25/12	Fri 6/29/12	Mon 7/23/12	2.63 days	2.4 days
29		Interior illustra	Thu 7/5/12	Wed 7/25/12	Fri 6/29/12	Mon 7/23/12	2.63 days	2.5 days
30		☐ 1st Pages revie	Thu 7/26/12	Fri 10/5/12	Mon 7/23/12	Mon 9/3/12	2.5 days	24.5 days
31		Proofread ar	Thu 7/26/12	Fri 8/24/12	Mon 7/23/12	Mon 8/6/12	2.5 days	14.5 days
32		Incorporate	Mon 8/27/12	Fri 9/21/12	Mon 8/6/12	Mon 8/20/12	14.5 days	24.5 days
33		Send proofe	Fri 9/21/12	Fri 9/21/12	Mon 8/20/12	Mon 8/20/12	24.5 days	24.5 days
34		Enter page c	Mon 9/24/12	Fri 9/28/12	Mon 8/20/12	Mon 8/27/12	24.5 days	24.5 days
35		Cover design	Mon 10/1/12	Fri 10/5/12	Mon 8/27/12	Mon 9/3/12	24.5 days	24.5 days
36		☐ 2nd Pages revi	Mon 10/8/12	Fri 10/19/12	Mon 9/3/12	Mon 9/17/12	24.5 days	24.5 days
37		Proof and re	Mon 10/8/12	Fri 10/12/12	Mon 9/3/12	Mon 9/10/12	24.5 days	24.5 days
38		Send proofe	Fri 10/12/12	Fri 10/12/12	Mon 9/10/12	Mon 9/10/12	24.5 days	24.5 days
39		Final review	Mon 10/15/12	Fri 10/19/12	Mon 9/10/12	Mon 9/17/12	24.5 days	24.5 days
40		☐ Design book's c	Mon 10/8/12	Fri 10/12/12	Mon 9/3/12	Mon 9/10/12	24.5 days	24.5 days
41		Create mock	Mon 10/8/12	Wed 10/10/12	Mon 9/3/12	Thu 9/6/12	24.5 days	24.5 days
42		Review with	Thu 10/11/12	Fri 10/12/12	Thu 9/6/12	Mon 9/10/12	24.5 days	24.5 days
43		☐ Color prep and pr	Mon 10/22/12	Thu 12/20/12	Mon 9/17/12	Fri 11/16/12	24.5 days	24.5 days
44		Send to color h	Mon 10/22/12	Mon 10/22/12	Mon 9/17/12	Tue 9/18/12	14.5 days	14.5 days
45		Generate proof	Tue 10/23/12	Mon 11/5/12	Tue 9/18/12	Tue 10/2/12	24.5 days	24.5 days
46		Print and ship	Fri 11/9/12	Thu 12/20/12	Fri 10/5/12	Fri 11/16/12	24.5 days	24.5 days

Ready   New Tasks : Auto Scheduled

In this table, you can view the scheduled, baseline, and variance values per task.

Here are some additional tips and suggestions for viewing slipped tasks:

● All filters are available to you via the Filter button on the Data group of the View tab. The name of the active filter appears in this button; click the arrow next to the filter name to see other filters. If no filter is applied to the current view, *No Filter* appears in the Filter box. When a filter is applied, the text *Filter Applied* appears on the status bar.

● You can see the criteria that most filters use to determine which tasks or resources they will display or hide. On the View tab, in the Data group, in the Filter box, click More Filters. In the More Filters dialog box, click a filter and then click Edit. In the Filter Definition dialog box, you can see the tests applied to various fields for the filter.

- You can quickly display late tasks—tasks that are late in relation to whatever status date you set. To set a status date, on the Project tab, in the Properties group, click Project Information. Then on the Format tab, in the Bar Styles group, check the Late Tasks check box. The Gantt bars of tasks that were scheduled to be completed by the status date but are incomplete are formatted black.

- The Slipping Tasks report describes tasks that are off schedule. To view a Slipping Tasks report, on the Project tab, in the Reports group, click Reports. In the Reports dialog box, double-click Current, and then double-click Slipping Tasks.

- In this exercise, you have viewed variance for a task. To see variance for assignments to a task, switch to the Task Usage view, and then apply the Variance table (to see scheduled variance) or the Work table (to see work variance).

Project Management Focus: Getting the Word Out

If you work in an organization that is highly focused on projects and project management, chances are that standard methods and formats already exist within your organization for reporting project status. If not, you might be able to introduce project status formats that are based on clear communication and project management principles.

Techniques that you can use in Project to help you report project status include the following:

- Print the Project Summary report (to do this, on the Project tab, in the Reports group, click Reports and then click Overview).

- If you have Microsoft Excel 2003 or later or Microsoft Visio 2007 or later, print a status-focused visual report (to do this, on the Project tab, in the Reports group, click Visual Reports).

- Copy Project data to other applications—for example, use Copy Picture (to do this, on the Task tab, in the Clipboard group, click the down arrow next to the Copy button) to copy the Gantt Chart view.

- Save Project data in other formats (to do this, on the File tab, click Save As, and in the Save As Type box, select the format that you want), such as an editable format like Excel Workbook, or in Portable Document Format (PDF) or XML Paper Specification (XPS) format for high-fidelity viewing.

All of these status-reporting tools are described elsewhere in this book. For hands-on practice with information-sharing features, see Chapter 17, "Sharing Project Information with Other Programs."

Examining Task Costs

The schedule's status (Did tasks start and finish on time?), although critical to nearly all projects, is only one indicator of overall project health. For projects that include cost information, another critical indicator is cost variance: Are tasks running over or under budget? Task costs in Project consist of fixed costs applied directly to tasks, resource costs derived from assignments, or both. When tasks cost more or less than planned to complete, cost variance is the result. Evaluating cost variance enables you to make incremental budget adjustments for individual tasks to avoid exceeding your project's overall budget.

Although tasks and resources (and their costs) are directly related, it's informative to evaluate each individually.

In this exercise, you view task cost variance. You'll start by displaying the Cost table.

1. On the **View** tab, in the **Data** group, click **Tables** and then click **Cost**.

   The Cost table appears in the Task Sheet view.

	Task Name	Fixed Cost	Fixed Cost Accrual	Total Cost	Baseline	Variance	Actual	Remaining
0	⊟ **Children's book sched**	$0.00	Prorated	$104,506.50	$93,742.00	$10,764.50	$73,717.50	$30,789.00
1	⊞ **Editorial staff meeting**	$0.00	Prorated	$2,223.00	$2,223.00	$0.00	$2,223.00	$0.00
15	⊞ **Acquisition**	$0.00	Prorated	$17,940.00	$17,400.00	$540.00	$17,940.00	$0.00
21	⊟ **Editorial**	$0.00	Prorated	$16,381.00	$15,670.00	$711.00	$16,381.00	$0.00
22	Organize manuscrip	$0.00	Prorated	$3,213.00	$3,060.00	$153.00	$3,213.00	$0.00
23	Copyedit	$0.00	Prorated	$8,460.00	$8,100.00	$360.00	$8,460.00	$0.00
24	Author review of cc	$0.00	Prorated	$1,098.00	$900.00	$198.00	$1,098.00	$0.00
25	Copyedit incorp	$0.00	Prorated	$3,610.00	$3,610.00	$0.00	$3,610.00	$0.00
26	Handoff to Producti	$0.00	Prorated	$0.00	$0.00	$0.00	$0.00	$0.00
27	⊟ **Design and Production**	$0.00	Prorated	$56,192.50	$46,679.00	$9,513.50	$37,173.50	$19,019.00
28	Set pages	$0.00	Prorated	$7,590.00	$7,590.00	$0.00	$7,590.00	$0.00
29	Interior illustration	$0.00	Prorated	$13,485.00	$13,050.00	$435.00	$13,485.00	$0.00
30	⊟ **1st Pages review**	$0.00	Prorated	$22,938.50	$13,860.00	$9,078.50	$16,098.50	$6,840.00
31	Proofread and in	$0.00	Prorated	$5,166.00	$900.00	$4,266.00	$5,166.00	$0.00
32	Incorporate 1st P	$0.00	Prorated	$10,932.50	$6,120.00	$4,812.50	$10,932.50	$0.00
33	Send proofed pa	$0.00	Prorated	$0.00	$0.00	$0.00	$0.00	$0.00
34	Enter page correc	$0.00	Prorated	$4,040.00	$4,040.00	$0.00	$0.00	$4,040.00
35	Cover design	$0.00	Prorated	$2,800.00	$2,800.00	$0.00	$0.00	$2,800.00
36	⊟ **2nd Pages review**	$0.00	Prorated	$6,345.00	$6,345.00	$0.00	$0.00	$6,345.00
37	Proof and review	$0.00	Prorated	$1,800.00	$1,800.00	$0.00	$0.00	$1,800.00
38	Send proofed pa	$0.00	Prorated	$0.00	$0.00	$0.00	$0.00	$0.00
39	Final review	$0.00	Prorated	$4,545.00	$4,545.00	$0.00	$0.00	$4,545.00
40	⊟ **Design book's comp**	$0.00	Prorated	$5,834.00	$5,834.00	$0.00	$0.00	$5,834.00
41	Create mockup	$0.00	Prorated	$2,610.00	$2,610.00	$0.00	$0.00	$2,610.00
42	Review with auth	$0.00	Prorated	$3,224.00	$3,224.00	$0.00	$0.00	$3,224.00
43	⊟ **Color prep and printin**	$0.00	Prorated	$810.00	$810.00	$0.00	$0.00	$810.00
44	Send to color house	$0.00	Prorated	$310.00	$310.00	$0.00	$0.00	$310.00
45	Generate proofs	$500.00	End	$500.00	$500.00	$0.00	$0.00	$500.00
46	Print and ship	$0.00	Prorated	$0.00	$0.00	$0.00	$0.00	$0.00

Ready   New Tasks : Auto Scheduled

In this table, you can see each task's baseline cost, scheduled cost (in the Total Cost column), actual cost, and cost variance. The variance is the difference between the baseline cost and the scheduled cost. Of course, costs aren't scheduled in the same sense that work is scheduled; however, costs derived from work resources (excluding fixed costs and costs associated with material and cost resources) are derived directly from the scheduled work.

Recall from Chapter 5, "Formatting and Sharing Your Plan," that task 0 is the project summary task; its cost values are the project's cost values, and match the values you would see in the Project Information dialog box. These values include the following:

○ The current cost value is the sum of the actual (that is, completed) and remaining (uncompleted) cost values.

○ The baseline cost value is the project's planned cost when its baseline was set.

○ The actual cost is the cost that's been incurred so far.

○ The remaining cost is the difference between the current cost and actual cost.

Next, you'll focus on the top-level costs.

2. On the **View** tab, in the **Data** group, click **Outline** and then click **Outline Level 1**.

Project hides all subtasks and nested summary tasks, leaving only the top-level tasks visible.

Looking at the Variance column, you can see that the *Design and Production* phase (task 27) accounts for nearly all the project's variance.

To conclude this exercise, you will use filters to help you zero in on tasks that have cost variance.

3. On the **View** tab, in the **Data** group, click **Outline** and then click **All Subtasks**.

Project expands the task list to show all subtasks.

4. On the **View** tab, in the **Data** group, click the arrow next to **Filter:** and then click **More Filters**.

5. In the **More Filters** dialog box, click **Cost Overbudget** and then click **Apply**.

Project filters the task list to show only those tasks that had actual and scheduled costs greater than their baseline costs. Scanning the task list you can see that tasks 31 and 32 both incurred substantial variance; you note this for further investigation later.

	Task Name	Fixed Cost ▼	Fixed Cost Accrual ▼	Total Cost ▼	Baseline ▼	Variance ▼	Actual ▼	Remaining ▼
0	⊟ Children's book schedu	$0.00	Prorated	$104,506.50	$93,742.00	$10,764.50	$73,717.50	$30,789.00
15	⊟ Acquisition	$0.00	Prorated	$17,940.00	$17,400.00	$540.00	$17,940.00	$0.00
19	Author review of cc	$0.00	Prorated	$4,140.00	$3,600.00	$540.00	$4,140.00	$0.00
21	⊟ Editorial	$0.00	Prorated	$16,381.00	$15,670.00	$711.00	$16,381.00	$0.00
22	Organize manuscrip	$0.00	Prorated	$3,213.00	$3,060.00	$153.00	$3,213.00	$0.00
23	Copyedit	$0.00	Prorated	$8,460.00	$8,100.00	$360.00	$8,460.00	$0.00
24	Author review of cc	$0.00	Prorated	$1,098.00	$900.00	$198.00	$1,098.00	$0.00
27	⊟ Design and Production	$0.00	Prorated	$56,192.50	$46,679.00	$9,513.50	$37,173.50	$19,019.00
29	Interior illustration	$0.00	Prorated	$13,485.00	$13,050.00	$435.00	$13,485.00	$0.00
30	⊟ 1st Pages review	$0.00	Prorated	$22,938.50	$13,860.00	$9,078.50	$16,098.50	$6,840.00
31	Proofread and in	$0.00	Prorated	$5,166.00	$900.00	$4,266.00	$5,166.00	$0.00
32	Incorporate 1st P	$0.00	Prorated	$10,932.50	$6,120.00	$4,812.50	$10,932.50	$0.00

6. On the **View** tab, in the **Data** group, click the arrow next to **Filter:** and then click **Clear Filter**.

Project removes the filter.

What caused the task cost variance in the new book project? Because this project's costs are almost entirely derived from work performed by resources, we can conclude that more work than scheduled has been required to complete the tasks to date.

As we noted earlier, task and resource costs are closely related; in most cases, task costs are mostly or fully derived from the costs of resources assigned to tasks. Examining resource costs is the subject of the next exercise.

Here are some additional tips and suggestions for working with cost data:

- To see tasks that are over budget, you can use the Overbudget Tasks report. To generate the Overbudget Tasks report, on the Project tab, in the Reports group, click Reports. In the Reports dialog box, double-click Costs, and then double-click Overbudget Tasks.

- If you have Excel 2003 or later, you can use the Budget Cost Report. To create the Budget Cost Report, on the Project tab, in the Reports group, click Visual Reports. In the Assignment Usage tab of the Visual Reports dialog box, click Budget Cost Report and then click View.

- Apply the Late/Overbudget Tasks Assigned To filter for a specific resource. To do this, on the View tab, in the Data group, click the arrow next to Filter: and then click More Filters.

- Display work variance in the Work table in a task view. To do this, on the View tab, in the Data group, click Tables and then click Work. Remember that for a project plan where most costs are derived from work resources, examining work variance is one way to examine cost variance.

- You can compare timephased baseline and scheduled work in a usage view. For example, in the Task Usage view, on the Format tab, in the Details group, click Baseline Work.

- In this exercise, you have viewed cost variance for a task. To see cost variance over time for assignments to a task, switch to the Task Usage view, and then apply the Cost table. While in a usage view, you can also show Cost, Baseline Cost, and Actual Cost details via the Add Details dialog box. On the Format tab, in the Details group, select the options you want.

Examining Resource Costs

Project managers sometimes focus on resource costs as a means of measuring progress and variance within a project. However, resource cost information also serves other people and other needs. For many organizations, resource costs are the primary or even the only costs incurred while completing projects, so closely watching resource costs might directly relate to the financial health of an organization. It might not be a project manager, but instead an executive, cost accountant, or *resource manager* who is most interested in resource costs on projects as they relate to organizational costs.

Another common reason to track resource costs is for billing either within an organization (for example, billing another department for services your department has provided) or externally. In either case, the resource cost information stored in project plans can serve as the basis for billing out your department's or organization's services to others.

Expenses in the new book project are for the most part derived from the costs of resource assignments. You've already seen the task costs, so next you'll focus on resource cost variance.

In this exercise, you use different views, tables, and sorting to see resource cost variance.

1. On the **View** tab, in the **Resource Views** group, click **Resource Sheet**.

   The Resource Sheet view appears.

2. On the **View** tab, in the **Data** group, click **Tables**, and then click **Cost**.

   The Cost table appears.

	Resource Name	Cost	Baseline Cost	Variance	Actual Cost	Remaining
1	Carole Poland	$11,182.50	$11,182.50	$0.00	$9,082.50	$2,100.00
2	Color Setting Service	$0.00	$0.00	$0.00	$0.00	$0.00
3	Copyeditors	$18,864.00	$13,500.00	$5,364.00	$18,864.00	$0.00
4	Dan Jump	$11,362.75	$8,644.75	$2,718.00	$9,248.75	$2,114.00
5	Hany Morcos	$24,391.25	$21,988.75	$2,402.50	$15,306.25	$9,085.00
6	Jane Dow	$19,580.00	$19,580.00	$0.00	$11,990.00	$7,590.00
7	Jun Cao	$546.00	$546.00	$0.00	$546.00	$0.00
8	Luis Sousa	$14,280.00	$14,000.00	$280.00	$8,680.00	$5,600.00
9	Printing Service	$0.00	$0.00	$0.00	$0.00	$0.00
10	Tad Orman	$0.00	$0.00	$0.00	$0.00	$0.00
11	Travel	$3,500.00	$3,500.00	$0.00	$0.00	$3,500.00
12	Bound galley proof	$300.00	$300.00	$0.00	$0.00	$300.00

In the Cost table, you can see each resource's cost, baseline cost, and related cost values. In most cases here, the cost values for work resources are derived from each resource's cost rate multiplied by the work on their assignments to tasks in the project plan.

Currently, the resource sheet is sorted by resource ID. Next, you will sort it by resource cost.

3. Click the **AutoFilter** arrow in the **Cost** column heading, and in the menu that appears, click **Sort Largest to Smallest**.

Project sorts the resources by cost from highest to lowest. Note that the resources are sorted according to the values in the Cost column, which is the sum of their actual (or historical) costs, and their remaining (or expected) costs.

	Resource Name	Cost	Baseline Cost	Variance	Actual Cost	Remaining
5	Hany Morcos	$24,391.25	$21,988.75	$2,402.50	$15,306.25	$9,085.00
6	Jane Dow	$19,580.00	$19,580.00	$0.00	$11,990.00	$7,590.00
3	Copyeditors	$18,864.00	$13,500.00	$5,364.00	$18,864.00	$0.00
8	Luis Sousa	$14,280.00	$14,000.00	$280.00	$8,680.00	$5,600.00
4	Dan Jump	$11,362.75	$8,644.75	$2,718.00	$9,248.75	$2,114.00
1	Carole Poland	$11,182.50	$11,182.50	$0.00	$9,082.50	$2,100.00
11	Travel	$3,500.00	$3,500.00	$0.00	$0.00	$3,500.00
7	Jun Cao	$546.00	$546.00	$0.00	$546.00	$0.00
12	Bound galley proof	$300.00	$300.00	$0.00	$0.00	$300.00
2	Color Setting Service	$0.00	$0.00	$0.00	$0.00	$0.00
9	Printing Service	$0.00	$0.00	$0.00	$0.00	$0.00
10	Tad Orman	$0.00	$0.00	$0.00	$0.00	$0.00

This sort quickly tells you who are cumulatively the most and least costly resources (as indicated in the Cost column), but it doesn't help you see variance patterns. You will do that next.

4. Click the **AutoFilter** arrow in the **Variance** column heading, and in the menu that appears, click **Sort Largest to Smallest**.

Project re-sorts the resources by cost variance from highest to lowest.

	Resource Name	Cost	Baseline Cost	Variance	Actual Cost	Remaining	A
3	Copyeditors	$18,864.00	$13,500.00	$5,364.00	$18,864.00	$0.00	
4	Dan Jump	$11,362.75	$8,644.75	$2,718.00	$9,248.75	$2,114.00	
5	Hany Morcos	$24,391.25	$21,988.75	$2,402.50	$15,306.25	$9,085.00	
8	Luis Sousa	$14,280.00	$14,000.00	$280.00	$8,680.00	$5,600.00	
1	Carole Poland	$11,182.50	$11,182.50	$0.00	$9,082.50	$2,100.00	
2	Color Setting Service	$0.00	$0.00	$0.00	$0.00	$0.00	
6	Jane Dow	$19,580.00	$19,580.00	$0.00	$11,990.00	$7,590.00	
7	Jun Cao	$546.00	$546.00	$0.00	$546.00	$0.00	
9	Printing Service	$0.00	$0.00	$0.00	$0.00	$0.00	
10	Tad Orman	$0.00	$0.00	$0.00	$0.00	$0.00	
11	Travel	$3,500.00	$3,500.00	$0.00	$0.00	$3,500.00	
12	Bound galley proof	$300.00	$300.00	$0.00	$0.00	$300.00	

With the resource list sorted by cost variance, you can quickly zero in on those resources with the greatest variance—the Copyeditors in this case. You note this for future investigation.

5. On the **View** tab, in the **Data** group, click **Sort**, and then click **by ID**.

Project re-sorts the resources by ID.

Note that the dollar amount of variance, while important, doesn't tell you the whole story. What would be useful to know is what tasks had the highest percentage of variance. A task with a $1,000 baseline and $1,200 actual cost has a lower percentage of variance than does a cost with a $100 baseline and $200 actual cost. In complex projects, understanding what tasks are prone to greater percentages of variance can help you avoid similar problems in the future. In the next section, you will see one way to begin to analyze variance in this way.

Here are some additional tips and suggestions for working with resource costs:

- You can use the Overbudget Resources report to list resources who are over budget. To do this, on the Project tab, in the Reports Group, click Reports. In the Reports dialog box, double-click Costs, and then double-click Overbudget Resources.

- You can also see timephased cost values in a usage view. For example, in the Resource Usage view, on the Format tab, in the Details group, click Add Details. In the Details Styles dialog box, show the Baseline Cost and Cost fields. This also works in the Task Usage view.

- If you have Excel 2003 or later, you can use the Resource Cost Summary Report. To do this, on the Project tab, in the Reports group, click Visual Reports. In the Resource Usage tab of the Visual Reports dialog box, click Resource Cost Summary Report and then click View.

Reporting Project Cost Variance with a Stoplight View

There are many different ways to report a project's status in terms of task or budget variance or other measures. There is no shortage of features in Project that support reporting project status, but the main thing to keep in mind is that the method by which you report project status is less a technical question than a communications question. For example, what format and level of detail do your stakeholders need to see? Should project sponsors see different aspects of a project's performance than those seen by its resources? These questions are central to the project manager's job. Fortunately, as noted earlier, Project is a rich communications tool that you can use to construct the type of project status information that best meets the needs of your stakeholders.

Next, you focus on creating what is often called a stoplight report. This status report represents key indicators for tasks, such as schedule or budget status, as a simple red, yellow, or green light. Such status reports are easy for anyone to understand, and they quickly provide a general sense of the health of a project. Strictly speaking, what you'll create here is not a report in Project, so we'll call it a *stoplight view* instead.

In this exercise, you create a view using custom fields to visually focus on project variance.

1. On the **View** tab, in the **Task Views** group, click **Other Views** and then click **Task Sheet**.

   Project displays the Task Sheet view. It currently contains the Cost table.

   To save you time, we have customized a field in this Project file containing a formula that evaluates each task's cost variance. Next, you will view the formula to understand what it does and then view the graphical indicators assigned to the field.

2. On the **Format** tab, in the **Columns** group, click **Custom Fields**.

   The Custom Fields dialog box appears.

3. In the **Type** box located in the upper-right corner of the dialog box, click **Number** on the drop-down list.

4. In the list box, click **Overbudget (Number3)**. This is the customized field we've set up for you.

The Number3 field has been renamed "Overbudget" and customized with a formula and graphical indicators.

5. Under **Custom attributes**, click **Formula**.

The Formula dialog box appears.

When writing a formula, use these buttons to insert Project fields or functions into your formula.

This formula evaluates each task's cost variance. If the task's cost is 10 percent or less above baseline, the formula assigns the number 10 to the task. If the cost is between 10 percent and 20 percent above baseline, it is assigned a 20. If the cost is more than 20 percent above baseline, it receives a 30.

6. Click **Cancel** to close the **Formula** dialog box.

7. In the **Custom Fields** dialog box, under **Values to display**, click **Graphical Indicators**.

   The Graphical Indicators dialog box appears. Here, you specify a unique graphical indicator to display, depending on the value of the field for each task. Again, to save you time, the indicators are already selected.

   Depending on the value returned by the formula, Project will display one of these three graphical indicators in the Overbudget column.

8. Click the first cell under the **Image** column heading (it contains a green smiley face), and then click the drop-down arrow.

   Here, you can see the many graphical indicators that you can associate with the values of fields.

9. Click **Cancel** to close the **Graphical Indicators** dialog box, and then click **Cancel** again to close the **Custom Fields** dialog box.

10. In the **Task Name** column, click the minus sign next to the name of task 1, the *Editorial staff meeting* recurring summary task.

    The recurring task list collapses to show just the recurring summary task.

    To conclude this exercise, you will display the Overbudget (Number3) column in the Cost table.

11. On the right side of the table, click the **Add New Column** column heading.

    A list of available fields appears.

12. In the list of fields, click **Overbudget (Number3)** on the drop-down list.

    You will also see the same customized field named *Number3 (Overbudget)* in the list of fields.

    Tip When selecting items from a list like this, you can begin typing the name of the item you want and when its full name appears, select it.

    Project displays the Overbudget column in the Cost table.

	Task Name	Fixed Cost	Fixed Cost Accrual	Total Cost	Baseline	Variance	Actual	Remaining	Overbudget
0	Children's book schedu	$0.00	Prorated	$104,506.50	$93,742.00	$10,764.50	$73,717.50	$30,789.00	
1	Editorial staff meeting	$0.00	Prorated	$2,223.00	$2,223.00	$0.00	$2,223.00	$0.00	
15	Acquisition	$0.00	Prorated	$17,940.00	$17,400.00	$540.00	$17,940.00	$0.00	
16	Manuscript receiver	$0.00	Prorated	$0.00	$0.00	$0.00	$0.00	$0.00	
17	Content edit	$0.00	Prorated	$6,300.00	$6,300.00	$0.00	$6,300.00	$0.00	
18	Original art review	$0.00	Prorated	$7,500.00	$7,500.00	$0.00	$7,500.00	$0.00	
19	Author review of cc	$0.00	Prorated	$4,140.00	$3,600.00	$540.00	$4,140.00	$0.00	
20	Handoff to Editorial	$0.00	Prorated	$0.00	$0.00	$0.00	$0.00	$0.00	
21	Editorial	$0.00	Prorated	$16,381.00	$15,670.00	$711.00	$16,381.00	$0.00	
22	Organize manuscrip	$0.00	Prorated	$3,213.00	$3,060.00	$153.00	$3,213.00	$0.00	
23	Copyedit	$0.00	Prorated	$8,460.00	$8,100.00	$360.00	$8,460.00	$0.00	
24	Author review of cc	$0.00	Prorated	$1,098.00	$900.00	$198.00	$1,098.00	$0.00	
25	Copyedit incorp	$0.00	Prorated	$3,610.00	$3,610.00	$0.00	$3,610.00	$0.00	
26	Handoff to Producti	$0.00	Prorated	$0.00	$0.00	$0.00	$0.00	$0.00	
27	Design and Production	$0.00	Prorated	$56,192.50	$46,679.00	$9,513.50	$37,173.50	$19,019.00	
28	Set pages	$0.00	Prorated	$7,590.00	$7,590.00	$0.00	$7,590.00	$0.00	
29	Interior illustration	$0.00	Prorated	$13,485.00	$13,050.00	$435.00	$13,485.00	$0.00	
30	1st Pages review	$0.00	Prorated	$22,938.50	$13,860.00	$9,078.50	$16,098.50	$6,840.00	
31	Proofread and in	$0.00	Prorated	$5,166.00	$900.00	$4,266.00	$5,166.00	$0.00	
32	Incorporate 1st P	$0.00	Prorated	$10,932.50	$6,120.00	$4,812.50	$10,932.50	$0.00	
33	Send proofed pa;	$0.00	Prorated	$0.00	$0.00	$0.00	$0.00	$0.00	
34	Enter page correc	$0.00	Prorated	$4,040.00	$4,040.00	$0.00	$0.00	$4,040.00	
35	Cover design	$0.00	Prorated	$2,800.00	$2,800.00	$0.00	$0.00	$2,800.00	
36	2nd Pages review	$0.00	Prorated	$6,345.00	$6,345.00	$0.00	$0.00	$6,345.00	
37	Proof and review	$0.00	Prorated	$1,800.00	$1,800.00	$0.00	$0.00	$1,800.00	
38	Send proofed pa;	$0.00	Prorated	$0.00	$0.00	$0.00	$0.00	$0.00	
39	Final review	$0.00	Prorated	$4,545.00	$4,545.00	$0.00	$0.00	$4,545.00	
40	Design book's comp	$0.00	Prorated	$5,834.00	$5,834.00	$0.00	$0.00	$5,834.00	

Ready   New Tasks : Auto Scheduled

Tip To see a graphical indicator's numeric value in a ScreenTip, just point to the indicator.

As each task's cost variance changes, so do the graphical indicators according to the ranges specified in the formula. This is a handy format for identifying tasks whose cost variance is higher than you'd like, as indicated by the yellow or red lights. You can see that tasks 31 and 32, and consequently their summary task 30, experienced both a high dollar amount of variance and a high percentage above baseline, as indicated by the red sad face indicators. Tasks 33 and later have no variance because they have not yet started.

Up to now, you've identified schedule and budget variance in a task view and budget variance in a resource view—each an important measure of project status. This is a good time to remind yourself that the final qualifier of project status is not the exact formatting of the data in Project, but the needs of your project's stakeholders. Determining what these needs are requires your good judgment and communication skills.

✖ CLEAN UP Close the Reporting Status file.

Key Points

- Schedule variance is caused by tasks that have slipped from their planned start or finish dates (as recorded in a baseline). You can use a combination of views, tables, filters, and reports to identify which tasks have slipped and caused variance.

- Schedule and cost variance are closely related—if a project plan has one, it likely has the other. As with schedule variance, you can apply a combination of views, tables, filters, and reports to locate cost variance.

- You can use formulas and graphical indicators in custom fields to create a highly customized view, such as a stoplight view, to communicate key project health indicators to your stakeholders.

Chapter at a Glance

Resolve missed deadlines by rescheduling tasks, page 300.

Identify tasks on the critical path, page 300.

Add additional resources to reduce task durations, page 300.

Replace resources with less expensive resources, page 307.

Inactivate tasks (Project Professional) or delete tasks (Project Standard) to reduce overall project scope, page 311.

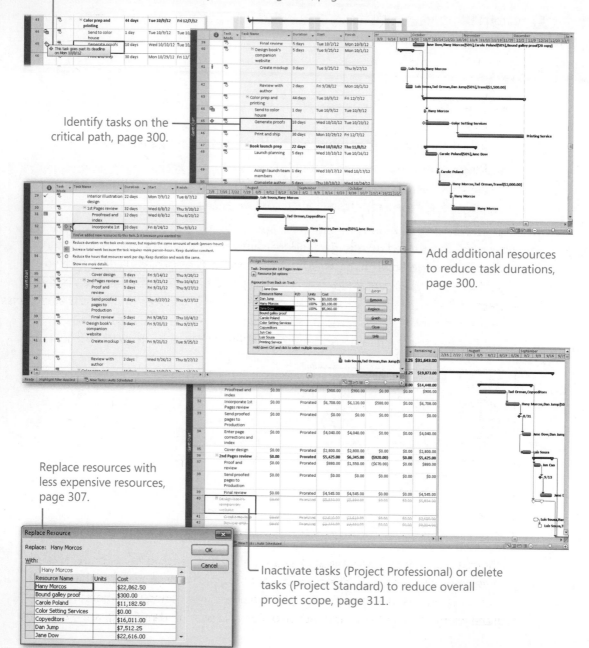

14 Getting Your Project Back on Track

In this chapter, you will learn how to:

✔ Assign additional resources to tasks to reduce task durations.

✔ Replace resources assigned to tasks.

✔ Delete or inactivate tasks.

After work has started on a project, addressing *variance* is not a one-time event, but instead is an ongoing effort by the project manager. The specific way in which you should respond to variance depends on the type of variance and the nature of the project. In this chapter, we'll focus on some of the many variance problems that can arise during a project as work progresses. We'll frame these problems around the *project triangle*, described in detail in Appendix A, "A Short Course in Project Management."

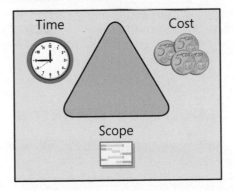

In short, the project triangle model frames a project in terms of *time* (or duration), *cost* (or budget), and *scope* (the project work required to produce a satisfactory *deliverable*). In this model time, cost, and scope are interconnected; therefore, changing one element can affect the other two. For purposes of identifying, analyzing, and addressing problems in project management, it's useful to fit problems into one of these three categories.

In virtually any project, one of these factors will be more important than the other two. The most important factor is sometimes called the driving constraint because meeting it drives your actions as a project manager. For example, for a project that must be concluded by a specific date, you might need to make cost and scope compromises to meet the deadline. Working with the project triangle provides you with a good method to analyze the trade-offs that nearly always must be made. Just as importantly, it gives you a clear way of explaining the pros and cons of trade-offs to the project's *resources, sponsors,* and other *stakeholders.*

The specific issues that we'll focus on in this chapter are not necessarily the most common problems you'll face in your own projects. Because every project is unique, there's no way to anticipate what you'll run into. However, we've attempted to highlight the most pressing issues at the midpoint of the new children's book project at Lucerne Publishing that we have been discussing throughout this book and apply solutions to common problems. You've already worked with most of the features used in this chapter, but here your intent is different—getting the project plan back on track.

> **Practice Files** Before you can complete the exercises in this chapter, you need to copy the book's practice files to your computer. A complete list of practice files is provided in "Using the Practice Files" at the beginning of this book. For each exercise that has a practice file, simply browse to where you saved the book's practice file folder.

Important If you are running Microsoft Project Professional, you may need to make a one-time setting change. This helps ensure that the practice files you work with in this chapter do not affect your Project Server data. For more information, see Appendix C, "Using the Practice Files if Connected to Project Server."

Troubleshooting Time and Schedule Problems

Schedule variance will almost certainly appear in any lengthy project. Maintaining control over the schedule requires that the project manager know when variance has occurred and to what extent, and then take timely corrective action to stay on track. To help you identify when variance has occurred, the new children's book project plan includes the following:

- A deadline date applied to a time-sensitive task
- A project baseline against which you can compare actual performance

The deadline date and project baseline will help you troubleshoot time and schedule problems in Project.

In this exercise, you address a missed deadline and shorten the durations of some tasks on the critical path.

 SET UP Start Project if it's not already running.

You need the Back on Track_Start project plan located in your Chapter14 practice file folder to complete this exercise. Open the Back on Track_Start project plan, and then follow these steps.

1. On the **File** tab, click **Save As**.

   The Save As dialog box appears.

2. In the **File name** box, type **Back on Track**, and then click **Save**.

   To begin troubleshooting the time and schedule issues, you'll get a top-level view of the degree of schedule variance in the project plan to date.

3. On the **Project** tab, in the **Properties** group, click **Project Information**.

   The Project Information dialog box appears.

4. Click **Statistics**.

   Project Statistics for 'Back on Track'

	Start	Finish
Current	Mon 4/2/12	Fri 12/7/12
Baseline	Mon 4/2/12	Fri 11/16/12
Actual	Mon 4/2/12	NA
Variance	0d	15.5d

	Duration	Work	Cost
Current	179d	2,520.9h	$98,462.25
Baseline	163.5d	2,249.5h	$87,908.00
Actual	88.72d	1,396.9h	$60,903.25
Remaining	90.28d	1,124h	$37,559.00

   Percent complete:
   Duration: 50%   Work: 55%

   Close

   As you can see, the new book plan has both schedule variance and cost variance. The schedule variance is listed in the intersection of the Finish column and Variance row. Also note that in terms of overall duration, this project plan is 50 percent complete.

5. Click **Close** to close the **Project Statistics** dialog box.

   The Statistics dialog box includes the project's finish date. However, to monitor the finish date as you work on the schedule, you can keep your eye on the Finish date for task 0, the project summary task.

	ⓘ	Task Mode	Task Name	Duration	Start	Finish	Mar 25, '12	Apr 1, '12	Apr 8, '12	Apr 15, '12	Apr 22, '12
0			⊟ Children's Book Schedule	179 days	Mon 4/2/12	Fri 12/7/12					
1	⟳✓		⊞ Editorial staff meeting	60.13 days	Mon 4/9/12	Mon 7/2/12					
15	✓		⊟ Acquisition	37 days	Mon 4/2/12	Tue 5/22/12					
21	✓		⊟ Editorial	29.78 days	Wed 5/23/12	Tue 7/3/12					
22	✓		Organize manuscript for copyedit	5 days	Wed 5/23/12	Tue 5/29/12					
23	✓		Copyedit	10.5 days	Wed 5/30/12	Wed 6/13/12					
24	✓		Author review of copyedit	12.2 days	Wed 6/13/12	Fri 6/29/12					
25	✓		Copyedit incorp	5 days	Tue 6/26/12	Tue 7/3/12					
26	✓		Handoff to Production	u days	Tue 7/3/12	Tue 7/3/12					
27			⊟ Design and Production	68.23 days	Tue 7/3/12	Mon 10/8/12					

Note the current project finish date in task 0's Finish field. You know that this date must be pulled in to meet your book printing date. Before you address the overall project duration, you'll examine the missed deadline for the *Generate proofs* task.

6. In the **Task Name** column, click the name of task 45, *Generate proofs*.

7. On the **Task** tab, in the **Editing** group, click **Scroll to Task**.

   Tip To select a task quickly, even a task you can't see in the current view, press Ctrl+G and, in the ID field of the Go To dialog box, enter a task number, and then click OK.

8. Point to the missed deadline indicator in the **Indicators** column for task 45, *Generate proofs*.

┌─ Positioning the mouse pointer over the
  missed deadline indicator displays a ScreenTip
  in which you can see the details of the deadline.

Enough changes to the schedule have occurred to cause the scheduled completion of this task to move out beyond its deadline date of October 8. Next, you'll adjust the view to better see tasks on the *critical path*—that is, the tasks that are driving the finish date of the project plan.

9. On the **View** tab, in the **Zoom** group, in the **Timescale** box, click **Weeks**.

10. On the **View** tab, in the **Data** group, click **Highlight** and then click **Critical**.

   Project applies a yellow highlight to the tasks in the table portion of the Gantt Chart view that are on the critical path.

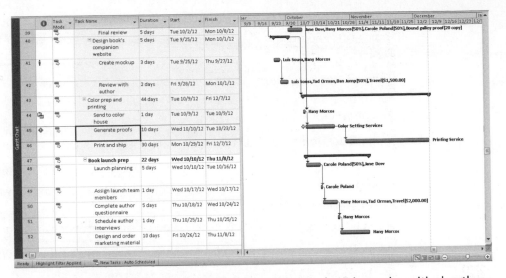

With the view displayed this way, you can see that task 45 is on the critical path, as is its successor task 46, *Print and ship*. Task 47 and its subtasks, however, are not on the critical path; their scheduling is currently not driving the project's finish date. This is an example where task ID order does not match chronological sequence.

To continue addressing the missed deadline on task 45, you'll focus on its predecessor tasks that have not yet been completed.

11. In the **Task Name** column, select the name of task 31, *Proofread and index*.

12. On the **Task** tab, in the **Editing** group, click **Scroll to Task**.

The Gantt bar for task 31 comes into view.

This is the next task to start, as indicated by the "task complete" check marks in the Indicators column and the progress bars through the Gantt bars of tasks 29 and earlier.

The new book's author, Tad Orman, and a copyeditor are assigned to the task. After consulting with the assigned resources, you all agree that task 31 can be completed in a slightly shorter duration: 12 days.

13. In the **Duration** field of task 31, type **12d**, and then press the Enter key.

Project reduces the duration of the task and reschedules the affected successor tasks, including task 45 and the project finish date.

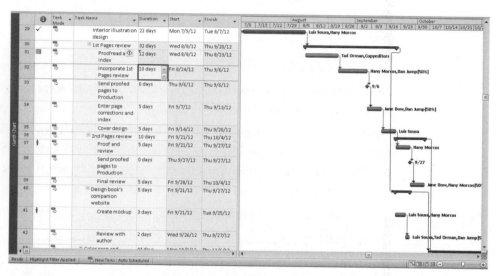

This adjustment isn't enough to fix task 45's missed deadline, however.

Task 32 should now be selected. For this task, you and the assigned resources agree that adding an additional resource should reduce the task's duration.

14. On the **Resource** tab, in the **Assignments** group, click **Assign Resources**.

The Assign Resources dialog box appears, with the names of the resources currently assigned to task 32 at the top of the Resource Name column.

15. In the **Assign Resources** dialog box, in the **Resource Name** column, click Jane Dow, and then click **Assign**.

After assigning the additional resource, you now need to tell Project how it should adjust the scheduling of the task.

16. Click the **Action** indicator in the **Task Name** field of task 32 (the small triangle in the upper-left corner of the field), and then click the **Action** button that appears.

The Action list appears.

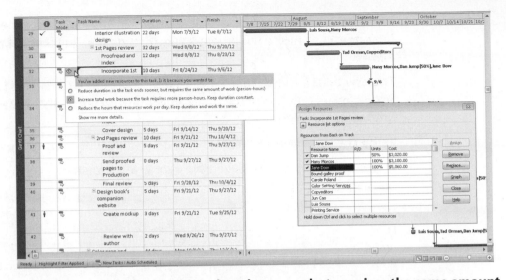

17. Click **Reduce duration so the task ends sooner, but requires the same amount of work (person-hours)**.

Project reduces the duration of task 32 from 10 days to 6 days. Because of the Action option you chose, Project kept the amount of work on the task the same, but that work is now distributed among the three assigned resources rather than the two resources.

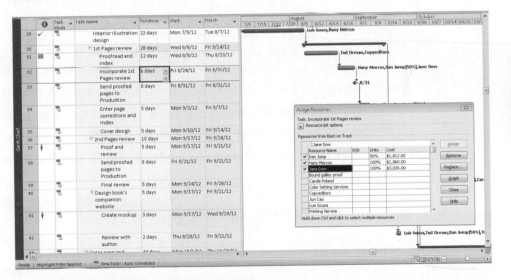

18. Click **Close** in the **Assign Resources** dialog box.

Checking the deadline indicator and the Gantt bar for task 45, you see that these actions have moved the completion date of task 45 closer to its deadline, but it's not there yet.

Looking over the remaining tasks that are predecessors of task 45, you see that tasks 34 and 35 have a finish-to-start relationship and different resources assigned. After consulting with the assigned resources, you decide these tasks could be completed in parallel. Next, you'll change their relationship type.

19. Scroll the table portion of the **Gantt Chart** view to the right to show the **Predecessors** column.

20. In the **Predecessors** field for task 35, type **34SS** and then press Enter.

Project changes the task relationship type to start-to-start.

Changing the predecessor relationship between these tasks to start-to-start decreases the overall duration of the project because these tasks are on the critical path.

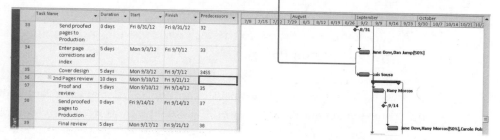

Now that these two tasks have a start-to-start relationship, the successor task's start date is moved in by five days. Checking the deadline indicator on task 45, you see that the missed deadline indicator is gone; you've sufficiently pulled in task 45's finish date (for now at least). The project's finish date has been correspondingly adjusted due to these schedule changes to tasks on the critical path.

This is an important deadline on task 45 so you plan to closely monitor the progress on its predecessor tasks as work progresses.

21. On the **View** tab, in the **Data** group, click **Highlight,** and then click **Clear Highlight**.

Reduce Task Durations by Assigning Resource Overtime Hours

One way to reduce a task's duration is to add overtime to the assigned resource. The trade-off may be additional costs, especially if the resource has an overtime pay rate. To add overtime to an assignment, follow these steps.

1. On the **View** tab, in the **Split View** group, click **Details**.

The Task Form appears below the Gantt Chart view.

2. Click anywhere in the **Task Form** and then on the **Format** tab, in the **Details** group, click **Work**.

3. For the task to which you want to add overtime, in the **Task Form,** enter the number of overtime work hours that you want in the **Ovt. Work** column, and then click **OK**.

When you add overtime work, the resource's total work on the task remains the same. After entering an overtime work value, however, that number of hours will be scheduled as overtime. The same amount of work will be performed, but in a shorter time span. Project also will apply overtime cost rates, if they have been set up, to the overtime portion of the assignment. If you plan to assign overtime hours for which an overtime pay rate should be applied, make sure you have a valid overtime pay rate set up for the assigned resource.

Troubleshooting Cost and Resource Problems

In projects where you've entered cost information for resources, you might find that you must fine-tune resource and assignment details to address cost or budget problems. Although this might not be your intention, changing resource assignment details not only affects costs, but it can affect task durations as well.

In addition to schedule variance, the new book project plan has some cost variance. As it is currently scheduled, the project plan will end up costing about $11,000 more than planned, or about 12 percent over budget. Recall from Chapter 13, "Viewing and Reporting Project Status," that the new book plan's cost variance is the result of some longer-than-expected task durations, and the delays increased the costs of the assigned resources. To address cost variance in this project, you'll focus on resource costs. While examining resource cost issues, you'll also look for opportunities to address any resource overallocation problems that have crept into the project plan.

In this exercise, you examine resource cost values and replace one resource assigned to a task with another resource.

1. On the **View** tab, in the **Resource Views** group, click **Resource Sheet**.

    You will use the Resource Sheet view to identify your most costly resources for the remaining tasks—costly not in hourly pay rate, but in the total expense in this project plan based on their assignments.

2. On the **View** tab, in the **Data** group, click **Tables**, and then click **Cost**.

    The Cost table appears in the Resource Sheet view.

	Resource Name	Cost	Baseline Cost	Variance	Actual Cost	Remaining
1	Carole Poland	$11,182.50	$11,182.50	$0.00	$9,082.50	$2,100.00
2	Color Setting Service	$0.00	$0.00	$0.00	$0.00	$0.00
3	Copyeditors	$16,011.00	$13,500.00	$2,511.00	$15,111.00	$900.00
4	Dan Jump	$7,512.25	$8,040.75	($528.50)	$3,586.25	$3,926.00
5	Hany Morcos	$22,862.50	$21,058.75	$1,803.75	$12,167.50	$10,695.00
6	Jane Dow	$22,616.00	$19,580.00	$3,036.00	$11,990.00	$10,626.00
7	Jun Cao	$286.00	$546.00	($260.00)	$286.00	$0.00
8	Luis Sousa	$14,280.00	$11,200.00	$3,080.00	$8,680.00	$5,600.00
9	Printing Service	$0.00	$0.00	$0.00	$0.00	$0.00
10	Tad Orman	$0.00	$0.00	$0.00	$0.00	$0.00
11	Travel	$3,500.00	$2,000.00	$1,500.00	$0.00	$3,500.00
12	Bound galley proof	$300.00	$300.00	$0.00	$0.00	$300.00

At this point, about half the project's duration has elapsed, so the most expensive resources overall might not be the most expensive resources for the work not yet completed. To identify the most expensive resources for the remaining work, you'll sort the table.

3. Click the **AutoFilter** arrow in the **Remaining** column heading, and in the menu that appears, click **Sort Largest to Smallest**.

	Resource Name	Cost	Baseline Cost	Variance	Actual Cost	Remaining
5	Hany Morcos	$22,862.50	$21,058.75	$1,803.75	$12,167.50	$10,695.00
6	Jane Dow	$22,616.00	$19,580.00	$3,036.00	$11,990.00	$10,626.00
8	Luis Sousa	$14,280.00	$11,200.00	$3,080.00	$8,680.00	$5,600.00
4	Dan Jump	$7,512.25	$8,040.75	($528.50)	$3,586.25	$3,926.00
11	Travel	$3,500.00	$2,000.00	$1,500.00	$0.00	$3,500.00
1	Carole Poland	$11,182.50	$11,182.50	$0.00	$9,082.50	$2,100.00
3	Copyeditors	$16,011.00	$13,500.00	$2,511.00	$15,111.00	$900.00
12	Bound galley proof	$300.00	$300.00	$0.00	$0.00	$300.00
2	Color Setting Service	$0.00	$0.00	$0.00	$0.00	$0.00
7	Jun Cao	$286.00	$546.00	($260.00)	$286.00	$0.00
9	Printing Service	$0.00	$0.00	$0.00	$0.00	$0.00
10	Tad Orman	$0.00	$0.00	$0.00	$0.00	$0.00

You can see that Hany Morcos and Jane Dow have the largest remaining cost values at this point in the project plan's duration. Managing costs for these two resources is one way that you can help limit additional cost variance. Note also that Hany's name is formatted red, indicating that she is overallocated.

4. On the **View** tab, in the **Task Views** group, click **Gantt Chart**.

   Project displays the Gantt Chart view. Next, you'll look at the tasks to which Hany and Jane are assigned.

5. If necessary, drag the vertical divider bar to the right to display the **Resource Names** column, then click the **AutoFilter** arrow in the **Resource Names** column heading. Then, in the menu that appears, click **(Select All)** to clear all the resource names, and then select *Hany Morcos* and *Jane Dow*.

6. Click **OK**.

   Project filters the task list to display only those tasks to which Hany or Jane is assigned.

7. Scroll the Gantt Chart view down to show later tasks.

	ⓘ	Task Mode	Task Name	Duration	Start	Finish	Predecessors	Resource Names	
26	✓	🖥	Handoff to Production	0 days	Tue 7/3/12	Tue 7/3/12	25	Hany Morcos	Hany Morcos
27		🖥	⊟ Design and Production	57.23 days	Tue 7/3/12	Fri 9/21/12	21		
28	✓	🖥	Set pages	15 days	Tue 7/3/12	Wed 7/25/12		Jane Dow	Jane Dow
29	✓	🖥	Interior illustration design	22 days	Mon 7/9/12	Tue 8/7/12	28SS	Luis Sousa,Hany Morcos	Luis Sousa,Hany Morcos
30		🖥	⊟ 1st Pages review	23 days	Wed 8/8/12	Fri 9/7/12	29		
32		🖥	Incorporate 1st Pages review	6 days	Fri 8/24/12	Fri 8/31/12	31	Hany Morcos,Dan Jump[50%],Jane	Hany Morcos,Dan Jump[50%
33		🖥	Send proofed pages to Production	0 days	Fri 8/31/12	Fri 8/31/12	32	Hany Morcos	◆ 8/31
34		🖥	Enter page corrections and index	5 days	Mon 9/3/12	Fri 9/7/12	33	Jane Dow,Dan Jump[50%]	Jane Dow,Dan Jump[
36		🖥	⊟ 2nd Pages review	10 days	Mon 9/10/12	Fri 9/21/12			
37	ⓘ	🖥	Proof and review	5 days	Mon 9/10/12	Fri 9/14/12	35	Hany Morcos	Hany Morcos
38		🖥	Send proofed pages to Production	0 days	Fri 9/14/12	Fri 9/14/12	37	Hany Morcos	◆ 9/14
39		🖥	Final review	5 days	Mon 9/17/12	Fri 9/21/12	38	Jane Dow,Hany Mo	Jane D
40		🖥	⊟ Design book's companion website	5 days	Mon 9/10/12	Fri 9/14/12	30		
41	ⓘ	🖥	Create mockup	3 days	Mon 9/10/12	Wed 9/12/12		Luis Sousa,Hany Morcos	Luis Sousa,Hany

Looking at the uncompleted tasks, you can easily spot Hany Morcos's overallocation: she's assigned to tasks 37 and 41, which overlap. That is why the red "overallocated resource" indicators appear in the Indicators column for these tasks.

You could fix Hany's overall allocation by resource leveling, but that is likely to extend the project's finish date and won't help reduce the project's overall cost. Instead, you'll replace Hany with a less expensive resource on one of her assignments.

8. Click the **AutoFilter** arrow (shaped like a funnel because the filter is applied) in the **Resource Names** column heading, and in the menu that appears, click **(Select All)** to check all the resource names, and then click **OK**.

   Project unfilters the task list to show all tasks.

9. In the **Task Name** column, click the name of task 37, *Proof and review*.

   This is a task that a less experienced (and cheaper) editor should be able to handle, so you'll replace Hany.

10. On the **Resource** tab, in the **Assignments** group, click **Assign Resources**.

    The Assign Resources dialog box appears. Note the cost of Hany's assignment to task 37: $1,550.

11. In the **Assign Resources** dialog box, in the **Resource Name** column, click *Hany Morcos*, and then click **Replace**.

    The Replace Resource dialog box appears. In this dialog box, you see the total cost per resource, based on their cost rates and assignments to tasks in the project plan.

12. In the **Resource Name** column in the **Replace Resource** dialog box, click *Jun Cao*, and then click **OK**.

Project replaces Hany with Jun on this assignment.

Jun's lower cost on the assignment, $880, appears in the Assign Resources dialog box. Note also that the red "overallocated resource" indicators no longer appear in the Indicators column; you have resolved Hany's overall allocation. Finally, note also that the finish date of task 37 was moved in by one day. This is due to Jun's "four by ten" working calendar that you set up in Chapter 3, "Setting Up Resources."

13. In the **Assign Resources** dialog box, click **Close**.

Troubleshooting Scope-of-Work Problems

A project's scope should include all the work required—and only the work required—to deliver the product of the project successfully to its intended customer. After project work has started, managing its scope usually requires making trade-offs: trading time for money, quality for time, and so on. You might have the goal of never making such trade-offs, but a more realistic goal might be to make the best-informed trade-offs possible.

After consulting with the management of Lucerne Publishing, you've been asked to shave about $5,000 from the remaining tasks in the new book project plan. This project plan's finish date is fine as is, but the actual cost has gone somewhat over budget, and you need to reduce work to reduce the remaining costs.

In this exercise, you view tasks' remaining costs and remove some tasks from the project plan.

1. On the **View** tab, in the **Data** group, click **Tables**, and then click **Cost**.

   Your focus here is on the tasks not yet completed, so you'll filter the task list.

2. On the **View** tab, in the **Data** group, click the arrow next to **Filter:** and then click **Incomplete Tasks**.

   Project filters the task list to show only the tasks that are not yet complete.

	Task Name	Fixed Cost	Fixed Cost Accrual	Total Cost	Baseline	Variance	Actual	Remaining
0	Children's Book Schedule	$0.00	Prorated	$98,380.25	$87,908.00	$10,472.25	$60,903.25	$37,477.00
27	Design and Production	$0.00	Prorated	$48,758.25	$40,845.00	$7,913.25	$23,051.25	$25,707.00
30	1st Pages review	$0.00	Prorated	$14,448.00	$13,860.00	$588.00	$0.00	$14,448.00
31	Proofread and index	$0.00	Prorated	$900.00	$900.00	$0.00	$0.00	$900.00
32	Incorporate 1st Pages review	$0.00	Prorated	$6,708.00	$6,120.00	$588.00	$0.00	$6,708.00
33	Send proofed pages to Production	$0.00	Prorated	$0.00	$0.00	$0.00	$0.00	$0.00
34	Enter page corrections and index	$0.00	Prorated	$4,040.00	$4,040.00	$0.00	$0.00	$4,040.00
35	Cover design	$0.00	Prorated	$2,800.00	$2,800.00	$0.00	$0.00	$2,800.00
36	2nd Pages review	$0.00	Prorated	$5,425.00	$6,345.00	($920.00)	$0.00	$5,425.00
37	Proof and review	$0.00	Prorated	$880.00	$1,550.00	($670.00)	$0.00	$880.00
38	Send proofed pages to Production	$0.00	Prorated	$0.00	$0.00	$0.00	$0.00	$0.00
39	Final review	$0.00	Prorated	$4,545.00	$4,545.00	$0.00	$0.00	$4,545.00
40	Design book's companion website	$0.00	Prorated	$5,834.00	$5,834.00	$0.00	$0.00	$5,834.00
41	Create mockup	$0.00	Prorated	$2,610.00	$2,610.00	$0.00	$0.00	$2,610.00

One set of tasks in the plan that could be cut without affecting the result of the new book plan is task 40 and its subtasks, *Design book's companion website*. The remaining cost of this work is slightly more than the $5,000 you've been asked to cut from the plan. After consulting with the project's sponsors, you all agree that this looks like a good set of tasks to remove from the plan.

3. Select the name of task 40, the summary task *Design book's companion website*.

4. Do one of the following:

   ○ If you are running Project Professional, continue with step 5.

   ○ If you are running Project Standard, skip ahead to step 6.

Tip Not sure which edition of Project you have? Here's one easy way to tell. Project Professional users should see the Inactivate command in the Schedule group on the Task tab, while Project Standard users will not see the Inactivate command at all. You can also see your edition identified in the Help pane of the Backstage (to check this, click the File tab, click Help, and then look for your edition name on the right side of the Help pane).

5. On the **Task** tab, in the **Schedule** group, click **Inactivate**.

Project inactivates the summary task and its subtasks.

In Project Professional inactivated tasks appear like this.

Important If you need a refresher on inactivating tasks in Project Professional, see Chapter 7, "Fine-Tuning Task Details."

These inactivated tasks will remain in the project plan, but they have no scheduling or cost impact now. Note that the Remaining cost value for task 0, the *project summary task,* and for task 27, the *Design and Production* summary task, are correspondingly reduced.

Note Project Professional users should skip to the end of this procedure. Project Standard users proceed from step 4 directly to step 6.

6. With the name of task 40 selected, right-click and in the shortcut menu that appears, click **Delete Task**.

A Planning Wizard message may appear, asking you to verify that you want to delete this summary task and its subtasks. If it appears, click OK.

Project deletes the summary task and its subtasks and renumbers the remaining tasks.

After deleting tasks, subsequent
tasks are renumbered.

	Task Name	Fixed Cost	Fixed Cost Accrual	Total Cost	Baseline	Variance	Actual	Remaining
0	Children's Book Schedule	$0.00	Prorated	$92,546.25	$87,908.00	$4,638.25	$60,903.25	$31,643.00
27	Design and Production	$0.00	Prorated	$42,924.25	$40,845.00	$2,079.25	$23,051.25	$19,873.00
30	1st Pages review	$0.00	Prorated	$14,448.00	$13,860.00	$588.00	$0.00	$14,448.00
31	Proofread and index	$0.00	Prorated	$900.00	$900.00	$0.00	$0.00	$900.00
32	Incorporate 1st Pages review	$0.00	Prorated	$6,708.00	$6,120.00	$588.00	$0.00	$6,708.00
33	Send proofed pages to Production	$0.00	Prorated	$0.00	$0.00	$0.00	$0.00	$0.00
34	Enter page corrections and index	$0.00	Prorated	$4,040.00	$4,040.00	$0.00	$0.00	$4,040.00
35	Cover design	$0.00	Prorated	$2,800.00	$2,800.00	$0.00	$0.00	$2,800.00
36	2nd Pages review	$0.00	Prorated	$5,425.00	$6,345.00	($920.00)	$0.00	$5,425.00
37	Proof and review	$0.00	Prorated	$880.00	$1,550.00	($670.00)	$0.00	$880.00
38	Send proofed pages to Production	$0.00	Prorated	$0.00	$0.00	$0.00	$0.00	$0.00
39	Final review	$0.00	Prorated	$4,545.00	$4,545.00	$0.00	$0.00	$4,545.00
40	Color prep and printing	$0.00	Prorated	$810.00	$810.00	$0.00	$0.00	$810.00
41	Send to color house	$0.00	Prorated	$310.00	$310.00	$0.00	$0.00	$310.00
42	Generate proofs	$500.00	End	$500.00	$500.00	$0.00	$0.00	$500.00

Note that the Remaining cost value for task 0, the *project summary task,* and for task 27, the *Design and Production* summary task, are correspondingly reduced.

You confer with the project sponsors, who are pleased that you can wrap up the new book project at a lower cost. Although completing the remaining work within the given time and cost constraints will be a challenge, you're optimistic about the project's future performance given your project management skills and knowledge of Project.

✖ CLEAN UP Close the Back on Track file.

Key Points

- When addressing variance in a project plan, it is useful to evaluate your plan (and variance) in terms of time, cost, and scope: the three sides of the project triangle.

- When addressing schedule problems, focus your remedies on tasks on the critical path; these drive the finish date of the project.

- When addressing cost or scope problems, focus on expensive resources, and especially on their longer assignments.

Part 3

Special Subjects

Chapter at a Glance

Add details to a Gantt view, page 318.

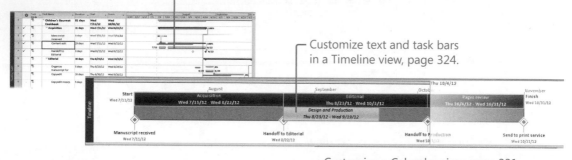

Customize text and task bars
in a Timeline view, page 324.

Change the details in
a Network Diagram
view, page 327.

Customize a Calendar view, page 331.

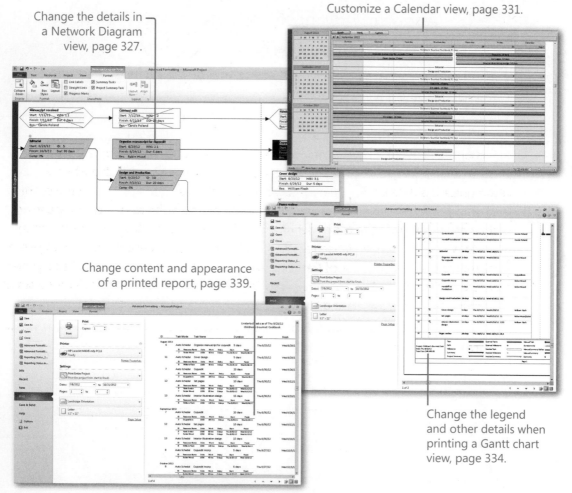

Change content and appearance
of a printed report, page 339.

Change the legend
and other details when
printing a Gantt chart
view, page 334.

15 Applying Advanced Formatting and Printing

In this chapter, you will learn how to:

- ✔ Customize a Gantt chart view.
- ✔ Format a Timeline view.
- ✔ Adjust details shown in nodes of a Network Diagram view.
- ✔ Add additional bar types to a Calendar view.
- ✔ Adjust page setup options and generate a PDF or XPS snapshot of views.
- ✔ Change content and appearance of a report.

This chapter introduces you to some of the more advanced formatting features in Microsoft Project 2010. A well-formatted project plan can be valuable when communicating details to *resources,* customers, and other *stakeholders.* Some of the formatting capabilities in Project are similar to those of a style-based word processor, such as Microsoft Word, in which defining a style once affects all content in the document to which that style has been applied. In Project, you can use styles to change the appearance of a specific type of Gantt bar, such as a summary bar, throughout a project plan. Other formatting options introduced in this chapter focus on the different ways of identifying tasks and formatting some of the more commonly used views.

> **Practice Files** Before you can complete the exercises in this chapter, you need to copy the book's practice files to your computer. A complete list of practice files is provided in "Using the Practice Files" at the beginning of this book. For each exercise that has a practice file, simply browse to where you saved the book's practice file folder.

> **Important** If you are running Project Professional, you may need to make a one-time setting change. This helps ensure that the practice files you work with in this chapter do not affect your Project Server data. For more information, see Appendix C, "Using the Practice Files if Connected to Project Server."

Formatting a Gantt Chart View

You can format specific items (a *milestone,* for example) directly in a Gantt chart view to change the look of a Gantt Chart view in limited ways. If you completed Chapter 5, "Formatting and Sharing Your Plan," you worked with the Gantt Chart Style box. In this section, you will customize specific items, such as Gantt bars and gridlines, in ways that the Gantt Chart styles cannot.

> **Tip** Remember that several views are Gantt chart views, even though only one view is specifically called the Gantt Chart view. Other Gantt chart views include the Detail Gantt, Leveling Gantt, Multiple Baselines Gantt, and Tracking Gantt. The term Gantt chart view generally refers to a type of presentation that shows Gantt bars organized along a timescale.

In addition to changing the formatting of items that appear by default in a Gantt chart view (such as a task's Gantt bar), you can add or remove items. For example, it may be useful to compare baseline, interim, and actual plans in a single view. Doing so helps you evaluate the schedule adjustments you have made.

In this exercise, you customize a Gantt chart view.

SET UP Start Project if it's not already running.

You need the Advanced Formatting_Start project plan located in your Chapter 15 practice file folder to complete this exercise. Open the Advanced Formatting_Start project plan, and then follow these steps.

1. On the **File** tab, click **Save As**.

   The Save As dialog box appears.

2. In the **File name** box, type **Advanced Formatting**, and then click **Save**.

   To begin, you will display the Tracking Gantt view.

3. On the **View** tab, in the **Task Views** group, click the down arrow below the **Gantt Chart** button, and then click **Tracking Gantt**.

   Project displays the Tracking Gantt view.

Next, you will customize this view. You will add the interim plan bars to the view.

4. On the **Format** tab, in the **Bar Styles** group, click **Format** and then click **Bar Styles**.

The Bar Styles dialog box appears. In this dialog box, the formatting changes that you make to a particular type of Gantt bar (a *summary task,* for example) apply to all such Gantt bars in the Gantt chart.

> **Tip** You can also display this dialog box by double-clicking the background of the chart portion of a Gantt chart view or by right-clicking in the background and selecting Bar Styles from the shortcut menu.

5. Scroll down the list of the bar styles, and in the **Name** column, click **Summary Progress**.

6. Click **Insert Row**.

Project inserts a row for a new bar style in the table. Project draws Gantt bars in the order in which they are listed in the Bar Styles dialog box. Inserting a new bar style above the Summary Progress bar style will help ensure that it won't be obscured by another type of Gantt bar.

7. In the new cell in the **Name** column, type **Interim**.

Interim is the name you'll give to the new task bar that will appear on the chart portion of the view.

> **Tip** The names of most task bars will appear in the legend of printed Gantt chart views. If you do not want a task bar name to appear in the legend, type an asterisk (*) at the beginning of the task bar name. For example, if you wanted to prevent Interim from appearing in the legend, you would enter its name here as *Interim. In the Bar Styles dialog box, you can see that the Manual Milestone task bar name (among others) is prefaced with an asterisk, so it does not appear in the legend of the printed Gantt chart view.

8. In the same row, click the cell under the **Show For...Tasks** column heading, and then click **Normal** on the drop-down list.

The Show For ... Tasks value indicates the type of task the bar will represent (such as a normal task, a summary task, or a milestone) or the status of the task (such as critical or in progress).

9. Click the cell under the **Row** column heading, and in the drop-down list, click **2**.

This causes Project to display multiple rows of Gantt bars for each task in the view.

10. Click the cell under the **From** column heading, and in the drop-down list, click **Start1**.

11. Click the cell under the **To** column heading, and then, in the drop-down list, click **Finish1**.

The From and To values represent the start and end points for the bar.

The *Start1* and *Finish1* items are the fields in which the first interim plan values were previously set for you in the project plan. The current start date and finish date of each task in the project were saved to these fields when the interim plan was set. If you completed Chapter 12, "Tracking Progress on Tasks and Assignments," you have already been introduced to interim plans.

You have now instructed Project to display the first interim plan's start and finish dates as bars.

Next, focus your attention on the lower half of the Bar Styles dialog box.

12. In the **Shape** box, under the **Middle** label, click the full-height bar, the second option from the top of the list.

13. In the **Pattern** box, under the **Middle** label, click the solid bar, the second option from the top of the list.

14. Click the **Color** box and, under **Standard Colors**, click green.

Tip Point to a color to see its name in a ScreenTip.

Because this customized view focuses on the interim plan, next you'll format the interim bars to include their start and finish dates.

15. In the **Bar Styles** dialog box, click the **Text** tab.

16. In the **Left** box, click **Start1** in the drop-down list.

Tip When selecting items from a list like this, you can often begin typing the name of the item you want, and when its full name appears, select it. For example if you type **s**, Project shows the values that begin with the letter *s*. If you then type **t**, Project shows the values that begin with the letters *st*.

17. In the **Right** box, click **Finish1** in the drop-down list.

Selecting these values will cause the Start1 and Finish1 dates to appear on either side of the bar.

18. Click **OK** to close the Bar Styles dialog box.

    Project displays the interim bars on the Tracking Gantt view. Next, you will add horizontal gridlines to the chart portion of the Gantt Chart view so you can associate Gantt bars with their tasks more easily.

19. On the **Format** tab, in the **Format** group, click **Gridlines**, and then click **Gridlines**.

20. Under **Lines to change**, leave **Gantt Rows** selected, and in the **Type** box under **Normal**, select the small dashed line (the fourth option), and then click **OK**.

    Project draws dashed lines across the chart portion of the Gantt Chart view.

    To conclude this exercise, you will get a better look at the Gantt bars.

21. On the **View** tab, in the **Zoom** group, click the down arrow next to the **Timescale** box and click **Weeks**.

22. In the **Task Name** column, click the name of task 3, *Content edit*.

Here you can see that the completed task 3 (shown as a solid blue bar at the top of the task row) corresponds exactly to its interim plan bar (the green bar at the bottom of the task row) and that both were scheduled later than the baseline (the patterned gray bar in the middle of the task row). This occurred because, after the baseline was set, changes to the schedule were made that pushed out the scheduled start date of the task. Then the interim plan was saved.

Project supports several additional Gantt chart formatting features besides those you've worked with in this section. If you wish to explore other formatting options, look at these commands on the Format tab:

- **The Text Styles button in the Format group** For formatting text associated with a specific task type, such as summary task text

- **The Layout button in the Format group** For formatting link lines and Gantt bar visual effects

Formatting a Timeline View

As you may recall from Chapters 1 and 5, the Timeline view is a handy way of seeing the "big picture" of the project plan. If you completed Chapter 5, you customized a timeline view and adjusted the visual display of some tasks, such as switching the display of a task from a bar to a callout. You may find that the default text formatting of the Timeline meets your needs, but you're also able to customize its look.

In this exercise, you format some text and task bar elements in the Timeline view.

1. On the **View** tab, in the **Split View** group, click the **Timeline** check box.

Project displays the Timeline view.

2. Click anywhere in the **Timeline** view.

This contextual tab dynamically changes based on the active view or selected item.

Putting the focus on the Timeline causes the commands on the Format tab to change. Remember that the Format tab is contextual; it adjusts based on what is currently selected.

First, you will adjust the formatting of an entire category of text values in the Timeline. Some people with whom you've shared Timeline snapshots have said the date values are too small, so you'll make them larger.

3. On the **Format** tab, in the **Text** group, click **Text Styles**.

The Text Styles dialog box appears. With this dialog box, you can alter the formatting of all occurrences of a specific type of information in the view.

4. In the **Item to Change** box, click **Task Date**.

5. In the **Font style** box, click **Bold**, and in the **Size** box, click **10**.

6. Click **OK**.

    Project applies the text style change to all task dates in the Timeline view.

    Next, you'd like to visually distinguish the *Design and Production* task in the Timeline.

7. In the **Timeline** view, click the *Design and Production* task bar.

    A colored highlight appears around the task bar, indicating that it is selected.

I

Italic

8. On the **Format** tab, in the **Font** group, click **Italic**.

    Project applies the italic text effect to the task bar's label (the task name) and its dates.

Background
Color

9. On the **Format** tab, in the **Font** group, click the arrow next to the **Background Color** button and then, under **Standard Colors,** click yellow.

Project changes the task bar color to yellow. This makes the white text difficult to read, however. You'll fix this next.

A

Font Color

10. On the **Format** tab, in the **Font** group, click the arrow next to the **Font Color** button and then click black.

Project changes the task bar's text to black.

11. On the **View** tab, in the **Split View** group, clear the **Timeline** check box.

Project hides the Timeline view.

Because the Timeline view is simpler than most other views in Project, it has fewer formatting options.

Formatting a Network Diagram View

In traditional project management, the Network Diagram is a standard way of representing project activities and their relationships. Tasks are represented as boxes, or nodes, and the relationships between tasks are drawn as lines connecting the nodes. Unlike a Gantt chart, which is a timescaled view, a Network Diagram enables you to view project activities in a manner more closely resembling a flowchart format. This is useful if you'd like to place more focus on the relationships between activities rather than on their durations.

Project provides rich formatting options for the Network Diagram. In this section, you will use only a few of these formatting options to customize the information that appears within nodes. If you're a heavy-duty Network Diagram user, you'll want to explore the formatting options in greater detail on your own.

In this exercise, you format items in the Network Diagram view.

1. In the **Task name** column, click the name of task 7, *Copyedit*.

2. On the **View** tab, in the **Task Views** group, click **Network Diagram**.

   The Network Diagram view appears. In this view, each task is represented by a box or node, and each node contains several pieces of information (or fields) about the task.

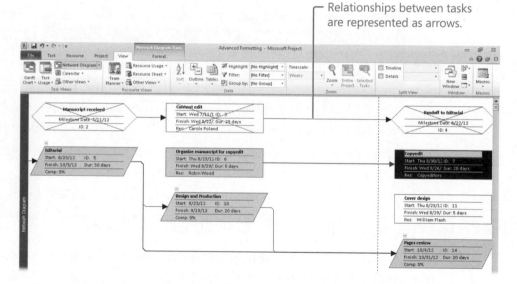

Relationships between tasks are represented as arrows.

Nodes with an X drawn through them represent completed tasks. Nodes with parallelogram shapes represent summary tasks.

In this exercise, you'd like to replace the task ID values with the *Work Breakdown Structure (WBS)* codes. Unlike task ID numbers, WBS codes indicate each task's location in the hierarchy of the project.

3. On the **Format** tab, in the **Format** group, click **Box Styles**.

   Recall that commands on the Format tab change depending on the type of active view; the Format tab is a contextual tab.

   The Box Styles dialog box appears.

On the Style Settings For list, you can see all the node box styles available in Project. The Preview box shows you the specific labels and fields displayed in each box style.

4. Click **More Templates**.

   The Data Templates dialog box appears. In this context, "Templates" determine what fields appear in boxes (nodes) as well as their layout (not to be confused with file templates).

5. In the **Templates in "Network Diagram"** list, make sure that **Standard** is selected, and then click **Copy**.

   The Data Template Definition dialog box appears. You want to add the Work Breakdown Structure (WBS) code value to the upper-right corner of the node.

6. In the **Template name** box, type **Standard + WBS**.

7. Below **Choose cell(s)**, click **ID**. This is the field you will replace.

8. In the drop-down list of fields, click **WBS**.

9. Click **OK** to close the **Data Template Definition** dialog box, and then click **Close** to close the **Data Templates** dialog box.

10. In the **Box Styles** dialog box, under **Style settings for**, select **Critical**, and while holding down the Shift key, click **Noncritical Milestone**.

   The four types of subtasks are selected.

11. In the **Data template** box, select **Standard + WBS** from the drop-down list.

12. Click **OK** to close the **Box Styles** dialog box.

Project applies the revised box style to nodes in the Network Diagram.

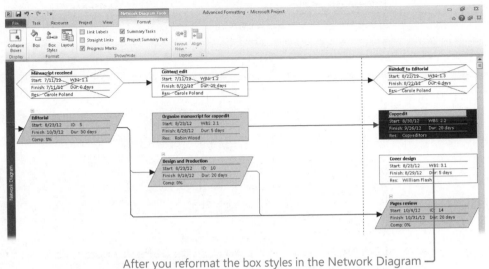

After you reformat the box styles in the Network Diagram
view, the WBS code replaces the task ID for select box styles.

Now, for these box styles, the WBS value appears in the upper-right corner of each box rather than the Task ID.

Here are some additional things to consider when working in the Network Diagram view:

- In the Network Diagram view, you can format all boxes with the Box Styles command on the Format tab, or you can format just the active box with the Box command. This is similar to the Bar Styles and Bar commands available on the Format tab when you have a Gantt chart view displayed.

- If you have Microsoft Visio 2007 or later, you can generate a Visio visual report that is similar to a network diagram view. Visio visual reports are pivot diagrams that you can customize. For more information about visual reports, see Chapter 17, "Sharing Project Information with Other Programs."

Formatting a Calendar View

The Calendar view is probably the simplest view available in Project; however, even the Calendar view offers several formatting options. This view is especially useful for sharing schedule information with resources or stakeholders who prefer a traditional "month-at-a-glance" format rather than a more detailed view, such as the Gantt Chart view.

In this exercise, you reformat summary and critical tasks in the Calendar view.

1. On the **View** tab, in the **Task Views** group, click **Calendar**.

   The Calendar view appears.

   The Calendar view resembles a traditional "month-at-a-glance" calendar and displays tasks as bars spanning the days on which they are scheduled to occur.

This view displays four weeks at a time, and it draws task bars on the days on which tasks are scheduled. The visible weeks are indicated by the orange blocks in the monthly calendars on the left side of the view.

2. On the **Format** tab, in the **Format** group, click **Bar Styles**.

   The Bar Styles dialog box appears. The additional item type that you would like to show on the Calendar view is a summary bar.

3. In the **Task type** box, click **Summary**.

4. In the **Bar type** box, click **Line** in the drop-down list.

   The next item type to reformat is critical tasks.

5. In the **Task type** box, click **Critical**.

6. Click the **Color** box, and, under **Standard Colors**, click red.

7. Click **OK** to close the **Bar Styles** dialog box.

   Project applies the format options to the Calendar view.

After you reformat the Calendar view, critical tasks appear red and summary tasks appear as lines.

As with the other views that you've customized in this chapter, the Calendar view has additional formatting options available on the Format tab.

Printing Views: Advanced Options

Project offers customization options for printing views beyond what you worked with in Chapter 5. Because views such as the Gantt Chart view are often shared with resources and other project stakeholders, you may find that you need to add additional details to the views you print.

In this exercise, you adjust the page setup and legend of the Gantt Chart view, and specify what table columns to include on the printed view.

1. On the **View** tab, in the **Task Views** group, click the down arrow below the **Gantt Chart** button and then click **Gantt Chart**.

    The Gantt Chart view appears.

2. On the **View** tab, in the **Zoom** group, click **Weeks** in the **Timescale** box.

    Project adjusts the zoom setting.

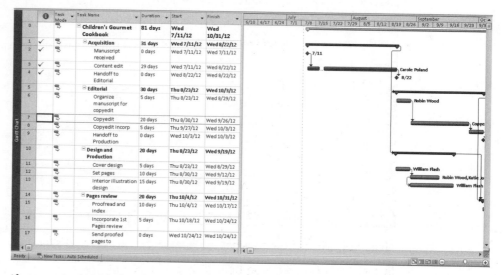

If you completed Chapter 5, you've already seen the Gantt Chart view in the Print Preview window in the Backstage view. There, you adjusted some print options, like printing a specific date range and adjusting scaling to fit the printed view on one page. Next, you'll explore some advanced printing options.

3. On the **File** tab, click **Print**.

The Print Preview screen appears in the Backstage view with the Gantt Chart in the preview. As currently set up, this view will require four pages to print. Note the "1 of 4" status message below the print preview.

Note If you have a plotter selected as your default printer or have a different page size selected for your default printer, what you see in the Print Preview screens may differ from what's shown here.

4. Click **Page Setup**; this link appears at the bottom of the controls, to the left of the print preview.

The Page Setup dialog box appears.

5. Make sure the **Page** tab is visible, and then under **Scaling**, click **Fit to** and type or select **1** page wide by **2** tall.

Next, you will customize what appears in the Gantt chart's legend.

6. In the **Page Setup** dialog box, click the **Legend** tab.

7. On the **Legend** tab are three alignment tabs. Click the **Left** tab.

Here, you can see the text and field codes that appear in the legend.

Project will print the project title and current date on the left side of the legend. You also want to print the project plan's estimated cost value in the legend.

8. Click at the end of the second line of text, and then press the Enter key.

9. Type **Total Cost:** followed by a space.

10. In the **Project fields** box, click **Cost** from the drop-down list, and then click **Add**.

Project adds the cost code to the Left legend text.

To conclude the page setup customization, you'll specify what columns from the table in the Gantt Chart view get printed.

11. Click the **View** tab.

12. Click **Print all sheet columns**, and then click **OK** to close the **Page Setup** dialog box.

Project applies the changes you specified to the legend. To get a closer look, zoom in on the legend.

13. In the Print Preview screen, click the lower-left corner of the page with the magnifying-glass pointer.

Project zooms in to show the page at a legible resolution.

New In
2010

Next, you'll shift focus from output formatting options to output file types. Two common file formats of printed output are Portable Document Format (PDF) and XML Paper Specification (XPS). PDF represents an Adobe Acrobat document. XPS is a format supported by Microsoft. Both formats provide a high-fidelity online representation of what would appear on a printed page. To conclude this exercise, you'll generate a PDF or XPS output file of the Timeline view.

14. On the **View** tab, in the **Split View** group, click the **Timeline** check box.

Project displays the Timeline view.

15. Click anywhere in the **Timeline** view.

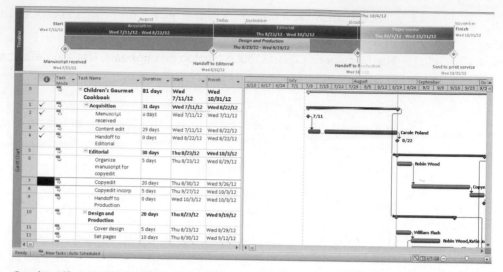

16. On the **File** tab, click **Save & Send**.

This pane of the Backstage view includes options for several ways of sharing or collaborating online.

Important If you are running Project Standard, you will not see some options relating to Project Professional and some SharePoint functionality.

17. Under the **File Types** heading on the left side of the **Save & Send** tab, click **Create PDF/XPS Document**.

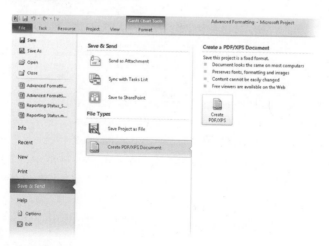

Some explanation of PDF and XPS documents appears on the right side of the tab.

18. Click **Create PDF/XPS**.

The Browse dialog box appears. Use the file name and location given in the dialog box.

19. In the **Save as type** box, select either **PDF Files** or **XPS Files** (depending on what format you want to see), and then click **OK**.

   The Document Export Options dialog box appears. Use the default settings.

20. Click **OK**.

   Project generates the PDF or XPS document.

21. In Windows Explorer, navigate to the Chapter15 folder and double-click the PDF or XPS document that you created.

   Note You may need to install a PDF or XPS viewer to complete this exercise. A free version of Adobe Acrobat Reader is available from *www.adobe.com*. A free XPS viewer is available from *www.microsoft.com*.

Printing Reports: Advanced Options

As you may recall from Chapter 5, *reports* are predefined formats intended for printing Project data. Unlike views, which you can either print or work with onscreen, reports are designed only for printing.

Although reports are distinct from views, some settings that you specify for a view might affect certain reports. For example:

- If subtasks are collapsed or hidden under summary tasks in a view, reports that include task lists will show only the summary tasks, not the subtasks.

- In usage views, if assignments are collapsed or hidden under tasks or resources, the usage reports (Task Usage or Resource Usage) likewise hide assignment details.

In this exercise, you see a report in the Print Preview screen, and then you edit its definition (that is, the set of elements that make up the report) to change how the report's information is presented.

1. On the **Project** tab, in the **Reports** group, click **Reports**.

   The Reports dialog box appears, displaying the broad categories of reports available in Project.

2. Click **Current**, and then click **Select**.

   The Current Activity Reports dialog box appears.

   Tip You also can do this by double-clicking the Current category.

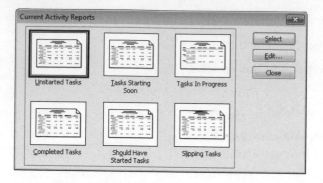

This dialog box lists reports that convey task status.

3. In the **Current Activity Reports** box, click **Unstarted Tasks**, and then click **Select**.

Project displays the Current Activity report in the Backstage view's print preview.

This report is a complete list of unstarted tasks and assignment schedule details. You'd like to see this data presented in a different way, so you'll edit this report.

4. On the **Project** tab, in the **Reports** group, click **Reports**.

The Backstage view closes, and the Gantt Chart view reappears. Next, you'll modify this report.

5. Click **Current**, and then click **Select**.

6. Click **Unstarted Tasks**, and then click **Edit**.

   The Task Report dialog box appears.

7. In the **Period** box, click **Months** in the drop-down list.

   Choosing Months groups tasks by the month in which they occur. Because the report now includes a time-period element, the Timescale options in the Backstage view become available, enabling you to print data within a specific date range if you want.

8. In the **Table** box, click **Summary** in the drop-down list.

Tip The tables listed in the Task Report dialog box are the same as those that you can apply to any view that displays tasks in a table. When editing a report format, you can apply predefined or custom tables and filters, choose additional details to include in the report, and apply a sort order to the information—all in the dialog box for the report you're editing.

9. Click **OK** to close the **Task Report** dialog box.

10. In the **Current Activity Reports** dialog box, make sure that **Unstarted Tasks** is selected and then click **Select**.

    Project applies to the report the custom report settings that you chose, and the report appears in the Print Preview screen of the Backstage view. Next, you will zoom in to see the report in more detail.

11. In the Print Preview area of the Backstage view, click twice in the upper-left corner of the first page with the magnifying-glass pointer.

This custom report shows the fields displayed in the Summary Task table, but it divides the tasks by month.

12. Click the **Task** tab.

The Gantt Chart with Timeline view reappears.

CLEAN UP Close the Advanced Formatting file.

Key Points

- Use the Bar Styles dialog box to change the appearance of a specific type of Gantt bar, such as all summary tasks. To display the Bar Styles dialog box, on the Format tab, in the Bar Styles group, click Format and then click Bar Styles.

- In the Timeline, you can directly modify text or all text styles, such as all task names, with the commands in the Font and Text groups on the Format tab.

- Nodes represent tasks and summary tasks in the Network Diagram view. You can customize the information that appears in a node.

- The Calendar view is especially helpful for those who prefer a traditional "month-at-a-glance" format.

- You can adjust page layout and legend text for Gantt chart views in the Backstage view.

- Report layouts can be customized in the Backstage view.

Chapter at a Glance

Work with the Organizer to share customized elements between project plans, page 346.

Record a VBA macro to perform an often-repeated sequence of actions, page 351.

Edit VBA macro code in the Visual Basic Editor, page 356.

Create a custom tab, page 362.

16 Customizing Project

In this chapter, you will learn how to:

✔ Copy a customized element, such as a calendar, from one project plan to another by using the Organizer.

✔ Record and play back a macro.

✔ Edit a macro in the Visual Basic for Applications (VBA) Editor.

✔ Customize the Quick Access toolbar and the ribbon.

This chapter describes some of the ways that you can customize Microsoft Project 2010 to suit your own preferences. Project 2010 adopted the *ribbon interface,* which offers new customization options. Project has other customization features, such as the Organizer and global template, that are unique to it. In addition, Project has customization features, such as recording Microsoft Visual Basic for Applications (VBA) macros, that are similar to what you might be familiar with from other Microsoft Office applications.

Important Some of the actions that you perform in this chapter can affect your overall settings in Project regardless of the specific project plan you are using. To keep your Project environment unaffected or at the "factory settings" throughout this chapter, we include steps to undo some actions.

> **Practice Files** Before you can complete the exercises in this chapter, you need to copy the book's practice files to your computer. A complete list of practice files is provided in "Using the Practice Files" at the beginning of this book. For each exercise that has a practice file, simply browse to where you saved the book's practice file folder.

Important If you are running Project Professional, you may need to make a one-time setting change. This helps ensure that the practice files you work with in this chapter do not affect your Project Server data. For more information, see Appendix C, "Using the Practice Files if Connected to Project Server."

Sharing Custom Elements Between Project Plans

Project uses a feature called the *global template,* named Global.mpt, to provide the default views, tables, and other elements that you see in Project. The very first time you display a view, table, or similar element in a project plan, it is copied automatically from the global template to that project plan. Thereafter, the element resides in the project plan. Any subsequent customization of that element in the project plan (for example, changing the fields displayed in a table) applies to only that one project plan and does not affect the global template. The global template is installed as part of Project and you normally don't work with it directly.

Initially, the specific definitions of all views, tables, and other elements listed here are contained in the global template. For example, the fact that the default usage table contains one set of fields and not others is determined by the global template. The list of elements provided by the global template includes the following:

- Views
- Reports
- Tables
- Filters
- Calendars
- Groups

In addition, you can copy modules (VBA macros), maps, and custom fields to the global template or between project plans.

When you customize an element like a view, the customized element remains in the project plan in which it was customized. With views and tables, you have the option of updating the version of that element in the global template with your customized view or table. If you create a new element, however, such as a new view, that new element is copied to the global template and thereafter becomes available in all other project plans you may work with.

One exception, however, is calendars. When you create a custom calendar, it remains just in the project plan in which it was created. A customized standard calendar that meets your needs in one project plan could redefine working times in other project plans in ways that you do not intend. For this reason, Project has a feature that allows you to share custom calendars (and other elements) between project plans in a controlled way. That feature is the *Organizer.*

The complete list of elements that you can copy between project plans with the Organizer was listed previously and is indicated by the names of the tabs in the Organizer dialog box, which you will see shortly.

You could use Project extensively and never need to touch the global template. However, when you do work with the global template, you normally do so through the Organizer. Some actions that you can accomplish relating to the global template include the following:

- Create a customized element, such as a custom calendar, and make it available in all project plans that you work with by copying the custom view into the global template.

- Replace a customized element, such as a view or table, in a project plan by copying the original, unmodified element from the global template to the project plan in which you've customized the same element.

- Copy one customized element, such as a custom calendar, from one project plan to another.

The settings in the global template apply to all project plans that you work with in Project. Because we don't want to alter the global template that you use, in this exercise, we'll focus on copying customized elements between two project plans. Keep in mind, though, that the general process of using the Organizer shown here is the same whether you are working with the global template and a project plan or two project plans.

Important In the Organizer, when you attempt to copy a customized view, table, or other element from a project plan to the global template, Project alerts you as to whether you will overwrite that element with the same name in the global template. If you choose to overwrite it, that customized element (such as a customized view) will be available in all new project plans and any other project plans that do not already contain that element. If you choose to rename the customized element, it becomes available in all project plans but does not affect the existing elements already stored in the global template. It's generally a good idea to give your customized elements unique names, such as *Custom Gantt Chart*, so that you can keep the original element intact.

In this exercise, you will copy a custom calendar from one project plan to another.

 SET UP Start Project if it's not already running.

You need multiple project plans located in your Chapter16 practice file folder to complete this exercise. Begin by opening the Customizing A_Start project plan, and then follow these steps.

1. On the **File** tab, click **Save As**.

   The Save As dialog box appears.

2. In the **File name** box, type **Customizing A**, and then click **Save**.

3. Next, open **Customizing B_Start** and save it as **Customizing B**.

4. On the **View** tab, in the **Window** group, click **Switch Windows** and then click **1 Customizing A**.

   The Customizing A project plan contains a custom calendar named Monday-Wednesday that you created in Chapter 7, "Fine-Tuning Task Details."

5. Scroll the **Gantt Chart** view vertically until task 44, *Send to color house,* is visible, and then point the mouse pointer at the calendar icon in the **Indicators** column.

	ⓘ	Task Mode	Task Name	Duration	Start	Finish	Mar 25, '12 S M T W
43		🠗	⊟ Color prep and printing	44 days	Tue 10/9/12	Fri 12/7/12	
44	📅	🠗	Send to color	1 day	Tue 10/9/12	Tue 10/9/12	
45	◆		The calendar 'Monday-Wednesday' is assigned to the task. The task is set to ignore resource calendars for scheduling. ofs	10 days	Wed 10/10/12	Tue 10/23/12	
46				30 days	Mon 10/29/12	Fri 12/7/12	

This task uses the custom calendar, so it can occur only on a Monday, Tuesday, or Wednesday. You'd like to use this calendar in the Customizing B project plan.

6. On the **File** Tab, click **Info**, and then click **Organizer**.

   The Organizer dialog box appears.

7. Click several of the tabs in the dialog box to get a look at the types of elements you can manage with the Organizer, and then click the **Calendars** tab.

As you can see, every tab of the Organizer dialog box has a similar structure: elements in the global template appear on the left side of the dialog box, and the elements that have been used in the active project plan at any time (for example, views displayed) appear on the right.

Selecting an element on the left side of the dialog box and then clicking the Copy button will copy that element to the project plan listed on the right. Conversely, selecting an element on the right side of the dialog box and then clicking the Copy button will copy that element to the file listed on the left (the global template by default).

8. From the **Calendars available in** drop-down list on the left side of the **Organizer** dialog box, select **Customizing B**.

This project plan appears in the list because it is open in Project.

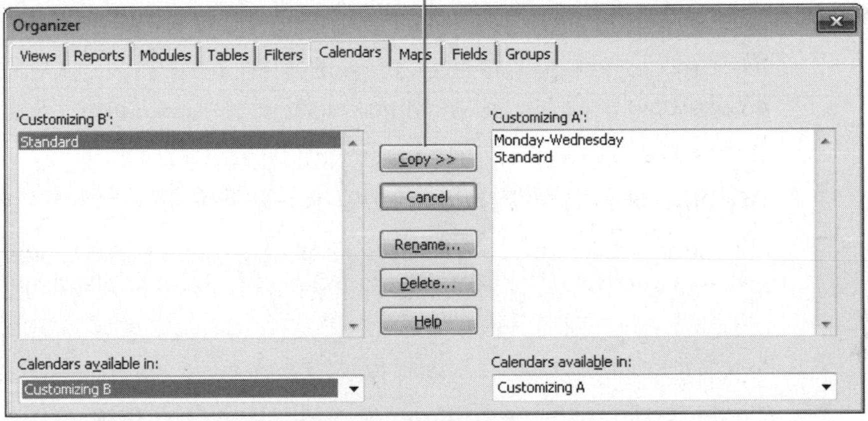

The side of the dialog box in which you've selected an element determines the direction in which you copy the element.

As you can see, the Customizing B plan (on the left) does not have the Monday-Wednesday custom calendar, and the Customizing A plan (on the right) does.

9. In the list of calendars on the right side of the dialog box, click **Monday-Wednesday**.

Tip Notice that the two arrow symbols (>>) in the Copy button switch direction (<<) when you select an element on the right side of the dialog box.

10. Click **Copy**.

Project copies the custom calendar from the Customizing A plan to the Customizing B plan.

After clicking the Copy button, the Monday-Wednesday calendar is copied from the Customizing A plan to the Customizing B plan.

Organizer

Views | Reports | Modules | Tables | Filters | Calendars | Maps | Fields | Groups

'Customizing B':
Monday-Wednesday
Standard

<< Copy
Close
Rename...
Delete...
Help

'Customizing A':
Monday-Wednesday
Standard

Calendars available in:
Customizing B

Calendars available in:
Customizing A

11. Click **Close** to close the **Organizer** dialog box.

Tip In this exercise, you used the Organizer to copy a custom calendar from one project plan to another. If you want to make a custom calendar available in all project plans, use the Organizer to copy it into the global template instead.

To conclude this exercise, you apply the custom calendar to a task in the Custom B plan.

12. On the **View** tab, in the **Window** group, click **Switch Windows**, and then click **2 Customizing B**.

Project switches to the Customizing B plan, which is the plan to which you just copied the custom calendar.

13. Select the name of task 19, *Send to color house*.

14. On the **Task** tab, in the **Editing** group, click **Scroll to Task**.

Note that this 1-day task is currently scheduled to occur on a Thursday.

	❶	Task Mode	Task Name	Duration	Start	Finish	Oct 28, '12	Nov 4, '12
14			⊟ **Pages review**	21 days	Thu 10/4/12	Thu 11/1/12		
15			Proofread and index	10 days	Thu 10/4/12	Wed 10/17/12		
16			Incorporate 1st Pages review	5 days	Thu 10/18/12	Wed 10/24/12	ble Poland	
17			Send proofed pages to Production	0 days	Wed 10/24/12	Wed 10/24/12	/24	
18			Enter page corrections and index	5 days	Thu 10/25/12	Wed 10/31/12		Katie Jordan,Robin Wood
19			Send to color house	1 day	Thu 11/1/12	Thu 11/1/12		Katie Jordan
20			Send to print service	0 days	Thu 11/1/12	Thu 11/1/12		11/1

15. On the **Task** tab, in the **Properties** group, click **Information**.

The Task Information dialog box appears.

16. Click the **Advanced** tab.

As you can see in the Calendar box, the default for all tasks is "None."

17. In the **Calendar** box, select **Monday-Wednesday** from the list of available base calendars, and then click **OK** to close the dialog box.

Project applies the Monday-Wednesday calendar to task 19 and reschedules the task to start on Monday, the next working day on which the task can occur. A calendar icon appears in the Indicators column, reminding you that this task has a task calendar applied to it. Note that the Monday-Wednesday calendar was not available in this project plan until you copied it via the Organizer.

18. Point to the calendar icon.

	ⓘ	Task Mode	Task Name	Duration	Start	Finish
14		🕑	⊟ Pages review	**23 days**	**Thu 10/4/12**	**Mon 11/5/12**
15		🕑	Proofread and index	10 days	Thu 10/4/12	Wed 10/17/12
16		🕑	Incorporate 1st Pages review	5 days	Thu 10/18/12	Wed 10/24/12
17		🕑	Send proofed pages to Production	0 days	Wed 10/24/12	Wed 10/24/12
18		🕑	Enter page corrections and index	5 days	Thu 10/25/12	Wed 10/31/12
19		🕑	Send to color	1 day	Mon 11/5/12	Mon 11/5/12
20			service	0 days	Mon 11/5/12	Mon 11/5/12

The calendar 'Monday-Wednesday' is assigned to the task.

As you customize views, tables, and other elements, you may find the Organizer to be a useful feature for managing your customized elements and the built-in elements in Project.

✖ **CLEAN UP** Close the Customizing B file. The Customizing A file should remain open.

Recording Macros

Many activities that you perform in Project can be repetitive. To save time, you can record a *macro* that captures keystrokes and mouse actions for later playback. The macro is recorded in Microsoft Visual Basic for Applications (VBA), the built-in macro programming language of the Microsoft Office system. You can do sophisticated things with VBA, but you can record and play back simple macros without ever directly seeing or working with VBA code.

The macros that you create are stored in the global template by default, so they are available to you whenever Project is running. The project plan for which you originally created the macro need not be open to run the macro in other project plans. For example, you can use the Organizer to copy the VBA module (which contains the macro) from the global template to another project plan to give it to a friend.

Creating a graphic image snapshot of a view is a great way to share project details with others. However, it's likely that the details you initially capture will become obsolete quickly as the project plan is updated. Capturing updated snapshots can be a repetitive task that is ideal for automation through a macro. When this task is automated, you can quickly generate a new GIF image snapshot of a project plan and save the GIF image to a file. From there, you could attach the GIF image to an e-mail message, publish it to a Web site, insert it into a document, or share it in other ways.

In this exercise, you record and run a macro.

1. On the **View** tab, in the **Macros** group, click the down arrow below the **Macros** button, and then click **Record Macro**.

   The Record Macro dialog box appears.

2. In the **Macro name** box, type **Capture_GIF_Image**.

   Tip Macro names must begin with a letter and cannot contain spaces. To improve the readability of your macro names, you can use an underscore (_) in place of a space. For example, rather than naming a macro CaptureGIFImage, you can name it Capture_GIF_Image.

   For this macro, we will not use a shortcut key. When recording other macros, note that you cannot use a Ctrl+ combination that is already reserved by Project, so combinations like Ctrl+F (the keyboard shortcut for Find) and Ctrl+G (Go To) are unavailable. When you click OK to close the dialog box, Project alerts you whether you need to choose a different key combination.

3. In the **Store macro in** box, click **This Project** to store the macro in the active project plan.

   When a macro is stored in a project plan, the macro can be used by any project plan when the project plan that contains the macro is open. The default option, Global File, refers to the global template. When a macro is stored in the global template, the macro can be used by any project at any time because the global template is open whenever Project is running. In this exercise, since we don't want to customize your global template, you'll store the macro in the active project plan.

4. In the **Description** box, select the current text and replace it by typing **Saves a GIF image of the Gantt Chart view.**

The description is useful to help identify the actions that the macro will perform.

5. Click **OK**.

Project begins recording the new macro. Project does not literally record and play back every mouse movement and passing second; it records only the results of the keystrokes and mouse actions that you make. Do not feel that you have to rush to complete the recording of the macro.

6. On the **View** tab, in the **Task Views** group, click the down arrow below the **Gantt Chart** button, and then click **Gantt Chart**.

Even though the project plan is already showing the Gantt Chart view, including this step in the macro thereby records the action so that, if the project plan were initially in a different view, the macro would switch to the Gantt Chart view.

7. On the **View** tab, in the **Zoom** group, in the **Timescale** box, click **Thirds of Months**.

Project adjusts the timescale to display more of the project.

8. Click the **Task Name** column heading.

9. On the **Task** tab, in the **Clipboard** group, click the arrow next to **Copy**, and then click **Copy Picture**.

   The Copy Picture dialog box appears.

10. Under **Render image**, click **To GIF image file**, and then click **Browse**.

11. In the **Browse** dialog box, navigate to the **Chapter16** folder, and then click **OK**.

12. Under **Copy,** click **Selected Rows**.

13. Under **Timescale**, in the **From** box, type or select **4/2/12**, and in the **To** box, type or select **12/7/12**.

    This date range matches the project plan's current start and finish date. You can see these dates for task 0, the *project summary task*.

14. Click **OK** to close the **Copy Picture** dialog box.

    Project saves the GIF image.

15. On the **View** tab, in the **Zoom** group, click **Zoom** and then click **Zoom**.

16. In the **Zoom** dialog box, click **Reset**, and then click **OK**.

    Now you are ready to stop recording.

17. On the **View** tab, in the **Macros** group, click the down arrow below the **Macros** button, and then click **Stop Recording**.

    Next, you will run the macro to see it play back.

18. On the **View** tab, in the **Macros** group, click **Macros**.

The Macros dialog box appears.

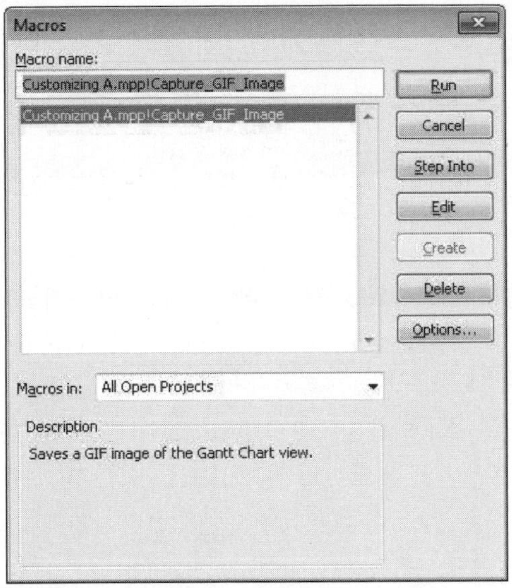

19. In the **Macro name** box, click **Customizing A.mpp!Capture_GIF_Image**, and then click **Run**.

The macro begins running, but pauses as soon as Project generates a confirmation message to replace the existing GIF image file (the one that you just created while recording the macro).

Important Your security level setting in Project affects Project's ability to run macros that you record or receive from others. You may not have set the security level directly, but it may have been set when you installed Project or by a system policy within your organization.

20. Click **Overwrite** to overwrite the previously created GIF image file.

The macro resaves the GIF image. Next, you'll see the results of the macro's actions.

21. In Windows Explorer, navigate to the **Chapter16** folder and double-click the **Customizing A** GIF image file to open it in your image editor or viewer application.

The GIF image appears in your image viewer application. In the following illustration, we are displaying the GIF image in a Web browser. Your screen should look similar to this.

22. Close your image viewing application, and then switch back to the Customizing A project plan in Project.

This macro would be very useful if the project manager at Lucerne Publishing needed to recapture the project plan snapshot frequently. For example, the project manager could recapture it at regular intervals during the planning stage (when the details are being developed) and then again during the execution stage (when the effects of actual progress change the remaining scheduled work).

Editing Macros

As handy as the Capture_GIF_Image macro is to use, it can be improved. Remember that when you ran it in the previous exercise, you had to confirm that Project should overwrite the existing GIF image. Because the intent of the macro is to capture the most current information, you would always want to overwrite the older information. You can change the macro code directly to accomplish this. The macro code resides in a VBA module, and you work with the code in the Visual Basic for Applications environment, commonly called the VBA Editor.

Tip The VBA language and VBA Editor are standard in many of the programs in the Microsoft Office system (including Project). Although the specific details of each program differ, the general way in which you use VBA in each is the same. VBA automation is a powerful tool you can master, and that knowledge can be used in many Microsoft programs.

In this exercise, you work in the VBA Editor to fine-tune and enhance the macro that you recorded in the previous exercise and then run it.

1. On the **View** tab, in the **Macros** group, click **Macros**.

2. Under **Macro name**, click **Customizing A.mpp!Capture_GIF_Image**, and then click **Edit**.

   Project loads the module that contains the macro in the VBA Editor.

   This VBA code was generated when
   Project recorded your macro.

   A full explanation of the VBA language is beyond the scope of this book, but we can walk you through some steps to change the behavior of the previously recorded macro. You might also recognize some of the actions that you recorded earlier by the names used in the VBA code.

3. Click at the beginning of the line **ViewApplyEx Name:="&Gantt Chart", ApplyTo:=0** and press the Enter key.

4. Click in the new line you just created, press the Tab key, and type **Application. Alerts False**.

   This line of code will suppress the prompt that you received when running the macro and accept the default option of replacing the existing GIF image file with the same name.

Here is the text you typed.

Tip Note that as you were typing, selection boxes and ScreenTips might have appeared. The VBA Editor uses such tools and feedback to help you enter text in a module correctly.

5. In the line that begins with **EditCopyPicture**, select the date and time **"4/2/12 8:00 AM"** (including the quotation marks) that follows **FromDate:=**, and type **ActiveProject.ProjectStart**.

This VBA code describes the project start date of the active project.

Here is the text string you typed to return the project start date.

This causes the macro to get the current start date of the active project for the GIF image that the macro creates.

6. In the same line, select the date and time **"12/7/12 5:00 PM"** (including the quotation marks) that follows **ToDate:=**, and type **ActiveProject.ProjectFinish**.

Here is the text string you typed to return the project finish date.

This causes the macro to get the current finish date of the active project for the GIF image that the macro creates. Now, if the project plan's start or finish date changes, the date range used when copying the GIF image will change as well.

Next, you'll add new macro capabilities while in the VBA Editor.

7. Click at the beginning of the line **SelectTaskColumn**, and press Enter.

8. Click in the new line you just created, press Tab, and type **FilterApply Name:="Incomplete Tasks"**.

   This line of code will apply the Incomplete Tasks filter to the current view.

9. Click at the beginning of the line **ZoomTimescale Reset:=True**, and press Enter.

10. Click in the new line you just created, press Tab, and type **FilterClear**.

    This line of code will remove the Incomplete Tasks filter from the current view.

Here are the two new lines of text you added to this macro.

11. On the **File** menu in the VBA Editor, click **Close and Return to Microsoft Project**.

    The VBA Editor closes, and you return to the project plan.

    You could run the updated macro now, but first, you'll record some progress on tasks.

12. Click the name of task 31, *Proofread and index*.

13. On the **Task** tab, in the **Schedule** group, click the down arrow to the right of the **Mark on Track** button and then click **Update Tasks**.

    The Update Tasks dialog box appears.

14. In the **Actual dur** field, type **16d**, and then click **OK**.

    Next, you'll record partial progress on another task.

15. Click the name of task 32, *Incorporate 1st Pages review*.

16. On the **Task** tab, in the **Schedule** group, click the down arrow to the right of the **Mark on Track** button and then click **Update Tasks**.

17. In the **Actual dur** field, type **5d**, and then click **OK**.

	ⓘ	Task Mode	Task Name	Duration	Start	Finish
21	✓	🗒	⊟ **Editorial**	**29.78 days**	**Wed 5/23/12**	**Tue 7/3/12**
22	✓	🗒	Organize manuscript for copyedit	5 days	Wed 5/23/12	Tue 5/29/12
23	✓	🗒	Copyedit	10.5 days	Wed 5/30/12	Wed 6/13/12
24	✓	🗒	Author review of copyedit	12.2 days	Wed 6/13/12	Fri 6/29/12
25	✓	🗒	Copyedit incorp	5 days	Tue 6/26/12	Tue 7/3/12
26	✓	🗒	Handoff to Production	0 days	Tue 7/3/12	Tue 7/3/12
27		🗒	⊟ **Design and Production**	**70.22 days**	**Tue 7/3/12**	**Wed 10/10/12**
28	✓	🗒	Set pages	15 days	Tue 7/3/12	Wed 7/25/12
29	✓	🗒	Interior illustration design	22 days	Mon 7/9/12	Tue 8/7/12
30		🗒	⊟ **1st Pages review**	**36 days**	**Wed 8/8/12**	**Wed 9/26/12**
31	✓	🗒	Proofread and index	16 days	Wed 8/8/12	Wed 8/29/12
32		🗒	Incorporate 1st Pages review	10 days	Thu 8/30/12	Wed 9/12/12
33		🗒	Send proofed pages to Production	0 days	Wed 9/12/12	Wed 9/12/12

Now you are ready to rerun the macro.

18. On the **View** tab, in the **Macros** group, click **Macros**.

19. Under **Macro name**, click **Customizing A.mpp!Capture_GIF_Image**, and then click **Run**.

The macro runs, and this time, you are not prompted to overwrite the previously saved file. To verify that the macro ran correctly, you'll view the updated GIF image in your image application.

20. In Windows Explorer, navigate to the **Chapter16** folder, and double-click the **Customizing A GIF** image file to open it in your image editor or viewer application.

The GIF image appears in your image application.

21. If you are viewing the image in Windows Internet Explorer, depending on your screen resolution you may be able to click the GIF image to magnify it.

ID		Task Mode	Task Name	Duration	Start	Finish
0			Children's Book Schedule	183 days	Mon 4/2/12	Thu 12/13/12
27			Design and Production	70.22 days	Tue 7/3/12	Wed 10/10/12
30			1st Pages review	36 days	Wed 8/8/12	Wed 9/26/12
32			Incorporate 1st Pages review	10 days	Thu 8/30/12	Wed 9/12/12
33			Send proofed pages to Production	0 days	Wed 9/12/12	Wed 9/12/12
34			Enter page corrections and index	5 days	Thu 9/13/12	Wed 9/19/12
35			Cover design	5 days	Thu 9/20/12	Wed 9/26/12
36			2nd Pages review	10 days	Thu 9/27/12	Wed 10/10/12
37			Proof and review	5 days	Thu 9/27/12	Wed 10/3/12
38			Send proofed pages to Production	0 days	Wed 10/3/12	Wed 10/3/12
39			Final review	5 days	Thu 10/4/12	Wed 10/10/12
40			Design book's companion website	5 days	Thu 9/27/12	Wed 10/3/12
41			Create mockup	3 days	Thu 9/27/12	Mon 10/1/12
42			Review with author	2 days	Tue 10/2/12	Wed 10/3/12
43			Color prep and printing	44 days	Mon 10/15/12	Thu 12/13/12
44			Send to color house	1 day	Mon 10/15/12	Mon 10/15/12
45			Generate proofs	10 days	Tue 10/16/12	Mon 10/29/12
46			Print and ship	30 days	Fri 11/2/12	Thu 12/13/12
47			Book launch prep	22 days	Tue 10/16/12	Wed 11/14/12
48			Launch planning	5 days	Tue 10/16/12	Mon 10/22/12
49			Assign launch team members	1 day	Tue 10/23/12	Tue 10/23/12
50			Complete author questionnaire	5 days	Wed 10/24/12	Tue 10/30/12
51			Schedule author interviews	1 day	Wed 10/31/12	Wed 10/31/12
52			Design and order marketing	10 days	Thu 11/1/12	Wed 11/14/12

Done

The updated screenshot includes the updated project finish date and displays only incomplete tasks because the macro applied the Incomplete Tasks filter (note that task 31, which is now completed, does not appear). Now you can run the macro as frequently as needed to capture the most up-to-date information.

22. Close your image viewing application, and then switch back to the Customizing A project plan in Project.

Here are some additional tips for working with VBA macros in Project.

- VBA is a rich and well-documented programming language. If you would like to take a closer look at VBA in Project, try this: On the View tab, in the Macros group, click the down arrow below the Macros button, and then click Visual Basic. In the "Microsoft Visual Basic for Applications" window, on the Help menu, click "Microsoft Visual Basic for Applications Help."

- While working in a module, you can get help on specific items such as objects, properties, and methods. Click a word, and then press the F1 key.

- To close the VBA Editor and return to Project, on the File menu, click Close and Return to Microsoft Project.

Customizing the Ribbon and Quick Access Toolbar

As with other Office applications, you have several choices concerning how to work with Project. Some of the many customization settings include the following:

- Add frequently used commands to the Quick Access toolbar.

- Customize an existing ribbon or create a new ribbon that includes any commands that you want.

In this exercise, you add a command to the Quick Access Toolbar and create a custom ribbon.

1. On the **File** tab, click **Options**.

   The Project Options dialog box appears.

2. In the **Project Options** dialog box, click the **Quick Access Toolbar** tab.

3. On the left side of the dialog box, in the **Choose commands from** box, click **Commands Not in the Ribbon**.

   Project displays the list of commands that you otherwise cannot access from the ribbon. Take a moment to look through this list for commands that you would like quick access to.

4. In the list of commands, click **Go To**, and then click **Add**.

   Project adds the Go To command to the right side of the dialog box.

The Go To command is a handy way to navigate to a specific task ID and scroll the timescale in the Gantt Chart view, all in one action.

5. Click **OK** to close the **Project Options** dialog box.

   Project adds the Go To command to the Quick Access toolbar.

   The Go To command now appears
   on the Quick Access toolbar.

Now try out the Go To command by doing the following steps:

6. On the **Quick Access** toolbar, click **Go To**.

7. In the **Go To** dialog box, type **43** in the **ID** box and then click **OK**.

   Tip In the Go To dialog box, you can also enter a date value in the Date field to scroll the Gantt Chart's timescale to a specific date.

Project jumps to task 43 and scrolls the chart portion of the Gantt Chart view to display its Gantt bar.

If you'd like to remove the command from the Quick Access toolbar, complete the following steps.

8. On the **Quick Access Toolbar,** right-click the **Go To** button and in the shortcut menu that appears, click **Remove from Quick Access Toolbar**.

To conclude this exercise, you will create a custom tab and add a command that runs the Capture_GIF_Image custom macro to it.

9. On the **File** tab, click **Options**.

10. In the **Project Options** dialog box, click the **Customize Ribbon** tab.

Project displays options for customizing the ribbon.

Here, you can get access to the commands and features supported by Project.

11. On the right side of the dialog box, under **Main Tabs**, click the name **View** and then click **New Tab**.

Project creates a new tab and group below (which on the Ribbon will be to the right of) the View tab.

12. On the right side of the dialog box, under **Main Tabs**, click the name **New Tab (Custom)** and then click **Rename**.

The Rename dialog box appears.

13. In the **Display name** field, type Custom and then click **OK**.

14. Click the **New Group (Custom)** item, and then click **Rename**.

The Rename dialog box appears.

15. In the **Display name** field, type My Commands and then click OK.

Now you are ready to add the custom macro to the new ribbon.

16. On the left side of the dialog box, In the **Choose commands from** box, click **Macros**.

The name of the custom macro appears.

17. Select the name of the **Customizing A.mpp!Capture_GIF_Image** macro, and then click **Add**.

Project adds the macro item to your custom group.

Next, you will rename the macro command and assign it an icon.

18. On the right side of the dialog box, select the name of the **Customizing A.mpp!Capture_GIF_Image** macro, and then click **Rename**.

19. In the **Display name** field, type **Copy GIF**, and in the **Symbol** box, select the picture image (sixth from the left in the second row).

Select this image.

20. Click **OK** to close the **Rename** dialog box, and then click **OK** to close the **Project Options** dialog box.

    Project adds your custom tab to the interface.

21. Click the **Custom** tab.

The custom tab and command now appear in the ribbon.

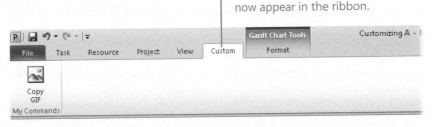

22. On the **Custom** tab, in the **My Commands** group, click **Copy GIF**.

    Project runs the macro. If you wish, navigate to the Chapter16 folder to view the GIF image.

    Finally, you will remove the custom ribbon to undo this customization.

23. Right-click the **Custom** tab, and in the shortcut menu that appears, click **Customize the Ribbon**.

24. On the right side of the **Project Options** dialog box, right-click **Custom (Custom)**, and in the shortcut menu that appears, click **Remove**.

    Tip You can also click the Reset button to undo all ribbon and Quick Access toolbar customizations that may have been made to your copy of Project.

25. Click **OK** to close the **Project Options** dialog box.

    Project has removed the custom tab.

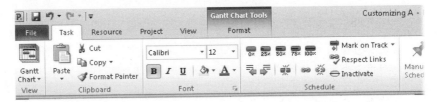

 CLEAN UP Close the Customizing A file.

Key Points

- In Project, elements such as custom calendars are managed through the global template via the Organizer.

- Project, like many other programs in the Microsoft Office system, uses the Visual Basic for Applications (VBA) macro programming language. Among other things, macros enable you to automate repetitive tasks.

- If you want to work directly with VBA code, you do so in the VBA Editor, which is included in Project as well as other Office applications.

- You can customize the Quick Access toolbar and ribbons in Project to include the commands and features that interest you the most.

Chapter at a Glance

Copy structured Project data, including column headings, to other programs, page 372.

Import data from other programs to Project, page 377.

Export structured Project data to other file formats, page 382.

Create a Visual Report to represent schedule details in Excel or Visio, page 386.

Synchronize task lists between Project and SharePoint (Project Professional only), page 391.

17 Sharing Project Information with Other Programs

In this chapter, you will learn how to:

✔ Copy and paste tabular data from Project to another program.

✔ Use Project to open a file produced in another program.

✔ Save Project data to other file formats using import/export maps.

✔ Generate Excel and Visio documents using the Visual Reports feature.

✔ See SharePoint and Project Professional task list integration.

In this chapter, you focus on various ways of getting data into and out of Microsoft Project 2010. In addition to the standard Windows copy and paste features with which you might be familiar, Project offers a variety of options for importing and exporting data.

Throughout this chapter, you'll see the following terms:

● The *source program* is the program from which you copy information.

● The *destination program* is the program to which you paste information.

> **Practice Files** Before you can complete the exercises in this chapter, you need to copy the book's practice files to your computer. A complete list of practice files is provided in "Using the Practice Files" at the beginning of this book. For each exercise that has a practice file, simply browse to where you saved the book's practice file folder.

Important If you are running Project Professional, you may need to make a one-time setting change. This helps ensure that the practice files you work with in this chapter do not affect your Project Server data. For more information, see Appendix C, "Using the Practice Files if Connected to Project Server."

Copying Project Data to Other Programs

Project supports copying information out of and pasting information into Project. However because Project information is highly structured, there are a few things to note.

When copying data from Project into other applications, you have some options for the results that you get:

New In
2010

- You can copy information (such as task names and dates) from a table in Project and paste it as structured tabular data in spreadsheet applications like Microsoft Excel, or as a table in word processor applications that support tables, like Microsoft Word. In most cases, the table's column headings for the data you copied will also be pasted, and summary/subtask relationships will be indicated by the subtasks being indented.

- You can copy text from a table in Project and paste it as tab-delimited text in text editor applications that do not support tables, like WordPad or Notepad.

- When pasting information from Project into an e-mail application, you probably will get tabular results if your e-mail application supports the Hypertext Markup Language (HTML) format.

- You can create a graphic image snapshot of the active view and paste the image into any application that supports graphic images. You worked with the Copy Picture feature (on the Task tab) in Chapter 5, "Formatting and Sharing Your Plan."

Tip Many Windows programs, such as Word and Excel, have a Paste Special feature. This feature provides you with more options for pasting data from Project into the destination program. For example, you can use the Paste Special feature in Word to paste formatted or unformatted text, a picture, or a Microsoft Project Document Object (an *OLE object*). You can also choose to paste only the data or paste it with a link to the source data in Project. When pasted with a link, the destination data in Project can be updated whenever the source data is changed.

You also have options when pasting data from other programs into Project:

- You can paste text (such as a list of task or resource names) into a table in Project. For example, you can paste a range of cells from Excel or a group of paragraphs from Word into Project. You can paste a series of task names that are organized in a vertical column from Excel or Word into the Task Name column in Project, for instance.

- You can paste a graphic image or an OLE object from another program into a graphical portion of a Gantt Chart view. You can also paste a graphic image or an OLE object into a task, resource, or assignment note, and into a form view such as the Task or Resource Form views.

Important Pasting text as multiple columns into Project requires some planning. First, make sure that the order of the information in the source program matches the order of the columns in the Project table. You can either rearrange the data in the source program to match the column order in the Project table or vice versa. Second, make sure that the columns in the source program support the same types of data—text, numbers, dates, and so on—as do the columns in Project.

In this exercise, you copy tabular data from Project and paste it into Excel and Word.

Note The following exercise requires Word and Excel. If you do not have access to one or both of these programs, you can experiment with pasting tabular data from Project into other applications. In general, you should get the expected pasting results if your destination application supports the HTML format.

SET UP Start Project if it's not already running.

You need the Sharing_Start project plan located in your Chapter17 practice file folder to complete this exercise. Open the Sharing_Start project plan, and then follow these steps.

1. On the **File** tab, click **Save As**.

   The Save As dialog box appears.

2. In the **File name** box, type **Sharing**, and then click **Save**.

   To begin, you'll copy some task names, durations, and start and finish dates from Project to Word.

3. In the **Entry** table on the left side of the **Gantt Chart** view, select from the name of task 5, *Editorial*, through task 13's finish date, *Wed 9/19/12*.

Tip One quick and easy way to select this range is to click the name of task 5, hold down the Shift key, and then click the finish date of task 13.

4. On the **Task** tab, in the **Clipboard** group, click **Copy**.

   Project copies the selected range to the Clipboard.

5. Start Word (or a comparable word processor application), create a new document, and then paste the Clipboard contents into the new document.

   If you have Word 2010, your screen should look similar to the following illustration.

Task Name	Duration	Start	Finish
Editorial	30 days	Thu 8/23/12	Wed 10/3/12
Organize manuscript for copyedit	5 days	Thu 8/23/12	Wed 8/29/12
Copyedit	20 days	Thu 8/30/12	Wed 9/26/12
Copyedit incorp	5 days	Thu 9/27/12	Wed 10/3/12
Handoff to Production	0 days	Wed 10/3/12	Wed 10/3/12
Design and Production	20 days	Thu 8/23/12	Wed 9/19/12
Cover design	5 days	Thu 8/23/12	Wed 8/29/12
Set pages	10 days	Thu 8/30/12	Wed 9/12/12
Interior illustration design	15 days	Thu 8/30/12	Wed 9/19/12

Pasting into Word generated a formatted table. The column headings from Project are included in the table, and the summary task and subtask outline structure from Project has been indicated as well.

Next, you'll paste tabular data from Project into a spreadsheet application.

6. Start Excel (or a comparable spreadsheet application) and create a new document.

   Now you will copy resource cost details from Project to Excel.

7. Switch back to Project.

8. On the **View** tab, in the **Resource Views** group, click **Resource Sheet**.

   The Resource Sheet view replaces the Gantt Chart view.

9. On the **View** tab, in the **Data** group, click **Tables** and then click **Cost**.

   This is the resource cost information you'd like to paste into Excel.

10. Click the **Select All** button in the upper-left corner of the **Cost** table.

Project selects the entire table, although only cells that contain values will be copied.

Click the Select All button to select the entire table.

11. On the **Task** tab, in the **Clipboard** group, click **Copy**.

Project copies the selected range to the Clipboard.

12. Switch back to Excel and then paste the Clipboard contents into the new document.

In Excel, if necessary, widen any columns that don't display the data values and instead display pound signs (##). If you have Excel 2010, your screen should look similar to the following illustration.

As with pasting into Word, note that pasting into Excel generated the correct column headings, and the cell values are the expected data types.

13. Close Word and Excel, and then switch back to Project.

The pasting of rich tabular data into Word or Excel does not work the same way in all applications. If you were to paste the same data into Notepad, for example, the result would be tab-delimited data and no column headings. Feel free to experiment with this.

Opening Other File Formats in Project

Information that you need to incorporate into a Project plan can come from a variety of sources. A task list from a spreadsheet or resource costs from a database are two examples. You might want to use the unique features of Project to analyze data from another program. For example, many people keep to-do lists and simple task lists in Excel, but accounting for basic scheduling issues, such as distinguishing between working and nonworking time, is impractical in Excel.

When saving data to or opening data from other formats, Project uses maps (also called *import/export maps* or data maps) that specify the exact data to import or export and how to structure it. You use import/export maps to specify how you want individual fields in the source program's file to correspond to individual fields in the destination program's file. After you set up an import/export map, you can use it over and over again.

For this exercise, a colleague has sent you an Excel workbook that contains her recommended tasks, durations, and sequence of activities for some work that Lucerne Publishing may do in the future.

Tip If you have Excel installed on your computer, open the workbook named Sample Task List in the Chapter17 folder. This is a file you will import into Project. The important things to note about the workbook are the names and order of the columns, and the presence of a header row (the labels at the top of the columns), and that the data is in a worksheet named "Tasks." When you are finished with the workbook, close it without saving the changes.

In this exercise, you open an Excel workbook in Project and set up an import/export map to control how the Excel data is imported into Project.

Important Project 2010 has a security setting that may prevent you from opening files from previous versions of Project, or files in other non-default formats. You'll change this setting to complete the following activity and then restore it to its original setting.

1. In Project, on the **File** tab, click **Options**.

   The Project Options dialog box appears.

2. Click the **Trust Center** tab.

3. Click **Trust Center Settings**.

   The Trust Center dialog box appears.

4. Click the **Legacy Formats** tab.

5. Under **Legacy Formats**, click **Prompt when loading files with legacy or non-default file format**.

6. Click **OK** to close the **Trust Center** dialog box, and then click **OK** again to close the **Project Options** dialog box.

    With this change to Project's settings completed, you're ready to import an Excel workbook.

7. Click the **File** tab, and then click **Open**.

8. Navigate to the Chapter17 practice file folder.

9. In the file type box (initially labeled **Microsoft Project Files**), select **Excel 97-2003 Workbook**.

    Tip   While scrolling through the file type box, you can see the file formats that Project can import. If you work with programs that can save data in any of these file formats, you can import their data into Project.

10. Select the **Sample Task List** file, and then click **Open**.

    The Import Wizard appears. This wizard helps you import structured data from a different format to Project.

11. Click **Next**.

    The second page of the Import Wizard appears.

The Import Wizard uses maps to organize the way that structured data from another file format is imported into Project. For this exercise, you will create a new map.

12. Make sure that **New map** is selected, and then click **Next**.

    The Import Mode page of the Import Wizard appears.

13. Make sure that **As a new project** is selected, and then click **Next**.

    The Map Options page of the Import Wizard appears.

14. Select the **Tasks** check box, and make sure that **Import includes headers** is selected as well.

    Headers here refer to column headings.

15. Click **Next**.

The Task Mapping page of the Import Wizard appears. Here, you identify the source worksheet within the Excel workbook and specify how you want to map the data from the source worksheet to Project fields.

16. On the **Source worksheet name** list, select **Tasks**.

"Tasks" is the name of the sheet in the Excel workbook. Project analyzes the header row names from the worksheet and suggests the Project field names that are probable matches.

On this page of the Import Wizard you
specify how Project should import data from
other file formats, in this case an Excel workbook.

Import Wizard - Task Mapping

Map Tasks Data

Source worksheet name:

Tasks

Verify or edit how you want to map the data.

(Choose a source table above)

From: Excel Field	To: Microsoft Project Field	Data Type
Name	Name	Text
Duration	Duration	Text

Add All   Clear All   Insert Row   Delete Row

Move

Preview

Excel:	Name	Duration	
Project:	Name	Duration	
Preview:	Analysis and desig	10 days	
	Typesetting	15 days	

Help   < Back   Next >   Finish   Cancel

Use the Preview area to see how the data from
another file format will be mapped to Project fields,
based on the settings you've made above.

17. Click **Next**.

The final page of the Import Wizard appears. Here, you have the option of saving
the settings for the new import map, which is useful when you anticipate importing
similar data into Project in the future. This time, you'll skip this step.

18. Click **Finish**.

A confirmation dialog box appears because Project is now attempting to open a
non-default file format.

19. Click **Yes**.

Project imports the Excel data into a new Project plan. (The dates you see on the timescale will differ from those shown because Project uses the current date as the project start date in the new file.)

Unless you've changed the default scheduling setting for new tasks, the task list is manually scheduled.

This is a simple task list with just task names and durations. The process for importing more complex structured data is similar, however.

20. Close the new file without saving the changes.

The Sharing project plan remains open in Project.

Saving to Other File Formats from Project

Pasting Project data into other programs as you did earlier might be fine for one-time or infrequent needs, but this technique might not work as well if you must export a large volume of data from Project. Instead, you can save Project data in different file formats, which can be accomplished in various ways, including:

- You can save the entire project as Extensible Markup Language (XML) format for structured data exchange with other applications that support XML.

- You can save only the data you specify in a different format. The supported formats include Excel workbook, Excel PivotTable, and tab-delimited or comma-delimited text. When saving to these formats, you choose the format in which you want to save, pick a built-in export map (or create your own), and export the data.

A financial planner at Lucerne Publishing has requested some project cost data. You'd like to give this data to the financial planner, but the financial planner uses a budget program that cannot work directly with Project files. You decide to provide her with cost data as tab-delimited text, which will allow her the greatest flexibility when importing the data into her budget program.

In this exercise, you save project cost data to a text file using a built-in export map.

1. On the **File** tab, click **Save As**.

    The Save As dialog box appears. Project suggests saving the file in the same location from which you opened the practice file.

2. In the **File name** box, type Sharing Costs.

3. In the **Save as type** box, click **Text (Tab delimited)** from the list, and then click **Save**.

4. A legacy file format confirmation dialog box appears; click **Yes**.

    The Export Wizard appears.

    Tip When you use import/export maps, it makes no difference what current view in Project is displayed. The current view does not affect what data can or cannot be exported.

5. Click **Next**.

    The second page of the Export Wizard appears.

6. Click **Use existing map**, and then click **Next**.

7. Under **Choose a map for your data**, select **Cost data by task**.

8. Click **Next**.

   On the next page of the wizard, you can see your options for the types of data to export, the delimiter between data values (tab or space), and other options.

9. Click **Next**.

Use these buttons to control what fields will be exported.

Here, you can see the detailed field mapping to be applied for this export. You can customize what data to export and how it is organized. For this export, however, you'll use the default settings.

10. Click **Finish**.

    Project saves the text file. To view it, you will open the file in Notepad.

11. On the **Start** menu, point to **All Programs**, click **Accessories**, and click **Notepad**.
    Notepad starts.

12. In Notepad, make sure that **Word Wrap** is turned off. (On the **Format** menu, **Word Wrap** should not be selected.)

13. On the **File** menu, click **Open**.

14. Open the document **Sharing Costs** in your Chapter17 folder.

In this file, the fields are separated by tabs. It might not be easy for you to read, but this format is imported easily into virtually any data-crunching program.

15. On the **File** menu, click **Exit**. Notepad closes, and you return to Project.

To conclude this exercise, you'll restore the Trust Center settings.

16. On the **File** tab, click **Options**.

17. Click the **Trust Center** tab, and then click **Trust Center Settings**.

18. Click the **Legacy Formats** tab.

19. Under **Legacy Formats**, click **Do not open/save file with legacy or non-default file formats in Project**.

20. Click **OK** to close the **Trust Center** dialog box, and then click **OK** again to close the **Project Options** dialog box.

Working with File Formats from Previous Versions of Project

Project 2000, 2002, and 2003 shared a common file format that could be opened by any version of Project from 2000 to 2003. In other words, if you were using Project 2000, 2002, or 2003, you didn't need to pay attention to the Project file format across these three versions of Project.

To accommodate the new functionality introduced in a new product release, Project 2007 introduced its own file format, as has Project 2010.

When running Project 2010, you may find you need to share project plans with users of previous versions of Project. There are a few ways of doing this.

The simplest strategy is to save in Microsoft Project 2000–2003 format or Microsoft Project 2007 format (these are both file formats listed in the "Save as type" box in the Save As dialog box). However, some data relating to new features in Project 2010 will be changed or discarded when saved. Manually scheduled tasks, for example, will be converted to automatically scheduled tasks.

Another strategy is to try to open a Project 2010 file in an earlier version of Project. Because the Project 2010 file format differs from that of all earlier versions of Project, you cannot open 2010 files in Project 2007 without first downloading a file converter from the Microsoft.com Web site. If a Project 2007 user tries to open a 2010 file, Project will prompt them to download the converter. Even when using the converter, new features introduced in Project 2010, such as manually scheduled tasks, are not supported in earlier versions of the software.

Generating Visual Reports with Excel and Visio

Project 2010 can generate visual reports that focus on sharing schedule details with other applications. Specifically, you can use the Visual Reports feature to export data from Project to either Excel or Microsoft Visio and, once there, visually represent schedule details in compelling formats.

A visual report can include task, resource, or assignment details. When you select a visual report in Project, it generates a highly structured database, called an Online Analytical Processing (OLAP) cube, from your project plan. Project then starts either Excel or Visio (depending on the visual report you selected), loads and organizes the data used by that application, and generates a graphical representation of that data (an Excel chart or a Visio diagram). The specific results you obtain depend on the type of visual report you choose:

- Excel visual reports use the PivotTable and PivotChart features in Excel. You can format the chart and modify the details in the PivotTable report from which the chart is derived. PivotTable reports are well suited to analyzing and summarizing the large volumes of data that Project plans can contain. You can create Excel visual reports with Excel 2003 or later.

- Visio visual reports use the PivotDiagrams feature in Visio. PivotDiagrams are well suited for presenting hierarchical data and can complement Project very well. Not only can you customize the visual report as a Visio diagram, but you can also filter and rearrange the data from which the diagram is derived. Visio visual reports require Visio 2007 or later.

Project includes several Excel and Visio visual report templates. You can also create your own visual reports from scratch or modify one of the supplied templates. If you are already familiar with Excel PivotTables or you are a Visio power user, and you have the need to analyze and present Project data, you'll find visual reports of interest. However, if you're not as experienced with Excel PivotTables or Visio diagrams, you can still look at the Visual Report feature so that you have some exposure to it.

In this exercise, you generate both Excel and Visio visual reports.

Important If the computer on which you are now working does not have Excel 2003 or later or Visio 2007 or later installed, you cannot complete this exercise. If this is the case, skip to the next section.

1. On the **Project** tab, in the **Reports** group, click **Visual Reports**.

    The Visual Reports dialog box appears.

This dialog box groups visual reports in a number of ways: all reports; only Excel or Visio reports; and task, resource, or assignment details (divided into summary and usage reports). The dialog box includes a simplified preview of the type of graphic (chart or diagram) associated with each visual report. If desired, you can click the various tabs in the dialog box to see how the visual reports are organized.

The first visual report you'll generate is Excel-based.

2. Click the **Resource Summary** tab.

3. Click **Resource Remaining Work Report** and then click **View**.

Project generates the data required by this report, starts Excel, and creates the report. You may need to adjust the zoom level to view the entire chart.

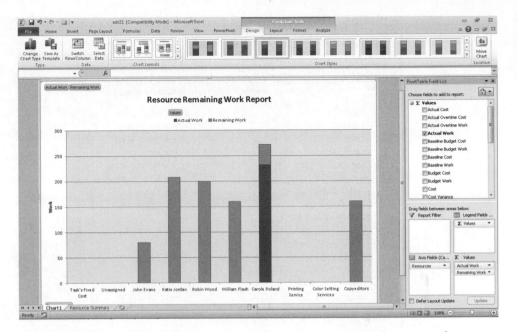

The PivotTable on which the chart is based is on the Resource Summary sheet. If you are familiar with PivotTables, you can view that sheet and modify the PivotTable settings if you wish.

Tip PivotTables is a powerful feature in Excel. To learn more, search for "**PivotTable**" in Excel Help.

4. When you are through working with the Excel chart, close Excel without saving the changes.

To conclude this exercise, you will generate a Visio-based visual report.

Important If the computer on which you are now working does not have Visio 2007 or later installed, you cannot complete this exercise. If this is the case, skip to the next section.

In Project, the Visual Reports dialog box should still be displayed.

5. Click the **Assignment Usage** tab.

6. Click **Baseline Report (US),** and then click **View**.

Project generates the data required by this report, starts Visio, and creates the Baseline Report diagram.

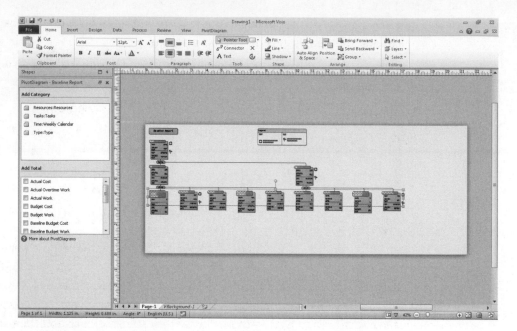

Next, you'll take a closer look at the items in this diagram.

7. Do either of the following:

- In Visio 2007, on the **View** menu, point to **Zoom**, and then click **100%**.

- In Visio 2010, in the Zoom slider, set the zoom level to **100%**.

8. If necessary, adjust the vertical and horizontal scroll bars until you can see the diagram details.

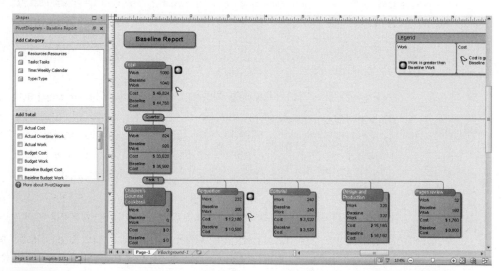

At this point, you could adjust the settings in the PivotDiagram pane in Visio to change the details included in the diagram.

9. When you are through working with the Visio diagram, close Visio without saving the changes.

10. In Project, click **Close** to close the **Visual Reports** dialog box.

 CLEAN UP Close the Sharing file.

Guided Tour: Synchronizing Task Lists Between Project and SharePoint (Project Professional only)

New In 2010 You can store Project 2010 (Standard and Professional) data files in a Microsoft SharePoint 2010 document library. In addition, with Project Professional 2010 you can synchronize tasks between Project and a new type of list in SharePoint called a Project Tasks list. You can either create the initial task list in Project and then synchronize it to the list in SharePoint, or create the initial task list in SharePoint and then create a new project plan based on the task list.

In both cases, the tasks in SharePoint behave like manually scheduled tasks; you can enter a start date and deadline for the tasks, but no active scheduling occurs. When a SharePoint task list is then synchronized with Project, the resulting tasks in Project are manually scheduled tasks. In Project, you can convert them to automatic scheduling and perform whatever task scheduling activities you wish, such as linking tasks, changing durations, and so on. However when you then synchronize from Project to SharePoint, the tasks in Project are converted back to manually scheduled tasks.

For the Project Professional user, you can think of task synchronization with SharePoint as serving two very useful purposes:

● You can create an initial task list in SharePoint and invite team members and other stakeholders to add tasks, durations, and other details in SharePoint. You can then synchronize the list with Project and do more scheduling work in Project. Then re-synchronize back to SharePoint so the team can see the results.

● You can create an initial task list in Project and then synchronize it with SharePoint. You can then invite team members and other stakeholders to adjust task details as needed. Then re-synchronize back to Project for additional schedule fine-tuning.

In both cases, you use the scheduling engine in Project and the collaborative, multi-user capabilities of SharePoint—the best combination of the strengths of both products.

In this section, you'll see how one project manager combines Project and SharePoint for collaboration on task lists.

Important This section does not use practice files or include hands-on activities for you to perform. We do not assume that you have access to both Project Professional and SharePoint as we illustrate them here. Instead, we present an illustrated narrative of how these products can be used together. If you do have access to both Project Professional and SharePoint, feel free to experiment with the kinds of activities illustrated here.

Hany Morcos is a project manager at Lucerne Publishing. Hany uses Project Professional to manage editorial and design work on the various books Lucerne has in its publishing pipeline. Recently, Lucerne has deployed SharePoint, and Hany wants to use the task list synchronizing features to involve her colleagues more directly in schedule development.

Hany has recently been given a basic task list from a colleague and wants to share it within her organization. She'd like her team to adjust the basic task list so it can be used for a new project they may take on. To begin, Hany will synchronize the task list from Project to SharePoint.

1. Hany opens the task list in Project.

2. Hany links the tasks to organize the tasks generally the way she wants them.

   This is what she'd like to synchronize with SharePoint and invite her team members to work with.

3. On the File tab, Hany clicks "Save and Send," and then clicks "Sync with Tasks List."

4. Hany enters the Uniform Resource Locator (URL) of the SharePoint site to which she wants to publish the task list, and then validates it.

Once Project validates the URL, Hany is ready to create the task list. She can either use an existing task list, or create a new one.

5. Hany enters a new name for the task list, and then clicks Sync.

   Project creates the SharePoint task list and then returns to the Gantt Chart view.

6. Next, Hany views the new task list in SharePoint.

With the task list now synchronized to SharePoint, Hany can invite her team members to review and modify the task list.

7. Hany's team members make changes to the task list, including adding new tasks and changing a due date.

8. Back in Project, Hany repeats the same synchronization process to refresh her view in Project of the tasks as they now appear in SharePoint.

The latest task list appears in Project. These remain manually scheduled tasks.

9. Hany fine-tunes the task list by entering some duration values, linking tasks, and other actions that produce a working schedule.

10. Finally, Hany again synchronizes the plan to SharePoint so that her team can see the latest details, and they continue to fine-tune the plan.

After additional rounds of fine-tuning the plan and synchronizing between Project and SharePoint, Hany converts that task list in Project to be scheduled automatically and makes other adjustments, like setting lead times, that are not supported by SharePoint.

From this point on, Hany will manage this plan in Project.

This section has illustrated just one scenario of Project and SharePoint integration via task list synchronization. Depending on the collaborative practices and tools of your organization, you may find that Project and SharePoint together make a powerful combination.

Key Points

- You can both copy from and paste into Project, just as you can with other Windows applications. However, when pasting data into a table in Project, take care to ensure that the data you want ends up in the correct fields.

- When opening other data formats in Project, Project uses import maps to help organize the imported data into the right structure for a Project table.

- Project supports saving data to common structured data formats, such as XML.

- Visual reports help you export Project data to nicely formatted Excel charts and Visio diagrams.

- Project Professional users can synchronize task lists with SharePoint.

Chapter at a Glance

Share resources from a central resource pool across several project plans, page 398.

See assignment details in a resource pool, page 404.

Create a consolidated project plan for a bird's-eye view across multiple projects, page 420.

Link tasks across different project plans, page 423.

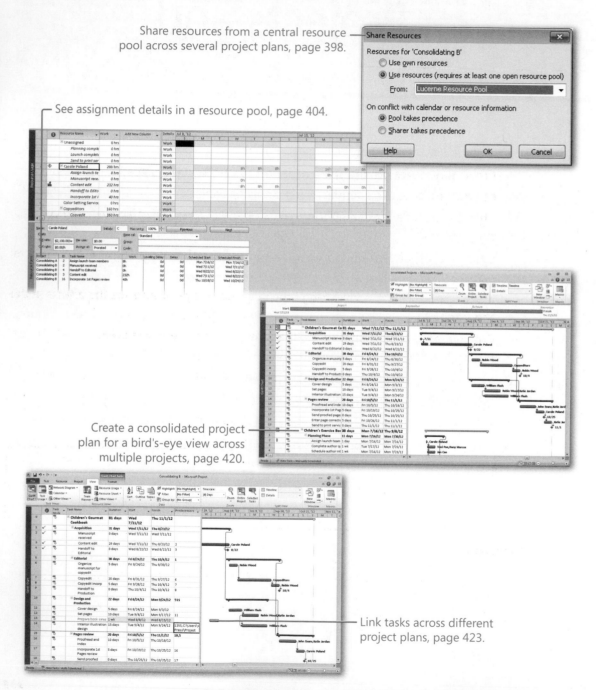

18 Consolidating Projects and Resources

In this chapter, you will learn how to:

✔ Create a resource pool to share resources across multiple projects.

✔ Look at resource allocation across multiple projects.

✔ Change resource assignments in a sharer plan, and see the effects in a resource pool.

✔ Change a resource's working time in a resource pool, and see the effects in a sharer plan.

✔ Make a specific date nonworking time in a resource pool, and see the effects in the sharer plan.

✔ Create a project plan, and make it a sharer plan for a resource pool.

✔ Update a resource pool manually from a sharer plan.

✔ Insert project plans to create a consolidated project.

✔ Link tasks between two project plans.

> **Practice Files** Before you can complete the exercises in this chapter, you need to copy the book's practice files to your computer. A complete list of practice files is provided in "Using the Practice Files" at the beginning of this book. For each exercise that has a practice file, simply browse to where you saved the book's practice file folder.

Important If you are running Project Professional, you may need to make a one-time setting change. This helps ensure that the practice files you work with in this chapter do not affect your Project Server data. For more information, see Appendix C, "Using the Practice Files if Connected to Project Server."

Creating a Resource Pool

When managing multiple projects, it is common for *work resources* (people and equipment) to be assigned to more than one project at a time. It might become difficult to coordinate the work resources' time among the multiple projects, especially if those projects are managed by different people. For example, an editor at a book publishing firm might have task *assignments* for a new book, a promotional Website, and a press release—three projects proceeding simultaneously. In each project, the editor might be *fully allocated* or even *underallocated*. However, if you add all her tasks from these projects together, you might discover that she has been overallocated, or assigned to work on more tasks than she can handle at one time. When working with cost resources in multiple projects, you might want to see not only the cost per project associated with a cost resource, but the cumulative costs across projects as well. Likewise, when working with material resources in multiple projects, you'd see cumulative consumed material resources in whatever unit of consumption you've used.

A *resource pool* can help you see how resources are utilized across multiple projects. The resource pool is a project plan from which other project plans draw their resource information. It contains information about all resources' task assignments from all project plans linked to the resource pool. You can change resource information—such as maximum units, cost rates, and nonworking time—in the resource pool, and all linked project plans will use the updated information.

The project plans that are linked to the resource pool are called *sharer plans*. The following is one way of visualizing a resource pool and sharer plans.

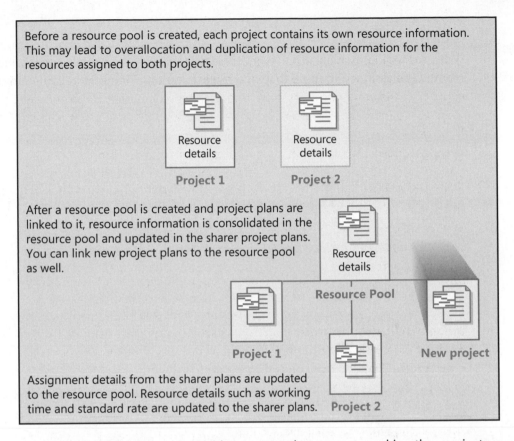

Before a resource pool is created, each project contains its own resource information. This may lead to overallocation and duplication of resource information for the resources assigned to both projects.

Resource details

Project 1

Resource details

Project 2

After a resource pool is created and project plans are linked to it, resource information is consolidated in the resource pool and updated in the sharer project plans. You can link new project plans to the resource pool as well.

Resource details

Resource Pool

Project 1

New project

Assignment details from the sharer plans are updated to the resource pool. Resource details such as working time and standard rate are updated to the sharer plans.

Project 2

If you manage just one project with resources that are not used in other projects, a resource pool provides you no benefit. However, if your organization plans to manage multiple projects, setting up a resource pool enables you to do the following:

- Enter resource information, such as nonworking time, in any of the sharer plans or in the resource pool so that it is available in other sharer plans.
- View resources' assignment details from multiple projects in a single location.
- View assignment costs per resource across multiple projects.
- View cumulative costs for work and cost resources across multiple projects.
- View cumulative consumption values for material resources across multiple projects.
- Find resources who are overallocated across multiple projects, even if those resources are underallocated in individual projects.

A resource pool is especially beneficial when working with other Microsoft Project 2010 users across a network. In those cases, the resource pool is stored in a central location, such as a network server, and the individual owners of the sharer plans (which might be stored locally or on a network server) share the common resource pool.

In this exercise, you create a project plan that will become a resource pool and link two sharer plans to it.

SET UP Start Project if it's not already running.

You need the Consolidating A_Start project plan located in your Chapter18 practice file folder to complete this exercise. Open the Consolidating A_Start project plan, and then follow these steps.

1. On the **File** tab, click **Save As**.

   The Save As dialog box appears.

2. In the **File name** box, type **Consolidating A**, and then click **Save**.

3. On the **File** tab, click **Open**.

   The Open dialog box appears.

4. Double-click the **Consolidating B_Start** file.

   Tip Double-clicking a file name here is a shortcut for selecting it and then clicking Open.

5. On the **File** tab, click **Save As**.

   The Save As dialog box appears.

6. In the **File name** box, type **Consolidating B**, and then click **Save**.

   These two project plans were previously created, and both contain resource information. When they were last saved, the Resource Sheet was the active view in both plans.

   Next, you will create a new project plan that will become a resource pool.

7. On the **File** tab, click **New**.

8. Under **Available Templates**, click **Blank project**, and then click **Create** on the right side of the Backstage view.

   Tip You can also double-click "Blank project."

   Project creates a new project plan, with the Gantt with Timeline view displayed.

9. On the **View** tab, in the **Resource Views** group, click **Resource Sheet**.

The Resource Sheet view replaces the Gantt Chart view.

10. On the **File** tab, click **Save As**.

11. Navigate to the **Chapter18** folder.

12. In the **File name** box, type **Lucerne Resource Pool**, and then click **Save**.

Tip You can give a resource pool any name you want, but it is a good idea to indicate that it is a resource pool in the file name.

Arrange All

13. On the **View** tab, in the **Window** group, click **Arrange All**.

Project arranges the three project plan windows within the Project window.

Note You do not need to arrange the project windows in this way to create a resource pool, but it is helpful to see the results as they occur in this chapter.

Looking at the resource names in the two project plans (Consolidating A and Consolidating B), you can see that several of the same resources appear in both project plans. These include *Carole Poland*, *Copyeditors*, *John Evans*, and others. None of these resources are overallocated in either project.

14. Click the title bar of the **Consolidating B** window.

15. On the **Resource** tab, in the **Assignments** group, click **Resource Pool**, and then click **Share Resources**.

    The Share Resources dialog box appears.

16. Under **Resources for 'Consolidating B'**, select the **Use resources** option.

    The Use Resources From list contains the open project plans that can be used as a resource pool.

17. In the **From** box, click **Lucerne Resource Pool**.

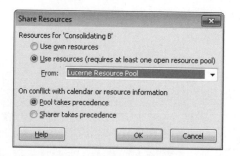

18. Click **OK** to close the **Share Resources** dialog box.

    You see the resource information from the Consolidating B project plan appear in the Lucerne Resource Pool plan. Next, you will set up the Consolidating A project plan as a sharer plan with the same resource pool.

19. Click the title bar of the **Consolidating A** window.

20. On the **Resource** tab, in the **Assignments** group, click **Resource Pool**, and then click **Share Resources**.

21. Under **Resources for 'Consolidating A'**, click the **Use resources** option.

22. In the **From** list, make sure that **Lucerne Resource Pool** is selected.

    Lucerne Resource Pool is selected by default. The Consolidating A project plan is already a sharer plan, and Project won't allow a sharer plan to be a resource pool for another project plan.

23. Under **On conflict with calendar or resource information**, make sure that the **Pool takes precedence** option is selected.

    Selecting this option causes Project to use resource information (such as cost rates) in the resource pool rather than in the sharer plan, should it find any differences between the two project plans.

24. Click **OK** to close the **Share Resources** dialog box.

You see the resource information from the Consolidating A project plan appear in the resource pool.

After these two sharer plans have been linked to the resource pool, the combined resource information appears in all files.

The resource pool contains the resource information from both sharer plans. Project will consolidate resource information from the sharer plans based on the name of the resource. John Evans, for example, is listed only once in the resource pool, no matter how many sharer plans list him as a resource.

Important Project cannot match variations of a resource's name—for example, John Evans from one sharer plan and J. Evans from another. For this reason, it is a good idea to develop a convention for naming resources in your organization and then stick with it.

Again, you do not have to arrange the project windows as you did in this exercise to link the sharer plans to the resource pool. However, it is helpful in this chapter to see the results as they occur.

Tip If you decide that you do not want to use a resource pool with a project plan, you can break the link. To do this, in the sharer plan, on the Resources tab, click Resource Pool and then click Share Resources. Under Resources For<*Current Project Name*>, select the Use Own Resources option.

Creating a Dedicated Resource Pool

Any project plan, with or without tasks, can serve as a resource pool. However, it is a good idea to designate as the resource pool a project plan that does not contain tasks. This is because any project with tasks will almost certainly conclude at some point, and you might not want assignments for those tasks (with their associated costs and other details) to be included indefinitely in the resource pool.

Moreover, a dedicated resource pool without tasks can enable people, such as *line managers* or resource managers, to maintain some information about their resources, such as nonworking time, in the resource pool. These people might not have a role in project management, and they will not need to deal with task-specific details in the resource pool.

Viewing Assignment Details in a Resource Pool

One of the most important benefits of using a resource pool is that it allows you to see how resources are allocated across projects. For example, you can identify resources that are overallocated across the multiple projects to which they are assigned.

Let's look at a specific example. As you might have noticed in the previous section, the resource Carole Poland, who was not overallocated in either of the individual project plans, did appear overallocated after Project accounted for all her assignments across the two project plans. When Carole's assignments from the two sharer plans were combined, they exceeded her capacity to work on at least one day. Although Carole most likely was aware of this problem, the project manager may not have known about it without setting up a resource pool (or hearing about the problem directly from Carole).

In this exercise, you view assignments across project plans in the resource pool.

1. Double-click the title bar of the **Lucerne Resource Pool** window.

   The resource pool window is maximized to fill the Project window. In the resource pool, you can see all the resources from the two sharer plans. To get a better view of resource usage, you will change views.

2. On the **View** tab, in the **Resource Views** group, click **Resource Usage**.

   The Resource Usage view appears.

3. In the **Resource Name** column, click the name of resource 1, *Carole Poland*.

4. On the **Task** tab, in the **Editing** group, click **Scroll to Task**.

   The timephased details on the right side of the Project window scroll horizontally to show Carole Poland's earliest task assignments. The red numbers (for example, 16 hours on July 16) indicate a day on which Carole is overallocated. Next, you will display the Resource Form to get more detail about Carole's assignments.

5. On the **View** tab, in the **Split View** group, click **Details**.

   The Resource Form appears below the Resource Usage view.

— In this combination view you can
  see both the resource's assigned tasks
  and details about each assignment.

		Resource Name	Work	Add New Column	Details	Jul 8, '12							Jul 15, '12				
						S	M	T	W	T	F	S	S	M	T	W	T
		Unassigned	0 hrs		Work												
		Planning comple	0 hrs		Work												
		Launch complete	0 hrs		Work												
		Send to print ser	0 hrs		Work												
1		Carole Poland	280 hrs		Work				8h	8h	8h			16h	0h	0h	8h
		Assign launch te	8 hrs		Work									8h			
		Manuscript rece	0 hrs		Work			0h									
		Content edit	232 hrs		Work				8h	8h	8h			8h	0h	0h	8h
		Handoff to Edito	0 hrs		Work												
		Incorporate 1st	40 hrs		Work												
2		Color Setting Service	0 hrs		Work												
3		Copyeditors	160 hrs		Work												
		Copyedit	160 hrs		Work												

Name:	Carole Poland		Initials:	C	Max units:	100%		Previous		Next	
Costs					Base cal:	Standard					
Std rate:	$2,100.00/w	Per use:	$0.00	Group:							
Ovt rate:	$0.00/h	Accrue at:	Prorated	Code:							

Project	ID	Task Name	Work	Leveling Delay	Delay	Scheduled Start	Scheduled Finish
Consolidating A	2	Assign launch team members	8h	0d	0d	Mon 7/16/12	Mon 7/16/12
Consolidating B	2	Manuscript received	0h	0d	0d	Wed 7/11/12	Wed 7/11/12
Consolidating B	4	Handoff to Editorial	0h	0d	0d	Wed 8/22/12	Wud 8/22/12
Consolidating B	3	Content edit	232h	0d	0d	Wed 7/11/12	Wed 8/22/12
Consolidating B	16	Incorporate 1st Pages review	40h	0d	0d	Thu 10/18/12	Wed 10/24/12

— The Resource Form shows assignments
  across multiple projects when using a
  resource pool.

In this combination view, you can see all resources in the resource pool and their assignments (in the upper pane), as well as the selected resource's details (in the lower pane) from all sharer plans. You can see, for example, that the *Content edit* task to which Carole is assigned is from the Consolidating B project, and the *Assign launch team members* task is from the Consolidating A project. Carole was not overallocated in either project, but she is overallocated when you see her assignments across projects in this way.

If you want, click different resource names in the Resource Usage view to see their assignment details in the Resource Form.

6. On the **View** tab, in the **Split View** group, clear the **Details** check box.

Tip In a resource pool, the Resource Form is just one way to see the details of specific assignments from sharer plans. You can also add the Project or Task Summary Name column to the table portion of the Resource Usage view. Doing so will show you which project each task assignment is from and that assignment's summary task name.

Updating Assignments in a Sharer Plan

You might recall that an assignment is the matching of a resource to a task. Because a resource's assignment details originate in sharer plans, Project updates the resource pool with assignment details as you make them in the sharer plan.

In this exercise, you change resource assignments in a sharer plan, and you see the changes posted to the resource pool.

1. In the **Resource Name** column heading in the Lucerne Resource Pool plan, select Resource 13, *Luis Sousa*.

   You can see that Luis has no task assignments in either sharer plan. (The value of his *Work* field is zero.) Next, you will assign Luis to a task in one of the sharer plans, and you will see the result in the resource pool as well as in the project.

Switch Windows

2. On the **View** tab, in the **Window** group, click **Switch Windows** and then click **Consolidating A**.

   Project displays the Consolidating A project plan. Currently, it has the Resource Sheet view displayed.

3. On the **View** tab, in the **Task Views** group, click **Gantt Chart**.

   The Gantt Chart view appears.

4. On the **Resource** tab, in the **Assignments** group, click **Assign Resources**.

   The Assign Resources dialog box appears.

5. In the **Task Name** column, click the name of task 5, *Design and order marketing material*.

6. On the **Task** tab, in the **Editing** group, click **Scroll to Task**.

7. In the **Resource Name** column in the **Assign Resources** dialog box, click **Luis Sousa**, and then click **Assign**.

   Project assigns Luis to the task.

8. Click **Close** to close the **Assign Resources** dialog box.

9. On the **View** tab, in the **Window** group, click **Switch Windows**, and then click **Lucerne Resource Pool**.

10. Make sure that resource 13, *Luis Sousa*, is selected, and then, on the **Task** tab, in the **Editing** group, click **Scroll to Task**.

As expected, Luis Sousa's new task assignment appears in the resource pool.

When the resource pool is open in Project, any changes you make to resource assignments or other resource information in any sharer plans immediately show up in all other open sharer plans and the resource pool. You don't need to switch between sharer plans and the resource pool, as you did in this chapter, to verify the updated resource assignments.

Updating a Resource's Information in a Resource Pool

Another important benefit of using a resource pool is that it gives you a central location in which to enter resource details, such as cost rates and working time. When a resource's information is updated in the resource pool, the new information is available in all the sharer plans. This can be especially useful in organizations with a large number of resources working on multiple projects. In larger organizations, people such as line managers, resource managers, or staff in a *program office* are often responsible for keeping general resource information up to date.

William Flash has told you that he will be unavailable to work on August 30 and 31.

In this exercise, you update a resource's working time in the resource pool, and you see changes in the sharer plans.

1. In the Lucerne Resource Pool plan, select the name of resource 8, *William Flash*.

2. Scroll the timephased portion of the view horizontally to the right until William's assignments for the week of August 26 appear.

3. On the **Project** tab, in the **Properties** group, click **Change Working Time.**

   The Change Working Time dialog box appears.

4. In the **For calendar** box, make sure that *William Flash* is selected.

   William's resource calendar appears in the Change Working Time dialog box. William has told you that he will not be available to work on Thursday and Friday, August 30 and 31, because he plans to attend a workshop.

5. On the **Exceptions** tab in the **Change Working Time** dialog box, click in the first row under **Name** and type **William at workshop.**

   The description for the calendar exception is a handy reminder for you and others who may view the project plan later.

6. Click in the **Start** field and type or select **8/30/12**.

7. Click in the **Finish** field and type or select **8/31/12**, and then press the Enter key.

8. Click **OK** to close the **Change Working Time** dialog box.

Now William has no work scheduled (he did previously).

Because August 30 and 31 have been set as nonworking days for this resource, no work is scheduled on these days and they are formatted as nonworking days for this resource.

To verify that William's nonworking time setting was updated in the sharer plans, you will look at his working time in one of those project plans.

Switch Windows

9. On the **View** tab, in the **Window** group, click **Switch Windows**, and then click **Consolidating A**.

10. On the **Project** tab, in the **Properties** group, click **Change Working Time.**

The Change Working Time dialog box appears.

11. In the **For calendar** box, click **William Flash**.

On the Exceptions tab, you can see that August 30 and 31 are flagged as nonworking days for William; the change to this resource's working time in the resource pool has been updated in the sharer plans.

Tip To scroll the calendar quickly to August 2012 in the Change Working Time dialog box, just select the exception name or the Start or Finish date for William's exception.

12. Click **Cancel** to close the **Change Working Time** dialog box.

Updating All Plans' Working Times in a Resource Pool

In the previous exercise, you changed an individual resource's working time in the resource pool, and you saw the change posted to a sharer plan. Another powerful capability of a resource pool enables you to change working times for a base calendar and see the changes updated to all sharer plans that use that calendar. For example, if you specify that certain days (such as holidays) are to be nonworking days in the resource pool, that change is posted to all sharer plans.

Important By default, all sharer plans share the same base calendars, and any changes you make to a base calendar in one sharer plan are reflected in all other sharer plans through the resource pool. If you have a specific sharer plan for which you want to use different base calendar working times, change the base calendar that sharer plan uses.

In this exercise, you set a nonworking time in a base calendar in the resource pool, and you see this change in all sharer plans.

Switch Windows

1. On the **View** tab, in the **Window** group, click **Switch Windows**, and then click **Lucerne Resource Pool**.

   The entire company will be attending a local book fair on August 13, and you want this to be a nonworking day for all sharer plans.

2. On the **Project** tab, in the **Properties** group, click **Change Working Time**.

   The Change Working Time dialog box appears.

3. In the **For calendar** box, select **Standard (Project Calendar)** from the drop-down list.

   Tip Base calendars, such as 24 Hours, Night Shift, and Standard, appear at the top of the list in the For Calendar box. Resource calendar names appear below the base calendars.

   Changes in working time to the Standard base calendar in the resource pool affect all project plans that are sharer plans of the resource pool.

4. On the **Exceptions** tab in the **Change Working Time** dialog box, click in the first row under **Name** and type **Local book fair**.

5. Click in the **Start** field and type or select **8/13/12**, and then click the **Finish** field.

   Project fills in the same value in the Finish Date field.

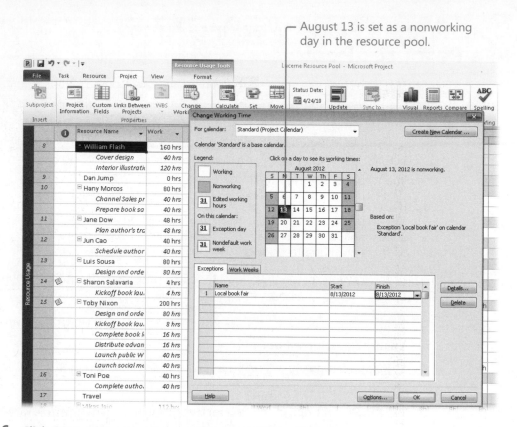

August 13 is set as a nonworking day in the resource pool.

6. Click **OK** to close the **Change Working Time** dialog box.

   To verify that this change to the Standard base calendar in the resource pool was updated in the sharer plans, you will look at working times in one of the sharer plans.

7. On the **View** tab, in the **Window** group, click **Switch Windows**, and then click **Consolidating A**.

8. On the **Project** tab, in the **Properties** group, click **Change Working Time**.

   The Change Working Time dialog box appears.

9. In the **For calendar** box, make sure that **Standard (Project Calendar)** is selected in the drop-down list.

   Note the *Local book fair* exception on August 13. All project plans that are sharer plans of the same resource pool will see this change in this base calendar.

In the sharer plans linked to the resource pool,
August 13 is set as a nonworking day in the
Standard base calendar.

10. Click **Cancel** to close the **Change Working Time** dialog box.

    If you want, you can switch to the Consolidating B project plan and verify that August 13 is also a nonworking day for that project.

11. Close and save changes to all open project plans, including the resource pool.

Important When working with sharer plans and a resource pool, it is important to understand that when you open a sharer plan, you must also open the resource pool if you want the sharer plan to be updated with the most recent changes to the resource pool. For example, assume that you change the project calendar's working time in the resource pool, save it, and close it. If you later open a sharer plan but do not also open the resource pool, that sharer plan will not reflect the updated project calendar's working time.

Linking New Project Plans to a Resource Pool

You can make a project plan a sharer plan for a resource pool at any time: when initially entering the project plan's tasks, after you have assigned resources to tasks, or even after work has begun. After you have set up a resource pool, you might find it helpful to make sharer plans of all new projects, along with the sharer plans of projects already created. In that way, you get used to relying on the resource pool for resource information.

Tip A definite time-saving advantage of creating new project plans as sharer plans of a resource pool is that your resource information is instantly available. You do not have to reenter any resource data.

In this exercise, you create a project plan and make it a sharer plan for the resource pool.

1. On the **File** tab, click **Open**.

   The Open dialog box appears.

2. Navigate to the Chapter18 folder, and double-click **Lucerne Resource Pool**.

   Project prompts you to select how you want to open the resource pool.

   Important The default option is to open the resource pool as read-only. You might want to choose this option if you and other Project users are sharing a resource pool across a network. If you store the resource pool locally, however, you should open it as read-write.

3. Click the second option to open the resource pool as read-write.

4. Click **OK**.

   The resource pool opens with the Resource Usage view displayed.

5. On the **View** tab, in the **Resource Views** group, click **Resource Sheet**.

   The Resource Sheet view appears.

6. On the **File** tab, click **New**.

7. Under **Available Templates**, make sure that **Blank project** is selected, and then click the **Create** button.

   Project creates a new project plan.

8. On the **File** tab, click **Save As**.

   The Save As dialog box appears.

9. Navigate to the Chapter18 folder.

10. In the **File name** box, type **Consolidating C**, and then click **Save**.

11. On the **Resource** tab, in the **Assignments** group, click **Assign Resources**.

    The Assign Resources dialog box is initially empty because you have not yet entered any resource information in this project plan.

12. On the **Resource** tab, in the **Assignments** group, click **Resource Pool** and then click **Share Resources**.

    The Share Resources dialog box appears.

13. Under **Resources for 'Consolidating C'**, select the **Use resources** option.

14. Make sure that **Lucerne Resource Pool** is selected in the **From** box, and then click **OK** to close the **Share Resources** dialog box.

    In the Assign Resources dialog box, you see all the resources from the resource pool appear.

Now these resources are ready to be assigned to tasks in this project.

15. Click **Close** to close the **Assign Resources** dialog box.

16. On the **File** tab, click **Close**. When prompted, click **Yes** to save your changes.

    The Consolidating C project plan closes, and the Lucerne Resource Pool remains open.

17. On the **File** tab, click **Close**. When prompted, click **Yes** to save your changes to the resource pool.

Important You save changes to the resource pool because it records the names and locations of its sharer plans.

Troubleshooting If a sharer plan is deleted, assignment information from that sharer plan is still stored in the resource pool. To clear this assignment information from the resource pool, you must break the link to the sharer plan. To do this, open the resource pool as read-write. On the Resource tab, in the Assignments group, click Resource Pool, and then click Share Resources. In the Share Resources dialog box, click the name of the now-deleted sharer plan and click Break Link. Note that what you see in the Share Resources dialog box for a resource pool differs from what you see for all other types of project plans.

Opening a Sharer Plan and Updating a Resource Pool

If you are sharing a resource pool with other Project users across a network, whoever has the resource pool open as read-write prevents others from updating resource information, such as standard cost rates, or making other project plans sharers of that resource pool. For this reason, it is a good idea to open the resource pool as read-only, and use the Update Resource Pool command only when you need to update the resource pool with assignment information. To do this, on the Resources tab, in the Assignments group, click Resource Pool, and then click Update Resource Pool. This command updates the resource pool with new assignment information; once that is done, anyone else who opens the resource pool will see the latest assignment information.

In this chapter, you are working with the resource pool and sharer plans locally. If you are going to use a resource pool over a network, it is a good idea to understand the updating process. This exercise introduces you to that process.

In this exercise, you change assignments in a sharer plan and then manually send updated assignment information to the resource pool.

1. On the **File** tab, click **Open**.

2. Navigate to the Chapter18 folder, and double-click the **Consolidating A** file.

   Because this project plan is a sharer plan linked to a resource pool, Project gives you the following options.

3. Click the **Open resource pool to see assignments across all sharer files** option, and then click **OK**.

    Choosing the second option, Do Not Open Other Files, allows you to see assignments only in the single sharer project plan.

    The resource pool opens as read-only in the background. (If you want to verify this, look at the items in the Switch Windows command on the View tab.) Next, you will change some assignments in the sharer plan.

4. On the **Resource** tab, in the **Assignments** group, click **Assign Resources**.

    The Assign Resources dialog box appears. First, you will assign a resource to a task.

5. In the **Task Name** column, click the name of task 3, *Complete author questionnaire.*

6. In the **Resource Name** column in the **Assign Resources** dialog box, click **Hany Morcos**, and then click **Assign**.

    Project assigns Hany to the task.

Next, you will remove a resource from a task.

7. In the **Task Name** column, click the name of task 5, *Design and order marketing material.*

8. In the **Resource Name** column in the **Assign Resources** dialog box, click **Toby Nixon** (located near the top of the **Resource Name** column), and then click **Remove**.

    Project removes Toby from the task.

You have made two assignment changes in the sharer plan. Because the resource pool is open as read-only, those changes have not been saved permanently in the resource pool. Next, you will update the resource pool.

9. On the **Resource** tab, in the **Assignments** group, click **Resource Pool**, and then click **Update Resource Pool**.

Project updates the assignment information in the resource pool with the new details from the sharer plan. Anyone else who opens or refreshes the resource pool now will see the updated assignment information.

Important Only assignment information is saved to the resource pool from the sharer plan. Any changes that you make to resource details, such as maximum units, in the sharer plan are not saved in the resource pool when you update. When you want to change the resource details, open the resource pool as read-write. After it is open as read-write, you can change resource details in either the resource pool or the sharer plan, and the other project plans will be updated.

Next, you will change an assignment in the sharer plan, close the sharer plan, and then update the resource pool.

10. In the **Task Name** column, click the name of task 8, *Kickoff book launch meeting*.

11. In the **Resource Name** column in the **Assign Resources** dialog box, click **Carole Poland**, and then click **Assign**.

Project assigns Carole to the task.

12. Click **Close** to close the **Assign Resources** dialog box.

13. On the **File** tab, click **Close**.

14. When prompted to save changes to the Consolidating A plan, click **Yes**.

Project determines that, because the resource pool was open as read-only, the latest assignment changes from the sharer plans have not been updated in the resource pool. You are offered the choices shown in the following illustration.

15. Click **OK**.

Project updates the assignment information with the new details from the sharer plan. The resource pool remains open as read-only.

16. On the **File** tab, click **Close**.

Because the resource pool was opened as read-only, Project closes it without prompting you to save the changes.

Consolidating Project Plans

Most projects often involve several people working on tasks at different times, sometimes in different locations, and frequently for different supervisors. Although a resource pool can help you manage resource details across projects, it might not give you the level of control that you want over tasks and relationships between projects.

A good way to pull together far-flung project information is to use a consolidated project. This is a project plan that contains other project plans, called inserted projects. The inserted projects do not reside within the consolidated project plan; rather, they are linked to it in such a way that they can be viewed and edited from it. If a project plan is edited outside the consolidated project, the updated information appears in the consolidated project plan the next time it is opened.

Tip Consolidated project plans are also known as *master projects*, and inserted project plans are also known as subprojects; however, this chapter uses the terms *consolidated* and *inserted*.

Using consolidated project plans enables you to do the following:

- See all tasks from your organization's project plans in a single view.

- "Roll up" project information to higher levels of management. For example, you might insert a team's project plan into the larger department's consolidated project plan and then insert that plan into the larger organization's consolidated project plan.

- Divide your project data into different project plans to match the nature of your project, such as by phase, component, or location. Then you can pull the information back together into a consolidated project plan for a comprehensive look at the whole.

- See all your projects' information in one location so that you can filter, sort, and group the data.

Consolidated project plans use Project's outlining features. An inserted project plan appears as a summary task in the consolidated project plan, except that its summary Gantt bar is gray and an inserted project icon appears in the Indicators column. When you save a consolidated project plan, you are also prompted to save any changes you have made to inserted project plans as well.

In this exercise, you create a new consolidated project plan and insert two project plans.

1. On the **File** tab, click **New**.
2. Under **Available Templates**, click **Blank project**, and then click **Create**.

Project creates a new project plan. This plan will become the consolidated plan into which you insert other projects.

3. On the **Project** tab, in the **Insert** group, click **Subproject**.

   The Insert Project dialog box appears.

4. Navigate to the Chapter18 folder, and while holding down the Ctrl key, select **Consolidating A** and **Consolidating B**.

5. Click **Insert**.

   Project inserts the two projects into the consolidated project as collapsed summary tasks.

6. On the **Task** tab, in the **Editing** group, click **Scroll to Task**.

   Project displays the Gantt bars of the collapsed summary tasks.

Note the Inserted Project icon in the Indicators column and the gray summary task bars.

Next, you will save the new consolidated project.

7. On the **File** tab, click **Save As**.

8. Navigate to the Chapter18 folder.

9. In the **File name** box, type **Consolidated Projects**, and then click **Save**.

   Next, you will display the details of the two inserted projects.

10. On the **View** tab, in the **Data** group, click **Outline** and then click **All Subtasks**.

    Project asks whether you want to open the resource pool. Project hasn't actually loaded the content of the inserted project plans yet, and showing the subtasks in the consolidated project is akin to opening them.

11. Make sure that **Open resource pool to see assignment across all sharer files** is selected, and then click **OK**.

    Project expands the two project plans. Note that the task IDs within both inserted projects start at 1, and the summary tasks representing the inserted projects are numbered 1 and 2.

    Next, you'll look at the details of the inserted projects.

12. On the **View** tab, in the **Zoom** group, click **Entire Project**.

Project adjusts the timescale in the Gantt Chart so that the full duration of the two inserted projects is visible.

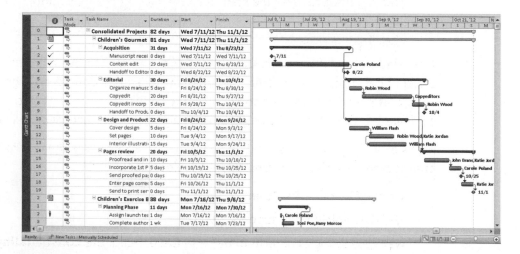

To conclude this exercise, you will display the project summary task of the consolidated project plan.

13. On the **Format** tab, in the **Show/Hide** group, click **Project Summary Task**.

Project displays the Consolidated Projects summary task.

The values of this summary task, such as duration and work, represent the rolled-up values of both inserted projects. As Lucerne Publishing develops more project plans, inserting them into the consolidated project plan in this way gives you a single location in which to view all activities of the organization.

14. Close and save changes to all open files.

Tip To create a consolidated project plan and insert projects that are open in Project quickly, on the View tab, in the Windows group, click New Window. Under Projects, select the open projects you want to insert and then click OK.

Creating Dependencies Between Projects

Most projects do not exist in a vacuum. Tasks or phases in one project might depend on tasks in other projects. You can show such dependencies by linking tasks between projects.

Reasons that you might need to create dependencies between projects include the following:

- The completion of one task in a project might enable the start of a task in another project. For example, another project manager might need to complete an environmental impact statement before you can start to construct a building. Even if these two tasks are managed in separate project plans (perhaps because separate departments of a development company are completing them), one project has a logical dependency on the other.

- A person or a piece of equipment might be assigned to a task in one project, and you need to delay the start of a task in another project until that resource completes the first task. The two tasks might have nothing in common other than needing that resource.

Task relationships between project plans look similar to links between tasks within a project plan, except that external predecessor and successor tasks have gray task names and Gantt bars. Such tasks are sometimes referred to as *ghost tasks* because they are not linked to tasks within the project plan, only to tasks in other project plans.

In this exercise, you link tasks in two project plans, and you see the results in the two project plans as well as in a consolidated project plan.

1. On the **File** tab, click **Open**.

The Open dialog box appears.

2. Navigate to the Chapter18 folder, and double-click the **Consolidating B** file.

3. Click **Open resource pool to see assignment across all sharer files**, and then click **OK**.

4. On the **File** tab, click **Open**.

5. Navigate to the Chapter18 folder, and double-click the **Consolidating A** file.

6. In the **Task Name** column, click the name of task 12, *Prepare book sales kit*.

   You need the book sales kit before you begin a task in the Consolidated B plan, so you will create a dependency between the two plans.

Switch Windows

7. On the **View** tab, in the **Window** group, click **Switch Windows**, and then click **Consolidating B**.

8. On the **View** tab, in the **Task Views** group, click **Gantt Chart**.

   The Gantt Chart view appears.

9. Click the name of task 13, *Interior illustration design*.

10. On the **Task** tab, in the **Editing** group, click **Scroll to Task**.

    Project scrolls the Gantt Chart view to display task 13.

11. In the **Gantt Chart** view, drag the vertical divider bar to the right until the **Predecessors** column is visible.

12. In the **Predecessors** field for task 13, click in the field so that the cursor appears directly after the existing predecessor value, *12SS*.

13. Directly after the existing predecessor value *12SS* type **,Consolidating A\12** (with no space between *12SS* and the comma and the subsequent text).

When creating an external predecessor link, Project requires the following format: *File Name\Task ID*.

14. Press Enter.

Project inserts the external predecessor task named *Prepare book sales kit* into the project. The external task represents task 12 from the Consolidating A project.

The external predecessor task appears in the project to which it is linked with its task name in gray.

The external task's Gantt bar is gray.

Tip If you point to the external task's Gantt bar, Project displays a ScreenTip that contains details about the external task, including the full path to the external project plan where the external predecessor task (the ghost task) resides.

Next, you'll look at the ghost task in the Consolidating A project plan.

15. On the **View** tab, in the **Window** group, click **Switch Windows**, and then click **Consolidating A**.

16. In the **Task Name** column, select the names of task 12, *Prepare book sales kit*, and task 13, *Interior illustration design*.

17. On the **View** tab, in the **Zoom** group, click **Selected Tasks**.

Project adjusts the chart portion of the Gantt Chart view to display the selected tasks.

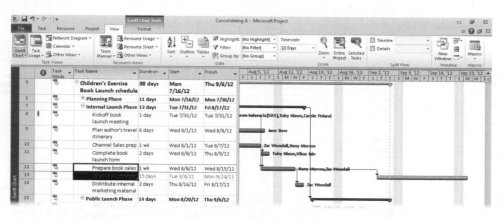

Here, you can see that task 12, *Prepare book sales kit*, is a predecessor for the external task 13, *Interior illustration design*. Because task 13 is a successor task with no other links to this project, it has no effect on other tasks here.

The link between these two project plans will remain until you break it. Deleting a task in the source plan or the ghost task in the destination plan deletes the corresponding task or ghost task in the other plan.

18. Close and save the changes to all open files.

To conclude this exercise, you will display the link between these two projects in the consolidated project plan.

19. On the **File** tab, click **Open**.

20. Navigate to the Chapter18 folder, and double-click the **Consolidated Projects** file.

21. Click **Open resource pool to see assignment across all sharer files**, and then click **OK**.

22. In the **Children's Exercise Book Launch** schedule plan (the second inserted project), click the minus sign next to the name of task 1, *Planning Phase*.

Project collapses this phase. This will allow you to see both the predecessor and successor tasks across the two inserted projects.

23. On the **Task** tab, in the **Editing** group, click **Scroll to Task**.

You can see the link line between the *Prepare book sales kit* task in one inserted project and the *Interior illustration design* task in the other inserted project.

In the consolidated project plan, the cross-project link appears as a normal task link.

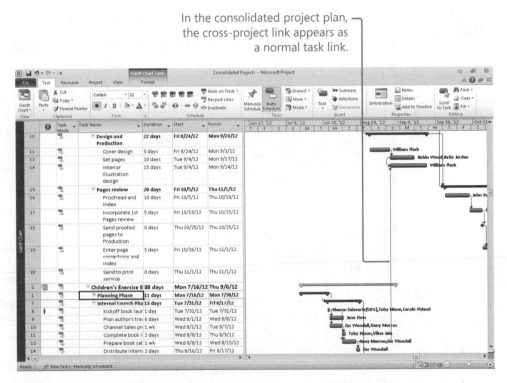

Because you are looking at a consolidated project plan that shows the tasks from both project plans, the cross-project link does not appear as a ghost task.

The following are a few additional tips and suggestions for working with consolidated projects and cross-project links:

- You can turn off the display of cross-project links if you wish. To do this, on the File tab, click Options. In the Project Options dialog box, on the Advanced tab, clear the Show External Successors and Show External Predecessors check boxes.

- When viewing a consolidated project, you can create cross-project links quickly by clicking the Link Tasks button on the Task tab. Dragging the mouse between two task bars will do the same thing.

- Each time you open a project plan with cross-project links, Project will prompt you to update the cross-project links. You can suppress this prompt if you would rather not be reminded, or you can tell Project to accept updated data from the linked project plan automatically. To do this, on the File tab, click Options. In the Project Options dialog box, on the Advanced tab, under Cross Project Linking Options For *<File Name>*, select the options that you want.

✖ CLEAN UP Close all open files.

Key Points

- If you have resource information duplicated in more than one project plan, a resource pool is an excellent way to collect resource information across project plans and spot problems, such as resource overallocation.

- Besides indicating various resources' nonworking time in a resource pool, you can edit the project calendar in a resource pool (for example, marking holidays as nonworking time) and that information will be propagated to all sharer plans of the resource pool file.

- Resource assignment details from all sharer plans are available for viewing (but not editing) in the resource pool file.

- Consolidating project plans into a single plan is useful when you want to see all the aggregate details in one place (the consolidated project plan) and yet continue to work with the individual project plans.

- When a task in one project plan has a logical dependency on a task in another project plan, you can link the two with a cross-project link. This produces what is sometimes called a ghost task (the predecessor or successor task) in both project plans.

Part 4

Appendices

A A Short Course in Project Management

Throughout this book, we've included advice on how best to use Microsoft Project 2010 while following sound project management practices. This appendix focuses on the basics of project management, regardless of any software tools you may use to help you manage projects. While project management is a broad, complex subject, in this appendix we focus on the *project triangle* model. In this model, you consider projects in terms of *time*, *cost*, and *scope*.

Understanding What Defines a Project

Succeeding as a project manager requires that you complete your projects on time, finish within budget, and make sure your customers are happy with what you deliver. That sounds simple enough, but how many projects have you heard of (or worked on) that were completed late, cost too much, or didn't meet the needs of their customers?

A Guide to the Project Management Body of Knowledge (published by the Project Management Institute)—referred to as the PMBOK and pronounced "pimbok"—defines a project as "a temporary endeavor undertaken to create a unique product or service." Let's walk through this definition to clarify what a project is—and what it is not.

Tip For more information about the Project Management Institute and the PMBOK, see Appendix B, "Roadmap for Developing Your Project and Project Management Skills."

First, a project is *temporary*. A project's duration might be just one week, or it might go on for years, but every project has an end date. You might not know that end date when the project begins, but it's out there somewhere in the future. Projects are not the same as ongoing operations, although the two have a great deal in common. *Ongoing operations*, as the name suggests, go on indefinitely; you don't establish an end date. Examples include most activities of accounting and human resources departments. People who run ongoing operations might also manage projects; for example, a manager of a human resources department for a large organization might plan a college

431

recruiting fair. Yet, projects are distinguished from ongoing operations by an expected end date, such as the date of the recruiting fair.

Next, a project is an *endeavor*. *Resources*, such as people and equipment, need to do work. The endeavor is undertaken by a team or an organization, and therefore projects have a sense of being intentional, planned events. Successful projects do not happen spontaneously; some amount of preparation and planning happens first.

Finally, every project creates a *unique product* or *service*. This is the *deliverable* for the project and the reason that the project was undertaken. A refinery that produces gasoline does not produce a unique product. The whole idea, in this case, is to produce a standardized commodity; you typically don't want to buy gas from one station that is significantly different from gas at another station. On the other hand, commercial airplanes are unique products. Although all Boeing 787 airplanes might look the same to most of us, each is, in fact, highly customized for the needs of its purchaser.

By now, you may realize that much of the work that goes on in the world is project-oriented work. In fact, a substantial portion of your work may be focused on project management—even if that's not your job title.

Project management has been a recognized profession for many decades, but project management work in some form has been occurring for as long as people have been doing complex work. When the Great Pyramids at Giza in Egypt were built, somebody somewhere was tracking resources, schedules, and specifications in some fashion.

Tip Project management is now a well-recognized profession in most industries. To learn more about organizations that train project managers and advance project management as a profession, see Appendix B.

The Project Triangle: Viewing Projects in Terms of Time, Cost, and Scope

You can visualize project work in many ways, but our favorite method is what is sometimes called the *project triangle* or triangle of triple constraints.

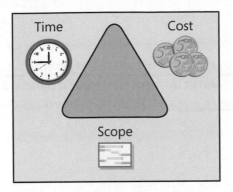

This theme has many variations, but the basic concept is that every project has some element of a time constraint, has some type of budget, and requires some amount of work to complete. (In other words, it has a defined scope.) The term *constraint* has a specific meaning in Project, but here we're using the more general meaning of a limiting factor. Let's consider these constraints one at a time.

Time

Have you ever worked on a project that had a deadline? (Maybe we should ask whether you've ever worked on a project that did not have a deadline.) Limited *time* is the one constraint of any project with which we are all probably most familiar. If you're working on a project right now, ask your team members to name the date of the project deadline. They might not know the project budget or the scope of work in great detail, but chances are they all know their immediate deadlines, and probably also the overall project deadline.

The following are examples of time constraints:

- You are building a house and must finish the roof before the rainy season arrives.
- You are assembling a large display booth for a trade show that starts in two months.
- You are developing a new inventory-tracking system that must be tested and running by the start of the next fiscal year.

Since we were children, we have been trained to understand time. We carry wristwatches, paper and electronic organizers, and other tools to help us manage time. For many projects that create a product or event, time is the most important constraint to manage.

Cost

You might think of cost simply in monetary terms, but in the context of projects, *cost* has a broader meaning: costs include all the resources required to carry out the project. Costs include the people and equipment doing the work, the materials being used, and all the other events and issues that require money or someone's attention in a project.

The following are examples of cost constraints:

- You have signed a fixed-price contract to develop an e-commerce website for a client. If your costs exceed the agreed-upon price, your customer might be sympathetic, but he or she probably won't be willing to renegotiate the contract.

- The president of your organization has directed you to carry out a customer research project using only the staff and equipment in your department.

- You have received a $5,000 grant to create a public art installation. You have no other funds.

For virtually all projects, cost is ultimately a limiting constraint; few projects could go over budget without eventually requiring corrective action.

Scope

You should consider two aspects of *scope*: product scope and project scope. Every successful project produces a unique product: a tangible item or service. Customers usually have some expectations about the features and functions of products they consider purchasing. *Product scope* describes the intended quality, features, and functions of the product, often in minute detail. Documents that outline this information are sometimes called *product specifications*. A service or event usually has some expected features as well. We all have expectations about what we'll do or see at a party, concert, or sporting event.

Project scope, on the other hand, describes the work required to deliver a product or service with the intended product scope. Project scope is usually measured in phases and tasks.

The following are examples of scope constraints:

- Your organization won a contract to develop an automotive product that has exact requirements—for example, physical dimensions measured to 0.01 mm. This is a product scope constraint that will influence project scope plans.

- You are constructing a building on a lot that has a height restriction of 50 feet.

- You can use only internal services to develop part of your product, and those services follow a product development methodology that is different from what you had planned.

Product scope and project scope are closely related. The project manager who manages project scope should also understand product scope or know how to communicate with those who do.

Time, Cost, and Scope: Managing Project Constraints

Project management gets most interesting when you must balance the time, cost, and scope constraints of your projects. The project triangle illustrates the process of balancing constraints because the three sides of the triangle are connected, and changing one side of a triangle affects at least one other side.

The following are examples of constraint balance:

- If the duration (time) of your project schedule decreases, you might need to increase budget (cost) because you must hire more resources to do the same work in less time. If you cannot increase the budget, you might need to reduce the scope because the resources you have cannot complete all the planned work in less time.

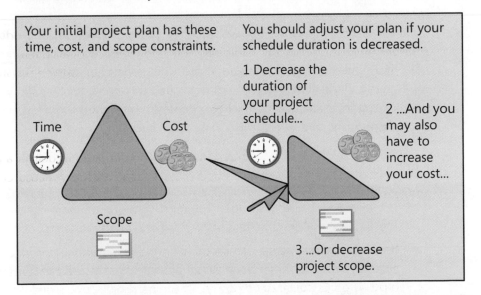

If you must decrease a project's duration, make sure that overall project quality is not unintentionally lowered. For example, testing and quality control often occur last in a software development project; if project duration is decreased late in the project, those tasks might be the ones to suffer with cutbacks. You must weigh the benefits of decreasing the project duration against the potential downside of a deliverable of poorer quality.

● If the budget (cost) of your project decreases, you might need more time because you cannot pay for as many resources or for resources of the same efficiency. If you cannot increase the time, you might need to reduce project scope because fewer resources cannot complete all the planned work in the time remaining.

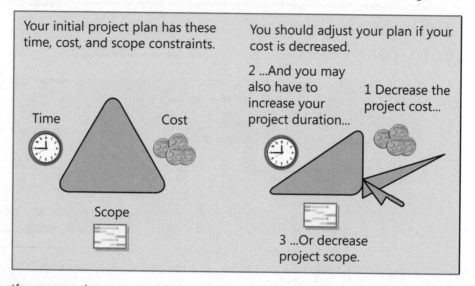

Your initial project plan has these time, cost, and scope constraints.

You should adjust your plan if your cost is decreased.

Time

Cost

Scope

2 ...And you may also have to increase your project duration...

1 Decrease the project cost...

3 ...Or decrease project scope.

If you must decrease a project's budget, you could look at the *grades* of material resources for which you had budgeted. A lower-grade material is not necessarily a lower-quality material. So long as the grade of material is appropriate for its intended use, it might still be of high quality. Here's one example we can all relate to: fast food and gourmet are two grades of restaurant food, but you may find high-quality and low-quality examples of each.

You should also look at the costs of the human and equipment resources you have planned to use. Can you hire less-experienced people for less money to carry out simpler tasks? Reducing project costs can lead to a poorer-quality deliverable, however. As a project manager, you must consider (or, more likely, communicate to the decision makers) the benefits versus the risks of reducing costs.

● If your project scope increases, you might need more time or resources (cost) to complete the additional work. When project scope increases after the project has started, it's called *scope creep*. Changing project scope midway through a project is not necessarily a bad thing; for example, the environment in which your project deliverable will operate may have changed or you've learned more about the nature of the work since beginning the project. Changing project scope is a bad thing only if the project manager doesn't recognize and plan for the new requirements—that is, when other constraints (cost, time) are not correspondingly examined and, if necessary, adjusted.

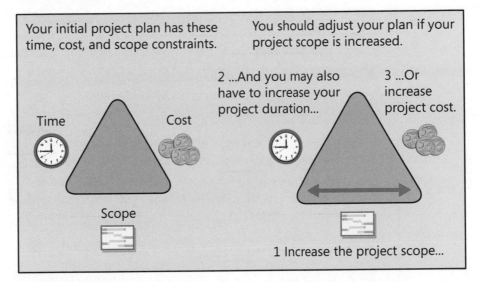

Time, cost, and scope are the three essential elements of any project. To succeed as a project manager, you should know how all three of these constraints apply to your projects and be able to communicate this to your stakeholders.

Here is our final word about the project triangle model. Like all simple models of complex subjects, this model is a useful learning tool but not always a reflection of the real world. If real projects always performed as the project triangle suggests that they should, you might see projects delivered late but at the planned cost or with the expected scope; or projects might be completed on time and with the expected scope, but at higher cost. In other words, you'd expect to see at least one element of the project triangle come in as planned. But the sad truth is that many projects, even with rigorous project management oversight, are delivered late, over budget, *and* with far less than expected scope of functionality. You've probably participated in a few such projects yourself. Project management is a demanding field. Success in project management requires a rare mix of skills and knowledge about schedule practices and tools, as well as skill in the domain or industry in which a project is executed.

Managing Your Projects with Project

The best project management tool in the world can never replace your good judgment. However, the right tool can and should help you accomplish the following:

- Track all the information you gather about the work, duration, and resource requirements for your project.

- Visualize your project plan in standard, well-defined formats.

- Schedule tasks and resources consistently and effectively.

- Exchange project information with *stakeholders* in a variety of ways.

- Communicate with resources and other stakeholders while leaving ultimate control in the hands of the project manager.

In the chapters of this book, you were introduced to the rich functionality of Project in a realistic context: managing a project from conception to completion. Not everything in this book might have applied to your needs, and you probably have needs that this book did not address. Yet, after completing this tutorial, you're off to a great start with Project.

B Roadmap for Developing Your Project and Project Management Skills

If you've completed most of or all the chapters in this book, you're well on your way to mastering Microsoft Project 2010. However, one book can get you only so far. To help further your knowledge of Project and project management, start with these sources.

Joining a Project Learning Community

If there's one thing we can say about Project users, it's that they love to talk about the program and their work with it and to share ideas with others. Whether you work in a large organization or independently, you're likely to find a community of Project users nearby.

If you're in a large organization, especially one with a strong project management focus, you might find an internal Project user group or support group there. Such groups often meet informally to provide peer training and support, critique project plans, and share best practices. If such a group does not exist in your organization, perhaps you can start one.

In the public realm, there are many Project user groups around the world. These groups typically meet on a regular basis to share tips and tricks about Project. Joining a user group is a great way to broaden your exposure to Project usage; it also can be a great source for informal product support, training, and career networking.

The following are a few places where you can investigate Project user groups and related resources:

- The Microsoft Project User Group (MPUG) is the official industry association for Project. MPUG offers information about a variety of Project and project management resources, as well as a directory of Project user groups around the world. Find it on the Web at *www.mpug.com*.

- The Project area of the Microsoft Office Online website includes a variety of tools and information from Microsoft and other Project users to help you manage your projects. Find it on the Web at *http://office.com*, and then navigate to the Project page.

- The official Project newsgroup offers help and discussions with other Project users, including Microsoft Most Valuable Professionals (MVPs). To get started, see the following websites:
  http://www.microsoft.com/office/community/en-us/default.mspx
  http://answers.microsoft.com/en-us/office/

- The Microsoft Project MVPs are independent Project experts (not Microsoft employees) officially given MVP status by Microsoft in recognition of their product expertise and work in helping the larger user community use Project successfully. MVPs frequently respond to questions in the newsgroups. Find Project MVP information at *https://mvp.support.microsoft.com/communities/mvp.aspx*, and then navigate to the Project page.

- The Enterprise Project Management (EPM) areas of the Microsoft Office Online website includes evaluation, deployment, and IT administration information for the Microsoft EPM solutions. Find them on the Web at *http://office.com*, and then navigate to the Project Server page.

- One of the authors of this book, Carl Chatfield, posts to a blog that focuses on Project, project management, and knowledge worker teams. Find the blog on the Web at *http://www.projhugger.com*.

To showcase your Project expertise formally, you can become certified. Microsoft developed Microsoft Certified Technology Specialist (MCTS) certifications for Project and enterprise project management solutions for Project 2007, and may offer similar certifications for Project 2010. To learn about training opportunities and requirements for Project certification, look on the Web at *www.microsoft.com/learning*.

Joining a Project Management Learning Community

Perhaps more than other desktop programs, Project requires you to be involved in a specific formal activity: project management. Project management can be an exciting mix of technical, organizational, and social challenges. The Project Management Institute (PMI) is the leading organization of professional project management. PMI focuses on setting project management standards, developing and offering educational programs, and certifying project managers. The most widely recognized PMI certification is the Project Management Professional (PMP) certification.

A Guide to the Project Management Body of Knowledge—published by the PMI and referred to as the PMBOK (pronounced "pimbok") describes generally accepted project management practices, knowledge areas, and terminology. In addition, the PMI publishes the journals *Project Management Journal* and *PM Network*. You can learn more about the PMI on the Web at *www.pmi.org*. If you are professionally invested in the practice of project management, you should be in the PMI.

Final Words

There are, of course, many worthwhile commercial and nonprofit organizations dedicated to Project and project management besides those we have described here. Project enjoys a leading position in the diverse, sometimes contentious, but always interesting world of project management. Wherever you are in your own Project and project management knowledge and career development, you can find a great variety of supporting organizations and peers today. The authors wish you the greatest success!

C Using the Practice Files if Connected to Project Server

This appendix addresses some adjustments you may need to make if you are running Microsoft Project Professional and connected to Microsoft Project Server. The appendix also gives you some preliminary information about Project Server and enterprise project management, and links to additional information.

Changing Account Settings if Connected to Project Server

If you have Project Professional and it is set up to connect to Microsoft Project Server, there are some adjustments that you should make to avoid inadvertently publishing this book's practice files to your Project Server.

1. On the Windows taskbar, click the **Start** button.

   The Start menu appears.

2. On the **Start** menu, point to **All Programs**, click **Microsoft Office**, and then click **Microsoft Project 2010**.

   Depending on how your enterprise options have been set in Project Professional, you might be prompted to choose a Project Server account. If so, complete step 3. Otherwise, skip to step 4.

3. If the **Login** dialog box appears, in the **Profile** box, select **Computer**, and then click **OK**.

   Choosing this option sets Project Professional to work independently of your Project Server and helps ensure that the practice file data used in this book won't accidentally be published to your Project Server.

   Project appears. Next, you'll review or adjust some enterprise options.

4. On the **File** tab, click **Info**, and then click **Manage Accounts**.

The Project Server Accounts dialog box appears.

5. Note the **Current** account value:

   ○ If the **Current account** value is something other than *Computer*, under **When starting,** click **Choose an account**, and then click **OK**.

   Or

   ○ If the **Current account** value is *Computer*, click **Cancel**.

   Selecting "Choose an account" will cause Project Professional to prompt you to choose an account to work with when you start Project Professional. This helps ensure that the practice files used in this book won't accidentally be published to your Project Server.

   When you need to work with information from your Project Server, when prompted at Project startup to choose a profile, click your Project Server profile name.

6. Exit and restart Project Professional. If prompted to choose a profile, click **Computer**, and then click **OK**.

   Project Professional appears. You are now able to work with the practice files as described in the chapters of this book.

Introduction to Enterprise Project Management

This appendix introduces some of the key differences between desktop project management (as you've practiced it in this book) and Project Server–based *enterprise project management*. Project Server is the cornerstone of the Microsoft Enterprise Project Management (EPM) Solution (we'll refer to this as *Project Server–based EPM*). EPM is one of the more complex but potentially rewarding practices that a large organization can adopt.

Some organizational benefits of Project Server–based EPM include:

● Capturing your organization's best practices with regard to workflow models and resource skills in enterprise templates

● Gaining insight into resource workload and availability across all projects and other activities in your organization

● Developing consistent ways of describing and tracking project activities across your organization

● Collecting a broad range of data relating to projects and reporting this data in timely and informative ways

Although you might be the sole user of Project in your organization, the real "user" of EPM is the entire organization; thus, the software toolset is correspondingly more complex than Project running on a single computer. For this reason, fully addressing the details of EPM is far beyond the scope of this book. However, we want to introduce Project Server–based EPM here so that you can start to determine whether it can serve a useful role in your organization. For most organizations, we think the answer will be "Yes," but getting from initial interest in Project Server–based EPM to full implementation is a series of complex steps. We hope that this brief introduction can help you formulate some ideas of how Project Server–based EPM can improve your organization's performance.

If you've completed the previous chapters in this book, you have a good introduction to project management on the scale of a single project manager with projects that have dozens of resources working on hundreds of tasks. You may be practicing project management at this scale now. Indeed, with a resource pool and multi-project features, such as consolidated projects, a single project manager should be able to stay on top of several different projects in various stages of completion with Project running on a single computer.

Now, imagine dozens of project managers planning and tracking hundreds of projects, each with hundreds or even thousands of resources and tasks—all within a single organization. Project management at this scale requires a high degree of planning, coordination, and standardization. This is the realm of EPM: a large organization planning, coordinating, and executing a large number of projects simultaneously.

Think about any past or current experiences you've had working on projects in a large organization, and try to answer these questions:

- Were potential projects evaluated against the goals and objectives of the organization such that the projects selected for execution aligned well with the strategic goals of the organization?

- Were the projects defined and scoped in a consistent way that would enable apples-to-apples comparisons?

- Were resource assignments made with full knowledge of each resource's skills, location, and availability?

- Did the executive leadership of the organization have a clear picture of the status of each project?

If your answer to these questions is "No," the organization was probably not practicing EPM effectively. There is no question that many large organizations can gain great benefits by adopting EPM; however, this is no easy task, or they would have implemented EPM already. Succeeding with EPM requires a strong willingness from the leadership of the organization (executive sponsorship), a well-trained group of administrators, project and resource managers, and a software infrastructure capable of enabling it.

The following are some resources to help with your evaluation, planning, and deployment of a Project Server–based EPM solution:

- Explore the online collaboration options available for Project Professional. To do this, on the File tab, click Save & Send.

- Review all the relevant material on the Project Server area of the Office Online website. Find it on the Web at *http://office.com,* and then navigate to the Project Server page.

- Consider attending classroom training on EPM deployment from Microsoft Learning. Check the Microsoft Learning website for Project Server information: *http://www.microsoft.com/learning.*

- If you are in an organization that is relatively new to the project management discipline or lacks an experienced internal Information Technology (IT) group, consider working through the Project Server deployment process with a recognized Project partner. You can begin your search for a qualified partner firm here: *http://pinpoint.microsoft.com.*

We hope this brief introduction will give you and your organization a good start in exploring EPM tools and practices.

D Using *Microsoft Project 2010 Step by Step* in a Classroom: Suggestions for Instructors

This book is suitable for various learning environments and needs, including:

- Individual self-paced training
- Instructor-led classroom training

If you are an instructor preparing training material for classroom delivery, this appendix offers some suggestions for how to best integrate this book into your syllabus or lesson plans.

Matching Content to Instructional Needs

The following table describes the organization of this book and how you as an instructor can incorporate this book into your classroom training environment.

Book Level	Training Focus
Entire book	Assign for the duration of your course, or the portion of the course that focuses on Microsoft Project 2010 skills development.
Part	Part 1, "Simple Scheduling," includes Chapters 1 through 6. Chapter 1 is an introduction to Project, and is especially well suited for those new to Project. Chapters 2 through 5 cover a complete project life cycle and introduce simpler task, resource, assignment, formatting, and tracking features of Project. The chapters in Part 1 follow a logical sequence. If your students have some experience with Project 2010, you may elect to skip Part 1.
	Part 2 (Chapters 7 through 14), "Advanced Scheduling," covers a complete project life cycle and introduces more advanced features relating to task, resource, assignment, formatting, and tracking activities in Project. The chapters in Part 2 follow a logical sequence.
	Part 3 (Chapters 15 through 18), "Special Subjects," covers some subjects that are not part of a project life cycle but are important for well-rounded training in Project. The chapters in Part 3 are not in any particular sequence.
Chapter	Each chapter is a complete learning solution that focuses on a major feature set of Project. Most chapters in this book require the use of at least one and sometimes multiple practice files.
	If you have specific feature areas that you want to cover, you can assign chapters based on subject matter. For example, if you want to focus on resource features in Project, you could assign Chapter 3, "Setting Up Resources," followed by Chapter 8, "Fine-Tuning Resource Details," and possibly Chapter 18, "Consolidating Projects and Resources" (if you want to address resource pools).
	Several chapters include "Project Management Focus" sidebars, in which project management principles or issues are brought up in the context of Project functionality. These sidebars are a great opportunity to broaden classroom discussions and activities to encompass project management practices.
Section	Each chapter consists of several sections. At the beginning of each chapter, you will find the learning objectives addressed in that chapter. The objectives state the instructional goals for each section so you and your students understand what skills they will master.
	In this book, the sections are strongly sequential within the chapter; students are expected to complete sections in the order in which they appear. If you need to assign just some sections of a chapter, check what state the chapter's practice file(s) should be in at the start of each assigned section. In some cases, you may need to create section-specific versions of sample files.

Book Level	Training Focus
Explanatory portion of section	Each section is roughly divided between an explanatory portion, which defines core concepts, and the hands-on activity (the enumerated procedure). When presenting core concepts to students, you may want to elaborate on the supplied content. For example, if you are teaching project management in an engineering course, you may wish to provide more engineering-specific examples and terms in your explanation.
Hands-on activity per section	The hands-on activity per section is intended to be completed by students or by an instructor while observed by students. The procedures are heavily illustrated so students can check their results against the illustrations.
	Students might work through the hands-on activities outside the classroom, or in the classroom if it is equipped with computers. For lab environments, you may find it helpful to pair up students so one completes the hands-on activity while the other reads the instructions, and both discuss the results. They can then alternate roles between sections.
Practice files	This book includes instructions on downloading the practice files used in the hands-on activities throughout this book. Should your practice files become unsuitable for new users (for example, students complete activities but overwrite the original practice files), you can reinstall fresh practice files from the Web.

The sections and chapters in this book vary in terms of page count and, for the hands-on activities, completion time. For this reason, we recommend that you complete the activities yourself that you intend to assign to students so you can better estimate how long the assignments should take. An experienced Project user should be able to complete any chapter in this book within one hour; a new Project user, however, may require substantially more time.

Depending on your classroom environment and training objectives, you may find a variety of instructional strategies to be effective, including:

- Instructor leads a lecture or discussion through the explanatory portion of a section, and then demonstrates the hands-on activity in Project.

- Instructor leads a lecture, and then assigns students to complete the hands-on activity at computers in the classroom or lab.

- Instructor leads a lecture, and then assigns students to complete the hands-on activity outside the classroom.

- Instructor assigns reading and completion of hands-on activities to students, to be completed outside the classroom.

These are just a few possible options.

Teaching Project Management with Project

A core principle of this book's instructional strategy is that success with Project is built on success with basic project management practice. Although Project is a feature-rich application, mastery of its features alone is no guarantee of success in project management. For this reason, you will find material about project management practice throughout this book. See for example the following:

● The many "Project Management Focus" sidebars throughout the chapters

● Appendix A, "A Short Course in Project Management"

● Appendix B, "Roadmap for Developing Your Project and Project Management Skills"

This book does not prescribe a specific project management methodology, but in general aims to be in alignment with the Project Management Institute's (PMI's) *A Guide to the Project Management Body of Knowledge* (PMBOK) and generally accepted project management practices.

That said, it is important to acknowledge that some core areas of project management are beyond the scope of activities performed with Project. Resource recruiting and procurement, for example, are critical activities for many projects, but they are not activities that Project directly supports. If your instructional context is more focused on Project features than project management practice, please explore this issue with your students so they gain a fuller understanding of the broad domain of project management and where specifically Project can best support them.

Glossary

8/80 rule A general guideline regarding the estimation of task duration. Task durations between 8 hours (or one day) and 80 hours (10 working days, or two weeks) are generally sized to a manageable duration.

accrual The method by which a project incurs the cost of a task or a resource. The three types of accrual are start, prorated, and end.

actual A detail about task progress recorded in a plan in Microsoft Project. Prior to recording actuals, the project plan contains scheduled or planned information. Comparing planned project information to actuals helps the project manager better control project execution.

allocation The portion of the capacity of a resource devoted to work on a specific task.

assignment The matching of a work resource (a person or a piece of equipment) to a task. You can also assign a material or cost resource to a task, but those resources have no effect on work or duration.

AutoFilter In a table, a quick way to view or organize only the task or resource information that meets the criteria you choose.

automatically scheduled task A task for which Microsoft Project dynamically adjusts the start or finish date to account for schedule changes in a project plan.

base calendar A calendar that can serve as the project calendar or a task calendar. A base calendar also defines the default working times for resource calendars. Microsoft Project includes three base calendars named Standard, 24 Hours, and Night Shift. You can customize these, or you can use them as a basis for your own base calendar.

baseline The original project plan, saved for later comparison with the revised or updated project plan. The baseline includes the planned start and finish dates, durations and work values of tasks and assignments, as well as their planned costs. Project plans can have up to 11 baselines.

bottom-up planning A method of developing a project plan that starts with the lowest-level tasks and organizes them into broad phases.

calendar The settings that define the working days and time for a project, resources, and tasks.

consolidated project A plan in Microsoft Project that contains one or more inserted project plans. The inserted projects are linked to the consolidated project so that any changes to the inserted projects are reflected in the consolidated plan, and vice versa. A consolidated project plan is also known as a *master project*.

constraint A restriction, such as Must Start On (MSO) or Finish No Later Than (FNLT), that you can place on the start or finish date of a task.

contour The manner in which a resource's work on a task is scheduled over time. Microsoft Project includes several predefined work contours that you can apply to an assignment. For example, a back-loaded contour schedules a small amount of work at the beginning of an assignment and then schedules increasing amounts of work as time progresses. You can also contour an assignment manually by editing work values in a usage view, such as the Resource Usage view. Applying a predefined contour or manually contouring an assignment causes Project to display a work contour icon in the Indicators column.

cost The resources required to carry out a project, including the people who do the work, the equipment used, and the materials consumed as the work is completed. Cost is one side of the project triangle model.

cost rate table The resource pay rates that are stored on the Costs tab of the Resource Information dialog box. You can have up to five separate cost rate tables per resource.

cost resource A type of resource used to represent financial costs associated with tasks in a project. Use cost resources to account for standard categories of costs that you want to track in a project, such as costs for travel or catering. A cost resource does no work and has no effect on the scheduling of a task to which it is assigned.

critical path A series of tasks that, if delayed, will push out the end date of a project.

deadline A date value that you can enter for a task that indicates the latest date by which you want the task to be completed. If the scheduled completion date of a task is later than its deadline, Microsoft Project notifies you. The benefit of entering deadline dates is that they do not constrain tasks.

deliverable The final product, service, or event that a project is intended to produce.

dependency A link between a predecessor task and a successor task. A dependency controls the start or finish of one task relative to the start or finish of the other task. The most common dependency is finish-to-start (FS), in which the finish date of the predecessor task determines the start date of the successor task.

destination program The program into which you place the data when exchanging data between Microsoft Project and another program.

duration The span of working time that you expect it will take to complete a task.

effort-driven scheduling A scheduling method in which the work of a task remains constant regardless of the number of resources assigned to it. As resources are added to a task, the duration decreases, but the total work remains the same and is distributed among the assigned resources. Effort-driven scheduling is turned off by default, but it can be turned on for fixed-unit or fixed-duration tasks. Effort-driven scheduling is always turned on for fixed-work tasks.

elapsed duration The uninterrupted span of time that it will take to finish a task, based on a 24-hour day and a 7-day week. Elapsed duration is not limited by project, resource, or task calendars; it is continuous.

enterprise project management (EPM) Project management practiced in a formal, consistent way throughout an organization.

Entry table The grid on the left side of the default Gantt Chart view.

export map The specifications for exporting fields from Microsoft Project to other file formats, such as Tab-delimited format. Project includes several export maps, which you can use as they are or modify.

field The lowest-level information about a task, resource, or assignment.

filtering In a view, a way to see or highlight only the task or resource information that meets the criteria you choose.

fixed consumption rate A fixed quantity of a material resource to be consumed in the completion of an assignment.

fixed cost A set amount of money budgeted for a task. This amount is independent of resource costs and task duration.

fixed duration A task type in which the duration value is fixed. If you change the amount of work that you expect a task to require, Microsoft Project recalculates the resource assignment's peak units for each resource. If you change duration or units, Project recalculates the work.

fixed units A task type in which a resource assignment's units value is fixed. If you change the duration of a task, Microsoft Project recalculates the amount of work scheduled for the task. If you change units or work, Project recalculates the duration.

fixed work A task type in which the work value is fixed. If you change the duration of the task, Microsoft Project recalculates the resource assignment's peak units for each resource. If you change units or work, Project recalculates the duration.

flexible constraint A constraint type that gives Microsoft Project the flexibility to change the start or finish dates (but not the duration) of a task. As Soon As Possible (ASAP) and As Late As Possible (ALAP) are examples of flexible constraints.

free slack The amount of time that a task can be delayed without delaying the start date of another task.

fully allocated The condition of a resource when the total work of his or her task assignments is exactly equal to his or her work capacity.

Gantt Chart view A predefined view in Microsoft Project consisting of a table (the Entry table by default) on the left and a graphical bar chart on the right that shows the project plan over time.

ghost task A task that represents a link from one plan to another in Microsoft Project. Ghost tasks appear as gray bars.

Global template A template in Microsoft Project named Global.mpt that contains the default views, tables, filters, and other items that Project uses.

group A way to reorder task or resource information in a table and display summary values for each group. You can specify several levels of groups. (The term *group* is also used to refer to the Resource Group field, which is unrelated.)

Group field A resource field in which you can specify a group name (such as a department) with which you want to associate a resource. If you organize resources into groups, you can sort, filter, or group resources by group.

hyperlink A link to another file, a specific location in a file, a page on the Internet, or a page on an intranet.

import/export map A set of specifications for importing specific data to or from fields in Microsoft Project. Project includes several built-in maps, which you can modify or use as they are. Import and export maps are sometimes referred to as *data maps*.

inflexible constraint A constraint type that forces a task to begin or end on a certain date. Must Start On (MSO) and Must Finish On (MFO) are both inflexible constraints.

inserted project In Microsoft Project, a plan that is inserted into another plan, called a *consolidated plan*. An inserted project is also known as a *subproject*.

interim plan A task's start and finish values, saved for later comparison. Each plan in Microsoft Project can have, at most, 10 interim plans.

lag time A delay between tasks that have a task relationship. For example, lag time causes the successor task in a finish-to-start (FS) relationship to begin some time after its predecessor task concludes.

lead time An overlap between tasks that have a task relationship. For example, lead time causes the successor task in a finish-to-start (FS) relationship to begin before its predecessor task concludes. In Microsoft Project, you enter lead time as negative lag time.

line manager A manager of a group of resources; also called a *functional manager*. A line manager might also have project management skills and responsibilities, depending on the organization's structure.

link A logical relationship between tasks that controls sequence and dependency. In the Gantt Chart and Network Diagram views, links appear as lines between tasks.

macro A recorded or programmed set of instructions that carry out a specific action when initiated. Macros in Microsoft Project use Microsoft Visual Basic for Applications (VBA).

manually scheduled task A task for which Microsoft Project does not set a start or finish date or duration automatically. Such a task can include any type of value you want in most fields.

material resources The consumables that are used up as a project progresses. As with work resources, you assign material resources to tasks. Unlike work resources, material resources have no effect on the total amount of work scheduled on a task.

maximum units The maximum capacity (as entered in the Max. Units field) of a resource to accomplish tasks. If you allocate the resource beyond its capacity, Microsoft Project alerts you that the resource is overallocated.

milestone A significant event that is reached within the project or imposed upon the project. In Microsoft Project, milestones normally are represented as tasks with zero duration.

negative slack The amount of time that tasks overlap due to a conflict between task relationships and constraints.

Night Shift base calendar A base calendar included with Microsoft Project designed to accommodate an 11:00 P.M.–8:00 A.M. "graveyard" work shift.

noncritical tasks The tasks that have slack. Noncritical tasks can finish within their slack time without affecting the project completion date.

note The information (including linked or embedded files) that you want to associate with a task, resource, or assignment.

Object Linking and Embedding (OLE) A protocol that enables you to transfer information, such as a chart or text (called an *object*), to documents in different programs.

ongoing operation An activity that has no planned end date and is repetitive in nature. Examples include accounting, managing human resources, and some manufacturing tasks.

Organizer In Microsoft Project, a dialog box with which you can copy views, tables, filters, and other items between the Global.mpt template and other plans or between two different plans.

outline A hierarchy of summary tasks and subtasks within Microsoft Project, usually corresponding to major phases of work.

overallocated The condition of resources when they are assigned to do more work than is their normal work capacity.

phase A sequence of tasks that represent a major portion of the project's work. In Microsoft Project, phases are represented by summary tasks.

planning The first major phase of project management work. Planning includes all the work in developing a project schedule up to the point where the tracking of actual work begins.

predecessor A task whose start or end date determines the start or finish of another task or tasks, called *successor tasks*.

product scope The quality, features, and functions (often called *specifications*) of the deliverable of the project.

program office A department within an organization that oversees a collection of projects (such as producing wings and producing engines), each of which contributes to a complete deliverable (such as an airplane) and the organization's strategic objectives.

progress bar A graphical representation on a bar in the Gantt Chart view that shows how much of a task has been completed.

project A temporary endeavor undertaken to create a unique product or service.

project calendar The base calendar that is used by the entire project. The project calendar defines normal working and nonworking days and times.

project scope The work required to produce a deliverable with agreed-upon quality, features, and functions.

project summary task A summary task that contains top-level information such as duration, work, and costs for the entire project. The project summary task has a task ID of 0 and is displayed through the Show/Hide group of the Format tab.

project triangle A popular model of project management in which time, cost, and scope are represented as the three sides of a triangle. A change to one side will affect at least one of the other two sides. There are many variations on this model.

recurring task A task that repeats at established intervals. You can create a recurring task that repeats for a fixed number of times or that ends by a specific date.

relationship The type of dependency between two tasks, visually indicated by a link line. The types of relationships include finish-to-start (FS), start-to-start (SS), finish-to-finish (FF), and start-to-finish (SF). Also known as a *link*, a *logical relationship*, a *task dependency*, or a *precedence relationship*.

report A format designed for printing. Microsoft Project includes several predefined reports, each focusing on specific aspects of your project data. You can also define your own reports. Another type of report is a visual report, which exports structured data to Microsoft Excel or Microsoft Visio for graphical representation and analysis.

resource calendar The working and nonworking days and times of an individual work resource.

resource leveling A method of resolving resource overallocation by delaying the start date of an assignment or an entire task or splitting up the work on a task. Microsoft Project can level resources automatically, or you can do it manually.

resource manager A person who oversees resource usage in project activities, specifically to manage the time allocation and costs of resources. A resource manager might also have project management skills and responsibilities, depending on the organization's structure.

resource pool In Microsoft Project, a plan that other projects use for their resource information. Resource pools contain information about resources' task assignments from all project plans (called *sharer plans*) linked to the resource pool.

resources People, equipment, and material (and the associated costs of each) needed to complete the work on a project.

ribbon interface A user interface design used by Microsoft Office 2010 applications. In the ribbon interface, commands are organized into groups and tabs for quick access.

risk An event that decreases the likelihood of completing the project on time, within budget, and to specification (or, less likely, an opportunity to improve project performance).

scheduling formula A representation of how Microsoft Project calculates work, based on the duration and resource units of an assignment. The scheduling formula is Duration × Units = Work.

scope The products or services to be provided by a project and the work required to deliver it. For project planning, it's useful to distinguish between product scope and project scope. Scope is one side of the project triangle model.

semi-flexible constraint A constraint type that gives Microsoft Project the flexibility to change the start and finish dates of a task within one date boundary. Start No Earlier Than (SNET), Start No Later Than (SNLT), Finish No Earlier Than (FNET), and Finish No Later Than (FNLT) are all semi-flexible constraints.

sequence The chronological order in which tasks occur. A sequence is ordered from left to right in most views that include a timescale, such as the Gantt Chart view.

sharer plan A project plan that is linked to a resource pool. Sharer plans use resources from a resource pool.

shortcut menu A menu that you display by pointing to an item on the screen and then right-clicking. Shortcut menus contain only the commands that apply to the item to which you are pointing.

slack The amount of time that a task can be delayed without delaying a successor task (free slack) or the project end date (total slack). Slack is also known as *float*.

sorting A way of ordering task or resource information in a view by the criteria you choose.

source program When exchanging data between Microsoft Project and another program, the program in which the data resided originally.

split An interruption in a task, represented in the Gantt bar as a dotted line between segments of a task. You can split a task multiple times.

sponsor An individual or organization that both provides financial support and champions the project team within the larger organization.

stakeholders The people or organizations that might be affected by project activities (those who "have a stake" in its success). These also include the resources working on the project as well as others (such as customers) external to the project work.

Standard base calendar A base calendar included with Microsoft Project designed to accommodate an 8:00 A.M.–5:00 P.M., Monday through Friday work shift.

status date The date that you specify (not necessarily the current date) that determines how Microsoft Project calculates earned value data.

successor task A task whose start or finish is driven by another task or tasks, called *predecessor tasks*.

summary task A task that is made up of and summarizes the subtasks below it. In Microsoft Project, phases of project work are represented by summary tasks.

table A spreadsheet-like presentation of project data, organized in vertical columns and horizontal rows. Each column represents one of the many fields in Microsoft Project, and each row represents a single task or resource. In a usage view, additional rows represent assignments.

task A project activity that has a starting and finishing point. A task is the basic building block of a project.

task calendar The base calendar that is used by a single task. A task calendar defines working and nonworking times for a task, regardless of settings in the project calendar.

task ID A unique number that Microsoft Project assigns to each task in a project. In the Entry table, the task ID appears in the far-left column.

task priority A numeric ranking between 0 and 1000 of a task's importance and appropriateness for resource leveling. Tasks with the lowest priority are delayed or split first if necessary. The default value is 500.

task type A setting applied to a task that determines how Microsoft Project schedules the task, based on which of the three scheduling formula values is fixed. The three task types are fixed units, fixed duration, and fixed work.

template In Microsoft Project, a file format that enables you to reuse existing project plans as the basis for new project plans. Project includes several templates that relate to a variety of industries, and you can create your own templates.

time The scheduled durations of individual tasks and the overall project. Time is one side of the project triangle model.

throughput metric A measurement of the quantity of a deliverable that can be completed over a given time period, usually expressed as a ratio. For example, "paint one wall per day" describes a quantity of a deliverable (a painted wall) that can be produced in a given time period (a day). Note that the time period used in a metric is work, not elapsed duration.

timephased field A task, resource, or assignment value that is distributed over time. The values of timephased fields appear in the timescale grid on the right side of a view, such as the Task Usage or Resource Usage view.

timescale The timescale appears in a view, such as the Gantt Chart or Resource Usage view, as a band across the top of the grid and denotes units of time. To customize the timescale, do this: On the View tab, in the Zoom group, click the down arrow to the right of the Timescale box and then click Timescale.

top-down planning A method of developing a project plan by identifying the highest-level phases or summary tasks before breaking them into lower-level components or subtasks.

total slack The amount of time that a task can be delayed without delaying the project's end date.

tracking The second major phase of project management work. Tracking includes all the collecting, entering, and analyzing of actual project performance values, such as work on tasks and actual durations.

underallocated The condition of resources when they are assigned to do less work than their normal work capacity. For example, a full-time resource who has only 25 hours of work assigned in a 40-hour work week is underallocated.

units A standard way of measuring the capacity of a resource to work when you assign the resource to a task in Microsoft Project. Units are one variable in the scheduling formula: Duration × Units = Work.

variable consumption rate A quantity of a material resource to be consumed that will change if the duration of the task to which it is assigned changes.

variance A deviation from the schedule or budget established by the baseline plan.

view A visual representation of the tasks or resources in your project. The three categories of views are charts, sheets, and forms. Views enable you to enter, organize, and examine information in a variety of formats.

work The total scheduled effort for a task, a resource, a resource assignment, or an entire project. Work is measured in person-hours and might not match the duration of the task. Work is one variable in the scheduling formula: Duration × Units = Work.

work breakdown structure (WBS) The identification of every task in a project that reflects that task's location in the hierarchy of the project.

work resources The people and equipment that do the work of the project.

Index

About the Authors

Carl Chatfield

Carl is a principal content project manager at Microsoft. In this role, Carl oversees development of assistance material, user interface (UI) text, and Web content for a variety of V.1 products and services. Carl also teaches software user assistance in the Human Centered Design and Engineering department at the University of Washington. Carl is a graduate of the master's program in Technical Communication at the University of Washington and is certified as a Project Management Professional (PMP) by the Project Management Institute. Carl blogs regularly about Microsoft Project, project management, and knowledge worker teams at *www.projhugger.com*.

Tim Johnson

Tim's first connection with Project began as a product support professional at Microsoft, starting with Project 3.0. Later, Tim worked on the Project user assistance team, where he brought his firsthand knowledge of Project customers' issues to new learning solutions for Project. Tim remains involved in the computer industry and continues to look for ways to help customers better understand and use their computer applications.

What do you think of this book?

We want to hear from you!

To participate in a brief online survey, please visit:

microsoft.com/learning/booksurvey

Tell us how well this book meets your needs—what works effectively, and what we can do better. Your feedback will help us continually improve our books and learning resources for you.

Thank you in advance for your input!

Microsoft®
Press

Stay in touch!

To subscribe to the *Microsoft Press*® *Book Connection Newsletter*—for news on upcoming books, events, and special offers—please visit:

microsoft.com/learning/books/newsletter